The Art of Natural Building

DESIGN | CONSTRUCTION | RESOURCES

SECOND EDITION

D0556604

EDITORS

Joseph F. Kennedy ◆ Michael G. Smith ◆ Catherine Wanek

Copyright © 2015 by Catherine Wanek, Joseph Kennedy and Michael G. Smith. All rights reserved.

Cover design by Diane McIntosh. Cover: Thierry Dronet's workshop/stable in France
is a hybrid natural building incorporating straw bales, cordwood masonry,
lime plaster and a living roof. Photo © Catherine Wanek.

Printed in Canada. First printing January 2015.

New Society Publishers acknowledges the financial support of the Government of Canada
through the Canada Book Fund (CBF) for our publishing activities.

Inquiries regarding requests to reprint all or part of *The Art of Natural Building*
should be addressed to New Society Publishers at the address below.

To order directly from the publishers, please call toll-free (North America)
1-800-567-6772, or order online at www.newsociety.com

Any other inquiries can be directed by mail to:

New Society Publishers
P.O. Box 189, Gabriola Island, BC V0R 1X0, Canada
(250) 247-9737

LIBRARY AND ARCHIVES CANADA CATALOGUING IN PUBLICATION

The art of natural building : design, construction, resources / editors,
Joseph F. Kennedy, Michael G. Smith, Catherine Wanek.—Second edition.

Includes bibliographical references and index. Issued in print and electronic formats.
ISBN 978-0-86571-771-8 (pbk.).—ISBN 978-1-55092-560-9 (ebook)

1. Architecture, Domestic—Environmental aspects.   2. Ecological
houses—Design and construction.   3. Dwellings—Design and construction—
Environmental aspects.   4. Building materials—Environmental aspects.
I. Wanek, Catherine, author, editor   II. Kennedy, Joseph F., author, editor
III. Smith, Michael G. (Michael George), 1968–, author, editor

NA2542.35.A77 2014   690′.8047   C2014-907511-1
                                                            C2014-907512-X

New Society Publishers' mission is to publish books that contribute in fundamental ways to building an
ecologically sustainable and just society, and to do so with the least possible impact on the environment,
in a manner that models this vision. We are committed to doing this not just through education, but
through action. The interior pages of our bound books are printed on Forest Stewardship Council®-
registered acid-free paper that is 100% post-consumer recycled (100% old growth forest-free),
processed chlorine-free, and printed with vegetable-based, low-VOC inks, with covers produced using
FSC®-registered stock. New Society also works to reduce its carbon footprint, and purchases carbon
offsets based on an annual audit to ensure a carbon neutral footprint. For further information, or to
browse our full list of books and purchase securely, visit our website at: www.newsociety.com

MIX
Paper from
responsible sources
FSC® C016245

Contents

Part Three: Natural Building Materials and Techniques

Part Four: Building the Global Village

The information in this book is based on the experience and opinions of the individual authors and has not been independently verified by the editors. Some of the techniques described herein are quite new and still under development; others are ancient, but may lack extensive scientific and technical study. The resurgence of natural building is still in an experimental stage. Claims as to the insulation value, structural strength, fire safety, health benefits, environmental benefits and so on of the various materials and techniques should be considered preliminary. Always do your own research and testing and/or consult a qualified professional before embarking on a building project.

Foreword to the First Edition

by Albert Bates

Time is most often thought of as a progression, a movement along an axis from past to present to future. We think of human progress in the same terms—today we are better or worse off than we were yesterday or collectively were a century ago. We feel trends afoot. Tomorrow will bring another step.

Some aboriginal societies—and by "aboriginal" I mean any culture still grounded in its origins—look at time as a circle. The Earth spins on its axis and another day is born. The moon goes once around and a month has passed. We circle the sun as seasons come and go, then come again.

In a linear model of progress, the human population continues to expand until its ever-enlarging technical prowess enables it to cross space and colonize the solar system, even leaping out to the stars. In another version, our exhaustion of natural resources and incautious dismemberment of natural evolutionary barriers with glitzy nano-bio-robo abandon devolve Earth's inhabitants into bubbling gray goo.

Here is a different view. This loop we are on is at its apogee and about to change not only its direction but also everything we think about in terms of human settlements and lifestyles. Instead of planned obsolescence, we will want planned evolution. The focus is on quality, not quantity. We need comfort, privacy, and self-respect. We want warmth that transcends temperature.

We want beauty. We want to be in touch with the eternal.

The chapters that follow are sublimely poised as a clue to our future.

This book is an invitation to get your hands muddy. [Credit: Nigel Fusella]

ALBERT BATES *is the author of 15 books on law, energy, history and the environment, including* Climate in Crisis (1990) *and* The Biochar Solution (2010). *He has been the director of the Global Village Institute for Appropriate Technology since 1984 and of the Ecovillage Training Center at The Farm since 1994, where he has taught sustainable design, natural building, agriculture and technology to students from more than 60 nations.*

Taos Pueblo: the oldest continually inhabited dwelling in North America. [Credit: Joseph F. Kennedy]

Foreword to the Second Edition

by Bill Steen

It was once commonly thought that the utilization of nature's resources was a linear process that would inevitably lead to unlimited material progress. Nature was seen as useless, unless human labor transformed it into something productive. It was inconceivable that this path might lead ultimately to a degraded environment and a dark future for future generations.

The creation of human habitat revolves around borrowing inputs from the environment and then transforming them into a form we think of as civilization. That process requires the expenditure of a great deal of energy, much of which is lost to entropy as a particular product or service is produced. In essence,

that energy becomes unavailable, warming the planet in the process.

Over the past two centuries, the building process as we know it has largely been driven by the fossil fuels that made the first and second Industrial Revolutions possible. These energy sources allowed for previously unimaginable expansion and growth in conjunction with unprecedented societal wealth and the widespread enjoyment of goods and services.

However, most of these benefits were misleading in that they required the burning of vast amounts of fossil fuels, releasing huge amounts of carbon dioxide into the Earth's atmosphere in the process. The result was

Athena and Bill Steen, applying clay plasters to a straw bale wall, demonstrate the artistry involved in natural building.
[Credit: Catherine Wanek]

BILL STEEN, *together with his wife Athena, co-founded The Canelo Project in southern Arizona, where he teaches workshops on straw bale and natural plaster. Co-authors of* The Straw Bale House, Small Strawbale *and* The Beauty of Strawbale Homes, *they have worked extensively with people in northern Mexico, and taught, lectured and created art throughout Europe and the United States.* **caneloproject.com.**

climate change; in other words, our debt to the Earth's atmosphere.

The construction and operation of buildings consumes approximately one-half of all the energy used in industrialized countries. Natural building is about learning how to build and operate our buildings so that we can live within our planetary means, by not consuming nature's endowment faster than the biosphere can recycle the waste and replenish the natural resources. Ultimately, this is the only sustainable path. Changing the way we build is also every bit as essential for our mental, emotional and spiritual health as it is for the planet.

We stand poised to enter an exciting new era of natural building, one that can help ensure a habitable planet, diversity of species, clean air and a healthy climate. The opportunities are endless. There are an increasing number of movements worldwide that focus on local production of human necessities. On a global scale, the Internet is converging with renewable energies to become the means by which we could manage collaborative green energy distribution. Imagine an ever-increasing number of homes built from sustainable, local and natural materials, that produce much or all of their own green energy, which can be distributed wherever needed through an "energy Internet."

However, utilizing efficient technologies and choosing the most appropriate natural materials is only part of the solution. Given today's emphasis on speed and the use of mass-produced materials, buildings have become largely impersonal, boring, predictable and devoid of creativity and artistry.

Natural materials give us the opportunity to change the rhythm of how we build. They slow us down. They relax the rigidity and homogeneous character of contemporary building practices by encouraging artistic expression characterized by soft organic curves and forms. Their colors and textures connect us to the surrounding landscape, the place where we live, or, in other words, the place *who* we are. Unexpectedly, they may indirectly lead us to realize that the beauty within ourselves and the beauty of nature are one and the same.

A diversity of ages and genders can be involved in the building process. In that sense, natural materials are inclusive, indirectly and almost invisibly building connections in a very disconnected world. Of these, one of the most important is the connection to the place where we dwell. What an extraordinary thing it is to be able to help sculpt and shape one's home with one's own hands—an experience no longer a common part of everyday life. How marvelous it is to feel the touch of clay, of wood and stone. In that touch, our connection with nature is immediately reestablished, and the art of living becomes reality.

This book is a compilation of contributions from those who have explored the world of natural building in a variety of different ways and have contributed to its evolution. It is also an invitation to you, the reader, to become part of that same journey, and in so doing, to bring beauty and artistry into your own life and the lives of others.

Acknowledgments

Our thanks go to the dozens of colleagues who have selflessly shared their hard-won experience to make possible not only this book, but the natural building movement as we know it. We are grateful to be part of a community that recognizes that the surest way to create positive change is to educate others. This book in fact represents the efforts of thousands of people on several continents who have been engaged for the last quarter-century or so in the process of developing new natural building techniques and rediscovering old ones, one building at a time.

Many of the contributing authors have supported us through multiple back-and-forth iterations of their chapters, helping to fine-tune the information to be as complete, up-to-date, and accessible as possible. Most have also gathered and contributed amazing photographs of their work, and we are grateful to them for allowing us to use their images. Special thanks go to David A. Bainbridge, Jacob Deva Racusin, Derek Roff, Carol Venolia, Mark Piepkorn and Martin Hammer for editorial assistance and advice.

We are indebted to our mentors, some of the natural building pioneers who have followed the threads of ancient wisdom to inspire the current natural building revival, as well as to our families and mates, who have supported us in assembling this anthology. And thank you, our readers, for *your* interest!

To the team at New Society, especially copy editor extraordinaire, Murray Reiss and designer Greg Green, our gratitude for the opportunity and support to bring this much-improved second edition to fruition.

Joseph F. Kennedy
[Credit: Halil Güven]

Michael G. Smith
[Credit: Cathy Suematsu]

Catherine Wanek
[Credit: Lora Colins]

Introduction: An Open Door

Michael G. Smith

He who dedicates himself to the duration of his life, to the house he builds,
to the dignity of mankind, dedicates himself to the earth and reaps from it the harvest
that sows its seed and sustains the world again and again.

« Albert Camus, *The Rebel* »

Natural building is nothing new. It is as old as the paper wasps who construct insulated hives out of chewed wood fiber, the aquatic caddis fly larvae who make protective shells by cementing together grains of sand, the prairie dogs who excavate enormous towns of interconnecting tunnels, and the chimpanzees who build temporary rain shelters out of sticks and leaves. For thousands of years, our own species followed this same path, building our shelters out of locally available materials.

Each group to settle in a new area developed a unique culture with its own architectural style, which evolved through small improvements from generation to generation, becoming increasingly better suited to local needs and opportunities. But always the basic materials stayed the same: the earth and stones beneath our feet, the trees and grasses that grew nearby. Building was a necessary skill shared by most people, a part of the traditional knowledge of how to live wisely and comfortably in a place, passed down through the centuries.

FIGURE I.1. People the world over are rediscovering the many advantages of building their own homes from natural materials.
[Credit: Joseph F. Kennedy]

Michael G. Smith *helped start the Cob Cottage Company in 1993 and the Natural Building Colloquium in 1994. He has taught well over 100 hands-on natural building workshops and been involved with the design or construction of at least 50 natural structures. He is the author of* The Cobber's Companion *and co-wrote* The Hand-Sculpted House. *Find out more at* **strawclaywood.com.**

Only in the last few generations has our relationship to building begun to change. The Industrial Revolution came like a big splash in a small pond. It started in Western Europe and is still spreading into less-developed parts of the globe. This wave has carried changes into nearly every aspect of our lives, not least the way we shelter ourselves. New materials appear on the market every year, promising more strength and speed than the old ones. The new building techniques are often more complicated and require specialized training and equipment, so most people in industrialized cultures no longer build their own homes.

The industrialization of building has made possible an enormous increase in the amount of construction that takes place every year. But not all of the consequences are positive. The energy expended in extracting, manufacturing and transporting building materials is a major contributor to the looming climate crisis and other environmental problems, too numerous to list here. Manufactured products can be toxic to the workers in the factories where they are made, the builders on the construction sites where they are employed and the families who live in the houses where these materials end up. They also create enormous waste disposal problems. Industrial building tends to be expensive: manufactured materials are transported great distances and specialized labor is often involved. What results is high-cost housing and increasing homelessness in industrialized countries.

Some individuals have always challenged the industrial building paradigm, preferring to build for themselves using local materials and traditional techniques. During the back-to-the-land movement of the 1960s and 1970s, thousands of people in the United States chose to build their own homes from available resources, without professional assistance, much training or money. Some were inspired and aided by contemporary pioneers like Helen and Scott Nearing (authors of *Living the Good Life* and other classics) and Ken Kern (whose book, *The Owner-Built Home*, was the bible for a generation).

The energy crisis of the mid-1970s focused public attention on our use of natural resources and the energy efficiency of our buildings. Around that time, a great deal of research and writing was done on passive solar building, alternative energy systems and sustainable resource use. But much of that knowledge was swept under the carpet by government policy and public apathy during the '80s. Some of the responses to the new interest in energy efficiency actually turned out to be detrimental to human health, as airtight buildings made of synthetic materials contrib-

FIGURE I.2. Natural building emphasizes the use of inexpensive tools and simple, easy-to-learn techniques. Here, a mallet fashioned from a log is being used to tap straw bales into place. This building was the first straw bale demonstration project organized by the American Indian Housing Initiative at the Crow Indian Reservation in Montana in 1999.
[Credit: Michael Rosenberg]

uted to environmental illness and other health problems.

Although it was no longer receiving much popular press, the experimental work of conservation-minded builders continued. In the late 1980s, a flurry of activity surrounded the rediscovery in the southwestern United States of straw bale building, a technique that had gained brief popularity in Nebraska in the early part of the 20th century. In Tucson, Matts Myrhman and Judy Knox started Out On Bale, (Un) Ltd., an organization devoted to popularizing this elegant and inexpensive construction system.

Around the same time, Ianto Evans and Linda Smiley, inspired by the centuries-old earthen homes in Britain, built their first cob cottage in Western Oregon. The interest generated by this wood-free wall building technique, which had proven itself well-suited to cool, rainy climates, led them to found the Cob Cottage Company. Meanwhile, Iowa-based Robert Laporte was teaching natural house building workshops that combined traditional timber-framing techniques from Japan and Europe, light-clay (a German infill of clay-coated straw) and earthen floors and plasters. In upstate New York, Rob and Jaki Roy taught cordwood masonry and earth-sheltered housing at their Earthwood Building School. Persian architect Nader Khalili established CalEarth, a center in Southern California devoted to developing, educating about and gaining code acceptance for earthbag construction. Also in California, David Easton was breaking into the contract-building market, first with monolithic rammed earth walls, and then with a sprayed-on soil-cement technique he dubbed PISE.

By the mid-1990s, there were dozens of individuals and small organizations in the United States researching, adapting and promoting traditional building systems. These visionaries proceeded with their work independently, each largely unaware of the existence of the others. Then the straw bale boom in the Southwest began to attract the interest of the mainstream national media. When movie star Dennis Weaver moved into a passive solar earth-bermed house made of recycled tires and soda cans, he brought instant fame to New Mexico architect Michael Reynolds, developer of the

FIGURE I.3. Natural Building Colloquia have inspired a great deal of collaboration and cross-pollination between practitioners of different building techniques. When the "straw bale people" met the "cob people" at the 1995 Colloquium, this hybrid dome was the result. [Credit: Catherine Wanek]

"Earthship" concept. As increasing numbers of hands-on workshops were offered around the country, the isolated teachers and innovators began to hear about one another.

In 1994, Ianto Evans, Linda Smiley and myself, directors of the Cob Cottage Company, organized the first Alternative Building Colloquium, inviting natural builders and teachers from around the country to spend a week together on a farm in Oregon. The idea was for these leaders to meet each other, share the building techniques each knew best and begin to join our various philosophies and experiences into a more cohesive system of knowledge.

The following year, Catherine Wanek hosted a follow-up gathering at her lodge in New Mexico. When publicizing that event, she coined the term "natural building" to define the commonality among these varied building materials and methods without limiting their potential with the marginalizing term "alternative." Joseph Kennedy, representing CalEarth, was one of nearly a hundred participants at that event, as were at least a dozen other authors represented in this book. We had all stumbled together through a doorway that we had glimpsed but had not been able to see clearly until that moment, into a world where decisions about the built environment are informed by traditions of the past yet rooted in a deep concern for the future of humanity and of the planet itself.

Since then, during the annual Natural Building Colloquia that followed on various sites around North America, thousands of people from diverse backgrounds (including students, architects and builders, code officials, artists, entrepreneurs and urban squatters) have attended workshops on wall building systems ranging from adobe to wattle and daub; roofing techniques including sod and thatch; and foundation systems including the rubble trench, dry stone and rammed earthbags. Through lectures, slides and demonstrations, innovators have presented their work with structural testing and building codes; composting toilets and grey water systems; designing with sacred geometry and natural forces; ecovillages and co-housing; and a hundred other topics.

FIGURE I.4. Kaki Hunter and Doni Kiffmeyer lead an earthbag building project at a Natural Building Colloquium at the Black Range Lodge in New Mexico. These gatherings combine hands-on building, skill-sharing, lectures and slide presentations and networking among natural builders. [Credit: Mark Mazziotti]

The energy and enthusiasm of these groups have been expressed physically in the construction of ornate timber frames, experimental straw bale vaults and multi-colored lime fresco murals. Ideas and techniques have collided and merged, coalescing into hybrid structures including a straw bale/cob dome and a straw bale/cob/light-clay/wattle and daub cottage on a stone and earthbag foundation. From the seed of these colloquia, a new movement has been born. The many disparate efforts to relearn ways of building with local materials and adapt them to modern needs have been brought together into a single conceptual basket with an easily understood name: natural building.

In the early years of the movement, authoritative written information was scarce, and in some cases there was substantial disagreement about best building practices. Terminology was divergent, as practitioners in different areas developed their own language to describe aspects of their work. The exceptions were stone masonry, adobe in the Southwest and timber framing, especially in the Northeast, since these techniques had never been "lost." In the 1990s, a new wave of practical guidebooks started to appear, starting with *The Straw Bale House* by Athena and Bill Steen, David Eisenberg and David Bainbridge in 1994. By the turn of the century, new how-to manuals had been published on cob, rammed earth, cordwood and Earthships, among other techniques. But there were still many critical gaps in the natural building literature.

Following the 1997 Colloquium, again hosted at Catherine's Black Range Lodge, Joseph and Catherine put together a booklet of information culled from the presentations. A great deal of technical information was put down in writing for the first time. Joseph and I had begun teaching two-week workshops on natural building and design, and compiled a large packet of Xeroxed handouts for our students. The packet was getting unwieldy and expensive to produce, and it still had some significant omissions. The three of us decided to join forces on a book aimed at introducing the emerging field of natural building in a comprehensive fashion to newcomers, while filling in gaps in the knowledge of readers already familiar with some pieces of the puzzle. We brainstormed our dream team of authors, selecting those who not only knew their material intimately but were clear and experienced presenters, and asked them to write chapters on their areas of expertise. Nearly all of them agreed, and that collaboration became the first edition of this book.

Representing every major natural building technique, and written by some of the most prominent innovators and advocates in the field, the first edition strove to document the current state of the art of the movement circa the year 2000. In addition to a survey of techniques, it provided a philosophical framework for the entire natural building movement, as well as a set of design principles broadly applicable to ecological design projects everywhere. In mapping out such a broad territory, we necessarily sacrificed some depth; we made up for that by including a comprehensive up-to-date list of resources for further information.

The book was a success, but time passes and things change. So many new resources have become available in the last decade, both in print and electronic form, that the first edition is no longer current. And the natural building movement is still young enough that a lot of new understanding can develop in a decade. By 2014, it was clearly time for a second edition.

FIGURE I.5. Natural building projects like this cob bench can provide an empowering creative outlet for urban youth, while teaching technical concepts and teamwork skills. [Credit: Joseph F. Kennedy]

When the three of us sat down to discuss our visions for the new edition, we were surprised to note that in the intervening decade and a half there had been almost no additions of major building techniques to the natural building palette. What had occurred instead was a significant fine-tuning and professionalization of the field. Whereas the natural builders of the 1990s have been characterized as a collection of mavericks, misfits and mad scientists, developing new techniques on desert lots and deep in the woods, often removed from public scrutiny, the latest generation of practitioners is more focused on gaining mainstream legitimacy for natural building techniques. This latest wave of natural builders has been examining traditional building systems through the new lens of building science, resulting in a much better understanding of how natural materials interact with each other and with their environments. They have also been evaluating the performance of early natural buildings in order to develop more effective designs and details. These trends have allowed a recent proliferation of high-performance natural buildings in challenging settings such as cold, wet climates and urban contexts. We wanted the present edition to reflect this sea change.

As both the knowledge base for natural building techniques and the public's acceptance of them increase, and as worsening climate and economic crises create disillusionment with industrial models of building and development, many organizations have begun to apply natural building methods to the housing needs of populations around the world. For this edition, we created an all-new section called "Building the Global Village," which showcases some of these successful efforts.

From the introduction of ancient Egyptian and Iraqi techniques for building earthen domes and vaults in sub-Saharan Africa, to empowering a social movement in Thailand with adobe and cob, to the increasing acceptance of straw bale buildings in China and Pakistan, each of these stories offers valuable lessons about how new and old techniques need to be adapted for best results in different contexts. We also wanted to feature some of the groundbreaking work ecovillages around the world are doing, as laboratories for both social and physical reorganization. As a planetary "village," we may be entering a new era of reinventing ourselves, our cultures, our settlement patterns and construction techniques to be more harmonious with the laws of nature. No corner of the Earth will be unaffected by the changes to come, so the time is ripe to learn successful resource-management strategies, both ancient and contemporary, wherever they can be found.

Our aspirations in this book go beyond just informing our readers of what other people are doing. Our greatest desire is that this book will be a doorway through which many of you will step in order to join the natural building movement. We hope that the profiled projects and the photographs throughout will help get you excited about handcrafting your own personalized structure.

The chapters describing construction techniques should give you a good basis for determining which ones appeal to you and make the most sense under specific circumstances, but they will

FIGURE I.6. Come on in—the door is open! This family home in British Columbia, built by Cobworks in collaboration with the homeowners, combines cob walls, local stone foundations, milled and unmilled wood and natural plasters. [Credit: Misha Rauchwerger]

not give you all the details you need to start building. Therefore, at the end of each chapter, we have once again listed a selection of the best books, periodicals and websites where you can find more information about that technique, as well as providers of workshops and other hands-on learning opportunities. We strongly encourage you to take advantage of the latter; a few days spent practicing

a natural building technique with a skilled instructor will give you more confidence and ability than all the volumes ever written.

So come on in; the door is open. We're very pleased to take you on a tour of the rambling, varied and often surprising world of natural building, and to introduce you to some of our friends, colleagues and teachers along the way.

PART ONE

The Context
for Natural Building

There is some of the fitness in a man's building his own house
that there is in a bird's building its own nest. Who knows
but if men constructed dwellings with their own hands,
and provided food for themselves and their families simply and
honestly enough, the poetic faculty would be universally developed,
as birds universally sing when so engaged.

« Henry David Thoreau, *Walden*, 1854 »

The Case for Natural Building

MICHAEL G. SMITH

Natural building is any building system that places the highest value on social and environmental sustainability. It assumes the need to minimize the environmental impact of our housing and other building needs, while providing healthy, beautiful, comfortable and spiritually uplifting homes for everyone. Natural builders emphasize simple, easy-to-learn techniques using locally available, renewable resources. These systems rely heavily on human labor and creativity instead of capital, high technology and specialized skills.

Natural building is necessarily regional and idiosyncratic. There are no universally appropriate materials and no standardized designs. Everything depends on local ecology, geology and climate; on the character of the particular building site and on the needs and personalities of the builders and users. This process works best when the designers, the builders, the owners and the inhabitants are the same people. Natural building is personally empowering because it teaches that everyone has, or can easily acquire, the skills they need to build their own home.

Natural building is not a new idea. In many parts of the world, almost all building still conforms to these criteria. Until the Industrial Revolution, the advent of cheap transportation and the professionalization of building and architecture, the same was true throughout Europe and America. Pioneer families in the United States built their own homes out of local materials, as First Peoples here and everywhere have always done. Our modern building industry with its

FIGURE 1.1. Everywhere on Earth, vernacular building traditions evolved that used local resources to their best advantage to meet local climatic and cultural conditions. These reconstructed Inca homes at Machu Picchu borrowed both their materials and their forms from the immediate environment. [Credit: Michael G. Smith]

MICHAEL G. SMITH *teaches workshops on natural building and consults with owner-builders:* **strawclaywood.com**. *He is also a founder and several-time organizer of the Natural Building Colloquium.*

resource-extractive, energy- and capital-intensive, polluting and often toxic practices must be seen as a temporary deviation from this norm. Let's look at some of natural building's many advantages over conventional modern building practices.

Environmental Impact

It's no secret that the global ecosystem is ill. The housing industry is a major contributor to the problem. We in the Pacific Northwest see the evidence all around us: the trail from clearcut to sawmill to building site is easy to follow. Other major modern building components depend on destructive mining: gypsum for plasterboard; limestone for cement; iron ore for hardware, rebar and roofing, to name just a few. Every material used in a typical modern building is the product of energy-intensive processing. The mills that saw our lumber, the factories that make plywood and oriented strand board, the foundries that make steel, the plants that turn minerals into cement by subjecting them to enormous heat—all consume vast quantities of power, supplied either by the combustion of coal and oil, the damming of rivers or the splitting of atoms.

Manufacturing processes also release toxic effluent into the water and hazardous chemicals into the air. The manufacture of Portland cement, for example, is responsible for approximately five percent of global greenhouse gas emissions. And even after our building materials are made, modern construction depends on an endless stream of polluting trucks to deliver them to us, usually from hundreds of miles away. Now that human-induced climate change is an accepted reality, we urgently need to find ways to reduce our carbon footprint. Building with less-processed nat-

FIGURE 1.2. Natural building offers the best environmental advantages when on-site materials are used as much as possible. At Emerald Earth Sanctuary in California all lumber for construction is harvested on the land, often within sight of the building project. This allows residents to micromanage the forest for health and productivity and also to increase solar gain for the buildings. [Credit: Michael G. Smith]

ural materials from close by our sites is an important step in the right direction.

In some cases, we can choose to build with materials that are the by-products of other industries and would otherwise create a disposal problem. Until the end of the 20th century, nearly all the straw produced in California—enough to build tens of thousands of family homes every year—was burned in the fields. But clean-air legislation passed in the early 1990s has outlawed that practice. Faced with the problem of what to do with all the straw that they can no longer burn, California rice growers supported legitimizing straw bale building, with the result that in 1996 California became the second state to adopt a straw bale building code.

It's impossible to build a house with no environmental impact, but it's our responsibility to minimize and localize the damage. Many of us religiously protect the trees on our property, then go to the lumberyard to purchase the products of wholesale clear-cutting. If we choose to build with wood, it seems less hypocritical to take down a few select trees near our home sites and run them through a small portable mill, or to thin overcrowded woodlands of small-diameter poles and build

with those. Digging a hole in your yard for clay to make a cob house may look ugly at first, but it's a lot less ugly than strip mines, giant factories and superhighways.

Nature has an enormous capacity for healing small wounds—and that hole in your yard can be turned into a frog pond that supports many kinds of animals and plants. Building with natural, local materials also reduces our dependence on the polluting and energy-intensive manufacturing and transport industries. When our environmental footprint is

under our very noses, it helps ensure that we will minimize its impact. Since we see and walk through our local ecosystems every day, we are more likely to protect their health.

Human Health

Some of the most fervent supporters of natural building are people with acquired chemical sensitivities and other environmental illnesses. These people are particularly aware of how modern buildings can make us sick, but we all know it. In 1984, a World

FIGURE 1.3. At the Permaculture Institute of Northern California, designers pride themselves on "closing loops"—filling needs with local resources while minimizing waste and environmental impacts. For example, the clay for this cob and straw-clay hybrid office was dug from a hole (right front) that later served as a duck pond and part of the site's greywater recycling and rainwater collection system. [Credit: Michael G. Smith]

Health Organization report found that, globally, 30 percent of new and remodeled buildings led to health complaints. These problems result from inadequate ventilation, mold and volatile organic compounds (VOCs) released from formaldehyde-based adhesives, carpets, paints and manufactured wood products.

Other industrial materials like fiberglass, plastics and insulating foams have a larger impact on the health of factory employees and construction workers. Natural materials like stone, wood, straw and earth, on the other hand, are not only non-toxic, they are life-enhancing. Clay, one of the most useful natural building materials, is also prized for its ability to manage moisture, absorb toxins and restore health. (It's also true that some people find straw irritating to their skin, and that inhaling fine particles of clay, straw or wood can cause respiratory illness, so use appropriate protection.)

There is increasing evidence that modern buildings can compromise our psychological and emotional health. Right angles, flat surfaces that are all one color and constant uniformity don't exist in the natural world where our ancestors evolved. Most modern homes certainly don't stimulate our senses with the variety of patterns, shapes, textures, smells and sounds that our pre-industrial ancestors experienced. The uniformity of our environments may contribute to our addiction to sensory stimulation through drugs and electronic media.

In contrast, people seem to get a good feeling from natural buildings that is difficult to describe. Even though conditioned to prefer the new, the shiny and the flawless, we respond at a deep level to unprocessed materials, to idiosyncrasy and to the personal care expressed in craftsmanship. Nearly all the natural buildings I have seen, regardless of the builders' level of expertise, are remarkably beautiful. When I lived in a hand-crafted cob house, I grew to expect the looks of mesmerized awe I saw on the faces of first-time visitors, and the difficulty they had prying themselves from the fire-warmed earthen bench when it was time for them to leave.

Empowerment

We grow up being told you can't build a house unless you're a professional builder. If we want a house, we have to work full-time at a job we often dislike to make enough money to pay a builder who may not like his or her job, either. But it doesn't have to be that way. By using local, unprocessed materials like earth and straw, building smaller than the conventional house and providing much of the labor yourself, you can create a home that is almost unbelievably affordable.

As the price tag drops from the hundreds of thousands to the tens of thousands or even a few thousands of dollars, it becomes easier to shrug off the yoke of

FIGURE 1.4. Natural building techniques allow people with minimal training to work together to build an inexpensive home. These systems often require a lot of labor but little cost in materials and tools. Here, workshop participants apply a base coat of clay plaster to a straw bale wall. [Credit: Catherine Wanek]

loans and mortgages. Save yourself money with a more efficient house that uses simple passive-solar technology for heating and cooling. You may find your cash needs dropping. You can cut down the hours you work and spend more time with the kids or grow a big vegetable garden that will save you even more money while increasing your happiness and health.

Techniques that rely on human labor and creativity produce a different social dynamic than those that depend on premanufactured building components, expensive machines and specialized skills. When you build with straw bales, cob or adobe, the whole family can get involved. A building site free of power tools is a safe and supportive environment for children to

learn valuable skills. Or invite your friends and neighbors for an old-fashioned barn-raising. Offer them food and an education in exchange for their time and energy. It's a good deal for everyone and a lot of fun. While building your home, you're also building a different kind of social structure where people depend upon themselves and each other—instead of on governments, corporations

RESOURCES

Books

• Chiras, Daniel. *The Natural House: A Complete Guide to Healthy, Energy-Efficient, Environmental Homes*, Chelsea Green, 2000. A homeowner's guide to a wide range of natural building systems, comparing the advantages and disadvantages of each. Contains excellent chapters on energy independence, sustainable water systems and site considerations.

• Elizabeth, Lynne and Cassandra Adams, eds. *Alternative Construction: Contemporary Natural Building Methods*, John Wiley and Sons, 2000. A thorough and scholarly treatment of the contemporary natural building revival, with good introductory material, as well as in-depth descriptions of specific techniques. Excellent bibliography and resource list.

• Snell, Clarke and Tim Callahan. *Building Green: A Complete How-To Guide to Alternative Building Methods*, Lark Books, 2nd Edition, 2009. Excellent practical overview of natural building for the owner-builder, with emphasis on straw bale, cob and cordwood. Amazing photos in full color throughout.

Periodicals

• The Last Straw: **thelaststraw.org**. This journal of straw bale and natural building, available in both print and electronic editions, features the latest technical developments and case studies from all over the world.

The website includes a comprehensive listing of workshops and events.

Videos

• *A Sampler of Alternative Homes: Approaching Sustainable Architecture*. Produced by Kelly Hart, Hartworks, Inc., 1998, 120 minutes. Available from **hartworks.com**. This two-hour video features a number of different natural building alternatives, including adobe, earthbags, Earthships, papercrete, rammed earth, straw bale and more.

• *Mud, Hands, a House (El barro, las manos, la casa)*, 2007, 116 minutes. A collaboration between Argentine natural builder/instructor Jorge Belanko and director Gustavo Marangoni, this well-organized, beautifully shot and professionally produced documentary starts with a convincing introduction to natural building and why it is important and moves on to clearly introduce nearly a dozen earth-building techniques. In Spanish with English subtitles. Available from **handprintpress.com/mud-hands-a-house**.

Organizations

• The Natural Building Network: **nbnetwork.org**. Membership organization for natural builders with links to websites and a calendar of events.

and professionals—to meet their basic needs.

From the many gatherings and collaborations of people interested in natural building, a few things have become clear. One is that we are all working together. Even though we may have chosen to focus on different techniques or aspects of natural building, we are all motivated by the same concerns, and our personal experience makes up part of a larger body of collective knowledge. Two, we are not alone. As word gets out to the greater public, we find enormous interest and support from a growing community of owner-builders, professional builders and designers, activists, educators, writers and conservationists.

And lastly, together we hold a great deal of power. The power in our ideas and collective action can influence the way our society thinks, talks and acts regarding building and resource use. We are helping to create a society where, someday, natural building will again be the norm in the United States, as it still is in some parts of the world, and where a new cob house with a thatched roof in any American town will draw only an appreciative nod.

FIGURE 1.5. What kind of world do we want to leave for our children? Natural building empowers children and youth to participate in the creation of their own homes and to envision a more healthy, creative and democratic future. [Credit: Michael G. Smith]

Natural Building: A Global Tradition

CATHERINE WANEK

Our ancestors discovered how to create all the elements of a building, from foundation to roof, using a combination of onsite or local natural materials. From caves to castles, through observation and experience, building designs evolved in each region to make the best use of whatever stone, soil, trees and other plants were at hand, as well as the skin, blood and bones of animals. These natural building solutions have, in many cases, been durable and sustainable for centuries, even millennia.

Recently, across the planet, most traditional building methods have been abandoned in favor

of capital- and energy-intensive building technologies that are seen as unilaterally better and more "modern." Nonetheless, the wisdom of vernacular design is still available to the perceptive designer and builder. These ancient designs embody the philosophy of natural building:

ecologically sound human-scale construction reliant on local resources and skills, within the economic reach of everyone.

North America

In different regions of North America, we can still see how native peoples created their

FIGURE 2.1. The Numatciki (referred as the Mander Indians) built their villages along the fertile floodplain of the Missouri River, in what is now North and South Dakota. The women of the tribes built sturdy pole structures and covered the exterior with reeds and branches, then an insulating layer of grasses, and finally earth, to create comfortable shelters for their extended families during the long, cold winters. Each earth lodge was circular with a dome-like roof and a square hole at the apex through which smoke could escape. These earth lodges were reconstructed at Fort Mandon, North Dakota. [Credit: Catherine Wanek]

CATHERINE WANEK *has traveled from Orange County to Red Square, learning about and documenting straw bale and natural building projects. Since 1992, she has authored three books, produced four straw bale videos, and spent five years managing and editing* The Last Straw: The International Journal of Straw Bale and Natural Building.

17

FIGURE 2.2. This historic mosque in Mali has a timeless feel. Earthen architecture is well-suited to the arid climate of North Africa. The thick cob walls and shade-creating design helps keep the interior of the building cool. The protruding wooden beams are permanent scaffolding for periodic plaster repair. [Credit: Beverly spears]

FIGURE 2.3. Ancient woodless techniques using earthen domes and vaults are now being promoted in the Sahel as a solution to deforestation. This domed structure is traditional in the desert region of Harran, Turkey. [Credit: Betty Wanek]

homes according to the local climate and resources. In the arid Southwest, ancient cultures lived in south-facing cliff dwellings, fashioned from stones, earth blocks and earthen mortar, saving precious trees primarily for roof structures. In the Northwest and East, where trees are abundant and rain more frequent, traditional buildings were typically made from planks and shingles. In colder climates, dwellings were often dug into a hillside or bermed, at least partially, underground, such as the earth lodges in North Dakota. Nomadic cultures of the Great Plains developed movable dwellings such as the tipi.

European settlers who colonized North America brought with them their own traditions of building, yet still had to create their defensible shelters from the materials they found at hand. Hence, the log cabin in forested regions, the adobe dwellings of the Southwest and the straw bale house in Nebraska.

Africa

Natural building in Africa is as varied as that vast continent. Many cultures originally utilized simple thatched beehive-shaped huts woven of small saplings, and a vanishing remnant still do.

Traditional African architecture is most often clustered, with extensive corrals of stone, brush or mud connecting and surrounding the small dwellings, reflecting extended family patterns.

Rammed earth and adobe are common in Morocco and other parts of North Africa, where designs incorporate passive cooling techniques such as courtyards, wind-catchers, shade structures and decorative building facades that simultaneously create shade and beauty. These cultures also developed sophisticated plastering techniques, such as *tadelakt*, a water-resistant finish consisting of many layers of lime-sand plaster, polished with a special soap.

While traditional African architecture is rapidly being lost in an increasingly urban Africa, some rural regions still keep the old ways. Here people still turn to the only materials available to them, chiefly the stones and earth beneath their feet.

Europe

In Europe, you have only to wander off the beaten track to discover centuries-old buildings of stone, timber, earth and straw, finished with lime plasters and thatched roofs. A spectrum of traditional buildings can be viewed at open-air folk museums across

FIGURE 2.4. Outstanding folk museums throughout Europe, like Weald and Downland Open Air Museum, England, offer an experience of how life was lived and homes were constructed without modern tools and using only natural materials. [Credit: Catherine Wanek]

the continent. In nearly every country, handsome historic structures have been saved from the bulldozer, restored in "villages" and finished with authentic furniture and tools, often accompanied by recreations of traditional crafts and cooking.

In the Nordic countries, wooden structures predominate, with the living space often built up on "legs" for security and to keep entrances above snow levels in the winter. Sturdy timber structures supported grass roofs that were waterproofed with a membrane of birch bark. The stave churches were typically waterproofed with thousands of hand-carved wooden shingles.

Elsewhere in Europe, the oldest surviving buildings are primarily stone masonry, a difficult

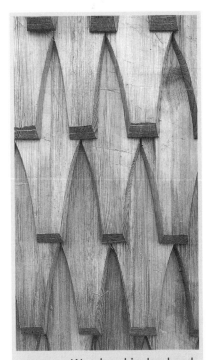

FIGURE 2.5. Wooden shingles, hand-crafted from rot-resistant trees, create a long-lasting weather-proofing exterior on a Norwegian Stave Church. [Credit: Tim Tolitson]

and valued craft, the most weather-resistant and defensible of structures. Also, many oak timber-frame structures are still in use today throughout central Europe—in Denmark, Germany, Austria, Switzerland and France. In Germany, this structural frame is known as *Fachwerk*. Walls may be infilled with wattle-and-daub, straw-clay (*Leichtlehm*), or, in more recent eras, with fired bricks, and are typically protected on the exterior with earth or lime plaster, and sometimes slate siding.

In parts of England and Wales, cob homes predominate, with earthen walls commonly two feet thick or more. Roofs on the oldest structures were often thatched with reeds, although slate was preferred where available. The French constructed their earthen buildings using *pisé* (rammed earth). All across the continent, there are traditions of earthen plasters, lime plasters and later "plaster of Paris," a gypsum-based plaster.

Careful research helped recreate Shakespeare's Globe Theatre on the bank of the Thames River in London, keeping it faithful to the materials and craftsmanship of the original. Set on a brick plinth wall, twenty huge oak timbers connected with mortise and tenon joinery form the three-story structural framework of the new Globe. Oak staves support strips of oak lath, which are plastered with a traditional mix of sand, slaked lime and animal hair to form its walls.

Traditional Building in China

The sophistication of early Chinese cultures is evident from their building practices. Most famous of these built structures is the so-called Great Wall of China. The earliest sections date to several centuries before Christ, and it was rebuilt and enlarged in the 1400s. Massive in scale, it towers twenty or more feet high and stretches 4,500 miles in length over jagged mountaintops and through swamps and deserts.

Some sections of the Great Wall were constructed from dry stacked stones. But much of the core structure is actually rammed earth, tamped by hand—or rather, millions of hands. The builders selected a nearby subsoil for the earthen mix, taking care that no organic material was introduced that could decompose, nor any seed that might sprout. This dampened clay/sand mix was compressed with wooden tampers inside forms, creating a wide fortified wall on which five soldiers could run abreast.

The strength of the structure is due to its trapezoidal cross-section, which provides built-in buttressing.

No less impressive are the construction of the Palace Museum, in Beijing, otherwise known as the Forbidden City, and the surviving Buddhist monasteries, some over 1,000 years old. Admittedly, these are not the homes of the ordinary people, but they reveal a superb understanding of design for longevity. These important buildings are always elevated several steps or more

FIGURE 2.6. No less impressive are the construction techniques of the Palace Museum in Beijing, otherwise known as the Forbidden City, and the surviving Buddhist monasteries, some over 1,000 years old. [Credit: Catherine Wanek]

above their surrounds, to protect them from ground moisture and potential flooding, and they have durable tile roofs with generous overhangs. Even the artistic arc of the roof serves the function of propelling rain away from the building.

Like elsewhere on the planet, the average rural Chinese family has for centuries lived in a home built from what was locally available and comfortable in their local climate, be that wood, earth, bamboo or even cave dwellings, in the Loess Plateau (see "Improving Vernacular Housing in Western China," p. 397). Today there are efforts underway to preserve China's ancient building traditions by making them more comfortable and energy-efficient.

Island Vernacular

Islands and coastal areas are subject to the caprices of ocean weather that can include hurricanes, tsunamis and earthquakes—not to mention normal rain, wind and surf. Homes in these regions are designed to shed water, sway in the wind and be flexible in earthquakes. They are typically built at least a couple of steps above the level of the surrounding ground to allow rain and abnormally high tides to flow under the structure without damage. Many of the Pacific islands are close to the equator, where the weather is warm year-round. Here insulation is not so important, but raising living spaces high to catch the passing breeze is the best way to keep cool.

FIGURE 2.7. This vernacular home in coastal Thailand is designed and constructed to stay high, dry and comfortable even with monsoon rains and flooding waters. [Credit: Kyle Holzheur]

Sustainable and Equitable Shelter

The goal for our ancestors was, as it still is for people all over the planet, to build a comfortable dwelling that is safe, secure, economically achievable and, ultimately, an artistic personal expression. Vernacular homes around the world show a remarkable similarity in structure and materials, and yet a wide range of creative solutions to common human needs. These homes have a lot to teach us about the art of natural building.

These age-old construction techniques can also benefit from modern building science. In recent years, laboratory testing has been performed on adobe, cob, rammed earth and straw bales. Structural, seismic, fire and other performance tests have validated these traditional techniques, while also pointing out directions for improvement. Accordingly, many contemporary visionaries, with a desire for a healthy home and concerned about their ecological footprint, are revisiting these age-old building technolo-gies, attracted also by the simple beauty of natural materials.

It is hoped that the current resurgence of interest and research into vernacular building systems will increase respect for these timeless ideas in their native lands, and that, in villages throughout the world, traditional technologies will gain greater respect as proven examples of low-impact building. It does seem fitting that we look to what has worked in the past, as we seek equitable and sustainable shelter for the century ahead.

RESOURCES

Books
• Bourgeois, Jean-Louis and Carolee Pelos. *Spectacular Vernacular: The Adobe Tradition*, Aperture Foundation, 2nd ed., 1996. An inspirational photo-essay focusing on earthen architecture in Africa. (Out of print but available used.)
• Kahn, Lloyd *Homework: Handbuilt Shelter*, Shelter Publications, 2004. Full-color photographic spectrum of hand-built houses throughout North America and the world.
• Kahn, Lloyd and Bob Easton, eds. *Shelter*, Shelter Publications, 2nd edition, 2000. This encyclopedic seminal work of writer/publisher/photographer Lloyd Kahn can be credited with inspiring the birth of the natural building movement.
• Komatsu, Eiko and Yoshio Komatsu. *Built by Hand: Vernacular Buildings Around the World*, Gibbs Smith, 2003. Perhaps the most beautiful photographic exploration of the world of traditional building.
• Oliver, Paul. *Dwellings: The Vernacular House Worldwide*, Phaidon Press, 2007. A scholarly but accessible discussion of the full range and history of human dwellings, with many beautiful photos, mainly in black and white.

• Rudofsky, Bernard. *Architecture without Architects: A Short Introduction to Non-Pedigreed Architecture*, University of New Mexico Press, reprint edition, 1987. Originally published in 1964, this slim but seminal work helped catalyze the modern appreciation for vernacular architecture. All photos in black and white.
• van Lengen, Johan. *The Barefoot Architect*, Shelter Publications, 2007. This English translation of an international bestseller is a must-have resource for natural builders. Prolifically illustrated, it covers design, construction details, natural heating and cooling, water and sanitation techniques, along with a wide variety of natural materials.

Websites
• naturalhomes.org. The single best Web portal for inspiration from the awesome creativity of people building natural building around the world. Created by Oliver Swann.
• wikipedia.org/wiki/List_of_open-air_and_living_museums. Comprehensive site with links to open-air museums throughout Europe and the world.

The Importance of Housing Ourselves

Ianto Evans

3

I once heard a Chilean named Ana Stern give a speech on "The Difference Between Peasants and Farmers in Mexico." Peasants, she said, satisfy their own basic needs: they grow their food, build the houses they live in and often make their own clothes. Most peasants collect medicinal herbs, treat medical emergencies and supply their family entertainment. They experience fully what they do every day; they have time; they feel joy. Their culture is integrated; it makes sense.

Farmers, by contrast, grow

IANTO EVANS *is an applied ecologist, landscape architect, inventor, writer and teacher, with building experience on six continents. With his partner Linda Smiley, he is responsible for reintroducing cob to North America. He is a founder and director of the Cob Cottage Company, co-founder of the Natural Building Colloquium and co-author of* The Hand-Sculpted House: A Practical and Philosophical Guide to Building a Cob Cottage *(Chelsea Green, 2002).*

things to sell. With what they earn from their products, they buy their groceries, building materials, clothes, entertainment and medical care. They must also buy into a system that demands they drive to market, pay taxes, perhaps send their kids to agricultural college. Increasingly they must buy machinery, seeds,

fertilizers and pesticides. Farmers have no time to enjoy directly satisfying their own needs, so they purchase their satisfactions: they buy ready-made clothing and convenience foods.

I've thought a lot about Ana's presentation. Her definition shook my worldview. In her terms we are all farmers — there are few

FIGURE 3.1. In village societies around the world, building a house was traditionally a cooperative venture among householders, extended family members and neighbors. Homes were often passed down through the generations, being expanded, repaired and remodeled over time. These men in South Yemen are preparing mud for continuing work on the cob and adobe complex in the background. [Credit: Danny Gordon]

FIGURE 3.2. Many natural building techniques are easy to learn, often without specialized training or expensive tools. This empowers people who would be excluded from the modern construction industry to participate in building their own homes. In Anapra, Mexico, these girls are learning to plaster with clay on the straw bale home that is being built for their family through a collaborative effort led by Builders Without Borders. [Credit: Catherine Wanek]

FIGURE 3.3. Katie Jean was a single mother in her mid-20s when she began building the first permitted cob home in California. Her only previous building experience was a week-long cob workshop. She was later able to secure a bank loan on the house to pay off the money she owed from purchasing the land. [Credit: Michael G. Smith]

peasants in the US. I've always felt comfortable in the traditional villages of Africa and Latin America, and now I understand why. The parts of my own life that I truly enjoy are the peasant parts, the parts I don't pay for, the parts that I myself create. A life of working for someone else and paying for basic needs is essentially unsatisfying. Why? Because our links to nature are severed when we live this way.

Why do we grow garden vegetables? It's not the easiest way to obtain food. The simplest cost-benefit analysis will show that it's hard to make the same money from growing lettuces as from going to the office. Otherwise wouldn't most of us be lettuce farmers?

We grow food (or flowers) for completeness, for the grounded understanding that comes from putting seeds in the ground, feeding, watering, picking and eating the plants that grow. To be complete, we need to have a constant awareness of our cosmic bearings, of where and how we fit into nature's patterns. If you compost your excrement as the Chinese do, use your own urine for fertilizer and grow your own vegetable seeds from the plants you raise, the cycle is complete: you have inserted yourself into a completely visible ring of cause and effect. You experience the whole natural process, and the better you observe how that process works, the easier you slide into it.

The peasant/farmer analogy works equally well for house building. For most of history, humans have created their own homes. The whole family helped when the work would otherwise be too heavy or too slow. Sometimes the entire community assisted, as with an Amish barn-raising. Only recently have we traded outside the circle of friends and family in order to have homes. At first we traded only for parts or techniques beyond the reach of the homemade. For example, the village blacksmith made the hinges and we gave him eggs. Later we paid money to skilled local artisans for more durable, better-made work. Then, not long ago, we started to pay complete strangers and distant corporations our hard-earned cash to supply us with skilled trades and manufactured components. To earn that money, we had to grow a surplus. The self-sufficient plot was no longer big enough.

Peasants became farmers. Yet small landholders often can't survive in a cash economy, and when they fail, their land is sold to a bigger operator. Not having land, they don't have access to the earth, rock, trees or straw that were previously at hand for building materials. In order to pay for housing, they turn to producing artifacts or services to sell.

That's the stage set. We go to jobs doing possibly meaningless work for 30, 40 or 50 years to pay for a house with which we no longer have any direct connection. How many of us have been in a steel mill or a plasterboard factory? If we have, did we enjoy what we smelled and heard and felt there? When schoolchildren take a field trip to the slaughterhouse, they often stop eating meat. When we see how building components are made, perhaps we will seek better ways to house ourselves.

The natural building movement has helped us reconnect with our tradition of self-reliant shelter, surely one of our natural rights. We take the free building materials from the ground beneath our feet—stones, soil, trees and grasses—and shape them into foundations, floors, walls, roofs, plasters: in short, homes.

A shift in attitude comes of making what you need for yourself. You change your outlook

RESOURCES

Books

• Evans, Ianto, Linda Smiley and Michael G. Smith. *The Hand-Sculpted House: A Practical and Philosophical Guide to Building a Cob Cottage*, Chelsea Green, 2002.

• Kahn, Lloyd. *Shelter*, Shelter Publications, 1973. An intoxicating celebration of owner-building in all of its forms, from vernacular architecture around the world to the unique artistic products of the American back-to-the-land movement. Many drawings and photos.

• ———. *Homework: Handbuilt Shelter*, Shelter Publications, 2004. An inspirational and idiosyncratic full-color exploration of hand-built houses throughout North America and the world.

• Kern, Ken. *The Owner-Built Home*, Scribner, 1972. The bible for a generation of owner-builders, this book provides practical instructions for first-time builders in site evaluation, design and planning and specific techniques such as poured concrete, stone masonry and roof framing.

• Nearing, Scott and Helen Nearing. *The Good Life: Helen and Scott Nearing's Sixty Years of Self-Sufficient Living*, Schocken, 1990. This book describes the Nearings' pioneering work in homesteading based on a philosophy of social justice and peace. Includes detailed descriptions of the process of building their slip-form stone and concrete house.

• Thoreau, Henry David. *Walden*, Dover, 1995. (Originally published in 1854.) A classic on the philosophy of simple living close to nature, this poetic journal particularly extols the virtues of building one's own simple shelter with available materials. Filled with timeless wisdom.

from "I want this. Where can I buy it?" to "What's here? What can I best do with it?" The first attitude is how a consumer society approaches life. The second is how people in traditional societies have always looked at their world. It's called creativity, and it's enormously satisfying. Now you see the role of roundwood thinnings in framing a roof and realize how easy it is to build door frames from poles, to shovel sod onto your roof, to set frameless glass shards for windows into a cob wall. Once you learn to create your basic building materials from the ground beneath your feet, your vision opens up.

Central to building your own natural house is the lifestyle change that frees you from tedium and debt. If you follow the thought processes and building principles explored in this book, your housing costs may almost disappear, creating an opportunity for you to take the time to build a house that really inspires you. Most importantly, remember that natural building is not something you do quickly to get a finished structure. Building and living in your house can be spiritual processes; joy, reflection and connection with nature can become daily experiences.

Natural Building and Social Justice

4

ROBERT BOLMAN

Elsewhere in this book there are various arguments for natural building from environmental, health and esthetic points of view. Here I wish to make the case for natural building from the standpoint of social justice. We all know that there is poverty in the world. The scale of that poverty and the root causes behind it must be understood and accounted for if we, as a society, are ever going to complement our concern for environmental responsibility with an equally passionate concern for social responsibility.

The unequal distribution of the world's wealth is not a coincidence. It is not an unfortunate inevitability. It is not a mechanical result of preexisting conditions that we are conveniently powerless to change. The poor

ROBERT BOLMAN *is a long-time meditator and founding director of Maitreya EcoVillage in Eugene, Oregon.*

distribution of the world's wealth is a direct and deliberate result of foreign policies first pioneered by colonizing European countries and then honed to a fine art by the United States. To a certain extent, wealth and prosperity in the US is directly related to poverty and suffering, often imposed at gunpoint, elsewhere in the world.

FIGURE 4.1. Throughout history, people with few economic resources have been able to build themselves adequate shelters, often both elegant and functional. This simple dwelling in highland Guatemala is made entirely from materials gathered from the forest nearby: a frame of saplings lashed together with vines, covered with split-palm trunk siding and palm frond thatch. People's capacity to house themselves according to these ancient traditions is rapidly being eroded by multiple forces, including the destruction of local ecosystems, loss of secure land tenure and economic and social forces that impel young people to seek work in the market economy, often leaving rural areas for cities. [Credit: Michael G. Smith]

(An examination of the history of the CIA will bear this claim out in shocking detail.)

For many decades, the Cold War served as a convenient pretext to impose US political will around the world. With the end of the Cold War, the push toward globalization serves as yet another pretext for the continued imposition of US economic order on the rest of the world's population—many of whom would choose something else if they had any say in the matter. The stated objective in promoting free-market capitalism the world over has been that only through economic growth and development can the world's poor be lifted up out of poverty. But this has only happened to a very limited extent. The far more pervasive reality is that the poor of the world are sinking into greater poverty while the wealthy are becoming much wealthier.

We must consider social realities when we contemplate building our houses. Since the 1940s, although families in the United States have gotten smaller, our houses have doubled in size. And there's no end to the consumer goods that big business is happy to help us fill these houses with—much of it entirely unnecessary and destined to end up in a landfill in a relatively short time. While there is some question as to whether or not there's any such thing as an environmentally responsible 5,000 sq. ft., (460 m²), million-dollar single-family house, there certainly is no such thing as a *socially* responsible house of that size and cost. We are doing our souls a disservice if we concern ourselves only with environmental issues while ignoring the immense, heartbreaking social issues that exist right in front of us.

The spirit behind natural building speaks to the all-consuming sickness of consumerism. Instead of using undue wealth to purchase toxic, energy-intensive building products made in a factory in Mexico, we could humbly assume our place in the world community by using our hands to build our houses out of naturally available, inherently safer materials—much as human beings have done since the dawn of civilization. Instead of buying pesticide-laden strawberries from Chile or lettuce from Mexico, we could grow natural, healthy food

FIGURE 4.2. Arriving in rapidly growing urban areas, poor people the world over must creatively shelter themselves with whatever materials they can find. This transitional home in Cape Flats, South Africa, is made of tarps and other salvaged materials. Cape Flats, an area of housing projects and informal settlements that sprang up during the second half of the 20th century near Cape Town, has been called "apartheid's dumping ground." [Credit: Joseph F. Kennedy]

FIGURE 4.3. This nearly 5,000 sq. ft. (450 m²) straw bale home was built for a family in Connecticut, USA. It may be natural, but is it socially responsible? As natural builders we must challenge ourselves and our clients to build smaller homes that use less energy and fewer resources. The original owners were challenged to make their payments and had to sell the house. [Credit: Catherine Wanek]

RESOURCES

Books

- Chomsky, Noam. *Hegemony or Survival: America's Quest for Global Dominance*, Holt, 2004. Just one of the dozens of hard-hitting and well-researched books on international politics and global capitalism written by this celebrated linguist.
- De Graaf, John, David Wann, and Thomas H. Naylor. *Affluenza: How Overconsumption Is Killing Us—And How to Fight Back*, 3rd edition, Berrett-Koehler, 2014. A thorough indictment of the waste and social problems caused by our societal obsession with overconsumption, with practical suggestions on how to escape from the trap.
- Galeano, Eduardo. *Open Veins of Latin America: Five Centuries of the Pillage of a Continent*, 25th Anniversary edition, Monthly Review Press, 1997. Superbly written exposé of the bloody history of exploitation in Latin America at the hands of colonial foreign powers (including the US), multinational corporations and local elites.

- Menzel, Peter. *Material World: A Global Family Portrait*, Sierra Club Books, 1995. Photographers selected a "statistically average" family in 30 countries, then shot portraits of the family with their home and belongings. A fascinating study of the disparity in global wealth, among other things.

Organizations

- Global Exchange: **globalexchange.org**. Among other services, this international human rights organization offers "Reality Tours" to educate travelers about the causes and solutions to global problems.
- Global Footprint Network: **footprintnetwork.org**. An international think-tank promoting a resource-accounting tool called the "Ecological Footprint" which measures how much of the Earth's area is required to sustain a certain lifestyle. You can take a quiz to calculate your own personal footprint.

in our own gardens. We would do this using the time that we have as a result of not working at a job we hate, to pay the mortgage on our over-sized, over-priced, environmentally clueless house.

The natural building movement exists hand in glove with the voluntary simplicity movement. Growing numbers of people in the US and other affluent countries are recognizing that not only will material abundance not make us happy but that the time spent working to accumulate it can make us miserable. Certainly, many recognize that material abundance doesn't just appear out of nowhere. "Our" fabulous wealth and "their" grinding poverty must somehow be related. As more people turn in the direction of simplicity, of finding happiness in activities other than material consumption, then hopefully more of the world's wealth can find its way into the lives of all the world's people—not just the wealthiest 20 percent. Natural building can play a major role in helping the human species evolve into a happier and more harmonious global family.

Sustainability and Building Codes

David Eisenberg

5

Our greatest responsibility is to be good ancestors.

« Dr. Jonas Salk »

Building codes are based on a societal decision that it is important to build in a way that protects peoples' health and safety. If, inadvertently, these codes actually jeopardize everyone's health and safety by ignoring our buildings' impacts on the environment, resulting in the destruction of the ecosystems that sustain us all, then we are obligated to reinvent the codes from that larger perspective. Certainly, it cannot be more important to protect individuals in specific buildings than to protect all of us and all future generations on this specific planet.

That was the opening premise of this chapter in the first edition of *The Art of Natural Building*. It is still valid well over a decade later, in spite of the many positive changes that have occurred in the interim. We still face the challenge of expanding the historically narrow selection of which hazards are taken into account by building codes, and which, regardless of size or seriousness, are ruled off limits and ignored. Without an expanded scope of concern that, at a minimum, recognizes both the life-cycle impacts of building and the role that codes play in those impacts, the code development process will be blind to many of the largest hazards created by buildings.

Life-cycle impacts begin long before the building is built and usually spread far from the building site. They include but are not limited to impacts on climate, resource depletion, wildlife destruction and the effects of pollution and toxicity on human and ecological health. They start with the acquisition of resources, their transportation, processing and eventual installation. They continue throughout the operation, maintenance and repair of the building and its components.

DAVID EISENBERG *co-founded and has led the Development Center for Appropriate Technology in Tucson, Arizona, since 1992. His decades of construction experience range from troubleshooting construction of the steel-and-glass cover of Biosphere 2 in Oracle, Arizona, to building a $2 million structural concrete house, a hypo-allergenic structural steel house and building with masonry, wood, adobe, rammed earth and straw bales. He was co-author of* The Straw Bale House, *and helped write the first load-bearing straw bale construction building code for the City of Tucson and Pima County, Arizona. He founded and chaired the USGBC Code Committee for 9 years.*

They extend all the way to the eventual demise of the building, including issues of disposal and cleanup. The exclusion of such issues from consideration in the code development process results in larger risks to larger populations over longer time frames and wider geographical areas. We cannot know whether any activity is safe without examining the full range of hazards produced, or having a process to assess and ideally to minimize and balance them.

The central relevance to natural building is that most natural building practices minimize these larger kinds of risk through the use of minimally processed, often local, natural materials. Pointing out the benefits of natural build-

ing in addressing these impacts helps bring into focus the way conventional building practices tend to amplify those hazards. The widespread assumption that currently accepted, conventional practices are safe needs to be challenged. Safety cannot be determined by limiting the scope of concern and investigation. The illustration below has proven to be effective in helping reframe this issue with code officials, by providing a way to more clearly visualize the issue.

As important as this expanded context is, for natural building to gain the level of acceptance we seek, it is also necessary to demonstrate that natural building practices can meet the performance requirements of codes.

One way to achieve both goals is by encouraging local building officials to consider the larger risk framework when they use their discretion in interpreting the code for alternatives to conventional practice. That process has been vital in growing awareness and acceptance for both green building and natural building within the building codes community. Local green building programs led to the creation of national organizations and programs, including the US Green Building Council (USGBC) and its Leadership in Energy and Environmental Design (LEED) rating system.

The rapid and widespread uptake and influence of LEED and green building in the design and building sector led the International Code Council (ICC, the US national organization of building code officials) to develop their International Green Construction Code (IGCC), first published in 2012. Similarly, the State of California developed green building provisions, which are now incorporated into the state's mandatory codes for all buildings.

Though natural building practices have yet to be incorporated directly into the body of these codes, the increasing awareness of the impacts of conventional

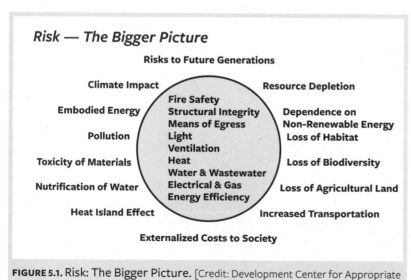

Risk — The Bigger Picture

Risks to Future Generations

Climate Impact

Embodied Energy

Pollution

Toxicity of Materials

Nutrification of Water

Heat Island Effect

Fire Safety
Structural Integrity
Means of Egress
Light
Ventilation
Heat
Water & Wastewater
Electrical & Gas
Energy Efficiency

Resource Depletion

Dependence on
Non-Renewable Energy

Loss of Habitat

Loss of Biodiversity

Loss of Agricultural Land

Increased Transportation

Externalized Costs to Society

FIGURE 5.1. Risk: The Bigger Picture. [Credit: Development Center for Appropriate Technology]

building opens the door for that to occur. As with acceptance for green building practices, local and regional development and acceptance for some natural building practices has led to wider knowledge and acceptance elsewhere. Nowhere is the viability of this process more apparent than in the approval of two new appendices for the 2015 International Residential Code (IRC, the most widely used residential building code in the US), one for straw bale construction and the other for light straw-clay construction. These both grew out of that local-to-national development process.

FIGURE 5.2. All construction begins with destruction. [Credit: Catherine Wanek]

Two factors have been key in this progress. The first is a growing sense of urgency about the need to greatly reduce the environmental and resource impacts of the built environment. The toxicity of materials and processes, resource intensity, climate impacts, embodied energy, indoor air and environmental quality have all become common topics in the codes community. In 2009, a senior staff member of the ICC invited proposals on straw bale construction and rammed earth for the first edition of the IGCC. A straw bale construction proposal was submitted, but not approved. However, it eventually led to the approved appendix for the IRC. At those public hearings in 2013, a telling statement was made. During the IRC Committee pre-vote discussion on the light straw-clay construction proposal, one committee member encouraged an approval vote, and finished by saying, "This is the future."

The second contributing factor is the long-standing efforts of a great many people and organizations in improving both technical knowledge and practice for a number of natural building methods. An excellent example of engagement with regional building authorities in support of sustainable building comes from the Alternative Solutions Resource Initiative (ASRI), formed in 2010 in Victoria, British Columbia. Their mission is "to promote affordable, environmentally sustainable and healthy buildings through the use of appropriate natural materials and systems" to be accomplished through research, education and development of technical guidelines and references. Their first product, the "Straw Bale Alternative Solutions Resource," is a comprehensive, well-researched and well-written technical guide that advances the prospects for that building system in Canada and elsewhere for professionals and owner-builders alike (see Resources).

Another technical resource for natural materials is the ASTM E2392 Standard Guide for Design of Earthen Wall Building Systems, covering adobe, rammed earth and compressed earth blocks. The Development Center for

Appropriate Technology (DCAT) initiated the development of the standard in 1999 in the ASTM (American Society for Testing and Materials, International) E6.71 Subcommittee for Sustainability in Buildings. The first version was published in 2005, followed by several years of work led by the Ecological Building Network to upgrade the original standard. The updated version (E2392-10) was published in 2010. There is interest in further improving the standard by making needed changes to meet ICC's criteria for a referenced standard in the International Residential Code and the International Building Code.

That standard is a good example of an effective approach to gaining new acceptance for an ancient building material that was actually being outlawed in

RESOURCES

Publication
• *The Last Straw: The International Journal of Straw Bale and Natural Building*: **thelaststraw.org**. The number one go-to resource for current straw bale information, this quarterly journal is available as pdf download and in print in full color. *The Last Straw* is up-to-date on the international natural building movement, human resources and technical developments.

DVD
• *Building Codes for a Small Planet: The Emerging Path Toward Sustainable Construction*, Development Center for Appropriate Technology (DCAT): **dcat.net**. Illuminates the unintended effects of current building regulations, proposes a major shift in focus for building codes and offers a vision for a future where buildings do more good than harm. 48 minutes.

Organizations
• Alternative Solutions Resource Initiative (ASRi): **asri .ca**. A non-profit based in Victoria, British Columbia, promoting natural materials and systems, through research, education and collaboration. Published *The Straw Bale Alternative Solutions*, available online.
• California Straw Building Association (CASBA): **strawbuilding.org**. The leading regional straw bale organization in the US. CASBA holds a spring Conference and fall Gathering.
• Cob Research Institute: **cobcode.org**. An NGO spearheading the effort to develop and implement building codes for cob.
• Development Center for Appropriate Technology (DCAT): **dcat.net**. DCAT's primary program is called

Building Sustainability into the Codes which seeks to create a sustainable context for building codes by working with national regulatory and green building organizations. Founder David Eisenberg offers inspiring presentations, and the website offers a free download of *Build It with Bales*. Tucson, Arizona, US.
• Ecological Building Network (EBN): **ecobuildnetwork.org**. An NGO developing and promoting green building technology since 1999, EBN is a collaborative group of builders, scientists, architects and engineers sharing practical technical guidance for designing and constructing better buildings anywhere in the world. San Rafael, California, US.
• Natural Builders Northeast (NBNE): **nbne.org**. A group of builders, designers, consultants, educators and professionals practicing the art of natural building and design throughout the northeastern United States.
• The Northwest EcoBuilding Guild: **ecobuilding .org**. A non-profit organization of ecological builders, designers, suppliers, homeowners and partners in the Pacific Northwest. The Guild empowers people through education to transform the built environment for long-term sustainability.
• Ontario Natural Building Coalition (ONBC): **natural buildingcoalition.ca**. An active organization that promotes and educates about straw bale and natural building in eastern Canada.

Websites
• US Adobe code: **astm.org/Standards/E2392.htm**
• Geiger Research Institute for Sustainable Building: **GRISB.org**. A good resource for code information and home plans from Dr. Owen Geiger.

some developing nations. Earthen building was seen in these places as unsafe, and classified as a poverty building system, unfit and undesirable for a modern society. Knowing that both old and new adobe and rammed earth buildings in the southwestern US were highly desirable, highly valued in the marketplace and capable of being designed and built to be safe even in high seismic regions, we surmised that if the US had a new earthen building standard, proponents of earthen building anywhere in the world could make the case that the US would not have developed a new standard for an unsafe building material. The key was to make sure that the standard would be appropriate for use in developing countries, not just in the US. The resulting standard is arguably the lowest-tech ASTM standard in existence, providing excellent design and construction guidance that can be used to build affordable, durable and safe earthen structures (see Resources).

Efforts are currently underway to develop a cob building code. Work continues on developing code commentary for both the straw bale and light straw-clay construction appendices in the 2015 IRC. Finding ways to support the continuing research, testing and development of these and other natural building materials and systems remains a challenge, but recent progress and the growing need for high-quality low-impact buildings may make it easier to fund these activities. An ongoing testing program for natural building materials and systems has been established at Santa Clara University in California. More such programs are needed.

Building codes are living documents. In the US, anyone can propose changes and additions to the building codes—the process is open to the public. Needed changes will come about most effectively when more people with direct knowledge of sustainable building practices engage in the code-development process. Through that involvement, both the codes and natural building practices can be improved. That positive outcome depends on the participation of those with both particular technical expertise and those with an understanding of the larger context of risk and responsibility, costs and benefits and the importance of ensuring that these technologies are accessible to those who need and want them. If you have concerns about this, the best way to address them is by participating in the process.

If, as seems likely, the emerging resource and climate crises continue to intensify, so will the need for buildings with smaller impacts on the climate and resources, buildings better able to withstand the greater variability and intensity of a changing climate. Buildings that utilize local, minimally processed, low-impact materials and systems to safely shelter their occupants when external utility connections fail will be in ever higher demand. Good codes, standards and well-developed guidance will be crucial, as will people with the skills to teach and build durable, high-performance buildings with these materials.

Recognizing the long and successful history of building with non-industrialized materials is the starting point for seeing the potential to meld our greater understanding of materials and building science with appropriate and beautiful design and the use of the natural materials that are available around the world. The biggest challenge the natural building movement may face will be a rapid increase in demand for knowledge about best design and building practices. That is a great kind of challenge and a great opportunity.

Can My Natural Home Get a LEED Rating?

6

JOSEPH F. KENNEDY AND ANN V. EDMINSTER

As concern about the environmental impacts of buildings has grown in recent decades, the US Green Building Council (USGBC) was formed to develop a building rating system to measure and compare the sustainability of buildings. This system is called LEED (Leadership in Energy and Environmental Design) and was first launched in 2000 to promote planning, design and construction strategies that address sustainability at every stage of a building's life-cycle, including design, construction, operations and maintenance. The natural building movement has always

JOSEPH F. KENNEDY *is a designer, writer and teacher of architecture.*

ANN V. EDMINSTER, *M.Arch., LEED AP, is a consultant and recognized national expert on green home design and construction. She is a principal author of the LEED for Homes Rating System and consults to builders, owners, developers, supply chain clients, design firms, investors and public agencies.*

been ahead of the curve in addressing sustainability concerns, and now many natural builders are becoming curious about how (or if) their buildings can be rated under LEED.

LEED takes a checklist approach to encourage greater sustainability in buildings. There are several different LEED checklists

for projects of different types and scales. We have chosen to investigate LEED for Homes to see how natural buildings can measure up, as most recent natural buildings are at a residential scale. LEED for Homes provides a set of 136 possible points distributed across seven categories (shown in the table on the following page) plus

FIGURE 6.1. This Sonoma Valley homestead by Daniel Smith & Associates Architecture features straw bale walls supplemented with solar collectors, mass storage and a variety of energy- and water-efficient measures that are integral to the design, including a living roof, greywater and rainwater harvesting. This house achieved LEED for Homes Platinum certification.
[Credit: Russell Abraham]

LEED for Homes

Category	How Natural Buildings Can Address This Issue
Innovation and Design Process (11 points maximum)	Good design process can be as easily applied to a natural building as any other. Innovative or Regional Design is an open category that takes an integrated approach, with particular emphasis on durability. This category gives natural builders an opportunity to garner credit for their design innovations, provided they pass muster with LEED assessment teams.
Location and Linkages (10 points maximum)	This category focuses on proximity to transit and services. A natural building located in a rural location, as many are, may earn relatively few points in this LEED rating category. As natural buildings are increasingly built in towns and cities that have better access to transportation and services, this section can more widely apply.
Sustainable Sites (22 points maximum)	This category emphasizes resource-efficient landscape design. Most natural builders take great pride in minimizing disturbance to sites and design their buildings accordingly. For most projects, these credits are relatively easy to earn. Credit for dense (multi-story) construction will be harder to earn for most natural buildings because of the structural limitations of many natural building systems.
Water Efficiency (15 points maximum)	Natural builders commonly integrate water catchment and greywater systems into their buildings, and are increasingly likely to incorporate water-efficient plumbing fixtures. As a result, they will score well in this category.
Energy and Atmosphere (38 points maximum)	Natural building systems, when properly selected, designed and detailed, can provide superior energy performance. One can earn points by following specified better-than-code standards for insulation, air infiltration, windows, HVAC, lighting, appliances and renewable energy.
Materials and Resources (16 points maximum)	This is the core strength of natural building, but while 8 of the category's 16 points are awarded for materials selection, relatively few—e.g., bamboo flooring, straw insulation and wood framing (which, though natural, isn't generally the focus of natural building)—lend themselves to natural materials. The other points are awarded for material-efficient framing (up to 5) and waste management (up to 3).
Indoor Environmental Quality (21 points maximum)	Natural materials are non-toxic and some (especially clay) can absorb toxins and help moderate humidity levels. (Proper building details are key here, however, especially when utilizing straw, wood or other materials that can mold if they get wet.) These qualities, however, don't earn credit in this category (all materials-related attributes are credited in the Materials and Resources category). Rather, the category focuses on proper ventilation, air filtering and contaminant control.
Awareness and Education (3 points maximum)	Credit is earned by providing the owner with an operations and maintenance manual, training in building operations and activities that promote public awareness of sustainable building and LEED.

an additional category (worth four points) for innovative approaches.

Depending on the number of points it scores, a project can be rated as LEED Certified (45–59 points), Silver (60–74 points), Gold (75–89 points) or Platinum (90–136). The points are awarded according to their relative significance to the overall performance of the building, as established by the US Green Building Council. While there has been some criticism in the past that LEED-certified buildings did not perform as well in practice as their point score would indicate, current versions of LEED have been updated to improve performance with regard to sustainability.

LEED places an emphasis on building energy performance— that is, reducing the energy used in building operations by emphasizing good insulation, an airtight building envelope, high-performance windows and so on. Increasing numbers of natural builders have begun to follow this example, as it has become clear that an energy-inefficient house counters any environmental benefits that may be gained by using natural materials. But the question remains: How do natural building materials and methods fit into these rating systems? The table on the previous page briefly addresses this question.

There is no penalty for using natural materials in the LEED system, and natural building approaches are likely to be awarded points in several categories,

Natural Building and LEED: An Architect's Perspective
by David Arkin

Natural building techniques and LEED certification are in no way mutually exclusive, and can certainly be mutually beneficial. Natural building systems can earn LEED credits for locally harvested resources (from within 500 miles of the building site). Low- and no–VOC (volatile organic compound) finishes, which are the norm in natural buildings, are mandatory under LEED. Innovative systems incorporating rapidly renewable resources qualify for points either specifically or as innovation credits. Straw bale walls can help a building sequester more carbon than is emitted during construction, and that will help us achieve the goals outlined in Architecture2030.org's 20/80 Pathway to curbing global climate change, which is arguably a more urgent goal than achieving LEED certification.

In a blower door and infrared study done on a straw bale cabin our firm designed, we showed that bale walls can be reasonably airtight, approaching the passive house standards for airtightness and thermal performance. We have investigated the thermal lag qualities of the earth-plastered straw bale walls at the Real Goods Showroom in Hopland, California. We have shown that these walls have the ideal 12-hour thermal lag that contributes to excellent passive solar performance in climates such as Hopland's that have diurnal temperature swings.

Identifying the credits that natural building techniques can earn early in the design process is key to ensuring they will both earn these credits and that the targeted features will remain intact through the design process. A handy guide from the USGBC, geared toward LEED for Homes, but probably similar for non-residential projects, can be found in the LEED resources below.

DAVID ARKIN is an award-winning architect who, together with his wife Anni Tilt, has designed numerous green and natural buildings.

FIGURE 6.2. This detail of the Sonoma Valley homestead illustrates the thick straw bale walls and energy-efficient windows of this LEED Platinum passive solar dwelling. [Credit: Daniel Smith & Associates Architecture]

FIGURE 6.3. This Passivhaus from Austria built for features high-quality "tilt and turn" windows. [Credit: Catherine Wanek]

although designers may have to educate the LEED auditors assigned to their cases, who may not be familiar with all of the benefits of natural building techniques. Architect Dan Smith writes:

We just completed a LEED Platinum straw bale house, where the bales certainly helped achieve high energy efficiency (80 percent better than Title 24 [the California state energy code]). This was as much for the plaster's thermal mass as for the straw bales' insulation. We also received credits for "rapidly renewable resources" and "local materials." However, on an early LEED Gold project, a 12,000 sq. ft. (1,100 m²) dining hall we designed, we had to fight to get straw bales to qualify as "rapidly renewable," since the basis was as a percentage of construction cost and they didn't cost enough.

It is clear that a natural building, like any other structure, should be constructed for energy efficiency and durability, with consciousness of the environment as it is being built, and awareness of how it should be maintained for optimum performance—all of which earn LEED credit. Because a LEED rating helps ensure these goals for natural buildings, it may add value, particularly as a guide to ensuring that the project is pursued through a lens of sustainability that is broader than simply the materials with which it is created.

Some LEED-Certified Natural Buildings

Sonoma Family Residence and Organic Farm (LEED Platinum). Designed by Dan Smith and Associates. Includes plastered straw bales. **dsaarch.com/projects/large_res/sonoma.html**

Monterey Ranger District Office in King City (LEED Silver). Rating success largely due to the use of straw bales. Skillful Means (John Swearingen and crew) did the straw bale walls and lime plaster finishes. **fs.usda .gov/detailfull/lpnf/home/?cid=stelprdb5423789&width=full**

Santa Clarita Transit Maintenance Facility (LEED Gold). Designed by HOK. Also includes straw bales. **inhabitat.com/hoks-leed-gold-certified-straw-bale-building/hokstrawbale4jpg/**

Western Pennsylvania Residence (LEED Platinum). Designed by Studio D'arc. Straw bales and straw clay and natural plasters. Built by Sota Construction. **sotaconstruction.com/project_details.asp?id=42**

RESOURCES

• Architecture 2030. Issued the challenge to make buildings carbon neutral by 2030. **architecture2030 .org/2030_challenge/the_2030_challenge**

• **Buildinggreen.com**. Environmental building news in sustainable design and construction.

• Building Performance Institute (BPI): **bpi.org**. BPI has created industry standards for the Building Performance industry. Building Performance contractors do the audits to determine energy and indoor quality issues in existing buildings, such as energy use, heating and cooling, air flow and moisture conditions, as well as performing any remedial work necessary.

• CalGreen: **bsc.ca.gov/Home/CALGreen.aspx**. The new California state green building code, CalGreen (Title 24, Part 11), has many similarities to LEED. Adopted in 2008, it is the first statewide green building code in the US. It applies not only to state-owned buildings, schools and hospitals but to all residential structures in the state. CalGreen provides a checklist of performance standards in five areas that are analogous to LEED's eight categories.

• Energy Star: **energystar.gov**. The US Environmental Protection Agency (EPA) system for the energy rating of buildings. According to their website, this rating is a simple 100-point scale that considers not only the impact of energy use in a building, but the impacts of the source energy, as this can vary widely by price and

emissions. This approach (site + source) focuses on variables that influence building energy performance. It is a foundation of the LEED for Homes Energy and Atmosphere category.

• LEED: **usgbc.org**. "LEED for Homes Guidance for Projects with Non-wood Framing" (including ICF, SIPs, Steel, CMU, Straw bale): **usgbc.org/Docs/Archive /General/Docs9155.pdf**

• Living Building Challenge: **ilbi.org/lbc**. The Living Building Challenge of the International Living Future Institute bills itself as the green building certification program that defines the most advanced measure of sustainability in the built environment possible today. Its categories are very similar to those of LEED, but projects must adhere to stricter standards.

• One Planet Communities: **oneplanetcommunities .org**. One Planet Communities has developed ten principles similar in intent to those of the Living Building Challenge, but in this case the emphasis is on community scale. Currently there are several official prototype communities under development, the initial one being the BedZed community in London.

• Passive House. A European standard gaining popularity in North America. Particularly suited to temperate climates similar to Europe. This standard is actually surpassed by California's CalGreen standards. **passive house.us/passiveHouse/FAQ.html**

Life-Cycle Cost and Value of Four Homes

7

DAVID A. BAINBRIDGE

The goal of the sustainable building movement is to improve the comfort and health provided by the built environment while maximizing the use of renewable resources, minimizing life-cycle costs and maximizing life-cycle benefits. Life-cycle costs and value provide an accounting for the entire lifetime of a building or project. In the US, a building may be in use for as little as 30 years, but 100 to 200 years or more is common in Europe. This is partly because economic incentives in the US favor depreciation, while in Europe, incentives more often favor quality construction and

long life. Loan repayment periods for homes are often 15 or 30 or years in the US, but can be as long as 100 years in Switzerland and Japan.

Life-cycle costs are the costs of constructing, maintaining and operating a building. Life-cycle benefits include the economic return and also the productivity, health and well-being of the users who live in or work in a building. We rarely consider life-cycle

value because there is a wide gap between economics as accountants and developers currently know it and a wiser, sustainable economics that considers human well-being and costs for future generations. Some traditional societies have more carefully considered the future, reflecting on possible outcomes and impacts for generations to come. For example, the leaders of the Haudenosaunee (Iroquois)

DAVID BAINBRIDGE *retired as associate professor of sustainable management at Alliant International University, San Diego, in 2010. His career has included research and development work in passive-solar heating and cooling, passive-solar hot water, sustainable agriculture and straw bale building. Thanks to Mark Smith of Pario Research for suggested improvements.*

FIGURE 7.1. Conventional construction, Moab, Utah. [Credit: Catherine Wanek]

Confederacy set their planning horizon at seven generations or approximately 150 years.

When evaluating costs and benefits over the lifetime of a building, comfort and health, energy and water use, waste and ability to be recycled are some of the key issues. Life-cycle considerations are particularly important for institutions and the elderly who cannot count on increased income to offset foreseeable large increases in costs for energy, water or other resources.

If we compare four hypothetical California houses, we can begin to see the impacts that design and materials choices have on life-cycle costs. The four houses include a conventional wood-frame house, a non-solar-oriented straw bale home and two solar-oriented straw bale homes, with one of them owner-built.

California produces more than one million tons of rice straw a year, and rice straw bales have proven well-suited for construction, providing better insulation (often double that of wood-frame) and good thermal mass for about the same cost as conventional construction. Owner-building can be easier with straw bales, but it still requires many skills to really reduce costs. Straw bale walls are easier to build than wood and are well-suited for community workshops, but they require more labor than wood-frame, so the overall cost of straw bale and conventional wood-frame houses is usually about the same if both are contractor-built. As studies by professor Tod Neubauer at the University of California, Davis, showed, utilizing both proper passive-solar orientation and window placement can reduce energy demand for heating and cooling by 80 percent or more, compared to a conventional house (Table 7.1).

This isn't the full cost, which also includes health and environmental costs from carbon dioxide,

Table 7.1 Finance, operating and opportunity costs

	Conventional	Straw bale	Solar straw bale	Owner-built SSB
Construction cost[1]	$210,000	$210,000	$210,000	$78,750
Utility capacity cost[2]	$3,000	$2,000	$0	$0
Home finance cost[3]	$360,925	$360,925	$360,925	$135,347
Heating & cooling energy (BTU/sf/year) [4]	$37,868	$24,892	$5,893	$5,893
Heating & cooling energy (kWh/year)	$15,400	$10,220	$2,380	$2,380
Energy cost over 30 years[5]	$92,400	$61,320	$14,280	$14,280
Home owner finance opportunity cost[6,7]	$620,320	$620,320	$620,320	$232,620
Home owner energy opportunity cost[6]	$158,807	$105,390	$24,542	$24,542
Utility finance opportunity cost[6]	$5,156	$3,437	$0	$0
Net cost over 30 years	$1,450,608	$1,363,392	$1,230,067	$485,539

[1] US dollars 2013

[2] Cost of natural gas peaker plant at $1,000 per kW of increased capacity

[3] Estimated at 30 year payback with 4 investment return and loan cost

[4] Energy use estimates adapted from L. Elizabeth and C. Adams, *Alternative Construction*, John Wiley and Sons, modeling by Jennifer Rennick, energy analyst, San Luis Obispo

[5] Based on estimated average cost 20¢ per kWh

[6] Opportunity cost is the often neglected cost of what money could earn if it was invested rather than spent.

[7] This is greater than finance cost because interest is compounded rather than fixed rate.

Table 7.2 Cost emissions 30 years

	Conventional	Straw bale	Solar straw bale	Owner-built SSB
CO_2e emissions, tons [1]	254	169	39	39
Cost emissions $36 ton [2]	$9,149	$6,071	$1,414	$1,414
Cost emissions $200 ton [3]	$50,800	$33,800	$7,800	$7,800

[1] PG&E utility emissions at 0.542 pounds CO_2e (or CO_2 equivalent effect of all GWG per kWh)
[2] 2013 CO_2 US GWG emission estimated cost $36 ton.
[3] Pindyck, R.S. 2013. "Pricing carbon when we don't know the right price." *Regulation*, Summer 43-46.

nitrous oxides, particulate matter, sulfur dioxide and global warming impacts from electricity generation. If we look at just the carbon dioxide equivalent (CO_2e) from power plant operation, we see the results shown in Table 7.2.

In most states, the emissions would be much worse, as California has much cleaner power than many others. Power plants in-state emitted a total of 41.6 million metric tons of Global Warming Gases (GWG) in 2012, according to the California Air Resources Board, but much dirtier out-of-state power plants provided about 30 percent of the state's electricity, mostly generated by burning coal. Estimates of the external costs of using

FIGURE 7.2. A straw bale house designed to take advantage of southern exposure. The highly insulating walls help to reduce conditioning costs, which is the largest expense over the life of a building. [Credit: Catherine Wanek]

western coal have not been made but ranged from 9–27 cents/kilowatt hour for eastern coal (Epstein et al., 2011). Residential emissions, primarily from natural gas heaters and water heaters added another 30 million tons. Total CO_2e emissions are about 12 tons per person per year. Considering the impacts of all of these emissions, the health costs of a new house (for asthma and pulmonary disease, among others) could easily exceed the finance cost. A 2008 National Resources Defense Council report estimated that controlling air pollution could save California three to five billion dollars a year in health care.

This estimate of life-cycle cost neglects the energy and emissions required to manufacture materials, buildings, power plants, drilling for gas, leaks while shipping gas, air-conditioner construction and repair, leaks of CFCs during AC repair and maintenance of the power system. The life-cycle costs of the power plant itself (rather than the energy produced) can also be significant (Spath and Mann, 2000), even without considering ecosystem impacts like nitrogen pollution (Bainbridge, 2009) and

RESOURCES

Publications

• Bainbridge, D.A. *Rebuilding the American Economy with True Cost Accounting*, Rio Redondo Press, 2009. Offers a comprehensive review of true cost accounting, including reviews of several companies. Free download at **sustainabilityleader.org**.

• Corbett, J., D.A. Bainbridge and J. Hofacre. *Village Homes Solar House Designs*, Rodale Press, 1979. Judy and Michael Corbett were the developers of this innovative sustainable neighborhood. Their primary interest was social—building community—but they did many other things very well too, including narrow streets, bicycle paths, aboveground drainage and community-managed orchards, vineyards and gardens.

• Epstein, P.R., J.J. Buonocore, K. Eckerle, M. Hendryx, B.M. Stout III, R. Heinberg, R.W. Clapp et al. "Full cost accounting for the life cycle of coal" in *Ecological Economics Reviews*, R. Costanza, K. Limburg and I. Kubiszewski, eds., Annals, New York Academy of Science 1219: 73–98. This detailed review covers eastern coal, but illustrates the complexity and very high cost of non-renewable fuels.

• Neubauer, L.W., G. Starr and B. Melzer. "Temperature control by passive solar house design in California," *Transactions of the ASAE*, 23(2):0449-0457, 1980. This report on the potential for temperature control by passive solar house design in central California shows that simply orienting homes correctly and providing adequate insulation could reduce heating bills by 80 percent.

• Spath, P.L. and M.K. Mann. "Life Cycle Assessment of a Natural Gas Combined Cycle Power Generation System," NREL/TP-570-27715, National Renewable Energy Laboratory, 2000. Life cycle costs of products and facilities are important, and this is a good one, showing how many interactions, impacts and costs are involved over the life of a power plant.

Websites

• Accounting for Sustainability: **accountingforsustainability.org**/ This organization supported by Prince Charles has been a leader in the development of more complete accounting. They have developed a new, innovative leadership seminar for Chief Financial Officers, jointly with the University of Cambridge Programme for Sustainability Leadership (CPSL).

• California Air Resources Board: **arb.ca.gov**. The California Air Resources Board reports state greenhouse gas emissions every year. What isn't measured isn't managed, so creating state requirements to report and audit emissions was a big step forward. This should be a national effort.

• Village Homes: **villagehomesdavis.org/public/about**. Visit this 220-unit solar subdivision from the 1970s and see how wise Judy and Mike Corbett were in building a community.

healthcare costs. These are often estimated as comparable to the current cost of energy, but are not well studied.

If we add just the lower estimate of GWG cost, we see the total cost over 30 years (rounded off):

Conventional $1,459,757
Straw bale $1,369,463
Solar straw bale $1,231,481
Owner-built Ssb $486,953

This also does not acknowledge other benefits. Statistically, reduced healthcare cost for families living in the straw bale solar house would be significant for the homeowner and for others experiencing reduced carbon emissions. Over 30 years, the straw bale solar house would not need to replace heaters and water heaters as often. Using rice straw for construction pro-vides two additional benefits— reducing methane emissions from rice straw decomposition in flooded fields and air pollution from straw burning.

The owner-built solar straw bale would clearly be the best choice for long-term value, with a life-cycle saving of $972,804 compared to a standard non-solar wood-framed home. This highlights the virtue of keeping construction costs low. The contractor-built solar straw bale home would reduce life-cycle costs about a quarter of a million dollars. The solar straw bale homes would also increase in value over time as resource costs and temperatures increase. We might also expect benefits to the homeowners similar to Village Homes (a solar subdivision in Davis, California) where home values were ten percent above comparable non-solar conventional developments.

Over the long term, the 100-year social and environmental costs of the conventional home would almost certainly exceed the construction cost. With a carbon tax of $200 per ton just for GWG, the construction of energy-inefficient homes would end. Incorporating the social and environmental costs would further incentivize better design and construction. If we had more flexible performance-based building codes and gave home photovoltaic installations the same subsidies we give utilities, it would probably be cost effective to build a solar stand-alone straw bale house with super-efficient appliances anywhere straw is available. Everyone except the utility company wins with sustainable design.

In Defense of Craft

8

PATRICK WEBB

*If you want a golden rule that will fit everything, this is it:
Have nothing in your houses that you do not know
to be useful or believe to be beautiful.*

« William Morris »

Food, clothes and shelter. That's where it all started for us as a species. Humans are fairly fragile creatures, but with our ability to procure such basic needs, we were able to not only survive but prosper. We got pretty good at it too, and fast! Rapid developments in agriculture, husbandry, textiles and building laid the grounds for what we today call civilization.

Mere survival was good and fine but ultimately not all that satisfying. So we started cooking, mixing and flavoring our food— culinary traditions were born, satisfying our senses of smell and taste. We wove colorful, intricate patterns into our garments from the softest wool and the finest linen, and a textile tradition was born, satisfying our tactile and visual senses. We began building shelters for our families that we called homes and ornamenting them with forms literal and iconic. We had finally arrived at a place at once personal, secure and restful.

A Definition of Craft

Our word "craft" came into Old English by way of an older Norse word that carried the meaning of

FIGURE 8.1. Finely detailed plaster meets exquisitely crafted timber frame in this "Econest" by builder Robert Laporte and architect Paula Baker-Laporte. [Credit: Paula Baker-Laporte]

PATRICK WEBB *is a traditional and ornamental plasterer. Currently he instructs as an Adjunct Professor of Architectural Plastering at the American College of the Building Arts in Charleston, South Carolina. Additionally, Mr. Webb serves as a technical consultant for heritage plaster manufacturer Plâtres Vieujot, providing services to architects to assist them in properly specifying plaster and plaster systems.*

49

"physical strength." By the time of Middle English, the meaning extended to include "mental power and skill." A related term that arrived by way of Latin and Italian was "artisan." It carried much the same sense as "craftsman" but indicated one especially instructed in the arts. (The terms craftsman and craftsmen are used throughout this article in reference to both men and women practicing craft.) So historically the meaning of "craft" was anything but pastiche or trivial—it was a serious expression of

FIGURE 8.2. Taking the time to hand-craft sculptural elements in your home can make the difference between a functional shelter and a habitable work of art. This window enhances a straw bale home on Waiheke Island, New Zealand. [Credit: Catherine Wanek]

human physical and mental ability; it was, if anything, sacred.

Four Misconceptions Concerning Craft

There are a number of ways in which craft is misunderstood. As a craftsman, I'd like to offer my opinion concerning some of the most frequent misunderstandings.

Craft is not labor. Somehow as a society we have come to view sweating and exerting oneself physically outside of sport as demeaning to the human spirit, an indication of low social status and inferior intelligence. This stigma has led some craftsmen to insist on a strict demarcation between labor and craft. I don't mean to deny that some menial labor commonly found in industry and construction meets the above description. However, one must always start off as a laborer in the process of acquiring the skill to grow to the level of a craftsman. There is nothing ignoble about it.

Quite to the contrary—in the course of his daily routine, even a master craftsman will find himself doing mundane tasks, sometimes very labor-intensive and not particularly skilled. That's just life. Frankly, there are times

when you appreciate the mental break so that straightening up the shop, sweeping the floor and taking out the trash is a comfort. Labor is only demeaning when there is a desire to progress but no ability and opportunity for advancement.

Craft is not art. During the 18th century Enlightenment, another line in the sand was drawn, this time between art and craft. Craft was at that time condescended to as a strictly technique-driven, practical function. By contrast, art or rather the "fine arts" were distinguished by creativity, uselessness and a conceptual nature. This was an entirely arbitrary distinction unrelated to recent historical precedent or common

FIGURE 8.3. The revival of a Roman technique of creating finely cobbled paved surfaces by setting flat rounded stones into a dry mortar bed. Built by Bruce Hauschildt. [Credit: Joseph F. Kennedy]

sense. Sculptors, plasterers and painters such as Michelangelo, Leonardo da Vinci and Rafael all had to begin as laborers or apprentices before mastering the practical techniques of their respective mediums and ultimately expressing their skill in highly creative discourse.

"No one does that kind of work anymore." I hear this all the time. I've heard it while I was actually on a scaffold doing that kind of work. Someone passing by will ask me what I'm doing—perhaps I'm placing some plaster ornament—and they'll say, "Too bad, no one does that kind of work anymore!" This idea is so firmly entrenched that despite the fact that the person sees craft happening right in front of their eyes, they still can't believe it. The educational system has told them that craft is dead, so that's it. The reality is quite different, of course. By and large, most architecture before World War II had a level of craft in its construction. That is a lot of inventory in the US that has to be maintained…by craftsmen! It is true that most new construction today primarily utilizes cheap, factory-made materials designed to be installed by unskilled labor; however, in the natural and traditional new build markets, craft continues to thrive.

Industry and technology are the future of production. Because craft costs too much. I challenge this view. I declare that industry and technology are clearly the undisputed present of production and have been so for many decades. And what kind of world have they produced for us to live in? A cheap one to be sure, though not so inexpensive. I'll state a few obvious facts. We know our contemporary homes are toxic. We know our contemporary homes are poorly constructed, unlikely to outlast the mortgage. We at least sense that our contemporary homes were poorly designed using cheap materials and cheaper labor. None of these facts contribute

FIGURE 8.4. Hand-applying ornamental gypsum plaster details. [Credit: American College of the Building Arts]

to the good of society or to our personal happiness.

The Value of Craft

As a craftsman myself, I see the value of craft as very personal. It has made me more "materialistic." I don't mean, of course, an empty desire to acquire more, but rather a deep and profound appreciation for materials themselves: the delicate grain of walnut that tells the story of its life; the intricate veining of a precious Nero Portoro marble that fractalizes in a symphony of color and pattern; the smooth, sensuous feel of earthen clay shaped by the power of my touch. At once I am the creator and the humblest devotee.

Leo Tolstoy once wrote, "There is no greatness where there is no simplicity, goodness and truth." In harmony with these words, I present this alternative: live honestly, with yourself and with others. Make no false justifications. Build or refurbish an authentic home that you want to live in. Fill it with craft that is both useful and beautiful. Employ men and women who care deeply about their work and want to give you the best. It may be at first a daunting concept, but eventually it is a liberation to realize that you can actually eat, drink, love and live in a place that contributes to your happiness.

RESOURCES

Websites
Below are three links to online sites that may be of interest. Of course, as Real Finishes is my own blog it may be a bit of a biased recommendation.
• Real Finishes: **realfinishes.blogspot.com/**
• The Original Green: **originalgreen.org/blog/**
• The American College of the Building Arts: **buildingartscollege.us**

Books
• Alexander, Christopher. *The Nature of Order: The Phenomenon of Life*, Routledge, 2004. (Book 1 of 4). These essays on the art of building and the nature of the universe encourage a view of the world that is at once deeply scientific, yet wholly engaged with our senses, evolved beyond our current mechanistic models.
• Bragdon, Claude Fayette. *The Beautiful Necessity: Seven Essays on Theosophy and Architecture*, Nabu Press, 2014. Explores the underlying spirituality and humanism that is the very foundation of traditional architecture.
• Coperthwaite, William. *A Handmade Life: In Search of Simplicity*, Chelsea Green, 2007. This rambling and stimulating excursion through the life and thoughts of a master craftsman and yurt-builder encourages the engagement of hand and heart with every aspect of our lives.
• Ruskin, John. *The Seven Lamps of Architecture*, Dover Publications, reprint edition, 1989 (original 1849). An invaluable collection of essays on the underlying moral virtues that must be present to imbue meaning to architecture.
• Scruton, Roger. *Beauty: A Very Short Introduction*, Oxford University Press, 2011. Lays the philosophical groundwork for grasping a supra-rational concept while making a compelling case for maintaining beauty in our lives.

PART TWO

Design and Planning

Have you ever watched millions of stars in the sky on a moonless night,
or seen the wind waver over a field of grass, or noticed the dust at play in a shaft of light,
or felt the warmth of another's hand…someone you cared for?
This is where architecture must come from.
Architecture must take measure of all that it is to be human
in a world that is whole.

« James Hubbell, 1974 »

Designing for Vitality

CAROL VENOLIA

9

There is much more to natural building than simply building with natural materials. To really embrace the potential of natural building, we must view a building as an ongoing process, not a static object. A building is a system within systems of human culture, resource flows, daily and seasonal cycles and numerous other natural rhythms.

The look and feel of earth, straw and bamboo stir our senses and remind us of our ancestral roots. The desire to build with material that is close to its own roots often comes from a desire to feel more alive and to behave more responsibly in relation to the larger environment. Natural building provides an opportunity for us to look at how our lives interact with our buildings and how our buildings can help us live in harmony with the greater biosphere.

In order to vitalize the process of creating and inhabiting buildings, we need to overcome some culturally ingrained habits. The buildings to which we have become accustomed in Western civilization reinforce the myth that humans are separate from the rest of nature. For the last several decades, our homes, schools and offices have increasingly cut us off from the world outside. Inside, we have created artificial systems for providing warmth, coolness, lighting, humidity, sound and scent—and often we have inadvertently created atmospheres of energy-sapping monotony, noise, odor and toxicity.

As we now know, the costs of such a narrow approach are many, including an excessive use of energy and other resources, the production of land-choking volumes of waste and damage to the health of inhabitants. But perhaps the greatest unexamined

FIGURE 9.1. We thrive with exposure to nature. [Credit: Carol Venolia]

CAROL VENOLIA is an architect, author and teacher who has pursued her passion for understanding the relationship between life and buildings for over 40 years. She has designed eco-homes, schools, healing centers and ecovillages; been honored by The Green Economy Post as one of ten pioneering women in green design; and named a Green Design Trailblazer by Natural Home Magazine. Carol is the Domestic Nature Goddess at ComeHomeToNature.com; author of Get Back to Nature without Leaving Home; co-author of Natural Remodeling for the Not-So-Green House with Kelly Lerner; and author of Healing Environments: Your Guide to Indoor Well-Being.

55

cost is in the attitudes we have learned—the myth of human separation. Conceivably, if we carry these attitudes into our new building creations, we can make buildings out of natural materials that are still toxic, soul-killing and grossly consumptive of our Earth's resources.

Building for human vitality can be the core of an approach that brings us back to life in all its dimensions. As we are beginning to remember, human vitality is inseparable from biospheric vitality.

FIGURE 9.2. This sensitively designed straw bale home not only avoids harming, but celebrates the existing tree. [Credit: Catherine Wanek]

The Paleolithic Touchstone

Looking to our biological origins provides us with a useful touchstone and suggests guidelines for living harmoniously with our environment. Our bodies are essentially the same as those of Paleolithic hunter-gatherers— anatomically, physiologically and psychologically. The human organism has evolved through millennia of constant interaction with sun, wind, rain, soil, fire, plants and animals in daily and seasonal cycles. Our Paleolithic ancestors lived tribally in the open air, stalked game, gathered plants and were acutely alert to sounds, smells, sights and changes in temperature, sunlight and air movement.

Contrast the sensory richness of Paleolithic times to life today, most of which we spend indoors breathing tainted, recycled air; being warmed by mechanically circulated, heated air; seeing with the aid of monotonous, artificial light; hearing the constant droning of equipment; surrounded by motionless walls and furnishings; and having our senses both understimulated and overstimulated in meaningless ways. It becomes clear that very few contemporary buildings are places where human beings can thrive.

By examining the sorts of "environmental nutrients" our body/being craves, we can create buildings that keep us dry and our activities private, while resynchronizing ourselves to natural cycles and restoring the rich sensory textures with which our nervous systems function best.

Natural Cycles

Daily and seasonal cycles of light and dark, warmth and coolness, are basic to our existence. Within our bodies, we experience daily biological rhythms that are synchronized to the sun—regulating sleep and wakefulness, body temperature, blood pressure, hormone secretion, cell division and virtually all bodily functions. There are also monthly physiological cycles in both women and men that may be synchronized to the changing light and the gravitational pull of the moon. And we have seasonal rhythms in mood, nutrient absorption, sex drive, growth and physical ability, also synchronized with seasonal fluctuations in sunlight.

Many researchers believe that we rely on environmental cues to reset our body clocks daily. The morning sunlight triggers and synchronizes certain internal rhythms, while the approach of darkness cues other rhythms to rise and fall. Changes in air temperature, the Earth's magnetic field and other environmental clues also stimulate biological cycles.

But our built environment typically estranges us from these natural cyclic clues. When our body rhythms get out of sync with each other or with the Earth, our health declines, often resulting in tiredness, depression, anxiety, sleep disturbances and general vulnerability. Electric lighting lengthens the days and blurs the distinction between the seasons. Street lighting entering bedrooms alters the essential darkness of night and obliterates the subtler periodicity of moonlight. Mechanical heating and cooling systems damp out natural temperature variations. And artificial electromagnetic fields overwhelm the Earth's electromagnetic field and its cyclic variations.

Light

Sunlight tells us a great deal about the type of lighting we need. Natural light is constantly changing in intensity, color and angle throughout the day and the year. We are biologically acclimatized to morning light that is warm in color, low in intensity and coming from a low angle, gently grading into noon light that is cool in color, high in intensity and coming from above. Those of us living outside of the tropics are also accustomed to shorter periods of light in winter and longer periods in summer. Any departure from these conditions challenges both our physiological functioning and our sense of esthetics and "rightness."

The obvious implication is to design for daylighting wherever feasible and to orient interior spaces for appropriate natural light. For example, an east-facing bedroom allows you to be awakened by the sun and to begin the day with your biological rhythms synchronized.

When you use artificial light, make sure there's some variety. Research shows that both monotony and overstimulation can lead to loss of visual acuity. We need variety in our visual field, and we need different kinds of light for different tasks—for example, brighter, cooler colored light for visual tasks and lower, warmer colored light for relaxing. Keep in mind that light is a stimulant: in this productivity-oriented culture, we use artificial lights to keep banks of chickens laying eggs all night long and fluorescent ceilings to keep office workers producing after dark.

Consider what it might do for your vitality if you let yourself wind down as the sun goes down. Lower lighting levels in the evenings—even going to bed when it gets dark—allow your body to repair itself and your mind to roam freely. Sleeping longer in the winter is a time-honored practice, too; perhaps there would be less Seasonal Affective Disorder if we got more exposure to daylight and allowed ourselves to hibernate in winter.

Heat

The sun was also our first source of heat, providing a combination of direct and indirect radiant warmth. We feel direct warmth when sunlight falls on us, and indirect warmth when nearby materials absorb the sun's heat and later reradiate it. Not surprisingly, studies have shown that radiant

FIGURE 9.3. A small niche is lovingly carved into a cob wall to contain this sculpture. [Credit: Joseph F. Kennedy]

heat is the most healthful form of heat for humans.

The sun remains our best source of radiant heat. Designing to admit an appropriate amount of sunlight, and incorporating thermal mass materials that can absorb and reradiate the sun's warmth, should be basic to most buildings; this is called direct-gain passive solar heating.

When passive solar heating is inadequate, installed radiant heating systems can fill the gap. Hydronic systems provide radiant heating via heated water that flows through radiators or tubes in the floor or walls. This warm water can also be heated by the sun from solar hot water panels on the roof. Electric-resistance radiant heating systems are also available but are not recom-mended due to their excessive fuel consumption and production of high electromagnetic fields.

Our thermal sense can also be a source of richness or tedium. Lisa Heschong, author of *Thermal Delight in Architecture*, feels that we have cut ourselves off from enjoying the potential sensuality, cultural meaning and symbolism of our thermal environment. Some people believe that by experiencing natural changes in temperature throughout the day and the year, we keep our inter-nal thermoregulatory mecha-nism tuned up and improve our immune systems. In her book, Heschong states a general princi-ple well: "Uniformity is extremely unnatural and therefore requires a great deal of effort and energy to maintain."

Sound

Our hearing evolved in a rela-tively quiet setting in which every sound had meaning; the ability to detect and understand subtle sounds was important to survival. The snapping of a twig, the call of an animal and the tone of the wind all provided a constant sonic picture of the state of things. The rare loud noises carried import-ant messages (rain is coming; a boulder is headed for you) and evoked an appropriate adren-aline rush. Today, most people are surrounded by inescapable background noise that dulls the senses, and the personal meaning of the sounds is minimal.

When building, you can re-store a meaningful sound envi-ronment in several ways. First, when possible, site your build-ing away from noise pollution. Second, insulate and weather-strip to block sound that you can't control—walls of earth and straw provide excellent sound insulation. Third, minimize the use of noise-producing appliances and mechanical equipment. And fourth, encourage a rich tap-estry of pleasant sounds: plant trees with leaves that rustle in the wind; plant fruit-bearing shrubs that attract songbirds; hang wind chimes; install a fountain.

FIGURE 9.4. We remain vital when all our senses are engaged. [Credit: Carol Venolia]

Air Quality

Our bodies process and eliminate toxic substances on a regular basis, but nothing in our evolution equipped us to handle the levels of pollutants currently found in our air, water and food. Although we can't immediately control many of these pollutants, we can make our homes and workplaces into oases of low toxicity where our bodies can rest and repair.

There is a threefold approach to keeping the level of indoor toxins low: eliminate, separate and ventilate. *Eliminate* means to "Just say No" to highly toxic carpets, paints, adhesives, sealers and other materials. You don't need them, and there are less toxic, affordable options available. How far you go with this approach depends on your health and your level of commitment, but it is your first and best defense.

RESOURCES

Books

• Bainbridge, David A. and Ken Haggard. *Passive Solar Architecture: Heating, Cooling, Ventilation, Daylighting, and More Using Natural Flows*, Chelsea Green, 2011. A beautiful, practical guide to direct use of natural resources (sun, breeze, shade, water) to achieve indoor comfort in harmony with the outdoors, including integrated design, natural/local materials and greywater reuse.

• Heschong, Lisa. *Thermal Delight in Architecture*, MIT Press, 1979. This small, pleasurable book explores the potential richness of the thermal environment as a sensory experience, looking to history (the hearth fire, the sauna, Roman and Japanese baths and the Islamic garden) as inspiration for ways to experience comfort without the blandness of technological overkill.

• Kellert, Stephen R., Judith H. Heerwagen and Martin L. Mador. *Biophilic Design: The Theory, Science, and Practice of Bringing Buildings to Life*, John Wiley & Sons, 2008. A compendium of essays by the best minds in biophilic (life-loving) design, ranging from biomimicry, the senses and neuroscience to the healing effects of nature, views and greenery in the built environment.

• Kellert, Stephen R. *Building for Life: Designing and Understanding the Human-Nature Connection*, Island Press, 2005. An introduction to biophilic design, including an overview of the "science and theory of connecting human and natural systems," the role of nature in childhood development and ways to harmonize nature with the built environment.

• Lewis, Charles A. *Green Nature, Human Nature: The Meaning of Plants in Our Lives*, University of Illinois Press, 1996. A classic work on the relationship between plants and humans, and how gardening and horticultural therapy can restore our vitality.

• Louv, Richard. *The Nature Principle: Human Restoration and the End of Nature-Deficit Disorder*, Algonquin Books, 2011. Louv, author of *Last Child in the Woods* and founder of the New Nature Movement, sums up his observations and collected research about how to meet our deep need for nature in our daily lives.

• Selhub, Eva M., MD, and Alan C. Logan, ND. *Your Brain on Nature: The Science of Nature's Influence on Your Health, Happiness, and Vitality*, John Wiley & Sons, 2012. This book sums up decades of research on our brain's need for stimulation from the green, living world, including how indoor plants and walks in the woods can restore us and improve our mental functioning and a look at "nutri-ecopsychology."

• Venolia, Carol. *Get Back to Nature Without Leaving Home: 10 Simple Ways to Feel Happier, Healthier, and More Connected in Everyday Life*. A workbook to help you better understand your roots as a natural being, and satisfy your need for daily communion with the living world in simple, low-cost ways: **comehometonature.com/ebook-get-back-to-nature-without-leaving-home**.

• Venolia, Carol and Kelly Lerner. *Natural Remodeling for the Not-So-Green House: Bringing Your Home into Harmony with Nature*, Lark Books, 2006. Helps you marry your own nature with the natural world around your house to massage your home into greater aliveness by looking first to the sun for heat and light and getting your cooling from shade and breezes, and creating outdoor rooms as your own personal eco-paradise.

Separate means that you minimize the impact of interior pollutant sources that are impractical to eliminate. For example, apply a sealer to cabinets that are made of materials that off-gas formaldehyde; locate office equipment or combustion appliances that create fumes in a separate room.

Ventilate is a good idea in any case. Fresh air is not only important to our health in itself, but it can dilute any pollutants that happen to be in our indoor air, rendering them less harmful. Ventilation can be as simple as an open window or as high-tech as a heat-recovery ventilator. If

FIGURE 9.5. Always create a strong connection with the outdoors. Design by Kelly Lerner. [Credit: Kelly Lerner]

you have a mechanical ventilation system, adding filtration can also remove some gases and particles from the air.

Implications for Design

The beauty of designing with natural cycles and for sensory richness is that it is also energy efficient. We are best adapted to the cyclically changing colors and intensity of light from the sun; therefore, design for daylighting—and save electricity. We are best adapted to the radiant warmth of the sun and the natural cooling of shade and breezes; therefore design for passive solar gain and natural cooling as appropriate—and again, save on the energy cost of heating and cooling. We thrive on the visual and auditory textures of rich landscapes and communion with other critters; therefore plant abundantly around buildings to attract songbirds, provide food, enrich vistas—and help with natural heating and cooling.

We can also get our environmental nutrients and conserve fuel by creating more indoor/outdoor living areas. Modern building has focused so thoroughly on enclosure and protection that we have lost much of the art of semi-enclosed spaces. But the blessings of screened porches,

outdoor kitchens, solariums and sleeping porches should not be forgotten. If the outdoor environment is at all appealing (and even the tiniest yard can be made more vital with plants, a fountain and wind chimes), tempering only the unwanted climatic influences can allow us to migrate to indoor/outdoor spaces as the time of day and season allow. Sometimes shade, a windbreak or protection from the rain are all we need to allow us to work, socialize or sleep outdoors. The fresh air, gentle breezes and sunlight can create deep feelings of satisfaction and vitality that are hard to find indoors.

The Heart of the Matter

You might have noticed something: all of the suggestions I'm making *feel* good. This is the most important part to keep in mind. Even if you forget all the theory and facts, you will always have this basic touchstone right at hand: what feels good to your body, mind, senses, emotions and spirit? Don't get so stressed out about saving the planet that you forget to have fun or to take good care of yourself. After all, if your energy is depleted, you can't help the planet much. So play, have a good time, let your friends help you and surround yourself with the things and feelings you love.

The Healthy House

PAULA BAKER-LAPORTE

Building-related illness, multiple chemical sensitivities, sick building syndrome, environmental illness, electro-hypersensitivity: these terms are recent additions to our vocabulary. Until about 35 years ago, indoor environmental pollution was a very limited phenomenon, but four basic things have changed in the evolution of building technology, resulting in the current widespread concern about environmental quality inside our homes.

First, the very fabric of our homes has changed. Postwar industrialization introduced mass-produced building components and transportation networks to distribute these products nationwide. Traditional building materials and methods, once regionally derived, have been replaced by manufactured components that promised to provide better performance for less cost. Have these products fulfilled this promise? Certainly not, when environmental and life-cycle costs are figured into the equation.

Furthermore, many of these new products have had a negative and costly impact on our health. Until very recent history, our built environments have been free of man-made chemicals. There are now more than four million registered man-made chemicals; between 70,000 and 80,000 of them are in common use. We know very little about the health effects of most of these substances and even less about what happens when they interact with one another in an enclosed environment. We do know that many chemicals found in building products, once thought to be safe, are now making people ill.

Second, as the cost of home heating and cooling skyrocketed, we recognized the need for more energy-efficient buildings. In solving this problem, however, we inadvertently created another, further contributing to the demise of our indoor environmental quality. For several decades now, new building technologies have been invented in order to increase insulation values and to seal homes more tightly, thus making them more energy efficient.

However, in order to maintain health, in weather conditions when natural ventilation is not viable, a well-sealed home requires a mechanical ventilation

PAULA BAKER-LAPORTE, *FAIA, has headed a prolific architectural practice in Santa Fe, New Mexico, and Ashland, Oregon, since 1986. Together with her husband, Robert Laporte, she co-founded the Econest Company. She lectures widely on the precepts of environmentally sound and health-enhancing architecture and is a seminar instructor for the Institute of Building Biology and Ecology. She is the primary author of* Prescriptions for a Healthy House *(3rd ed., New Society Publishers, 2008) and co-author of* EcoNest: Creating Sustainable Sanctuaries of Clay, Straw and Timber *(Gibbs Smith 2005).*

system to replace stale and humid air. Given the number of synthetic and petrochemically derived toxins that we have introduced into our homes, the need for fresh air is especially significant in standard home construction. And yet no mechanical fresh air exchange is required by law in most places, and most tight homes are insufficiently ventilated for optimal health.

Third, we have become accustomed to a new level of comfort and convenience undreamed of just one hundred years ago. These amenities have placed unanticipated performance demands on our buildings. We have introduced huge amounts of moisture into our homes through daily indoor bathing and the use of laundry and dishwashing appliances. In addition, with the advent of modern heating, ventilation and air-conditioning (HVAC) equipment, modern architecture abandoned climatically responsive vernacular design in favor of the mechanically dependent "machine for living in."

We have succeeded in equipping our homes with the capacity to provide uniform temperature continuously, regardless of climate and weather, and independent of architectural form. In the process, we have created extreme moisture and temperature differentials between the interior of our homes and the outside environment. These unprecedented stresses placed on our building envelopes, combined with our efforts to seal them tightly without a time-tested evaluation of the products we are using, has contributed to a proliferation of trapped moisture problems that result in mold.

Even since the first edition of this book was released, a fourth phenomenon is quickly becoming a significant source of environmental illness. We are being exposed to unprecedented levels of man-made electromagnetic radiation. The proliferation of wireless communication technology has led to greater convenience but has left in its wake an ever-increasing number of people who are negatively impacted by exposure to these technologies. Electromagnetic hypersensitivity is a relatively new disorder and one that appears to be growing rapidly as we blanket our world with ever-increasing electromagnetic radiation.

In response to the problem of building-related illness, two very different models for the healthy home have emerged. The first, more mainstream, approach involves eliminating as many pollutants as possible from within the building envelope and sealing

FIGURE 10.1. Katy Bryce and Adam Weismann converted a 17th-century cob granary in Cornwall, England, into a cozy, healthy home. The updated aesthetic includes bigger windows for daylighting and passive heating and a skillful combination of smooth clay plasters and rough-sawn lumber. [Credit: Ray Main]

it very tightly on the inside so that there is less need to worry about the chemical composition of the structure or insulation. Clean, fresh air is then mechanically pumped in, and pollution caused by human activity is purged from the home. This is a technology-based solution to a technology-created problem. In the last decade, this so-called green building has become much more popular, and the various score cards developed to rate green buildings take certain aspects of indoor environmental quality into account (see "Can My Natural House Get a LEED Rating?" p. 37).

The second approach involves designing and landscaping a building to be responsive to local climatic conditions and building the walls out of natural or non-toxic materials that allow for the free flow of vapor through them. The building is seen as a third skin (clothes being the second)—a permeable organism interacting with the natural world and facilitating a balanced exchange of air and humidity.

This approach is based on the precepts of *Bau-biologie*, or "building biology" in English. Bau-biologie is a health-based approach to building, popular throughout northern Europe, that recognizes humans to be part

FIGURE 10.2. This EcoNest home in Grass Valley, California, is constructed using natural materials, including timber framing, straw-clay walls and clay plasters. The design features passive solar heating and natural daylighting, all part of the recipe for a healthy house. [Credit: T.J. Heater]

of, and not apart from, a greater natural system. Although technological innovation has been somewhat successful in both dominating and replicating the natural environment, many of the subtle benefits provided by nature have been overlooked. For several decades, as mentioned before, the need for fresh air was one such subtlety (see "Designing for Vitality," p. 55).

The Bau-biologie vision of a healthy indoor environment encompasses several criteria that are not often considered in the more mainstream technology-based approach to the healthy home. These include the study of Earth energies and geopathic disturbances; the elimination of man-made electromagnetic fields; the benefits of color, light and harmonic proportions in building design; and the role that unsealed natural materials play in balancing humidity and electromagnetic climate inside a home.

Ironically, natural building materials, once the norm for us and still the norm for the majority of humankind, are not well understood in current mainstream building culture. Even though people have surrounded themselves with natural, permeable materials throughout human history, and even though enduring models of these buildings are found throughout the world, mainstream building practices and codes promote manufactured building commodities that are laboratory tested, standardized, stamped, packaged and shipped. In this current building climate, applying for a permit to build a natural home can be an "interesting" and educational process.

However, the natural building movement is gaining momentum, supported by the theories of Bau-biologie and a small but growing sector of environmentally concerned builders, designers and homeowners. Recent inclusion of straw bale and straw-clay wall systems into the International Residential Code

FIGURE 10.3. Timber frame elements and varying ceiling treatments create place within the open space of this compact EcoNest home. The walls are straw-clay with natural earthen plaster. [Credit: Laurie Dickson]

are indicators of this success. The keynote of this holistic approach is that issues of health, energy and the environment cannot be considered in isolation. Natural building, in its very essence, exemplifies a synergy of energy efficiency, health and a wise use of resources.

RESOURCES

Books

• Baggs, Sydney and Joan Baggs. *The Healthy House: Creating a Safe, Healthy, and Environmentally Friendly Home*, Harper Collins, 1996. Informed by Bau-biologie and *feng shui*, this book leads you on a journey through designing a healthy house, from sacred geometry to sewage treatment.

• Baker-Laporte, Paula, Erica Elliott and John Banta. *Prescriptions for a Healthy House: A Practical Guide for Architects, Builders & Homeowners*, 3rd ed., New Society Publishers, 2008. A thorough introduction to the problem of toxic building materials, including medical research. Clear suggestions on what you can do differently, and where to get products and information.

• Bower, John. *The Healthy House: How to Buy One, How to Cure a Sick One, How to Build One*, 4th ed., Healthy House Institute, 2000. This encyclopedic book for builders, buyers and remodelers identifies threats to indoor health and suggests strategies for improvement in a system-by-system fashion.

• Van Der Ryn, Sim. *Design for an Empathic World: Reconnecting People, Nature, and Self*, Island Press, 2013. A green building pioneer explains how to design our communities and buildings to improve the health of their inhabitants and users.

Organizations

• International Institute for Building-Biology and Ecology: **hbelc.org**. Offers books, videos, equipment, seminars and a correspondence course on building health, the environment and electromagnetic issues.

• The Healthy House Institute: **hhinst.com**. Independent resource center for designers, contractors and homeowners interested in healthy houses.

Eighteen Design Principles to Make Square Feet Work Harder

ROBERT GAY

Before you begin designing your home, do this four-part exercise in self-knowledge:

1. Study your lifestyle very carefully.
2. Think as freely as possible about the qualities of the spaces and places you have most loved and hated.
3. Fight to minimize your clutter and accumulations.
4. Free yourself up from advertising, media imagery and pressures to consume, since if you don't, the urge to buy will terrorize you.

Then, when you begin designing or working with a designer, use as many of the following principles as possible:

1. Minimize circulation space by reducing or eliminating hallways and paths to and from the doors. Excessive circulation space is one of the biggest drawbacks of many floor plans.
2. If you do have to have a hallway, enrich the pass-through experience with bookcases, niches, photos, mirrors, art objects, skylights or textures.
3. Avoid circulation paths that cut diagonally through a space. This almost always chops something up that would otherwise be an integral whole. (An exception is that sometimes a large space can successfully be cut into two groupings of furniture.)
4. Don't close rooms off from each other unless you have to. It's easy to see how this helps minimize interior walls.
5. Consider partial separations between rooms to create an ambiguity of connectedness: arches, interior windows, half-walls, curtained spaces, freestanding headboards (for beds), interior columns and similar features. Often there are reasons for partially separating one space from another, without needing to devote a separate room to each.
6. Let interior walls be as thin as possible. (This contrasts to the many compelling reasons for having thick exterior walls.) Something thinner than an inch (2.5 cm) can often serve as a wall, as with Japanese shoji doors.
7. Organize the floor plan around activities, such as eating dinner, doing a craft or hobby, or greeting visitors, rather than around preconceived rooms. Look for the centers of action, movement

ROBERT GAY, *an architect in private practice in Tucson, centers his largely residential practice on human needs and sustainable building practices, with a specialty in straw bale design. See* **radius-architects.com**. *He's also done university teaching, a college master plan, general contracting, furniture making, stonework and small playful art projects.*

and attention, then shape spaces around them.

8. Minimize the number of doors, after considering your real need for privacy.

9. If a door swing seems to take up too much space or unavoidably conflicts with something else, consider a sliding pocket door.

FIGURE 11.1. The varying ceiling height under the arched roof on the second story of Hilda Dawe's cob cottage (built by CobWorks in Canada), lends itself to different kinds of usage in different areas. Against the wall, the ceiling is too low for standing, but a desk makes perfect use of the skylight above. [Credit: Catherine Wanek]

10. Relate carefully to the different views in different directions; include connections with the heavens above, via roof windows, skylights or porch roofs high enough to let you see some sky from inside the house. Look also for ways to appreciate or enhance the smaller views, since intimate, small-scale views can be just as enjoyable as sweeping, dramatic ones. The perceptual effect of a view is to expand the space from which you see it.

11. Have easy connections between inside and outside spaces, such as patios, decks and outdoor showers, designing them as outdoor rooms with their own definition and sense of partial enclosure. Because of seasonal variations in your climate, you may need different outdoor spaces for winter and summer use.

12. Consider creating other planetary connections: a compass in the floor, a Stonehenge-like shaft of light at the equinoxes or solstices, a sundial or shadow-casting play place or prisms in a window that send rainbows flying around. These connections help make a house feel part of a much larger whole.

13. Avoid right angles as much as is permitted by your budget, your building system and your skill in building. Where you do have them, consider softening them by sculpting your wall material, and by using trim, ornament or a built-in feature like a fireplace or display cabinet.

14. Vary ceiling height by generally giving smaller spaces lower ceilings. This will dramatize the perceived size of the larger spaces by increasing the contrast between spaces.

Floor levels can also be varied—even a few inches of difference adds to the diversity and apparent size of a space. (This, of course, is at odds with the desire for maximum accessibility for potential wheelchair-bound or otherwise infirm users of a house.)

15. Avoid flat ceilings; instead, use open trusses, curved vaults or cornices. A shape that rises will pull your feelings up with it.

16. Have a diversity of windows. A single glass block or one-square-foot (0.1 m²) window can energize a large blank wall, and "Zen views" can make much of a small window.

17. Plan lighting to create pools of light, rather than uniform illumination everywhere.

18. To extend rooms and create diversity, add "non-room" spaces, such as window seats, sleeping alcoves, niches, built-in benches and recessed shelves. Thick-walled building systems like straw bale and rammed earth naturally allow these kinds of spaces, but

RESOURCES

Books

• Cline, Ann. *A Hut of One's Own: Life Outside the Circle of Architecture*, MIT Press, 1997. This intriguing book weaves together many threads: the failure of modern architects to meet the needs of their clients, historical accounts of downwardly mobile hut dwellers throughout the ages and the author's own experience of building and inhabiting a tiny teahouse.

• Kahn, Lloyd. *Tiny Homes, Simple Shelter: Scaling back in the 21st Century*, Shelter Publications, 2012. Over 1,300 color photos showcase handmade shelters (under 500 square feet), including homes on land, on wheels, in trees, plus studios, saunas, garden sheds and greenhouses. Inspiring!

• Salomon, Shay. *Little House on a Small Planet: Simple Homes, Cozy Retreats, and Energy Efficient Possibilities*, Lyons Press, 2006. Many valuable case studies from around North America with information on how you can design and build your own small house, live more happily in a small indoor space or subdivide your too-large house into smaller apartments.

• Shafer, Jay. *The Small House Book*, Tumbleweed Tiny House, 2009. One of the leaders of the tiny house movement shares inspiration and design ideas.

• Susanka, Sarah. *The Not So Big House*, Taunton Press, 2001. A thought-provoking book on techniques for designing houses that use less space while increasing quality of life for their inhabitants. The same author has several more recent books, with more plans and ideas.

• Walker, Lester. *The Tiny Book of Tiny Houses*, Overlook Press, 1993. A series of case studies of tiny (less than 300-square-foot [27 m²] houses), with excellent illustrations.

Organizations and Websites

• Small House Society: **SmallHouseSociety.net**. Founded in 2002 to support the small house movement, with many links to resources, designers and builders.

• Tiny House Blog: **tinyhouseblog.com**. Many photos, directory and links.

• The Tiny Life: **thetinylife.com**. Resources and links, primarily for tiny mobile houses.

thin-wall methods can also incorporate them. One result on the outside might be "bump-outs."

Of course, these guidelines aren't absolute, and sometimes the exceptions are as intriguing as the rules! Nevertheless, I believe that by using these principles, small spaces can be intensified to become richer and more enjoyable. A vibrant level of complexity will automatically unfold.

FIGURE 11.2. A bay window recessed into a thick straw bale wall serves as seating in the family room and a cozy queen-sized sleeping nook for overnight guests. This house was built by Bill Hutchins and landscape designer Beth Knox in Takoma Park, Maryland. [Credit: Catherine Wanek]

Designing with the Sun

Susie Harrington

The shape, orientation and siting of a house, combined with its window locations and roof overhangs, determine not only its direct experience of sun and shade but also how its internal climate responds to seasonal climatic conditions. Rather than controlling temperature by using mechanical devices powered by fossil fuels, we can rely on the three key components of solar design—insulation, insolation and thermal mass—to create a comfortable environment.

Insulation and Air Barriers

The more extreme the environment, the more insulation is appropriate, and the tighter the building should be constructed. It is simpler and over time less expensive to install high-quality windows, insulation materials and a well-detailed air barrier, than to heat a "leaking sieve." The use of passive heating or cooling strategies presupposes that the building is airtight and well enough insulated that the low-intensity heat of the sun or the coolness of nighttime breezes will make a difference.

Insolation

Insolation—bringing the sun's heat and light into a building— occurs through the windows. Infrared-spectrum energy can pass through window glazing and warm up the interior space. As often occurs in a greenhouse, insolation can easily lead to excessively high temperatures. In solar design, moderating influences are provided by seasonal shading strategies, night-flushing and other passive cooling strategies and interior levels of thermal mass.

Thermal Mass

Any material that has the capacity to absorb large amounts of heat can be called a thermal mass. Rock, earth, masonry, concrete and water are common thermal mass materials. These heavy, dense materials change temperature slowly, coming into equilibrium with the surroundings over a period of time.

In a solar-heated space, a thermal mass will slowly increase in temperature as the sun heats the ambient air. This is called *indirect gain*. If sunlight falls directly on the mass, heating will occur more rapidly—this is called *direct gain*. The factors influencing the efficacy of thermal mass include the exposure of the mass to the heat source (for example, sun hitting the mass directly), the surface area of the mass, the thickness of the mass, the color

SUSIE HARRINGTON *is an architect and landscape architect in Moab, Utah, specializing in sustainable buildings, especially straw bale walls and earthen finishes.*

and reflectivity of the surface (a black surface will absorb more energy than a white surface and a matte surface more than a shiny surface) and the thermal capacity of the mass (water has a higher thermal capacity than sand, for example).

A room with appropriate thermal mass will be less susceptible to overheating when the sun shines in through the windows. After the sun has set, the warm mass will cool down slowly, radiating heat to people within the room. Thus, thermal mass acts as a buffer, harnessing solar thermal energy during the day to provide heat during the night, without overheating at the peak insolation period. Thermal mass is most effective, especially for heating, if it is insulated from the exterior.

The same principles apply to summer cooling. It is a common experience to walk into a masonry building in the middle of the summer and find it refreshingly cool. That is because when nighttime temperatures are low enough, the mass of the building gives up its heat at night and then slowly heats up over the course of the day. The primary challenge in designing a passive solar house is to balance the amount of sun coming in the windows throughout the year with the amount of thermal mass.

The Magic of Sun Angles

Fortunately, it is easy to design a building to receive sunlight through south-facing windows in the winter but not in the summer. [Note: In the southern hemisphere the windows would face north.—Editors] During the summer months, the sun is high in the sky and its rays can be blocked by roof overhangs, trellises, awnings and other shading devices. Because the sun is low in the southern sky during the winter months, the winter sun can shine in below these shading devices, providing heat to the interior. Overhang dimensions and other shading strategies can be optimized for summer protection and winter penetration on south-facing windows.

Shading east- and west-facing windows is more challenging since the sun is low in the sky on summer mornings and evenings, diminishing the usefulness of overhangs. Ideally, most of the glass in a passive solar building will face south, with limited windows on other sides. To maximize the performance of passive solar design, a building should be elongated in an east-west direction

FIGURE 12.1. The basic components of passive solar design are orientation, insulation, glass and mass. In this straw bale home designed by Kelly Lerner, home, south- and east-facing windows let the sun shine in, and the solar heat is absorbed directly into the concrete (mass) floors, and indirectly into the wall plaster. [Credit: Catherine Wanek]

Window Selection

The most common insulated window glass has a low-e (for emissivity) coating. In addition to increasing a window's insulation, the standard low-e coating is effective at blocking the sun's heat, which is useful for cooling but counterproductive for south-facing windows in a solar-heated building. Thus, the coating and glazing strategies on the south walls will likely be different than those on the east, west and north walls, and the strategies for maximizing versus minimizing heat gain may differ depending on your climate. Fortunately, there are low-e coatings that allow the sun's heat to pass through, and which are increasingly available as a window option.

FIGURE 12.2. The clerestory windows of this off-the-grid straw bale home in Northern California are designed to maximize the entry of winter sun, while shade structures over windows facing south and west will help prevent overheating (Architects David Arkin and Anni Tilt; builder Tim Owen Kennedy, Vital Systems Natural Building & Design). [Credit: Catherine Wanek]

RESOURCES

Books
• Bainbridge, David A. and Ken Haggard. *Passive Solar Architecture*, Chelsea Green, 2011. Two solar pioneers compress 80 years of work into one masterful book.
• Rempel, Alexandra and Alan Rempel. "Rocks, clays, water, and salts: highly durable, infinitely rechargeable, eminently controllable thermal batteries for buildings," *Geosciences* 3(1):63–101, 2013. A very detailed review of thermal mass options, including very thoughtful guidelines for mass depending on building use.
• van Dresser, Peter. *Homegrown Sundwellings*, Lightning Tree Press, 1977. A great introduction to passive solar design for beginners. This delightful book highlights van Dresser's concern for sustainable materials and technology. His much harder-to-find book *A Land-* *scape for Humans* (Lightning Tree Press, 1972) lays out strategies for sustainable community development, based on local resources in northern New Mexico.

Websites
• Mother Earth News interview with Peter van Dresser: **motherearthnews.com/nature-and-environment /peter-van-dresser-zmaz75sozgoe.aspx**. Solar pioneer van Dresser was 30 years ahead of everyone else.
• Passive solar design: **works.bepress.com/david_a _bainbridge/11**. A slide show introduction.
• Solar resources: **builditsolar.com**. Very broad coverage of solar design, projects and how-to material. Browse and become inspired to take action.

Natural Building for Cold Climates

13

JACOB DEVA RACUSIN

The modern landscape of natural building varies widely across different regions, from the most effective building design to the most appropriate construction materials, techniques and detailing. While examples of similar techniques—earth and straw walls, clay and lime plasters, natural floors—can be found across the globe, the design and detailing varies widely. A good example of this is the straw bale wall. When straw bale was first revived as a building solution in the southwestern US, common design features included deep-set exterior windowsills, cement stucco renders and plastered walls built close to the ground. A decade later, when these features were replicated in the northeastern United States, failure from moisture damage set in rapidly in many of the pioneering buildings, and straw quickly gained a reputation for being unsuitable for use in the northeastern climate. We have since learned that with appropriate detailing—developed by a combination of common sense, existing precedent, trial-and-error and diligent observation—straw bale construction is not only feasible, but superior for addressing climate pressures in cold, wet climates.

Why did early straw bale buildings in the Northeast fail so quickly and catastrophically, even when constructed following best practices developed in the Southwest? A quick glance at these two regions reveals major differences. Yuma, Arizona, has an average rainfall of 3.3 in. (8.4 cm) and an average annual temperature of 75°F (24°C). Randolph, Vermont, gets on average 13 times as much rain (Vermont can easily see 3.3 in. in a single day) and a mean annual temperature of 41°F (5°C).

Long cold winters don't just mean greater heat loss and fuel consumption; they also create heightened potential for moisture damage and even structural damage from freeze-thaw cycles. Cold-climate buildings face relentless entropic pressure from rain and snow, heaving and soggy soils, and indoor-to-outdoor temperature differentials of up to 100°F (38°C). To endure, they require a solid design based on an understanding of building science fundamentals and a skilled build-out with well-executed details.

JACOB DEVA RACUSIN *is co-owner of New Frameworks Natural Building, LLC, offering services in green remodeling, new construction, consultation and education in natural building technologies. He is currently an instructor at the Yestermorrow Design/Build School, where he was formerly director of the Natural Building Intensive Program. A BPI-certified contractor and certified Passive House Consultant, Jacob's field research on moisture and thermal performance of straw bale wall systems is featured in his book* The Natural Building Companion, *co-authored with Ace McArleton.*

Heat and Buildings

In cold climates, heat must be kept inside the structure and cold air outside. This is easier said than done, but the doing is supported by good design, which is supported in turn by understanding how heat moves. In this era of energy, resource and carbon conservation, there is increasing focus on improving thermal envelopes. The *thermal envelope*, tasked with stopping heat loss, ideally wraps continuously around the conditioned part of the building—walls, ceiling, foundation and floor. It is composed of two parts: insulation and an air barrier. To work effectively, these two layers must always be touching (sometimes they are the same material), and be continuous around the whole building. This can be a challenge for any builder, and an even greater challenge when using natural materials.

Heat moves in three ways: conduction, convection and radiation. *Conduction* is heat transfer through materials, such as the framing or adobe blocks in your walls. Conductive heat transfer always moves from warmest to coldest. The part of the thermal envelope that stops conduction is the insulation: straw bales, cellulose or woodchip-clay, for example. The effectiveness of the insulation is calculated as an R-value. The higher the R-value, the better the insulation.

Convection is the movement of a hot fluid, such as warm air rising to the top of the building. Convective heat transfer always moves upwards, because the warm fluid is more buoyant and rises in the container as the cooler fluid drops. Two important things are happening here: movement and pressure. This is a classic illustration of the stack effect, when hot air in a building rises up to the second-floor ceil-

FIGURE 13.1. A "good hat, good boots and a coat that breathes" keep the rain off this straw bale studio in New Hampshire. The "good hat" is represented by generous overhangs and shingled gable ends that are furred out from the plane of the plaster, allowing for a positive drip edge. The "good boots" are supplied by the structural stone facade that supports the plaster 24 in. (60 cm) off of the ground, taking the brunt of the impact from splashing rain and piled snow. The "breathable" coat is a durable lime plaster that will resist erosion and moisture absorption, yet still allow water vapor to dry through to the outside. [Credit: Jacob Deva Racusin]

ing, generating high pressure that forces air out through leaks in the thermal envelope. A negative pressure environment is created at the bottom of the house, and cold drafts rush in. To stop these convective losses, an air barrier is needed. This could be plaster, airtight drywall or an airtight membrane.

Radiation is the movement of heat through space; it always moves from greatest to least concentration. Generally, if you can see something warmer than you (i.e., the sun), it is radiating energy to you, and vice versa. Our thermal envelopes (with the obvious exception of windows) do a good job of stopping radiation to deep space, but the colder the interior surface temperature of our walls, the more heat we will radiate to them, making us uncomfortable.

It is important here to draw a distinction between thermal mass and insulation. While insulation stops conductive heat flow, mass conducts and stores heat like a battery. When utilized inside a building, a mass material's thermal storage capacity moderates diurnal temperature swings. Building thick exterior walls out of massive materials such as stone, adobe and cob can work in regions where it is hotter during the day and colder at night than the standard indoor temperature of 70°F (21°C). In cold climates, however, that mass will steadily conduct heat outside for most of the year, and your body will radiate heat to the cold surfaces (think clammy, cold, stone castle). Accordingly, we keep our mass *inside* the thermal envelope, such as in earthen or stone floors, thick interior plasters, stone sills and counters or interior earthen walls and masonry heaters.

Let's look again at a straw bale wall. It's pretty easy to make the middle of the wall airtight and well insulated, as the bales provide excellent insulation and plaster is a great air barrier. Most of the challenges occur around the edges, where plastered bales transition to other materials such as roof framing, foundation and windows. For example, a gap usually forms where plaster meets a beam or window frame. Such gaps or *air bypasses* let a lot of cold air in (down low) and warm air out (up high). This convective heat

FIGURE 13.2. "Air fins," or gaskets, can help permanently block air leakage through the wall behind the plaster-to-wood crack. Here, strips of Masonite (hardboard made of compressed wood fibers) were glued to the exposed timber frame prior to installing the straw bales and plaster. As the plaster dries, and the expected crack between the plaster and timber opens up, the wall will still perform well, since the plaster is sealed to the fin, and the fin is sealed to the frame. [Credit: Jacob Deva Racusin]

loss can add up to a significant energy cost. One of the easiest and cheapest strategies to seal those gaps is to install gaskets or *air fins* that are sealed to the framing or trim prior to plastering. As the plaster dries, and the inevitable gap forms between the plaster and the framing, this gasket guarantees the integrity of the air barrier.

FIGURE 13.3. This double-stud wall eliminates thermal bridging and creates space for more insulation while incorporating standard framing practices. In this picture, two 3.5 in. (9 cm) stud walls with a 5 in. (12.7 cm) space in between for insulation create a super-insulated wall assembly. The structural loads can be borne either by the interior or exterior frames, or both. [Credit: Robert Riversong]

Conductive heat loss, or *thermal bridging*, occurs where rafter plates and other framing members penetrate the straw. Since wood is a poor insulator compared to straw, heat more readily passes through the wood and out of the house. Good design for cold climates involves looking very closely at these thermal bridges and managing them carefully. Double-stud wall construction with in-fill insulation addresses this by breaking the framing continuity through the wall assembly with an insulation plane.

Addressing thermal bridging in roofs requires adapting to a different set of structural parameters than in walls. Cathedral ceilings, where the living space is directly under the roof assembly (as opposed to an insulated ceiling with a cold attic below the roof), feature some of the same design challenges as walls: limited cavity depths for insulation, potential for thermal bridging through framing and moisture-management requirements such as drying potential. Parallel-cord trusses (essentially a "double rafter" frame) are one solution; running continuous foam board insulation above the roof sheathing is another.

With a lattice-frame approach to roof structure, primary 2×8 rafters are run vertically up the slope of the roof, with horizontal 2×8 purlins connected to the rafters with 10 in. (25 cm) timber screws. In this way, a full 16 in. (40 cm) insulation cavity is created, with only the points where rafters and purlins cross (and the occasional blocking) as thermal bridges. An additional benefit is the ease of creating generous overhangs not only on the eaves but also on the gable ends—traditionally a difficult area to engineer deep overhangs.

When proper detailing has been executed, natural building solutions can be superior to their conventional counterparts. Here in Vermont, our straw bale buildings regularly achieve wall insulation levels more than 30 percent higher than stick-frame construction.

Moisture and Buildings

Since cold, wet climates tend not to have significant fire risk, in these regions moisture is the single largest cause of building failure. In this era of super-insulation and airtight construction, moisture problems are all the more prevalent (see "The Healthy House," p. 61). Natural building solutions can be difficult to execute, given the lack of common knowledge of how to detail these systems correctly in cold and wet climates.

Water enters our buildings in lots of ways; we'll break them down by liquid phase and gaseous phase (water vapor).

Liquid Water

The majority of water damage in buildings occurs as a result of wind-driven rain or melting snow and ice penetrating the building. Some of the most common liquid moisture entry sources include:

- flashing around windows and doors, vents for fans/dryers/heaters, attached porches and other roof transitions and penetrations
- ground-source moisture such as surface runoff pooling against foundations, ground water leaking into basements, and erosive splash-back off roof eaves
- built-in moisture: wet construction techniques such as straw-clay, cob and natural plasters

Due to their polar charge, water molecules have the ability to wick upwards against gravity through porous materials, a phenomenon called capillary action. Builders working with wood, earth, fiber and plaster need to design with this in mind, since liquid moves readily through these materials. Good preventative strategies include capillary breaks between foundations and walls, and coatings such as limewash that reduce liquid absorption into plasters.

FIGURE 13.4. This lattice-frame roof structure creates a 16-in. (40.6-cm) cavity for insulation, while minimizing thermal bridging in the wooden frame. The 2×8 rafters run vertically, with 2×8 purlins attached horizontally on top.
[Credit: Ace McArleton]

Water Vapor

Water vapor—individual molecules of water suspended in air—is unlikely to cause substantial damage in buildings. However, vapor can *condense* into liquid when the concentration of vapor in the air rises and the temperature drops. Warm air can hold more vapor than the same mass of colder air. When air gets cooler, the relative humidity rises until the air cannot hold the vapor molecules in suspension and vapor condenses into liquid against adjacent surfaces. The *dew point* is the temperature at which this occurs.

Vapor can migrate into and around our buildings through multiple vectors:

- basements/foundations: vapor rising from the ground by infiltrating through cracks and penetrations (i.e., sump pumps, plumbing drains)
- use patterns: cooking, aquariums, bathing, coupled with inadequate ventilation
- built-in moisture: wet building assemblies drying by evaporation to the interior of the structure, such as drying timbers, curing concrete
- convection: currents of warm, humid air leaking into walls and roofs from inside the building (in a cold climate)
- diffusion: moisture moving through vapor-permeable materials, such as plaster and drywall

As humid air works its way through cracks in a wall or ceiling towards the outside of the building, it cools until it reaches the dew point and condenses into liquid. Because the insulation keeps the exterior of the thermal envelope cooler, there is less heat available to re-evaporate the moisture, and so it can persist, build up over time and cause damage.

Integrated Design Strategies

In a cold climate, it is especially important to integrate a building's thermal and moisture management strategies. Our approach is the "5 Ds of moisture control," adapted from Dr. John Straube.

Design: In *Design of Straw Bale Buildings*, John Straube writes, "The best moisture control strategies always involve design-

FIGURE 13.5. The vented rainscreen system is appropriate for marine climates and extreme moisture locations. It requires a minimum ¼ in. (0.6 cm) gap between the siding and a weather-resistant air barrier behind it (in this building, lime-stabilized earthen plaster). Flashing and trim details need to be worked out in advance. This straw-clay home in Ithaca, New York, was built by Sarah Highland. [Credit: Catherine Wanek]

ing problems OUT—not solving them after they have been needlessly designed into the enclosure."

Deflection: Keep rain and snow out through good flashing in roof and wall penetrations. Consider wood cladding for high-exposure locations. Design good overhangs and bottom-of-wall protection. Build airtight to keep vapor out of the assembly.

Drainage: Consider "drainscreens" or "rainscreens"— drainage planes behind the cladding or between layers of plaster that allow liquid to drain safely out of the assembly.

Deposition (Storage): Use building materials that can safely store concentrations of moisture in strategic locations. Given their high moisture absorption capacity, clay plasters are especially effective at managing interior moisture.

Drying: Understand which way the building assembly will dry (in cold climates, predominately towards the outside) and use vapor-permeable materials that allow vapor to migrate through walls and liquid to evaporate.

There is an old English adage, updated by contemporary natural builders: "Give a building a good hat, good boots and a coat that breathes, and it will stand the test of time." This refers to generous roof overhangs protecting the walls, good foundation detailing protecting moisture-sensitive components

RESOURCES

Books
- Allen, Edward. *How Buildings Work: The Natural Order of Architecture*, Oxford University Press, 1980. A terrific guide exploring the different systems of a building and how they relate to the building's environment.
- King, Bruce. *Design of Straw Bale Buildings: The State of the Art*, Green Building Press, 2008. The most authoritative resource on engineering data and analysis for straw bale construction, written in a style that is both well-researched and highly accessible.
- Racusin, Jacob Deva and Ace McArleton. *The Natural Building Companion: A Comprehensive Guide to Integrative Design and Construction*, Chelsea Green Publishing, 2012. The most up-to-date resource for natural building science and appropriate design and detailing for cold and wet climates.

Periodicals
- *Environmental Building News*: buildinggreen.com. The definitive periodical for the green building industry and a wealth of information across many styles of construction.

Organizations
- Building Science Corporation: **buildingscience.com.** A leading building science firm, offering a series of building guides, white papers, case studies and other publications tailored for specific climates.
- International Passive House Association (iPHA): **passivehouse-international.org**. The network for the Passive House Institute, the certifying body for the rigorous international Passive House building energy standard.
- Passive House Institute US (PHIUS): **passivehouse .us**. The counterpart to the PHI in the United States, certifying buildings across North America.

Websites
- Green Building Advisor: **greenbuildingadvisor.com.** Online forum for information about green building products and methods, including Q&A.

in the walls and floor and durable wall surface protection, such as lime plaster or wood cladding. To this, we add the importance of a good belt, buttons, zippers and suspenders. Flashing above and below windows and other penetrations and envelope transitions is oft-overlooked and misunderstood, and yet is all-important. Building an airtight assembly, coupled with appropriate ventilation and vapor absorbing materials, not only will keep the building much warmer with less fuel, but will keep vapor from building up and condensing in the walls and roof. The more we ask of our buildings, the more details we must address—and, ultimately, the better our buildings will serve us.

Hybrid Homes: Combining Natural Materials for Energy Efficiency

14

Catherine Wanek and Michael G. Smith

It's natural to use available, on-site materials to build our homes. Doing so conserves energy and resources—our own and the planet's. Understanding the specific qualities of onsite resources and how they can be combined helps us create efficient and elegant homes that require the least energy input to provide the greatest comfort.

Recently converted natural building enthusiasts are often determined to build their homes using the building system that first caught their attention. Perhaps they visited a sculptural cob home and fell in love at first sight. Or they were handed a newspaper clipping about straw bale building and felt a window of possibility open up in their heads. Or they stumbled upon an underground house during a desert vacation and thought, "This is the way to live! It just makes sense."

Indeed, each of these systems (and the others described in this book) makes good sense and can perform wonderfully under the right conditions. But when located in the wrong setting, natural building systems will not hold up to their residents' expectations; they can actually perform more poorly from an energy and comfort standpoint than conventional building materials. Or, worse yet, lead to maintenance nightmares and health problems.

Examples unfortunately abound. A young couple we know built a cob home in northern Missouri where winter temperatures may stay below freezing for weeks, only to find that the house was damp and difficult to keep warm and that they were developing allergies from mold exposure. An artfully finished straw bale kiosk at a California sustainability center had to be torn down after the bales were inundated in a flood (it had been built in a flood-plain). A German expatriate in Argentina built his passive solar home precisely by the book, following the published recommendations so faithfully that he failed to compensate for the

CATHERINE WANEK *is the author/photographer of* The Hybrid House: Designing with Sun, Wind, Water and Earth *and* The New Strawbale Home. *She lives in a historic stone and brick lodge that faces north, with leaky old windows and minimal insulation. The quest for energy-efficient comfort led her to add on a straw bale greenhouse, and subsequently onto the "straw bale trail," where she has visited many homes in diverse climates, learning from them all.*

MICHAEL G. SMITH *grew up in Massachusetts in a drafty house his father built largely from salvaged window sashes. Since then, he has lived on a tin-roofed wooden platform in the Costa Rican jungle; in a tiny aluminum trailer in the Oregon rainforest; in a century-old California settler's cabin; and in three small natural homes he built himself: one all cob, the next a straw bale and clay wattle hybrid and the last a very comfortable hybrid with straw bale, cob and straw-clay walls. His website is* strawclaywood.com.

flip from northern to southern hemispheres and ended up with a house that was cold in the winter and hot in the summer.

We advise prospective builders to let go of their preconceptions about what materials and techniques to use until they have considered the qualities and assets of their chosen building sites. Not only do the local climate and other site characteristics determine the most suitable family of building techniques for a particular structure, but the best choice can even vary in different parts of the same building. "Hybrid" natural homes, combining two or more wall systems, may be the most effective under many circumstances. To understand why, let's first explore the thermal properties of natural materials.

Earth and Straw for Thermal Mass and Insulation

Earth is common to nearly every building site—in fact, to build a sturdy foundation, it's generally necessary to excavate. After the topsoil is set aside for gardening or landscaping, the subsoil is available as a resource. Very often it can be combined with other natural materials to form walls. Wall systems using earth as the primary ingredient include rammed earth, compressed earth blocks, earthbags, cob and adobe; when combined with wood and/or with larger proportions of straw or other fiber, the list grows to include wattle and daub, straw-clay, woodchip-clay and many others.

The high compressive

FIGURE 14.1. A stone interior wall provides thermal mass to absorb heat from a greenhouse, helping to buffer temperature swings. Jane Koger's off-the-grid straw bale home in the Flint Hills of Kansas artfully contrasts different materials and finishes, including stone, wood, plaster and glass blocks. [Credit: Catherine Wanek]

strength of stone and earth makes them suitable as structural materials. Their density also gives them high thermal mass, which means that they absorb heat from the sun or from another direct heat source, or, to a lesser extent, from the warm air around them; then, as the interior air temperature drops, the mass slowly releases this stored heat into the building. Thermal mass materials are most effective for passive solar heating when they have a dark colored and non-reflective surface that the sun hits directly at the times of the year when heating is needed.

Used well, thermal mass can help to warm and cool our homes at appropriate times, but misunderstood it can be an energy drain and cause discomfort. For example, the "heat island" effect in some urban areas is due in part to excess thermal mass and lack of shading. Masonry buildings, asphalt streets and concrete sidewalks soak up the hot summer sun during the day and radiate it back out at night, keeping the city continually hot. This cycle can continue day after day, requiring massive energy inputs to create human comfort zones.

In some desert climates, there can be a large daily temperature swing from uncomfortably cold at night to uncomfortably hot during the day. Under these somewhat rare conditions, uninsulated mass walls can result in efficient buildings, since the thermal mass tends to equilibrate to the average temperature of the daily cycle. In areas with cold winters when outdoor temperatures stay below the human comfort zone all day long, thermal mass is only effective if it is well insulated. Even if the home has good solar orientation and design, excessive mass will overcool the building at night and during cloudy weather. Then, when the sun comes out or the heater is turned on, the cool mass will absorb much of the available heat; it will take a lot of time and heat input before the house feels warm again. Worse yet, dense earthen walls have poor insulation value, and will conduct heat outside the house. This doesn't mean that an uninsulated rammed earth house in Alaska can't be kept warm; only that it will require far more energy to heat than a better-insulated home would.

Straw is not so often found onsite as earth is, but it is available in nearly every region, as a by-product of grain production. Since humans first began to build shelters, straw (or grass) has been used as a building material, both alone and in combination with earth. When the baling machine was invented, it became possible to turn straw into big, well-insulating building blocks. In bale form, straw can be used structurally, and it provides something few other natural materials do—excellent insulation. The dead-air spaces within and between the hollow stalks make straw bales a good insulator, provided that any walls made with them are well sealed with plaster to prevent air infiltration.

Since thermal mass is positively correlated to the density of a material and insulation value is negatively correlated, we can imagine a spectrum of natural building materials ranging from stone on one end, with the most thermal mass and the least insulation, to straw bale at the other end, with the opposite characteristics. Earthen walls like rammed earth, compressed earth blocks, adobe and cob would lie close to stone on the dense end of the spectrum. Elsewhere along the continuum, we would find cordwood masonry, woodchip-clay, straw-clay, mineral clay, fidobe, papercrete and hempcrete. Definitive R-values have not yet been established for many of these wall systems, and furthermore, mix proportions and installation

R-Value Comparison Chart: Wall Section Thermal Characteristics (Source: US Department of Energy)

Wall Type[1]	R-value (h ft²°F/Btu)	U-value Btu/(h ft²°F)	Weight lb/ft²	Heat Capacity[2] Btu/ft²°F
Wood Frame[3]				
2×4 studs w/R11 batts	10.2	0.098	9.2	2.2
2×6 studs w/R19 batts	15.4	0.065	10.5	2.6
Compressed Straw Panel[4]				
uninsulated 4.8 in. panel	10.1	0.099	13.4	4.9
insulated 4.8 in. panel	18.4	0.054	13.7	4.9
Fibrous Concrete Panel[5]				
insulated 3 in. panel	16.7	0.060	16.9	4.7
insulated 4 in. panel	19.1	0.052	20.1	5.7
Straw Bale[6]				
23 in. bale @ R-1.8/in. (−25%)	42.7	0.023		
23 in. bale @ R-2.4/in.	56.5	0.018	21.4	6.4
23 in. bale @ R-3 0/in. (+25%)	70.3	0.014		
Foam Blocks[7,8]				
6 in. form w/concrete/adobe fill	26.3	0.038	40.8	7.5
8 in. form w/concrete/adobe fill	28.0	0.036	54.2	9.8
Adobe[9,10]				
uninsulated 10 in.	3.5	0.284	95.0	17.9
uninsulated 10 in.	11.9	0.084	95.3	18.0
uninsulated 24 in.	6.8	0.147	183.4	34.2
exterior insulated 24 in.	15.1	0.066	183.6	34.3

1. All walls have stucco exterior and drywall interior, except adobe and straw walls have plaster.
2. Heat capacity is the scientific measure of thermal mass.
3. Wood-frame walls have 25 percent (R-11) and 20 percent (R-19) stud areas. The R-19 batt compresses to R-18.
4. Compressed straw panel, insulated case, has 2 in. polystyrene on exterior.
5. Fibrous concrete panels have 1 in. polystyrene inside and out.
6. Straw bale wall R-value is calculated for 3 unit R-values for straw to cover potential variability.
7. Average material thickness across foam block wall sections is as follows: 6 in. foam has 2.9 in. polystyrene each side and 3.4 in. of fill; 8 in. foam has 3.1 in. polystyrene each side and 4.8 in. of fill.
8. Wall properties are based on 75 percent adobe and 25 percent concrete fill.
9. Adobe walls, insulated case, have 2 in. of polystyrene on exterior.
10. 24 in. wall is two 10 in. layers with 4 in. air gap.

technique can radically affect their thermal properties. For example, increasing either the amount of slip or the amount of tamping in a straw-clay wall will increase its density and reduce its insulation value. In mild climates where heating and cooling needs are minimal, wall systems with moderate insulation properties may be acceptable, provided that the home has good solar orienta-tion and design, a well-insulated roof and a well-sealed building envelope.

Hybrid Homes for Comfort and Efficiency

Good insulation in foundations, exterior walls and ceilings isolates indoor environments from daily and seasonal temperature swings and provides the greatest comfort for the least energy input—which is why we so often favor straw bales for exterior walls. But bales take up a lot of space and are less suitable as interior partitions where insulation usually isn't needed. A thermal mass material is most useful for interior walls, where it will serve to moderate temperature swings. Thin earthen walls such as wattle and daub are a good choice for interior par-titions. Cob, adobe, stone and

FIGURE 14.2. A south-facing trombe wall helps heat Jan and Tom Moffat's rammed earth home in Flagstaff, Arizona, a high-altitude climate that can get very cold in the winter. However, this wall proved to be too large, and actually over heated the bedroom space inside during part of the year. The lesson? Passive solar and mass systems must be oriented and sized properly, with appropriate overhangs for the latitude and climate. This size of wall might be perfect for a greenhouse or large common space, while a smaller trombe wall would have worked better for the bedroom. [Credit: Catherine Wanek]

earthbags can also serve admirably where their load-bearing capacity and greater thermal mass are desired.

A special use of thermal mass material for passive heating is called a "Trombe wall." This is a masonry wall (such as concrete, brick, rammed earth or adobe) on the south wall of a home (in the northern hemisphere). Outside the wall is a narrow airspace enclosed by a layer of glass. When the winter sun shines on the wall, its rays mostly pass through the glass and are absorbed by the masonry wall. At night and on cloudy days, the glass helps reduce heat loss from radiation so that most

of the solar gain works its way to the interior of the building. This is an especially effective strategy in places with cloudy winters, where the heat loss through south-facing windows can be greater than the gain. It also works well in urban areas where large south-facing windows are undesirable because of privacy concerns.

A greenhouse or sunspace attached to the south wall of a house performs a similar passive heating function, while also providing inexpensive semi-conditioned space for many possible uses. Some of these uses, such as growing food and entertaining guests, may not be

compatible, so be sure to clarify your design goals. Again, the wall separating the sunspace from the rest of the home can be of a thermal mass material, as long as the sunspace can be shaded in the summer to prevent unwanted heat from entering the home.

Design considerations sometimes put different structural demands on the different walls of a home. For example, in the northern hemisphere, the majority of the windows should be on the south face of a passive solar home. East- and southeast-facing windows are excellent for taking the chill out of a winter morning. Windows facing north and west are typically losers from a thermal standpoint, although they may be valuable for views and daylighting. If your design calls for many windows or doors on one wall, you will need a construction system that accommodates many openings with relatively narrow columns between; this is easier to accomplish using a framed wall infilled with hempcrete or straw-clay, for example, than it is with straw bales.

Considerations such as these have led many people planning natural homes in mild climates to arrive at designs utilizing straw bale walls on the north and cob, adobe or straw-clay on the south.

FIGURE 14.3. Architect Herwig van Soom built this hybrid home in Belgium. The north, east and west walls are straw bale, but the south wall is framed and sided with wood to enable the modern solar window design. [Credit: Catherine Wanek]

The east and west walls can be either one, or both, or something else altogether. This puts straw bales on the north where insulation is most important and places more thermal mass on the south, where solar warming will reduce heat losses through the less-well-insulated walls. In some cases, from the standpoint of thermal performance alone, using straw bales for all of the exterior walls might be a wiser choice. But, like any other design decision, the choice of wall systems is usually influenced by more than a single factor.

Other Advantages of Hybridization

People may choose to build a hybrid home for a large number of reasons. Some of these reasons are very practical, others more personal or whimsical. The more experience a builder has with a wide range of natural building options, the easier it becomes to mix and match. In particular, straw bale and cob seem to complement each other's properties in a remarkable fashion. While block-shaped straw bales lend themselves most easily to simple shapes, cob offers infinite possibilities for sculpting interior spaces and built-in furniture.

Another reason to use earth inside the home is for its ability to absorb sound, odors and moisture. Water vapor from bathing and cooking can build up inside a house and provide a perfect environment for mold and fungal growth, but earthen walls and

FIGURE 14.4. When Alejandra Caballero set out to renovate this adobe and stone structure in central Mexico, she chose straw-clay for the second-story walls because of its light weight and insulating properties. The thick thatched roof also provides good insulation. [Credit: Michael G. Smith]

plasters, with their enormous capacity to absorb and disperse humidity, moderate this buildup. Rather than building a straw bale bathroom, one might sculpt a shower enclosure from cob or adobe, protected where necessary by a water-resistant tadelakt finish. (Active ventilation is recommended for bathrooms and kitchens, especially in humid climates. Clay-plastered walls alone may not be sufficient to prevent moisture buildup, and can in fact transfer humidity deep into the wall system if not adequately ventilated.)

Clay has a preservative effect on straw and wood, reducing their vulnerability to moisture and rot. Similarly, earth and stone are much more fire-resistant than straw and wood. Many natural homes have sculptural hearths as their energetic focal point. A cob hearth will never burn, and, if properly designed, can store heat from the fire for slow release later, reducing fuel usage.

When building a two-story or taller house, it can make sense to use more massive wall systems below, lighter ones above. This not only reduces the amount of weight that must be lifted high during the construction process, it also reduces the size of structural beams and headers. During

an earthquake, heavy materials high up can weaken a structure, and they are more dangerous if a wall collapses. When adding onto an older adobe building in central Mexico, our friend Alejandra Caballero chose straw-clay walls and a thick thatched roof for the second story, resulting in a vertical hybrid home.

Sometimes the scheduling of the construction process can be a factor in choosing a hybrid design. Even when you are using machinery, walls made from cob, straw-clay, adobe or rammed earth are quite labor-intensive to build and can take a long time to dry, whereas bale walls can be raised more quickly and require no drying period for construction to continue. Owner-builders

FIGURE 14.5. Michael G. Smith transforms a rectangular framed opening into an earthen archway by sculpting straw-rich clay over an armature of green sticks, nails and baling twine. The lathed interior walls of this northern California home will later be filled with woodchips and clay, with a cob wall separating the living space from the solarium. Earthen plasters will seamlessly meld the different materials for a unified appearance. [Credit: Michael G. Smith]

are more likely to enclose their homes in a single building season if they build with both cob and straw bale than with cob alone. If help is available in short bursts, straw bales and adobe blocks are well-suited to getting walls up fast, whereas cob works best where labor is consistent. So if you know you will have three people available to work on your house all season long, with 30 more helpers joining in for occasional weekend work parties, a hybrid design might make the best use of labor resources. And, as workshop instructors intent on spreading knowledge about natural building in general, we lean towards hybrid buildings for their increased demonstration value.

Challenges to Address

Although combining different wall systems in the same building has many advantages, it also creates challenges that are best addressed in the design stage. Materials with very different densities and other properties sometimes behave differently over time, particularly as changes in temperature and humidity cause them to expand and contract. This can result in aesthetic and functional problems such as cracks in the plaster where wall systems meet. It's important to design good transitions where different wall systems meet and where walls meet floors, ceilings and windows (see "Natural Building for Cold Climates," p 73).

On a more dramatic scale, light and heavy walls may move differently when subjected to seismic forces, so strong unions are even more critical in areas with earthquakes. This is fairly easy with non-structural wall systems, where there is a continuous post and beam structure holding the building together. But if you wish to join load-bearing straw

RESOURCES

Books
• Bainbridge, David and Ken Haggard, Racusin, Jacob Deva and Ace McArleton. *The Natural Building Companion: A Comprehensive Guide to Integrative Design and Construction*, Chelsea Green, 2012. Excellent resource for building science applied to natural building systems, as well as much how-to information. Includes DVD.
• Wanek, Catherine, *The Hybrid House, Designing with Sun, Wind, Water and Earth*, Gibbs Smith, 2010. Features 14 climate-by-climate case studies of natural buildings with renewable energy systems. Full color.

Periodicals
• *The Last Straw: The International Journal of Straw Bale and Natural Building*: **thelaststraw.org**. Up-to-date articles on the international natural building movement, human resources and technical developments. This quarterly journal is available as a pdf download and in print in full-color. *The Last Straw Journal* CD-Rom includes the first 40 issues.

Workshops
• Emerald Earth Workshops: **emeraldearth.org**. Practical workshops in many aspects of natural building, emphasizing good design and detailing for hybrid buildings. Emerald Earth is the most comprehensive natural building demonstration site in the western US.
• Natural Building Colloquium: annually, at various locations. The gathering that brought the natural building movement into focus and has inspired the construction of many hybrid natural structures. More details can be found at **naturalbuildingnetwork.org**.
• Proyecto San Isidro: **proyectosanisidro.com**. Excellent workshops in a wide variety of natural building techniques, led by Alejandra Caballero and her team in central Mexico.

Websites
• **Naturalhomes.org**
• Natural Building Network: **nbnetwork.org**

bales with cob, for example, or either of these with a timber frame, then use caution and all of your creative problem-solving skills. It's often advisable to consult a structural engineer, especially if you are planning a large building or working in a seismically active zone.

Another complication is that different wall systems can require differing details in their foundations, window framing, plastering protocol and so on. For example, the foundation for a straw bale wall should be level on top, with a constant width determined by the dimension of the bales, whereas a foundation for cob ideally has an uneven surface to increase bonding, and may be of variable widths. This provides a lot of opportunity for learning and skill building in a single construction project. But it also requires more planning and creates more opportunities for error. In many cases, whether natural buildings are constructed by their owners or by professional builders, some or all of the crew have little or no experience with the systems being used. Learning takes time, and this slows down the building process. So the more there is to learn, the slower the going can be.

Despite these concerns, we believe that hybrid homes offer enormous potential for creating effective shelters from local and natural materials, and we expect to see many more of them in years to come. Understanding the properties of different natural materials and how they can complement each other will lead to healthy and energy-efficient built environments that nurture human life.

Remodeling With Natural Materials

15

JOSEPH F. KENNEDY AND JANINE BJÖRNSON

Some say that the most ecological way to build a house is not to build one at all, but to inhabit one that already exists. It usually takes less energy, materials, time and money to remodel an existing building than to build a new one. In many areas with stable or declining populations, large numbers of houses stand empty, falling slowly into disrepair as they wait to be lived in again or condemned and torn down. By staying in place rather than buying or building a new home elsewhere, we help bring stability to our communities.

It is estimated that 80 percent of the existing building stock in the US would benefit from upgraded energy and health performance. While there is certainly a place for high-tech solutions (multi-pane windows, heat exchangers, etc.), in many situations the appropriate use of local natural materials will achieve the desired improvements with lower financial and environmental costs. Given the huge numbers of existing buildings that require improvement, natural builders should consider applying their talents to address this need.

Many natural building materials can help transform poorly performing building stock into more beautiful, affordable, energy-efficient dwellings. Creative juxtapositions of new materials with old and traditional systems with conventional can produce many benefits. These include:

- improved aesthetics
- increased energy efficiency (for example when using straw bales or straw clay as insulation)
- reduced waste stream (conventional renovations produce excessive landfill waste)
- reduced ecological footprint compared to the use of industrially produced materials
- carbon sequestration (when using high carbon techniques such as straw bales)
- toxin absorption (especially when using clay finishes)
- a healthy living environment from choosing natural non-toxic materials in place of conventional off-gassing material choices, resulting in improved indoor air quality

JANINE BJÖRNSON *is a natural builder, educator and consultant who specializes in natural paints and plasters. She began her career in natural building in 1996 when she studied with Cob Cottage. Since then, she has taught over 90 workshops in Canada and the United States. She is the "natural materials" cyberpanelist at greenhomebuilding.com. She lives and builds in Sebastopol, California. You can reach her via* **claybonesandstones.com.**

JOSEPH F. KENNEDY *teaches at the New School of Architecture and Design and is a passionate advocate for adaptive reuse of our existing building stock using local and natural materials.*

- local employment (more of the money spent on the remodel goes to natural builders in the community rather than to distant corporations)
- expressing the architecture of a region by using local materials

Health

Some homeowners choose to remodel with natural materials due to health considerations. Natural materials are less likely to outgas or release toxic substances than industrially produced materials. Clay has even been shown to absorb toxins from the environment as well as moderating humidity

levels. For those with environmental illnesses or chemical sensitivities, natural materials can provide one of the few safe pathways to healthy construction or remodeling (see "The Healthy House," p. 61).

An important consideration is mold. Any carbonaceous material such as wood or straw is susceptible to mold growth when exposed to excessive moisture. It is important in natural building (as in all construction) to follow proper building practices, such as providing good foundations and drainage, sufficient roof overhangs and proper ventilation.

Many people believe that

natural materials can improve mental and emotional health as well. We crave the handmade, and we respond to textures that show a human touch. The natural technologies of earth and stone help to counter the stress of our hyperconnected world. Natural materials can satisfy our desire for mental and spiritual calm—the intangible feeling of wellness one experiences in the presence of earthen plasters, real stone, exposed timber and other materials close to their natural state.

Aesthetics

Every remodeling project is its own exciting journey, no matter what materials are used. Good design is necessary for good results. By selecting the natural colors and textures of materials in their raw state, a designer can add a new local element to the aesthetic, often completely transforming an existing structure. The sculptural forms of cob, earthen plasters and unmilled wood stand in contrast to the more precise qualities of industrially produced building elements. Making a clean and visually pleasing connection between extremely dissimilar techniques (i.e., existing wood-stud frame with new straw bales) can sometimes be a challenge so make sure to use common sense

FIGURE 15.1. Architect Mark Lakeman of Communitecture is masterful at using recycled and natural materials in his designs, in this case a residential remodel in Portland, Oregon. [Credit: Mark Lakeman]

and creativity to create elegant transitions.

Building Performance/ Carbon Neutrality

Most natural materials, especially those obtained locally, have very little embodied energy, so their contribution to the carbon problem is minimal. In fact, some natural building systems, especially straw bale construction and lime plasters, will sequester carbon from the atmosphere. Other types of natural materials (stone and earthen materials) contribute thermal mass to

FIGURE 15.2. Creating an insulating straw bale wrap around a steel shipping container. [Credit: Will Coquillette]

Remodeling "Do's" and "Don'ts"

Don't:

- Wing it. Do your research and testing. Consult local experts.
- Use the right materials in the wrong place, for example, use materials such as earth and straw in areas prone to water damage from high humidity, leaks, splash, etc. An earthen floor is a terrific idea in a living room, but is less than ideal under a claw-foot tub in a bathroom.
- Use materials incorrectly. Make sure you understand the function of your materials. Materials high in mass are very different from insulative materials. Make sure to use them in the appropriate places.

Do:

- Your homework. Understand the material requirements, weather requirements, sequencing, application techniques and appropriate uses of each building system you will be using.
- Use appropriate materials. They should be locally available and have a successful track record in your region. If you choose the wrong material, you may have increased maintenance or even failure. For example, exposed bamboo in a hot dry climate will rapidly crack. Clay plasters on the exterior of a building that gets a lot of wind-driven rain will erode.
- Make sure your new addition is structurally sound. Consult a professional if your remodel will change the structure of your building.
- Consider how your materials will respond to heating and cooling. Will the new materials expand and contract at a rate similar to your existing building?
- Bridge all dissimilar materials to create a cohesive and strong wall. Make sure to connect and reinforce all the parts adequately to prevent movement which could translate into cracks in your building over time.
- Use appropriate flashing for windows, doors and connections. Think like a water droplet. You need to be extra careful when working with materials that can be damaged by water contact or infiltration.

improve thermal performance (see "Combining Natural Materials for Energy Efficiency," p. 81). In any construction, the energy embodied in the building materials is minimal compared with the energy utilized to power a building over its lifetime. Thus it is important when remodeling a home to consider improving its energy efficiency by using passive heating, cooling and daylighting techniques.

Economy

Natural materials like earth and stone, as well as recycled materials such as concrete chunks, are often appropriate for use in renovation projects because they are local and available, and therefore inexpensive (or even free).

Challenges and Possibilities of Natural Materials

Certain natural materials lend themselves to particular situations. Straw bales, for example, can be used to wrap existing structures for improved thermal performance, and even as insulation in roofs. Cob is ideal (with proper foundations) for interior uses such as benches, fireplace surrounds and interior walls, while it finds even more uses outside for privacy and garden walls, garden furniture, sheds and other ancillary buildings. Lightweight infill materials such as straw clay and hempcrete (which is actually hemp and lime) can be installed between existing studs, and natural materials such as cellulose, cotton, perlite and wool are becoming more common as replacements for fiberglass and foam insulations.

Perhaps the most common use of natural building techniques in remodels is the application of interior clay or lime finishes (paints or plasters) over existing drywall. If the drywall has been coated with synthetic paint in the past, it will need to be primed

FIGURE 15.3. Plastered straw bales were used by Matts Myrhman and Judy Knox to make their concrete block home more comfortable in the exceptional temperature extremes of Tucson, Arizona. The shading veranda was added to create additional outdoor space and to protect the new straw bale wall. [Credit: Janine Björnson]

before applying a natural plaster. A common primer for this task is a mixture of white glue and sand (see "Earth Plasters and Alis," p. 339). If you intend to add a thick plaster to a slick wall surface, you may need to improve adhesion even more by securing lath to the wall. Conventional expanded metal lath will work, but natural alternatives can do the job as well or better. Some options include wooden lath or reed mat nailed or screwed to the wall, or burlap fabric soaked in a mixture of flour paste and clay slip and then stuck to the wall like wallpaper.

Earthen floors can be installed over existing concrete and wood floors. Concrete floors should be sealed first, especially on wet or poorly drained sites. Wooden floors must be strong enough to handle the additional weight. There cannot be any flexion or expansion of the wooden floors or cracking will result.

It is important to carefully detail the connections between new and old. First, make sure the existing structure can handle the addition of new materials. New foundations or other structural supports may be necessary, especially when adding heavy materials such as cob and stone. Dissimilar materials may need

FIGURE 15.4. This bike shop has been creatively remodeled with cob and recycled bicycle parts to create shelter for the day laborers who congregate at this spot. [Credit: Mark Lakeman]

to be connected through various means such as straps, cables, cross-bracing, wire fencing and other creative solutions. Don't forget that earthen materials such as cob, straw-clay and clay plaster shrink as they dry, and uncompressed straw bales may settle over time. It is often important to create expansion joints between dissimilar materials in order to address differing coefficients of expansion and contraction. Figuring out the details of the unions is an ongoing task, faced every day by growing numbers of people as natural building techniques are used to remodel more homes.

Pay special attention to detailing for building performance issues such as moisture and heat loss. It's crucial to keep water out of building assemblies as much as possible, and to create ways for moisture to escape when it does get in. Weather protection is particularly important where old meets new, especially at the roof connections.

Case Studies

Matts Myhrman and Judy Knox, two of the pioneers of the straw bale revival, owned a masonry block house in Tucson, Arizona. Unsatisfied with its thermal performance, they decided to wrap the entire home with straw bales. First, they insulated the flat roof with rigid foam insulation, choosing to use a petroleum product at this stage to reduce later use of petro-fuels for cooling and heating. Next, they added a deep porch to the south and east sides of the house, shading the walls and creating delight-ful outdoor living spaces. Then they wrapped the exterior of the house with straw bales. The bales rest on a "foundation" of treated wood spiked into the ground at the outer edge of the bales; the space between the house and the wood "toe-up" was filled in with pea gravel to discourage moisture from wicking up into the bales. Matts devised a clever tie system to cinch the bales to the existing block walls. Finally, they coated the bales with earth plaster. The "window wells" created by the bale wrap became outdoor window seats, finished in lime plaster to reflect light into the house. Now the house stays much cooler during the summer, and saves big on energy bills.

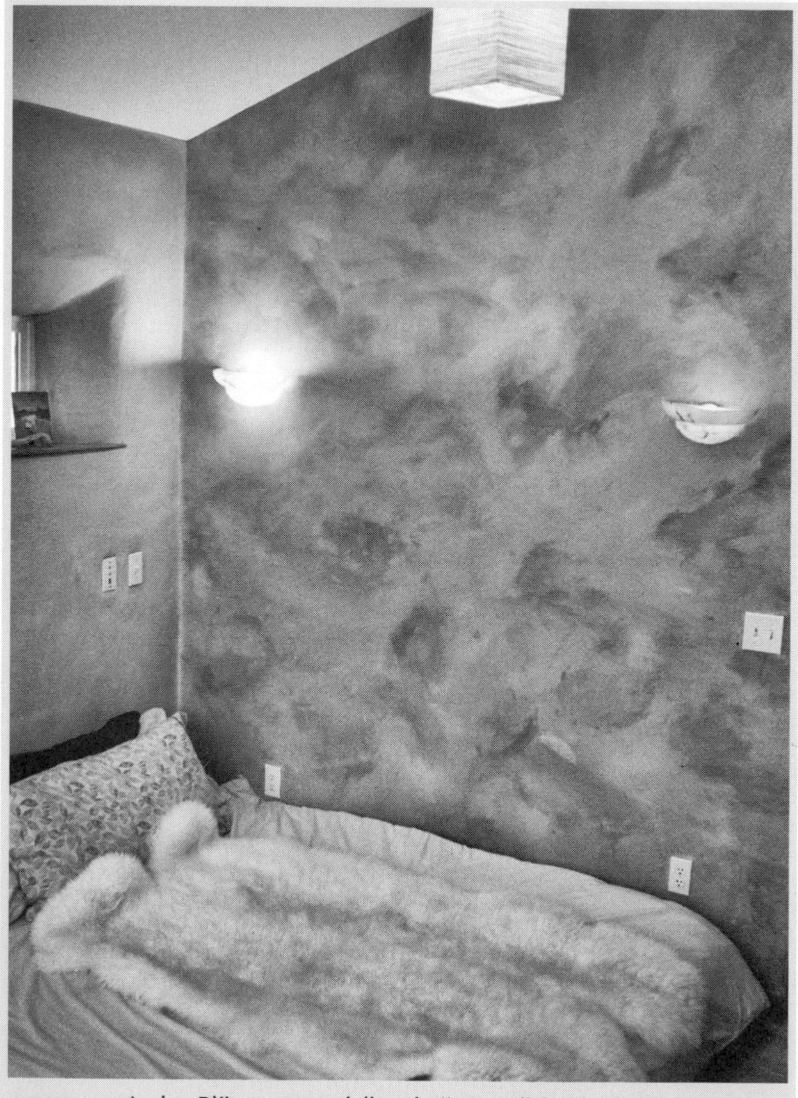

In Sonoma County, California, Dave Henson and Kendall Dunnigan needed to expand their tiny 70s-era solar prototype dwelling at the Occidental Arts and Ecology Center. They decided to use light straw-clay for the walls of their addition. This new addition illustrated the spirit of this environmentally progressive community through the use of local and non-toxic materials. Yet it had to connect with the existing house. After considering cob and straw bale, it was clear, due to inherent space constraints at their site, that a light straw-clay addition would allow them to maximize their square footage. Light straw-clay was also a fantastic choice because it made the connection between the new and the old sec-

FIGURE 15.5. Janine Björnson specializes in "naturalizing" existing homes, primarily through the use of earthen finishes, as demonstrated here in Dave Henson and Kendall Dunnigan's home in Sonoma County.
[Credit: Janine Björnson]

tions easy to join using conventional methods. This allowed for a seamless look between these two different sections.

The light straw-clay wall system was built using small dimension lumber (2×4s) instead of traditional post and beam construction. Two parallel walls were framed beside each other with a 3 in. (8 cm) wide space between them. This resulted in a 10 in. (25 cm) thick wall of light straw-clay, with an uninterrupted insulation space running down the middle of the wall. This results in sufficient insulation for the Sonoma County coastal climate, keeping the home cool in summer and warm in winters.

The walls were prepared for plaster using burlap and clay slip to cover all dissimilar materials and prevent cracking over time. Strips of burlap were coated in clay slip and held in place using staples (into the wood), or landscaping pins (into the straw). The exterior walls then received 1½ in. (4 cm) of earthen plaster (sand, clay, straw) and ¼ in. (0.6 cm) of lime plaster (lime putty, sand) and four coats of pigmented limewash to seal and prevent water erosion over time. Interior walls were finished with ½ in. (1.2 cm) of earth sub-plaster and ¼ in. (0.6 cm) of fine clay finish plaster.

Dave and Kendall decided to take advantage of earth's thermal mass qualities by installing a poured adobe floor over radiant heating tubes in their living room. They used bamboo flooring and tile in the rest of the house. The finished example is a space that is cohesive, beautiful and functional.

Naturalize Your Home

Janine Björnson has developed a process called "naturalizing a home," which focuses on transforming a conventional house through the use of natural wall finishes and materials. When approaching a home renovation, she considers where natural materials could be used instead of conventional ones.

Natural paints and plasters are a wonderful healthy option; because they cover so much of the home's interior surface, they provide a big bang for your buck. Natural paints and plasters can be installed on top of most existing wall and ceiling surfaces with minimal preparation. Earthen paints and plasters are excellent in most rooms, and lime is an excellent choice for bathrooms and kitchens. Tadelakt plaster finishes (a traditional plaster from Morocco made with burnished soap and lime) can also be used on shower walls and sinks, but you would need to hire an expert to install this type of finish.

Natural materials can also be used for floors and other areas.

RESOURCES

Books
• The Editors of Home Energy Magazine. *No-Regrets Remodeling, 2nd Edition: How to Create a Comfortable, Healthy Home That Saves Energy*, Home Energy Magazine, 2013. Educates homeowners about energy efficiency, comfort and health, including chapters on design and planning, air-sealing, heating, cooling, ventilation, insulation, selecting doors and windows and using water wisely.

• Venolia, Carol and Kelly Lerner. *Natural Remodeling for the Not-So-Green House: Bringing Your Home into Harmony with Nature*, Lark Books, 2006. This book invites you to look first to your home's site and climate as resources for lighting, heating, cooling and delight, adding technical upgrades where necessary and selecting appropriate materials to support your natural comfort strategies; illustrated with case studies, including the Myhrman-Knox home.

You might consider installing a poured adobe floor over a concrete floor, or using reclaimed wood or fabric for a wall finish. Instead of purchasing new furniture sprayed with fire retardants and other chemicals, you might consider building your own furniture into the home using straw bales, adobe bricks or cob. When you start thinking outside of the box, you'll be amazed at the materials at your disposal. Your home will become healthier by using these materials, but it will also become a thing of beauty. Including natural elements in your home inevitably results in a space that feels calm and grounded. People will feel it as soon as they walk through the door.

Siting a Natural Building

Michael G. Smith

16

Selecting a building site is one of the most critical design decisions you will ever make. The wrong choice can have long-lasting negative effects that are difficult (or impossible) to mitigate. Some of the characteristics that most strongly determine what it will be like to live in a place are not immediately obvious during a quick visit. To find the best building site, you will need to spend a lot of time on the land through different seasons and in extreme weather conditions.

If possible, spend a full year camping on the site, or visit it frequently, before pinning down the precise building location. Also speak to neighbors and look through county records to learn as much as you can about historical and planned usage of your land and surrounding properties. The care you take will pay off.

The following suggestions are intended specifically for siting dwellings on rural land, but most are applicable to other situations and building types (in the Southern Hemisphere, reverse north and south notations).

Physical Site Characteristics

Slope

Don't assume you need a level building site. Often it's best to build on a slope and leave the flattest places for gardening. Slopes can provide the best views and offer advantages in water and air drainage, since gravity will help move water and wastes. Excavating a flat pad on a sloped site can provide earth for building, gardening or landscaping. On the other hand, very steep slopes may complicate access, require excessive digging and massive retaining walls and be difficult to

get around on during construction. Another option is to build a level platform above ground on a post-and-pier foundation. This has the advantage of minimizing earth moving and the disruption of groundwater flows. Drawbacks include reduced earthquake safety, reduced interior climate stabilization from the loss of earth coupling, and increased use of structural lumber. Post-and-pier foundations are best suited to relatively light buildings in non-seismic areas.

Aspect

The direction a sloped site faces makes a big difference in ground temperature. South-facing slopes, with their surface more nearly perpendicular to the rays of the winter sun, collect more heat in the winter, which could translate into substantial energy savings.

MICHAEL G. SMITH *provides consultation to owner-builders on the placement and design of natural buildings:* strawclaywood.com.

It's also easier to design a passive solar home on a south-facing site.

Drainage

If possible, pick a naturally well-drained site. It will save work, expense, materials and repairs. Avoid marshy areas, floodplains and depressions. Stay away from seasonal creeks and gullies where surface water may flow during part of the year (or maybe only once every several years). If you can't be onsite during the heaviest rainfall of the year, imagine a storm of Biblical proportions and figure out where the water would flow. If you're stuck with poorly drained clay soil and a rainy climate, site the building on a slope so that you can create artificial drainage.

Subsurface Geology

One of the first things I do when exploring a potential building site is to dig a lot of holes. I want to know how far down it is to bedrock (which will inform my excavation plans and foundation design), how much topsoil there is and how suitable the subsoil is for building. If the site has deep, rich topsoil, then it might be better used for a garden or orchard. I also look for evidence of landslides and try to determine whether the site is seismically stable.

Microclimate

Solar Access

In any climate, you can save a lot of money and energy in heating and/or cooling your home by

FIGURE 16.1. When designing her own home near Moab, Utah, architect Susie Harrington looked to the site for inspiration. By choosing local materials and a form that reflects the surrounding landscape, she ensured that the building would look and feel like a natural outgrowth of the site. The walls of this passive solar home are straw bale and the undulating roof is covered with recycled plastic "eco-shakes." [Credit: Catherine Wanek]

using simple passive solar design strategies. Where winter heating is needed, windows on the south side (or an attached greenhouse) make a big difference, but only if you have winter sun on the building! (See "Designing with the Sun," p. 69.)

The best sites for passive solar heating (and for photovoltaic electricity) have an unobstructed view to the horizon from the southeast to the southwest. If trees to the south shade your site, consider respectfully harvesting or substantially pruning them. The number of trees you will save by decreased heating needs over the lifetime of the building can easily make up for the ones you remove now.

FIGURE 16.2. The Anasazi people who built this cliff side settlement at Mesa Verde, Colorado, nearly 1,000 years ago were well aware of the importance of good siting. This cave was selected partly because its southern aspect provided warmth in winter and protection from the baking sun in summer. [Credit: Catherine Wanek]

Shade

In hot summer climates, afternoon shading can make the difference between a cool, comfortable retreat and an oven. Look for tall trees to the southwest and west of the site. Deciduous trees are especially useful since they block the summer sun but drop their leaves and let the winter sun shine through. In general, trees and vegetation around a site will keep it cooler and moister (as will irrigation). Deciduous trees and vines can also be planted after the structure is complete.

Prevailing Wind Direction

Because of local topography, wind direction on a specific site can differ from the regional norm. Find out from which direction the biggest storms approach your site. (If you live in the woods, look for big fallen trees. Which direction did they fall in?) Will there be wind-driven rain, sleet or snow? Are you in a valley that channels cold winds past your site, increasing your future heating costs? Are you on a ridge with a spectacular view of the ocean but no protection from whipping gales?

Air Drainage

On clear winter nights, air cools off and condenses wherever it is exposed to the sky, flowing downhill as a viscous fluid. Wherever its passage is blocked by a rise in the ground, a line of trees or even a building, it may come to rest, creating frost pockets of much colder air. These are the places that freeze first—not a good location for your tomatoes, fruit trees or a cozy home. Valley floors are often the worst. If your site is on a slope, then make sure that cold air can drain away downhill. Also

FIGURE 16.3. Large trees near a building site can provide not only cooling shade but also a visual and energetic focal point. This straw bale home in Pagosa Springs, Colorado, was built by Kelly Mathews. [Credit: Catherine Wanek]

them about the most extreme weather conditions they can remember.

Site Planning
Master Plan
It's incredibly useful to have a good understanding of your likely overall land usage before you site any building. Look as far into the future as possible. What buildings, gardens, orchards, pastures, ponds, woodlots and wild areas might you eventually want on the property, and where does it make the most sense to put them? How can you position them relative to each other in a sensible way so that each part of the system meets the needs of the others and of the whole system?

For example, can you dig a pond to provide earth for your cob house, fire control and a home for the ducks and geese, which will also help with erosion and drought control, be part of your greywater system and irrigate your fruit orchard? This sort of design takes thought and careful planning.

position your buildings where early morning winter sun will warm them up sooner.

Fire
Wildfire runs uphill and in the direction of the wind. Ridges and hilltops are the most susceptible to burning. Waterways, roads and irrigated gardens all make effective firebreaks.

Floods
If you're near a river or stream, find out where the 100-year floodplain is and site any buildings beyond its reach. Get to know old-timers in your area and ask

Access
Although it's not always necessary to have a permanent road to a building site, it's important to think about these questions: how will you transport materials to the

site during construction? How will the inhabitants get themselves, their babies, groceries and the like to the building in rainy or snowy weather? What about emergencies—getting sick people out or fire engines in?

It's very romantic to build on a remote site with no vehicle access. But a few experiences of hauling heavy materials like sand, cement and foundation stones uphill via wheelbarrow makes me recommend that you seriously consider at least a temporary road, which can be decommissioned or shortened after construction is complete. If you do create a new permanent road, then plan it very carefully. Road building is expensive and can have a major detrimental effect on the local ecology, as well as channeling runoff and causing erosion problems.

Water and Utilities

Drinking water, wash water, electricity, phone lines—if you need them, where will they come from?

Avoid having to pump sewage uphill to a septic system or leach field. Plan for your greywater to be useful downhill from the building site in an orchard, garden, woodlot or pond. Wastewater considerations suggest that it may be best to avoid locating your home at the lowest point of the property.

Building Materials

If you plan to use materials from the land (such as earth, sand, stones, trees, straw or water)

FIGURE 16.4. Thierry Dronet built this homestead in northwestern France (also shown on the cover.) Before constructing your home, it's valuable to have a long-term site plan, including such elements as food production, outbuildings, vehicle access and parking, drainage and water features and wildlife habitat. That way, the various elements can be placed in beneficial relationship with each other, and earthmoving can be done all at once.
[Credit: Catherine Wanek]

in construction, where are they located and how will you transport them? It's much easier to roll stones downhill than up.

Social and Political Considerations

Zoning and Regulations

Different states and counties have different land use policies and varying abilities to enforce them. Within a county, areas are zoned for different purposes, such as residential, forestry or light industry. If your plans include agriculture, manufacturing, multiple residences or building with alternative materials and you pick the wrong location, then you may find yourself fighting your neighbors and the local government.

Relations with your neighbors are of primary importance, so nurture them. Try to a find an area where other people are doing the sorts of things you would like to do. Zoning and regulatory considerations should affect your choice of a building site on a much larger scale—at the neighborhood, county and state levels.

FIGURE 16.5. Jane Faith and Tony Wrench built this inexpensive, cement-free home at an ecovillage in Wales as a model of low-impact construction. The walls are cordwood with cob mortar. The roof is covered with a layer of straw bales, then a rubber pond liner and sod. Although the building is nearly invisible from the surrounding countryside, this ultimately did not prevent a legal battle with the local planning authority. See thatroundhouse.info for the story. [Credit: Catherine Wanek]

Privacy

Think about not only visual privacy but also protection from noise, smells and light pollution. A nearby highway may be loud on one side of the property and impossible to hear just around the side of the hill. Some kinds of noise and smells (hunting, field burning, etc.) are seasonal. If you want to keep a low profile, then figure out where your building site is visible from. Can it be seen from a neighbor's property, a driveway or a major highway? Remember that visibility can be much greater in winter when some trees drop their leaves.

Community

Would you like your home to be clustered near friends and neighbors for mutual support, safety and companionship? (For more information see "Ecovillages and Intentional Communities," p. 429.)

Easements

Owning the title to a piece of land doesn't mean that you own all the rights to it. A neighbor might already have permission to use your well or to put a road through your property. The phone or utility company may own a corridor where they plan to put a cable or pipeline. A mining company may own the mineral rights to your land, allowing them to drill or tunnel beneath the surface. These rights are called easements, and should be recorded on the property title.

Future Development

Find out who owns surrounding land and what they plan to do with it. Clearcut the forest? Build a housing development? Get to know your neighbors and ask them what rumors they've heard. Also check with your county planning department to find out about any plans to widen roads or change the zoning.

Other Important Considerations

Views

Although you can establish beautiful short views by landscaping your site, you can't do much about the long views; either you have them or you don't. Views of the sky and the distant horizon do a lot to combat feelings of claustrophobia and cabin fever, especially for people who live in the forest or in places with cold or gray winters, and for those who spend a lot of time at home. Sometimes you can open up long views by judiciously pruning or clearing trees around your site.

History

It's always useful to know what human beings before you have done on the land. Who were the original human inhabitants of this place? Are there sites of archeological or religious significance that it would be better not to disturb? In recent times, have people used chemicals that might still be present in the soil and water? If there's a history of manufacturing, agriculture or even previous building, it might be a good idea to get the soil tested for toxins.

Ecological Impact

It hardly seems necessary to suggest that you think seriously before cutting down a lot of trees or draining a wetland for your building site. But all outdoors places are habitat. Get to know the plants and animals that you will displace or kill during construction. Find out where deer trails pass through, where owls roost to hunt and who is living underground.

RESOURCES

Books
- Chiras, Daniel. *The Natural House: A Complete Guide to Healthy, Energy-Efficient, Environmental Homes*, Chelsea Green, 2000. Contains an excellent chapter on site considerations.
- Evans, Ianto, Michael G. Smith and Linda Smiley. *The Hand-Sculpted House: A Practical and Philosophical Guide to Building a Cob Cottage*, Chelsea Green, 2002. Contains detailed instructions on how to approach a building site with sensitivity, as well as more information on site selection and many useful anecdotes.
- Mollison, Bill. *Permaculture: A Designer's Manual*, Island Press, 1990. The bible of permaculture; lays out an entire system for master planning. See "The Permaculture House" for more recommended permaculture resources.
- Scher, Les and Carol Scher. *Finding and Buying Your Place in the Country*, Kaplan, 2000. An excellent guide to selecting rural property and navigating the complexities of real estate transactions.

Try to locate your building where it will cause the least disruption to natural cycles. Many people advocate developing the most damaged sites: clearcuts, logging depots or abandoned pastures. That way, through erosion control, revegetation and so on, you can actually improve the ecological health of your building site.

Feng Shui

The Chinese art of building placement is based on the inter-relationships of complex factors like geometry and subterranean waterways, but you don't have to be a trained specialist to use your intuition. Different places have different kinds of energy. Spend time on a proposed building site, meditating or just living, and see how it feels. Is the energy happy or sad, welcoming or resistant? Would you be comfortable with it in your home? Usually the most magical spots, like that special natural meadow in the back woods, are exactly the places where you should not put a building. Any intervention changes the feeling of a place, and building a house has an extreme impact. If the place is already as good as it can be, leave it alone.

The Permaculture House

PETER BANE

17

Permaculture is a system of design for managing energy that arose from the 1970s revolution in thinking about humankind's relation to the natural world. Permaculture works as a set of principles within a matrix of ethics. It encourages individual initiative toward care of the Earth, care of people, sharing surplus resources fairly and limiting our own consumption and population.

Informed by ecology and a growing awareness of global limits, permaculture is also a response to the failure of institutionalized development policies. Hunger in the world today is a problem not of production but of distribution of land and resources. In the same way, renewable energy solutions are limited not by technology or economics, but by politics and ignorance.

Homelessness and inadequate shelter will not be remedied by agencies or contractors but only by people empowered to build their own houses. In every case, says veteran permaculture teacher Lea Harrison, "the problems are large and complex, but the solutions are embarrassingly simple." Permaculture emphasizes ethics because to change behavior, attitudes and thinking must change first.

Originating from conversations between Australians David Holmgren, a student in ecological design, and Bill Mollison, a professor of environmental psychology, permaculture has spread through more than 60 countries and dozens of languages in rural villages, isolated farms and giant cities. Its basis of grassroots education—"each one, teach one"—

aims to empower individuals and local communities to restore degraded environments, create local employment and housing, generate energy and improve food security. While specific strategies vary with climate, culture and the resources available, the principles of good design are universal and form the core of permaculture education.

Permaculture design gives us a new way to see energy flows and material cycles in the world around us—a way that aligns us with the workings of the natural world. If we are to reduce the negative impacts of human activity on the biosphere or even repair the damage done, it's important that we apply this understanding to what we create. Permaculture design has tremendous relevance for the ways in which we cultivate

PETER BANE *publishes* Permaculture Activist, *the world's longest-running journal of permanent culture. A teacher, designer and co-founder of Earthaven Ecovillage in the North Carolina mountains, he is also the author of* The Permaculture Handbook: Garden Farming for Town and Country. *He divides his time between a suburban farmstead in Indiana and a rural one in Michigan.*

the Earth—agriculture and forestry—and for how we build our homes and towns. Applying permaculture principles can improve the comfort, durability, healthfulness and economy of any building by helping us make intelligent choices about placement and orientation, the design and layout of the space within and around the building and the way it harnesses and disposes of energy, water and waste.

Assessing Your Needs

Our first consideration in the creation of any structure should be our need for it. Built space is expensive—it's the most energy- and materials-intensive area of any property. Getting clear about our need for a building helps us meet those needs without taking on more than we can afford.

Though the standard American house is still being built for a married couple with two or three children, most families these days don't match that picture. It's possible to live comfortably in a very small space; I know because my partner and I lived in a 300 sq. ft. (27 m²) house. We built small to save money and avoid debt. Our house didn't include some things the typical American house is expected to have. We built a loft for our sleeping space, eliminating the need for a separate bedroom. We had no closets, though there were plenty of built-in or movable cupboards, shelves and hooks to keep the things we really used. Surplus belongings were stored in a nearby shed about the same size as the house; because it didn't have to be heated or finished to the same degree as the dwelling, the shed cost only one-third the price of our already inexpensive home. A small kitchenette met most of our needs for cooking. For major food processing, baking or entertaining, we had access to two larger community kitchens nearby.

Instead of building a bath and toilet inside the house, we shared these facilities with ten other households in our immediate neighborhood. We had access to a shower, a composting toilet and a sauna; we rarely had to wait to use any of them, always had enough hot water and did less maintenance on average than if we kept our own.

Our house, though small inside, had a large roof. The large overhang provided not only good protection for our exterior plasters and straw-clay walls but ample sheltered space for tool and fuel storage, cool food storage (on the north side), a small greywater treatment cell

FIGURE 17.1. Keeping your house as small as possible is the best way to reduce its environmental impact. This tiny self-sufficient straw bale cottage was built for a Buddhist teacher in Crestone, Colorado.
[Credit: Catherine Wanek]

and a sheltered walkway to access the cistern, which stored water collected from the roof.

Building small to meet our most essential needs allowed us to finish and move into our own home much sooner than if we had built a larger space. When we moved into our off-the-grid, debt-free home, we started saving money by not paying rent and by lowering our utility costs. We got on to the land we wanted to cultivate: gardens sprouted just outside the door, and other crops were soon growing within easy walking distance. This proximity gave us the chance to enrich our landscape by continuous care and to harvest and sell crops. The benefits of building small and debt-free were well worth the small inconveniences of limited space.

Building Siting and Design

Choosing where you will build is next in importance after assessing your real needs. The ideal situation is a small lot in a clean environment, with friendly and cooperative neighbors and reasonable local government regulation. Most of us can't make good use of more than a quarter-acre, which is enough land to grow all the vegetables for a dozen families. And if the land around ours is

clean and well managed in a compatible use, we benefit while not needing to pay taxes on it. The purpose of good placement for a building is to conserve and capture energy throughout the life of the structure. Poor placement is a "type one error," a mistake for which you will pay forever after—an energy sinkhole (see "Siting a Natural Building," p. 99).

As well as its site, the shape of

a building strongly affects its energy performance. The most compact shape in nature is a sphere; the most compact rectilinear space is a cube, which is easier to build. The longer a building is in relation to its depth and height, the less efficient it is at conserving heat. However, a longer south side (in the northern hemisphere) allows a building to capture more solar gain relative to its volume,

FIGURE 17.2. Chris Prelitz got a bargain on this steep, eroded lot in pricey Laguna Beach, California, because it was considered "unbuildable." His first step was to terrace the slope with urbanite (demolished concrete) retaining walls and plant a water-absorbing edible landscape. A lush food-bearing jungle downslope from the house now helps cool the home and protect it from wildfires. The house is made of straw bales and many salvaged materials. [Credit: Catherine Wanek]

so building shape and proportion is a tradeoff between these factors. In far northern or cloudy winter climates, where solar gain is less effective, buildings should take a more compact shape. In locations with more winter sun, buildings should stretch out on the east-west axis to a length that is from 1.4 to 1.7 times their north-south depth.

Buildings in hot climates should avoid large exposures on the west and south sides to limit daily heat gain. Ventilation is more important in hot climates, so the sector from which summer breezes blow should be planted in deciduous trees to cool and direct air toward the dwelling. In hot, humid climates, successful traditional buildings are usually elevated on posts to allow cooling and drying breezes to pass beneath the structure, and have deep overhangs to shade the windows and doors. Heavy, heat-retaining materials, such as masonry, should be limited in favor of lightweight materials like wood, straw and thatch. Hot, dry climates (which often have wide daily temperature variations) are well-suited to massive masonry or earthen walls, which can act as a thermal flywheel to hold cool evening temperatures throughout the day. In cold climates, highly insulating materials, such as straw bales, serve admirably.

Borrowing from successful traditional knowledge is important to permaculture. By starting with the best of what has worked for vernacular builders and then refining those ideas from our own experience and the learning of other innovators, we can determine an appropriate building design for our climate and circumstances.

Permaculture design means applying environmental considerations to the shaping of buildings and their surroundings. For example, the interior layout of rooms should reflect their function. Rooms benefiting from morning light (bedrooms, kitchen) ought to be placed on the east side of the house, rooms for living (kitchen, sitting room) to the south or sunny side and rooms and spaces with infrequent or nighttime use (bath, utility room, closets) to the north.

In choosing materials for a building, keep in mind their embodied energy costs. Aluminum, steel, concrete, brick and glass have relatively high environmental impacts because of their energy-intensive manufacturing processes. Wood is a wonderfully strong, light material that is easy to work with, but most commercial lumber is harvested unsustainably. If you can't acquire wood from sustainably harvested sources, limit its use to essential structural elements. Wood siding, for instance, doesn't make a lot of ecological sense even though it can be beautiful.

FIGURE 17.3. This trellis on the south face of Kristin and Mark Sullivan's straw bale home in central California has been planted with grape vines. As the vines mature, they will provide not only food but also deep shade to the outdoor sitting area and to the south-facing windows. In the winter, the vines will lose their leaves and allow the warming sun to pass through. [Credit: Catherine Wanek]

To build houses that are durable, comfortable, energy-efficient, non-toxic, friendly to the Earth and easy to reuse or recycle at the end of their useful life, we must build with materials that themselves meet these criteria.

In general, our buildings should be mostly constructed of local, abundant, cheap natural materials that do not damage the environment in which they are produced, used or disposed of. Not surprisingly, these are the same materials people have built with for millennia: earth, clay, straw, wood and local stone.

The use of natural materials is not a dogma but a practical means for making buildings inexpensive and recyclable, while minimizing environmental costs and toxicity. Low cost is not just about initial investment; it also means low energy, operating and maintenance costs. These goals can be far more easily achieved with the judicious use of a few high-tech modern materials: steel and rubber for roofs, glass for windows, closed-cell foam for subgrade insulation. The energy embedded in these materials can be justified by their limited use and by the amount of energy they allow us to capture and conserve over the life of a building. For the functions they

FIGURE 17.4. Colin Gillespie built this water feature to filter and aerate greywater from his family's straw bale home. The pond also cools the air near the outside living area—a great asset on this hot California site. Note the large oak tree providing afternoon shade to the southwest of the house. [Credit: Michael G. Smith]

FIGURE 17.5. These planters are built of recycled burlap chili sacks filled with local soil and covered with soil cement plaster. They are watered from a cistern that stores rain captured from the nearby barn roof. Tlholego Village, South Africa. [Credit: Joseph F. Kennedy]

perform, they represent appropriate technology.

Much of the energy impact of a house lies in its interactions with its surroundings, for buildings are not static. Even if our skillful design of the structure has limited the need for combustion heating by allowing for solar gain, the building's inhabitants will require food and water and will generate waste that must be managed. The energy benefits of good initial placement of the building can be augmented by planting trees for windbreaks and shade.

The judicious location of roads supports fire control and allows us to take advantage of gravity in moving heavy building materials, farm produce and so on, downhill.

With the modern food system wasting ten calories of energy in transport and processing

Permaculture Design Principles

To create human settlements that restore fertility, generate more energy than they consume and heal disrupted societies, it's necessary that all our planning, building, agriculture, forestry and commerce be based on the principles that underlie natural ecosystems. These communities provide the only evidence we have of sustainable, permanent systems of land use. Let's look at these principles and see how they can help redirect our thinking toward more harmony with the natural world.

Location and Connection

To properly manage our supply of energy and materials, we must place every element of a productive system (a town, farm, household or woodland) in beneficial functional relation to everything near it. To keep a house warm in winter, for example, locate it halfway up a south-facing slope so that frost and cold air drain away, winter winds and storms are blocked and free energy can fill the dwelling. To avoid pumping water, hook roof gutters up to a storage tank. Put the garden below the tank and irrigate by gravity.

Multiple Functions

If everything in the system serves multiple functions, we can do more with less. Permaculture means that you see your roof not only as shelter, but also as part of the water supply and as a producer of energy (solar collectors). Houses that stack functions to meet their own needs approach the elegance of living systems.

Redundancy

Let every essential function be met by multiple elements. Have more than one source of water, heat and income. Parts always fail; larger systems are more stable if their energy pathways are flexible.

Energy Cycling

Capture, use and recycle energy many times before it leaves the system. Turn sunlight into plants, plants into animals and animals into manure, meat, compost, heat and other animals. Catch water high and move it slowly through the landscape, building fertility with every turn.

Zones, Sectors and Elevations

Plan for energy efficiency by analyzing the influences from outside a system (sectors), the intensity of activity within a system (zones) and the differences of elevation on the landscape itself. Place elements requiring high levels of interaction (such as children, a plant nursery and small livestock) at the center of the system and more autonomous elements, such as a woodlot,

for every calorie of food value delivered, it's imperative that we shift food growing closer to home. The best place for a garden starts at the kitchen door of the house. If that garden emphasizes herbs and salads, includes some small fruits, and incorporates a few poultry and fish in a pond to add eggs and meat into the diet, we can eliminate much of the toxicity, nutrient and soil loss and wasted energy of industrial food production. If the water for the garden is harvested from the roof of the house (easily done with gutters and a tank or cistern), and the nutrients in the human waste stream are returned to the soil through composted or biologically treated humanure, then most of the major energy cycles of the domestic economy can be closed (see "Complementary

toward the outer fringe. Scatter hostile energies (noise, pollution, storms, cold winds) and focus beneficial ones (winter sunlight, good views, cooling summer breezes, customers, bird manure). Plan to move water, waste, fuels and construction materials downhill.

Use Biological Resources

Biological resources are cheaper and safer than industrial ones. Automobiles pollute the air, kill innocents and break down to junk, but horses run on grass, create food for mushrooms and replace themselves. Air conditioners cost kilowatts and destroy the ozone layer; deciduous trees can cool just as effectively while making rain, building soil, feeding animals and growing money.

Appropriate Technology

If you can't afford it, repair it, fuel it and recycle it locally, look for something else. Make sure that every element of your design meets the energy test: will it produce more energy and resources over its lifetime than were required to make it? Don't forget the cost of disposal. Atomic science hasn't learned to put its toys away yet.

Start Small

Build out from a controlled front. Bite off no more than you can chew and meet your own needs first; then you'll be in a better position to help others.

Succession and Stacking

Use time in your favor. Anticipate natural succession and plan for your house, garden or neighborhood to change. As things naturally grow up, plan to use all the layers and spaces in three dimensions. Harvest from the canopy as well as from the ground. The forest does; why shouldn't we?

Observe and Replicate Natural Patterns

Organic life has demonstrated what works cheaply and cleanly. If we pay more attention, we'll get along much better.

Incorporate Diversity and Edge

Diverse ecosystems are more stable than simple ones. Variety is the name of life itself. Edges are where the variety is greatest; that's where the action is.

Attitude Matters

Think positively. Turn problems into solutions. Work for the good of life itself and remember to share your surpluses. The natural world is abundant, and life begets life. Our individual efforts can and do make a difference.

Systems for Energy-Efficient Homes," p. 115).

Making beneficial and functional connections between a house and its surroundings is the essence of permaculture design.

When the yields of a landscape can supply the needs of its inhabitants and all the other elements of the cultivated system, we approach the standard that nature demands of us. If this good design can be implemented mainly with local materials, local labor and community financing, then we'll be well on our way to a whole different world.

RESOURCES

Books

• Alexander, Christopher, et al. *A Pattern Language*, Oxford University Press, 1977. This famous work of design, with its multicultural suite of six co-authors, draws on the heritage of humanity, expressed primarily in successful urban settings, to establish a core curriculum for humane and convivial built spaces ranging from the city and its region through streetscapes to details of the home.

• Aranya. *Permaculture Design: A Step-by-Step Guide*, Permanent Publications, 2012. A rare work that focuses on the permaculture design system through its core methods and modes of thinking, this book uses examples to illustrate holistic problem solving. Humorous and graphically strong, it is indispensable to the professional designer.

• Bane, Peter. *The Permaculture Handbook: Garden Farming for Town and Country*, New Society Publishers, 2012. A comprehensive introduction to permaculture principles and applications through the lens of adapting or creating a sustainable home on an urban or suburban lot or small rural acreage. The book offers a pattern language for the home economy of the near future.

• Mars, Ross. *The Basics of Permaculture Design*, Permanent Publications, 2003. A slender and accessible overview of permaculture fundamentals with many useful tips for the home designer.

• Mollison, Bill and Reny Mia Slay. *Introduction to Permaculture*, Tagari Publications, 2nd ed., 1994. The classic distillation of Mollison's work with David Holmgren in *Permaculture I* and *Permaculture II*. Plant examples and climatic emphasis for Australian conditions make this more appropriate for readers in the arid and sub-tropical Southwest, California or the Gulf States.

• Morrow, Rosemary. *The Earth User's Guide to Permaculture*, Permanent Publications, 2006. A very simply written text from one of the world's most experienced teachers of permaculture, accompanied by excellent illustrations. In addition to the elements of land and home design, it offers insights into social dynamics as well as practical guidance for dealing with natural disasters.

• van Lengen, Johan. *The Barefoot Architect*, Shelter Publications, 2008. Though it does not reference permaculture directly, this work is cut from the same cloth and provides an encyclopedic reference to appropriate technology for building. Generously illustrated with line drawings, it covers everything from site selection to plumbing details, emphasizing very low-cost methods and materials for tropical, subtropical and temperate climates.

Periodicals

• *Permaculture Activist*: **permacultureactivist.net**. A quarterly journal of grassroots permaculture work, primarily focused on North America. Each issue covers a major theme in permanent culture ranging from microbes to economics through plant migration, soil building and the practice of democratic community. Provides course listings for North and Central America and the Caribbean. The website provides ready access to permaculture groups around the world as well as a fine compendium of sources for nursery stock and open-pollinated and heritage seed varieties.

• *Permaculture Magazine*: **permaculture.co.uk**. A quarterly glossy magazine supporting the permaculture movement in Britain but widely distributed in North America as well, *PM* draws on writers from around the world to offer many practical and thoughtful articles on building, cultivation and settlement issues.

Complementary Systems for Energy-Efficient Homes

18

Michael G. Smith

If we aim to create truly sustainable homes that do not contribute to climate destabilization, pollute the land or air or deplete scarce resources, we must think far beyond what our houses are made of. Much more energy is consumed for heating and cooling, hot water, lighting, cooking and other domestic uses than by the construction industry. Over a 100-year lifespan, approximately 20 times more energy will be used inside a typical American house than went into its materials and construction. About half of that energy is used in heating and cooling the house itself. This is one of the simplest energy expenditures to address, using passive solar design, good insulation, efficient windows and careful detailing to keep drafts out (see "Designing with the Sun," p. 69 and "Natural Building for Cold Climates," p. 73).

The other main energy consumers in homes are water heating, cooking, refrigeration and other appliances, lighting and electronic devices such as computers and televisions. Expenditures in each of these categories can be reduced by good design, selection of energy-efficient appliances and, just as significantly, changes in lifestyle, such as using a clothesline instead of an electric dryer in the summer.

In addition to energy, our homes are also major consumers of water. The average US household of four uses 300 gal. (1,100 L) of water per day inside the house. This means that, over the course of a year, over 100,000 gal. (380,000 L) of clean drinking water are made dirty and sent down the drain. Wastewater is usually either lost into the ground, rivers or the ocean or else recycled for human consumption through an energy- and chemical-intensive treatment process.

We all know some simple ways to conserve energy and water: put on a sweater and turn down the thermostat; turn off the lights when we leave a room; take shorter showers. But if we are going to mitigate the impending disaster of global climate change, we need to think and act much bigger.

Imagine a properly oriented home that needs only half as much energy for heating and cooling, and has solar panels on the roof that generate more electricity than the home consumes. How about one that meets its water needs with roof catchment and reuses all of its wastewater for irrigating food crops? Imagine a carbon-neutral homestead where the carbon dioxide released from fuel use, electricity generation and even

Michael G. Smith *is a natural builder, designer, consultant, instructor, writer, editor, farmer and father:* strawclaywood.com.

manufacture of building materials and equipment is all caught and stored in growing trees? These are the sorts of strategies we will have to implement as a global community.

We don't need to wait for our governments and power utilities to lead the way in making these changes; in fact, we can't afford to wait. Whether we are building a new house or living in an older one, there are dozens of ways we can make our homes more efficient. Many of the strategies listed below are inexpensive and simple for the do-it-yourselfer to implement, with a little technical advice. The resources listed at the end of each section are a good place to start.

Mass Heating Strategies

The most common way to heat homes in North America is to heat air with a gas- or oil-burning

FIGURE 18.1. This sculptural masonry stove in Belgium combines a firebrick core with earthen exterior finishes. [Credit: Catherine Wanek]

furnace, then force that hot air through ducts and out of vents located around the house. This is an inefficient approach for several reasons. First, because warm air rises, much of the heat ends up in parts of your house where it does you no good, like up around the ceilings of high rooms, especially upstairs. Second, hot air forces its way out through leaks in the upper part of the building, creating a vacuum that pulls cold drafts in to replace it. Third, air doesn't hold much heat, and therefore a large volume of air needs to be circulated through the building to satisfy heating demands, leading to system inefficiencies and human discomfort from air turbulence.

Systems that heat water in boilers and then distribute it through radiators, baseboards or hydronic tubing make a bit more sense—at least the hot water is going to remain inside the house. A given volume of water also has much higher capacity to store heat than the same volume of air does, making it more efficient as a heat transfer system.

Radiant or hydronic heating systems use hot water or other fluids such as oil or glycol, often in combination with solid thermal mass, to store and radiate heat. During construction, flexible plastic tubes can be embedded in either a floor or a wall. Hydronic floors are best installed on a slab subfloor of earth or concrete, with insulation below. The surface of the floor can be sealed earth (see "Earthen Floors," p. 331), tile or flagstone. These floors heat your body by direct contact (conduction) as well as radiation. This makes them feel wonderful underfoot on a cold day. The heat remains in the mass for a long time, making them much more efficient than forced-air heating. Radiant and hydronic systems can also be combined with active solar water heating, in which case the fluid running through the tubes is heated directly by the sun.

An older and more low-tech radiant heating system is the masonry stove. Masonry stoves are massive wood-burning stoves, usually constructed from stone or brick, and placed in a central location in the home. They can be used for cooking and baking as well as heating. Hot gases from burning wood travel through many winding passageways inside the stove before exiting the building through the chimney, transferring most of their heat to the thermal mass. This is in contrast to a lightweight metal woodstove, where a great deal of the heat is lost immediately up the chimney.

In many traditional Chinese homes, a massive bed called a *kang* was made of earth or brick and used to store heat from the wood- or coal-fired cookstove in much the same way. If placed inside a south-facing window, a mass heater or bed can also be heated by direct solar gain.

Masonry stoves are a highly efficient option if you wish to heat your home with wood, but they can be expensive and technically difficult to construct. A low-cost DIY version is the rocket mass heater developed by Ianto Evans of the Cob Cottage Company. Rocket mass heaters use an inner core of bricks surrounded by a steel drum, the top of which serves as a cooking surface. Hot gases exit the drum via a metal stovepipe that can travel many yards through a cob bench or earthen floor before leaving the building.

All mass heating systems are slow to respond; they take a long time to heat up or cool down. They work best when heating needs are predictable, such as where winters are cold and cloudy, and when the building is intended to be kept at a consistent temperature throughout the season. With good design, the same thermal mass used for heating can also serve for cooling the home in the summer time.

Energy-Efficient Cooking and Water-Heating

Globally, at least one-third of all household energy usage is for cooking and heating water. In most places, the majority of this

FIGURE 18.2. This rocket mass heater heats Flemming Abrahamsson's cob studio in Denmark. The cob bench is kept warm by flue gases passing through it from the combustion unit, which can be constructed primarily from salvaged barrels and other waste materials. [Credit: Catherine Wanek]

work could be done by harvesting the sun's energy directly. Applied at a large scale, solar thermal technology could save enormous amounts of fuel and reduce carbon emissions substantially. The level of sophistication of these technologies varies from simple do-it-yourself systems using off-the-shelf parts to much more complex and expensive preassembled units.

You can heat water for a shower or bath simply by leaving a dark-colored tank of water or a coil of black hose or poly pipe in the sun. Run cold water in one end of the coil, and solar-heated water comes out the other end. The next level of sophistication is to place the coil inside a glass-topped box, tilted and oriented towards the sun. The box slows down heat loss from the water, so you can have a warm shower even after the sun goes down. To hold hot water through the night, you will need to store it in an insulated tank. If the tank is located higher than the heating coil, and both ends of the loop of pipe are plumbed into the tank correctly, hot water will rise into it via a thermosiphon, while cooler water gets recirculated through the heating element.

If you wish to drink the hot water, the pipe and tank need to be made out of a food-safe material like copper or stainless steel. In the developed world, household solar water systems often include factory-made sealed panels mounted on a south-facing roof of the house (in the northern hemisphere), insulated tanks, pumps and safety features to prevent pressure from building up inside the system and causing an explosion.

There are a number of ap-

RESOURCES FOR MASS HEATING

Books
• Evans, Ianto and Leslie Jackson. *Rocket Mass Heaters: Superefficient Woodstoves You Can Build (and Snuggle Up To)*, Cob Cottage Co., 2006. A how-to guide for creating your own low-cost version of a masonry heater.
• Lyle, David. *The Book of Masonry Stoves: Rediscovering an Old Way of Warming*, Chelsea Green, 1998. An expert in the field discusses the history of masonry stoves, along with many useful details for the builder.
• Matesz, Ken. *Masonry Heaters: Designing, Building, and Living with a Piece of the Sun*, Chelsea Green, 2010. Authoritative and up-to-date resource for anyone interested in buying, designing or building a masonry heater.

Periodicals
• Fine Homebuilding: **finehomebuilding.com**. High-quality publication available both on-line and in paper. Authoritative and readable instructions on many different topics, for professionals and owner-builders. The site includes a searchable database of articles, which can be downloaded for free.

Organizations
• Cob Cottage Company: **cobcottage.com**. Offers workshops on rocket mass heater construction. Coquille, Oregon, US.
• Firespeaking: **firespeaking.com**. Designs and installs masonry heaters, rocket mass heaters, Rumford fireplaces, wood-fired ovens and cookstoves. Also offers workshops. Oregon, US.
• Masonry Heater Association of North America: **mha-net.org**. Extensive and up-to-date information and resources on masonry heaters, for both builders and buyers.

Websites
• Hand Print Press: **handprintpress.com/resources/home-heat**. An archive of designs and experiments related to masonry heaters, rocket mass heaters and earthen ovens.

proaches to cooking with the sun (see "Solar Cookers," p. 128), some of which have caught on at large scale in developing economies such as India and China. Solar cookers are a great way to save energy and to get you out of your house and attuned to the weather.

My favorite way to save energy while cooking is called a haybox. This century-old technology is simply an insulated box with a tight lid, large enough to contain your cooking pot. I use a Styrofoam cooler lined with aluminum foil to increase heat reflectivity. When cooking anything that needs to simmer for a long time, such as grains, beans, soups and stews, I first bring the pot to a boil on my regular cookstove, then move it into the box to continue cooking with stored heat. I don't have to watch the pot, stir it, add more water or worry about the food (or the house!) burning, even if I leave it alone for hours. Hayboxes work in any kind of weather in the convenience of your own kitchen. They can also be made from fabric and loose insulation. Make yourself one and try it! You can find instructions online (see "Resources").

Many organizations develop and promote fuel-efficient cookstoves, especially in less-industrialized areas where cooking is done over an open flame. One approach that is catching on the United States, as well as in Latin America and Africa, is called the rocket stove. (These share the same design origins with the rocket mass heaters described above, but they do not include a thermal mass heat storage element as they are intended for cooking rather than space heating.) Rocket stoves burn small-diameter sticks at high temperatures and focus most of the heat of combustion onto the bottom of a cookpot. They are easy to construct from readily available materials including bricks, steel barrels and stovepipe. The latest development of this technology is the BioLite stove, which combines the rocket stove concept with a thermoelectric generator, converting waste heat into electricity to power a fan that further improves fuel efficiency and reduces harmful emissions.

An exciting new development in energy-efficient cooking is the micro-gasifier. Engineer Paul Olivier is working to perfect and promote a design that converts agricultural wastes such as rice hulls, coffee husks, nut shells and pelletized wood to syngas,

FIGURE 18.3. A kitchen at the Bethel Business and Community Development Center, a sustainability learning and demonstration center in rural Lesotho. Some of the technologies in use here include roof-integrated solar water heating, a parabolic solar cooker, photovoltaic panels for lighting, roof water harvesting and storage and vegetable production right outside the kitchen window. [Credit: Ivan Yahdnitsky]

a combination of carbon monoxide and hydrogen gas that can be safely burned in the home for cooking and water heating and even for micro-enterprises such as coffee roasting. These cookers are being marketed in Vietnam and elsewhere for approximately $50. They consume fuel that is practically free and produce a saleable commodity in the form of biochar pellets, which are highly prized as a soil amendment. For more details see "The Power of Small Gasifiers" by Paul Olivier: dl.dropboxusercontent.com/u/22013094/Paper/Summaries/Gasification.pdf

Home-Generated Electricity

Nearly all homes in the industrialized world get their electricity from the grid, a vast network of power lines controlled by utilities that generate electricity and/or purchase it from other utilities. Globally, the major sources of electricity production in 2008 were, in order, coal (41 percent), natural gas (21 percent), hydro-electric (16 percent) and nuclear (13 percent.) In the US, electricity generation from fossil fuels accounts for 40 percent of total greenhouse gas emissions. Besides large-scale hydro projects, which have been responsible for displacing human settlements and destroying habitat around the world, other forms of renewable electricity generation like wind and solar account for only a tiny fraction of global production.

The long distances energy must travel through the grid,

RESOURCES FOR ENERGY-EFFICIENT COOKING AND WATER HEATING

Books

• Denzer, Kiko. *Build Your Own Earth Oven*, Hand Print Press, 3rd ed., 2007. While it is debatable whether wood-fired earthen ovens should be classified as "energy-efficient," they have many excellent properties, including being a superb starter project for novice earth builders. This is an outstanding guide to building, firing and baking.

• Edleson, Max and Eva Edleson. *Build Your Own Barrel Oven*, Hand Print Press, 2013. Step-by-step instructions on how to build an efficient, quick-heating wood-burning oven.

• Ramlow, Bob and Benjamin Nusz. *Solar Water Heating*, New Society Publishers, 2006. A book for those who want to install their own solar thermal system, starting with the basics of solar water heating, including energy conservation, it then moves into the types of solar collectors, solar water and space-heating systems, system components, installation, operation and maintenance, system sizing and siting.

• Lane, Tom. *Solar Hot Water Systems: Lessons Learned*, Energy Conservation Services of North Florida, 2002. Aimed at the contractor who wants to know what works, and the homeowner who wants basic facts for comparison shopping, this book will help people use currently available solar water heating products while avoiding the mistakes of the past.

Periodicals

• Home Power Magazine: **homepower.com**. US-based bimonthly print and digital magazine with up-to-date technical articles on many topics including solar water heating. A good introduction to the topic is available for free on their website.

Organizations and Websites

• Aprovecho Research Center: **aprovecho.org**. Research, development and testing of improved cookstoves and other appropriate technology. Many useful publications.

• **Builditsolar.com**. "The renewable energy site for do-it-yourselfers," with details on hundreds of energy-saving projects.

• Global Alliance for Clean Cookstoves: **cleancookstoves.org**. Advocates a market-based approach to global adoption of clean cooking technology.

• The Thermal Cooker: **thermalcooker.wordpress.com**. Instructions for building and using hayboxes.

combined with its haphazard design and poor state of repair, lead to enormous inefficiencies. Depending on the utility, as little as 25 percent of electricity generated is actually delivered and used.

Generating your own power at a household or community level is one response to these problems. Depending on your climate and terrain, the best options might be photovoltaic solar panels, wind turbines or microhydro. Small-scale hydro power is suitable only where you have running surface water, such as a stream. A small water-powered turbine can generate electricity whenever the water is running, whereas wind turbines and solar panels are highly weather-dependent. Photovoltaics are the most widely adaptable home energy source, but you might want to consult an expert for help designing and installing your system.

Off-grid systems usually require batteries for electrical storage. Some devices like LED lights and laptop computers can run on direct current (DC) electricity straight from the batteries, but most appliances are designed to run on alternating current (AC). So off-grid systems usually include inverters to convert DC to AC, as well as charge-controllers and other components to

FIGURE 18.4. This stainless steel gasifier, designed by Paul Olivier, is being manufactured for distribution in Vietnam. It converts rice hulls and other agricultural wastes into cooking gas and biochar, a prized soil amendment. [Credit: Paul Olivier]

FIGURE 18.5. This natural homestead in Missouri is powered entirely by renewable energy from the sun and wind. [Credit: Mark Mazziotti]

improve safety, efficiency and ease of use. The cost of initial system installment plus replacement of short-lived parts like batteries adds up, making off-grid electricity more expensive than buying from the grid.

However, more and more households in the US are installing grid-tied systems, where the electricity they produce is stored not in onsite batteries but in the grid itself. This trend has been accelerated in recent years by net-metering laws that require utilities to buy excess power from consumers. When combined with federal tax credits and other incentives, which vary from state to state, home power generation can now more than pay for itself.

Depending on the incentives offered, the cost of electricity and the number of hours of sun the system receives, grid-tied photovoltaic systems usually pay for themselves in between 5 and 20

RESOURCES FOR HOME-GENERATED ELECTRICITY

Books

• Chiras, Dan. *The Homeowner's Guide to Renewable Energy*, New Society, 2006. This book covers the many ways we can slash energy bills while improving comfort in our homes, including solar hot water, solar space heat, passive cooling, solar, wind and microhydro generated electricity and emerging technologies such as hydrogen, fuel cells, methane digesters and biodiesel.

• Chiras, Dan. *Solar Electricity Basics*, New Society, 2010. Another well-written guide, by one of our most prolific authors, to choosing and living with grid-tied and off-grid systems.

• Davis, Scott. *Microhydro: Clean Power from Water*, New Society, 2004. Lavishly illustrated and practical, this book covers microhydro principles, design and site considerations, equipment options and legal, environmental and economic factors.

• Hren, Stephen and Rebekah Hren. *The Carbon-Free Home*, Chelsea Green, 2008. Meant as a guide for renovating existing homes, this book guides you through many small and large projects designed to save money on utilities and reduce carbon emissions.

• SEI. *Photovoltaics: Design & Installation Manual*, Solar Energy International, 2007. A manual on how to design, install and maintain a photovoltaic system. Includes a detailed description of PV system components, including PV modules, batteries, controllers and inverters. Also available in Spanish.

• Shaeffer, John. *Real Goods Solar Living Sourcebook*, 14 Edition, 2014, New Society Publishers. Encyclopedic yet accessible guide to nearly all aspects of home-scale renewable energy, including photovoltaic systems, wind generators, solar water heating, energy conservation, off-the-grid and grid intertie applications. There's an appendix with charts, maps and worksheets to help you design your own solar home and energy system.

• Woofenden, Ian. *Wind Power for Dummies*, For Dummies, 2009. Clearly written guide walks you through every step of the process of selecting, installing and operating a small-scale wind generator to power your home.

Periodicals

• Home Power Magazine: **homepower.com**. US-based bimonthly print and digital magazine that provides technical updates and how-to information for householders as well as professional installers. Their website also provides lots of useful free information.

Organizations and Websites

• Center for Renewable Energy and Green Building: **evergreeninstitute.org**. Founded by Dan Chiras, The Evergreen Institute provides high-quality workshops in renewable energy and green building. Gerald, Missouri.

• Solar Energy International: **solarenergy.org**. Offers solar and renewable energy trainings around the world and online. Carbondale, Colorado.

• Solar Living Institute: **solarliving.org**. A non-profit organization that offers online and onsite trainings in solar design and installation, other forms of home power and many other topics including biofuels and natural building. Hopland, California.

years. In some areas, contractors will install the panels for free and then collect the energy savings until the system is paid for. Due to technological improvements and the increased scale of production, the cost of solar electric panels is dropping rapidly in the United States.

It is theoretically possible for a home to be a net energy producer over its lifetime. However, one would need to factor in the energy needed to produce the components of the power system (the energy payback period is estimated at four years for the average rooftop photovoltaic system) plus all the other materials and components that go into the house itself. The average US household would need an unusually large and long-lived energy system to compensate for all the embodied energy of construction plus the energy used in the home.

A more economical strategy is to reduce the embodied energy of the building by using less-processed natural materials, to design for reduced heating and cooling needs, to use fewer and more efficient gadgets and appliances and to change one's habits to replace electric sources of livelihood, entertainment and socializing with biological ones. At that point, making up the balance of energy consumption with onsite production becomes much more feasible.

Water Catchment and Recycling

Where does the water that flows out of your faucets come from? If you are on a municipal water system, your water is most likely rain or snowmelt that has been captured in a reservoir, treated with chlorine and other processes to kill pathogens and often piped long distances to your home. If you live in the country, you may have your own spring or well. In either location, you may be able to save a lot of energy, reduce the use of toxic chemicals and even improve your water quality by catching rainwater off your roof and storing it in a tank or cistern.

Depending on the type of roofing material and the complexity of your storage and filtration systems, roof-collected water may not be suitable for human consumption, but it can safely be used for laundry, toilet flushing, fire safety and irrigation. My friend Mark Mazziotti and his family live in rural Missouri where the groundwater has been so badly contaminated by agricultural runoff that it cannot be drunk (see "Evolving a Village Vernacular in Missouri," p. 453). Like many of their neighbors, their only source of domestic water is rain collected off their powder-coated steel roof, stored in a cistern buried underneath their house and then pumped into their sink using an old-fashioned hand-powered pump. They seem quite happy with this system. For irrigating their garden and orchard, they use a large pond to catch surface runoff.

FIGURE 18.6. Water collection and storage don't have to be ugly. This pleasing "rain chain" collects rain from the living roof of a cob building at OUR Ecovillage in British Columbia, Canada. [Credit: Misha Rauchwerger]

No matter how the water gets to your house, you can save both water and energy by using it a second time. The term "greywater" describes water that has been used for washing in a sink, tub, shower, dishwasher or clothes-washing machine, whereas "blackwater" is toilet-flushing water that contains urine and feces. It's an excellent idea to keep these two kinds of waste-water separate, since greywater can be safely reused for irrigation and other purposes.

Home greywater systems can be as simple as a bucket under-neath the sink which you pour onto a tree outside (hopefully before it overflows). A slightly more complex system called the "branched drain" automatically distributes wastewater to a series of trees or other plantings near the house (see *Create an Oasis with Greywater* under "Resources" for instructions).

When greywater is collected and stored, grease rises to the top, solids settle to the bottom and

bacterial slime can grow; these need to be filtered out before the water can be used. (A better strategy is to use the greywater immediately, before it stagnates.) The most complex domestic greywater systems include filters, pumps and subsurface emit-ters. A constructed wetlands is a man-made marsh in which water is filtered and cleaned as it passes through sand, gravel and plant roots. After making its way through the system, the water may be clean enough to discharge

FIGURE 18.7. This greywater drain outlet empties into a mulched and vegetated infiltration basin that also harvests rainwater and surface runoff. The pipe discharges above the mulch to keep roots from growing into and clogging the pipe. (Reproduced with permission from *Rainwater Harvesting for Drylands and Beyond*, Volume 1, 2nd Edition, by Brad Lancaster. HarvestingRainwater.com.) [Credit: Brad Lancaster]

into surface or groundwater or used for wildlife habitat.

If you have the space and the time (it needn't take a lot of either), you can use wastewater to grow some of your food. Some house designs, including many Earthships (see "Earthships: An Ecocentric Model," p. 289) include containers for reusing greywater to grow plants inside the home. In cold and damp climates, growing a lot of plants inside can lead to increased humidity levels, condensation and moisture problems.

Another option is to build a greenhouse attached to the south wall of your house (in the northern hemisphere). This is especially advisable in cold winter climates, where a greenhouse

FIGURE 18.8. "Flowforms" are a cascading series of vessels, usually cast in concrete or ceramic, shaped in such a way that water swirls and tumbles from one to the next, absorbing oxygen and removing impurities. [Credit: Joseph F. Kennedy]

RESOURCES FOR WATER CATCHMENT AND RECYCLING

Books
- Berthold-Bond, Annie. *Better Basics for the Home: Simple Solutions for Less Toxic Living*, Potter Style, 1999. Learn to make your own natural cleaning products, along with many other useful tips.
- Lancaster, Brad. *Rainwater Harvesting for Drylands and Beyond, Vol. 1: Guiding Principles to Welcome Rain into Your Life and Landscape*, Rainsource Press, 2nd ed., 2013. The first in a three-volume guide that teaches you how to conceptualize, design and implement sustainable water-harvesting systems for your home, landscape and community.
- Ludwig, Art. *Create an Oasis with Greywater: Choosing, Building and Using Greywater Systems*, Oasis Design, 2006. The essential greywater resource, with many different ideas and designs from simple to complex.

- Ludwig, Art. *Water Storage: Tanks, Cisterns, Aquifers and Ponds*, Oasis Design, 2005. This book will help you design storage for just about any use, including domestic, irrigation and fire safety, in just about any context—urban, rural or village. Includes detailed instructions on building a ferrocement tank.

Organizations and Websites
- HarvestingRainwater.com. Brad Lancaster's website, with lots of valuable water wisdom, including information on what soaps and detergents you can or cannot use with a greywater system.
- Oasis Design: **oasisdesign.net**. In addition to publishing several greywater guidebooks and DVDs, Oasis provides enormous amounts of free information on their website.

allows greywater usage in the winter while also helping to heat the home. In milder climates, greywater-irrigated gardens are best located close to the house, slightly downhill.

Remember that anything you put into the water will have to be removed to make the water clean again. This is true whether you plan to reuse your greywater for irrigation, send it down the drain to be cleaned at the municipal

FIGURE 18.9. This composting toilet separates urine from feces so that the former can be diluted and used immediately as fertilizer while the latter is composted. Removing urine from the composting process helps to keep the temperature higher and reduces smells. [Credit: Catherine Wanek]

wastewater facility or dump it into the ground (perhaps after passing through your septic system) and let Nature do the job. It just makes sense not to send toxic chemicals down the drain.

Many soaps, detergents and cleaning supplies are poisonous to plants and animals and/or break down into compounds such as phosphate, sodium and boron that pollute the environment. You can make your own effective cleaning supplies from simple ingredients such as vinegar, baking soda and alcohol. Oasis sells laundry and dish soaps specially formulated to break down into plant nutrients.

Composting and Human Waste

In our homes, we produce several kinds of solid wastes that can be beneficially reused. More and more municipalities now offer curbside pickup for recyclable and compostable materials. It's also easy to make your own compost from food scraps, lawn trimmings and other yard wastes; that way you can keep the nutrients onsite and reuse them in your garden or landscape. A well-managed compost pile need not smell bad or attract pests; you can learn to make compost by reading a book or taking a local class.

If you follow recommended protocols, you can also safely recycle your own human wastes. Unlike feces, which carry harmful bacteria like *E. coli* and salmonella, urine poses no health risks and is an incredible source of nitrogen, potassium and phosphorus, the common elements in all fertilizers. It can either be added to a compost pile or diluted with water and used directly on many plants.

The biggest challenge for would-be urine users is likely to be collection. Special urine-diverting toilets have been developed for use in homes, public facilities, in campgrounds, on boats and even in space. But you can also make your own home urinal from materials as simple as a plastic milk jug.

Composting human feces is a bit more complicated but can also be done safely on a home scale. There are many approaches, from commercially produced composting toilets with sealed chambers and fans, to owner-built toilets of many different designs. All use heat (whether generated by the composting process itself or added by a solar collector) to kill pathogens. For fifteen years, I have safely used composting outhouses I built myself.

My preferred design has two

large composting chambers built out of concrete or plywood. The seat can be moved back and forth above the two chambers, but is left in one position until the chamber below is full. After each use, a scoop of dry carbonaceous material such as sawdust, lawn trimmings or leaves is added on top. This ensures the correct ratio of nitrogen and carbon needed for the composting process. In damp climates, urine should be separated out to prevent bad smells.

The chambers are built large enough that it takes at least six months to fill each one. While the second chamber is being filled, the first is allowed to compost.

FIGURE 18.10. This portable toilet is used during permaculture courses and other gatherings at the Bullock brothers' homestead on Orcas Island, Washington. At the beginning of an event, the toilet is placed over a fresh hole. When the hole is full of humanure and carbonaceous material (sawdust, straw or leaf litter), it is left to compost in place. Later, a tree will be planted in the hole. [Credit: Michael G. Smith]

FIGURE 18.11. This plastic infiltrator is the core of a "Watson wick," an alternative to conventional septic and leach field systems that processes human waste aerobically and delivers water and nutrients to perennial plants at their root zones. [Credit: Catherine Wanek]

Time as well as heat will kill most disease-causing organisms. By the time the second chamber is full, the material in the first chamber is broken down and ready to use on trees and ornamental plants. (Out of an abundance of caution, I avoid using humanure on crops where the edible parts grow in contact with the soil.) If necessary, it can also be taken through a secondary composting process by adding green plants and/or urine in a separate location.

Solar Cookers

by Patricia McArdle

Combustible fuel (wood, coal, dung, kerosene, natural gas) for cooking food and boiling water is becoming more expensive and less accessible every year for the three billion people who still cook every day over open fires. While international petroleum companies are rolling out plans to market subsidized, bottled cooking gas in some of the world's poorest countries, and international aid agencies spend millions to develop more efficient wood-burning stoves, too little attention has been paid to capturing Earth's most abundant source of cooking heat— the sun—in simple solar cookers.

Solar cooking technology was first adapted for contemporary use by a small group of visionaries in the mid-1950s. Following the oil crises in the 1970s, organizations were established in Europe and the US to promote solar thermal cooking technologies in refugee camps, in the developing world and in Western countries. Funding for research and development of this technology has always relied on small donations and on the volunteer work of individual researchers. Only the Chinese and Indian governments have subsidized solar cooker research.

The Chinese remain the largest users of this technology. Several million parabolic solar cookers are used on a daily basis in China's treeless western provinces, where the primary fuel for years has been coal. The Indian government has subsidized the distribution of family-sized parabolic solar cookers in some states as well as institutional-sized models at remote schools in northern India. The advantage of the parabolic solar cookers (which are shaped like satellite dishes) is that they can be used from sunup until sundown even in sub-zero weather, as long as the sun is shining. Many families keep a kettle of water continuously simmering in their backyard solar cooker, using it as a low-tech solar hot water heater. (Peer-reviewed studies have shown that up to one-third of household fuel consumption in developing countries is for heating water.)

Parabolic solar cookers direct a beam of concentrated light onto a pot and can generate temperatures of 450°F (230°C) or more, which is useful for boiling, frying and sautéing. Box cookers, on the other hand, work like an oven and are ideal for baking, stewing, roasting and food drying. They can hold several pots of food which are slowly heated to temperatures between 230°F and 350°F (110°C to 180°C). A smaller model, the panel cooker, works like a box cooker but at slightly lower temperatures. The advantage of a panel solar cooker is that it can be folded up into a compact square for easy storage and transport.

Another solar cooker design that can contribute to the sustainability of a home is a through-the-wall box cooker built into a south-facing wall (in the northern hemisphere). This allows people to solar cook from inside their

In some other home-built systems, composting takes place inside a large barrel, which can be replaced with an empty one as necessary. In *The Humanure Handbook*, author Joe Jenkins advocates a simple bucket toilet. Urine and feces are collected in a bucket with dry carbonaceous material, then the contents are transferred to a contained compost pile outdoors.

Even if you don't want to build a toilet or ever handle your own composted waste, there are toilet kitchens. Many institutions in India use a tracking parabolic solar cooker called the Scheffler, which also allows indoor solar cooking. Smaller versions of the Scheffler are used in community bakeries, health centers and schools.

In recent years, foodies, environmentalists and more recently the "prepper" (survivalist) community in the US have all embraced solar cooking technology. While a number of manufactured solar cookers are available for purchase online, the great advantage of this technology is that it can be easily produced using local materials. Many construction plans are available at the website of Solar Cookers International, a twenty-five-year-old NGO that promotes solar cooking around the world.

Resources

Solar Cookers International: **solarcookers.org**. Their website provides access to a vast trove of information, including country-by-country solar cooking projects, new designs, vendors and non-profits. It also contains multilingual instructional videos, training manuals and current news stories on solar cooking activities around the world. The *Solar Cooker Review*, their thrice-yearly publication, is available in hard copy and online and provides in-depth analysis and reporting on issues affecting the spread of this technology around the world.

Patricia McArdle is a retired Foreign Service Officer, a former Peace Corps volunteer and a US Navy veteran. She is the author of the award-winning, fictional war memoir Farishta, *which was inspired by the year she spent in northern Afghanistan with a British infantry unit. She is currently the editor of the* Solar Cooker Review.

FIGURE 18.12. Namibian children learning to solar cook at the Namib Desert Environmental Education Trust (NaDEET), a non-profit established in 2003. [Credit: NaDEET]

designs that allow you to capture and reuse nutrients that would be lost by flushing blackwater to the sewer or septic system. Anna Edey, at Solviva in Massachusetts, adapted a standard flush toilet to flush through a box filled with wood chips and leaves, where worms digest the solids. The liquid runoff is then filtered through a series of beds where plants absorb the remaining nutrients.

Tom Watson in New Mexico developed a system for flushing a toilet into a plastic infiltrator buried just under the surface of the ground. The infiltrator is surrounded by a bed of pumice rock covered with soil, which is planted with shrubs and trees. The plants consume both the water and the nutrients from the composting solids.

On a larger scale, biogas digesters that produce methane gas from the anaerobic decomposition of manure and other organic wastes have been in use for more than a century. In developing countries, simple home and farm-based anaerobic digestion systems offer the potential for low-cost energy for cooking and lighting. Since 1975, the governments of China and India have both supported the development and installation of small biogas plants. Some municipal wastewater facilities in the United States now digest collected food wastes together with blackwater to produce methane fuel. The liquid and solid by-products of anaerobic digesters can both be used as fertilizer.

Since the dawn of agriculture, human wastes and crop residues have both been returned to the soil. This nutrient recycling, among other sustainable practices, allowed rural families in places like China to farm the same fields for thousands of years without depleting the soil's capacity to grow food. In recent times, the nutrients in human wastes have mostly been flushed down toilets, processed in sewage treatment facilities and then lost into the ocean where they cause havoc to marine ecosystems. To make up for the missing nutrients, farmers pepper their fields with ever-increasing quantities of synthetic fertilizers derived from natural gas and from increasingly scarce minerals. All of these practices need to change. You can help lead the way towards a more healthy and balanced future with the changes you implement in your own household.

RESOURCES FOR RECYCLING HUMAN WASTE

Books
• Edey, Anna. *Solviva: How to Grow $500,000 on One Acre, and Peace on Earth*, Trailblazer Press, 1998. An autobiographical ramble by the pioneer of many ecological living systems, including the worm toilet.
• Jenkins, Joseph. *The Humanure Handbook: A Guide to Composting Human Manure*, 3rd ed., Joseph Jenkins, Inc., 2005. With surprisingly high entertainment value, Jenkins guides the reader through the whys and hows of safely composting human waste using an easy-to-build bucket toilet.
• Logsdon, Gene. *Holy Shit: Managing Manure to Save Humankind*, Chelsea Green, 2010. An Ohio farmer's readable treatise on the history and culture of human and animal manure management—how more sustainable cultures like the ancient Chinese recycled manures into the soil to reclaim their fertility, why it is imperative that modern society do the same and how to go about it on a farm or household scale.
• Steinfeld, Carol. *Liquid Gold: The Lore and Logic of Using Urine to Grow Plants*, EcoWaters, 2007. Practical handbook on how to separate urine and use it as safe and environmental fertilizer for all kinds of plants.

Regenerative Building: An Ecological Approach

19

Michael G. Smith

In the last few decades, restoration ecologists have developed techniques for healing damaged ecosystems, detoxifying hazardous chemicals, restoring interrupted flows of water and nutrients and reintroducing vanished species. This work is essential not only from an ethical standpoint, but because natural ecosystems ultimately provide human beings with most of what sustains us: soil, clean air and water, climate regulation, pest control for our crops and the genetic source of all our foods and most of our medicines.

The developing concepts of restoration forestry and ecological agriculture have spread this awareness among producers and consumers of food, fiber and forest products. Those of us concerned with shelter need to take a similar step. If we wish to heal the scars caused by the non-sustainable resource exploitation of the past and ensure the continuing health of our ecosystems into the distant future, we must do more than merely reduce our environmental impact by substituting natural building materials for processed ones.

How can regenerative builders improve ecological health? First, we can study ecology—the science of living systems. Before we can know what building materials are most appropriate to a particular place, we need to determine how their production, extraction, transportation, assembly and presence in a building will affect the environment on all levels.

Second, we can emphasize the use of local resources. A full ecological analysis will mandate that we eliminate long-distance transportation of bulk materials.

This requires that we get to know intimately the places where we live—not only our houses but our back yards, watersheds and bioregions.

Finally, we can incorporate site influences, energy flows and landscape interactions into our designs for homes, neighborhoods and towns. Our buildings consume, breathe and excrete like animals do but often on a far larger scale. We must understand their material and energy cycles in order to minimize the need for industrial energy and the production of hazardous wastes (see "The Permaculture House," p. 107).

As we come to understand how our local ecosystems work, we can see how our own behaviors and choices affect them. When we recognize our dependence on the landscape in which

*As he builds houses, grows food and raises his two children, **MICHAEL G. SMITH** likes to ponder how these activities were done in the ancient past and how they might take place in the distant future. He believes that a deep relationship to the surrounding landscape is an essential part of what it takes to be a healthy human: strawclaywood.com.*

we live, we are compelled to take responsibility for our actions. When we value the long-term stability of each ecosystem, we can develop integrated practices of building and resource management that will enhance the health of the nonhuman communities surrounding and protecting us. Let's look at an example of how this might work in practice.

The Hermitage

I worked with the staff of an environmental education center near my home in Northern California to design and build a small structure that demonstrates the principles of natural and regenerative building. Located in a small meadow surrounded by mixed forest, the Hermitage offers a temporary retreat for people wishing to slow down, relax, meditate, write or paint, observe and commune with the natural surroundings. It contains a bed, a desk, a tiny wood stove, an altar, comfortable sitting areas and a minimal kitchenette.

Soil from the site, a mix of clay and rock fragments ranging from sand to small cobbles, made an excellent base material for earthbags, cob, earthen floors and plasters. We also built a section of straw bale wall, pinned with bamboo stakes and covered with earth and lime plasters. We made the roof trusses from bamboo poles harvested 150 mi. (240 km) away. All of these techniques would be called natural building: they are very low-cost, low-embodied energy, non-toxic, easy-to-construct

FIGURE 19.1. The Hermitage serves both as a quiet woodland retreat and as an example of how natural buildings can contribute to the process of ecological restoration. [Credit: Paul Cohen]

systems that use few manufactured products and mostly local materials. But they don't necessarily cross the bridge into regenerative building by improving the health of the surrounding ecosystem.

We wanted to demonstrate true regenerative building in the Hermitage. Before beginning construction, we took a close look at the ecology of the site: what resources did it offer and in what ways had it suffered from past mismanagement?

Perennial native bunch grasses, herbs and shrubs once grew thick in the meadow where the building now stands. This ecological community underwent a major transformation due to the introduction of cattle and the suppression of wildfire. Quick-growing wild oats and other introduced annual grasses now predominate, out-competing the natives for light and nutrients.

We decided to push the ecological balance in favor of the native grasses. After collecting their ripe seeds in late summer, we mowed the meadow, setting aside the dry grass stalks for building material. Broadcasting some of the seed over the mown area, we grew the rest out in the nursery to be transplanted later into areas affected by the construction.

The forest surrounding the meadow still shows the effects of heavy logging decades ago. Fire

FIGURE 19.3. Small saplings and branches harvested as part of forest management practices can find many applications in natural buildings. Here, branches have been attached to the rafters in preparation for an earthen plaster in the author's home at Emerald Earth Sanctuary. [Credit: Michael G. Smith]

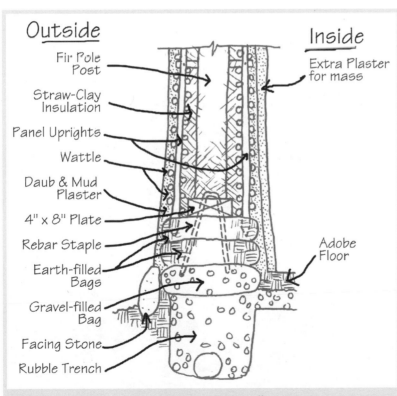

Outside

- Fir Pole Post
- Straw-Clay Insulation
- Panel Uprights
- Wattle
- Daub & Mud Plaster
- 4" x 8" Plate
- Rebar Staple
- Earth-filled Bags
- Gravel-filled Bag
- Facing Stone
- Rubble Trench

Inside

- Extra Plaster for mass
- Adobe Floor

FIGURE 19.2. A cross-section of the Hermitage wall system. [Credit: Joseph F. Kennedy]

suppression in the vicinity has allowed Douglas fir to grow back in thickets, crowding and shading out the hardwoods: live oak, madrone and bay laurel. Under Native American management, frequent low-temperature forest fires used to thin these groves, killing many of the fir seedlings. This also reduced the fuel load near the ground, making severe canopy fires less likely. As a result of recent fire suppression, the forest is now much more vulnerable to fire damage, and the population balance is shifting from native hardwoods and the wildlife they support, toward the reduced complexity of Douglas fir stands.

We went into the forest with saws and pruners, with the aim of "thinking like fire." We thinned overcrowded stands of fir by selectively harvesting young trees and pruned lower branches to increase light penetration and reduce fire danger. We wound up with fir poles of up to 9 in. (23 cm) in diameter and branches of all sizes.

Logging and grazing had compacted the soil and increased erosion from the area. To remedy this, we dug swales (on-contour ditches) to catch the winter rain runoff, increase infiltration and slow down the loss of topsoil and nutrients. By digging the swales

deep, we harvested extra earth for construction.

Our aim was to reverse ecological deterioration caused by former land management practices, and our efforts created an abundance of local, natural building materials, including clay soil, dry grass stalks, fir poles and branches. Putting these into the building was the link we needed to make our project truly regenerative.

From the larger poles we constructed a post and beam frame to

support the roof. On either side of these posts, we wove wattle wall panels using straight branches and small fir saplings. At the same time, we prepared our wall insulation by coating the dry grass with a thin clay slip to protect it from fire and insects. This hay-clay was sun-dried, then packed into the 8 in. (20 cm) cavity between the inner and outer wattle panels. The wattle was then covered with a daub made of clay soil, horse manure and chopped hay. Finally, the wall was plastered with a fine

FIGURE 19.4. Stuffing the Hermitage wall cavity with insulation made from site-harvested dried grasses and clay. The round-pole structural frame is also visible. [Credit: Michael G. Smith]

mix of screened clay, sand and horse manure or cattail fluff.

This experimental system combines traditional techniques: wattle and daub, light-clay straw and earthen plasters. The specific building method was chosen to make use of the materials yielded by ecological restoration, with an aim to improve the building's thermal efficiency by combining insulation and thermal mass in the most efficient way.

Bioregional Building

Over time local builders, if encouraged to observe and experiment, will develop construction methods and land management strategies ideally suited to their regions. Within several generations, we can imagine a distinctive architectural style

FIGURE 19.5. Workshop participants applying clay plaster to the interior of the Hermitage. The roof trusses were framed using locally harvested bamboo, the ceiling is made of woven bamboo mat, and the roof cavity is insulated with local wool. [Credit: Janine Björnson]

RESOURCES

Books
• Anderson, M. Kat. *Tending the Wild: Native American Knowledge and the Management of California's Natural Resources*, University of California Press, 2006. An in-depth and inspirational exploration of land practices used by native Californians to enhance ecological diversity and encourage useful plant and animal species.
• Drengson, Alan and Duncan Taylor. *Ecoforestry: The Art and Science of Sustainable Forest Use*, New Society Publishers, 1998. A superb introduction to the philosophy, science and sociology behind the current efforts to develop sustainable forest management practices.
• Pilarski, Michael, ed. *Restoration Forestry: An International Guide to Sustainable Forestry Practices*, Kivaki Press, 1994. A resource guide and anthology of articles about international efforts to heal the world's forests.

Organizations
• Emerald Earth Sanctuary: **emeraldearth.org**. An intentional community in Northern California with a focus on forest restoration as well as natural building and permaculture. You can visit during a workshop or a work party.
• Occidental Arts and Ecology Center: **oaec.org**. This sustainability education center in Northern California offers excellent workshops in permaculture and many other topics. They also have a Wildlands Biodiversity program aimed at exploring the concepts in this article.

evolving in each bioregion, along with a unique system of food production, materials use and energy systems, all of which will reflect what local people know about their climate, resources and ecosystems. This process—now in its incipient stages—has been called "reinhabiting the landscape," or "re-indigenization."

Building can be considered the art and practice of creating homes. But in the industrialized world especially, building our homes too often destroys the homes of other creatures. Some of us are moving toward a way of building that respects those other homes and the rights of their animal and plant dwellers to inhabit the Earth indefinitely. The next step involves creating homes for ourselves in ways that repair the damage we have already done to the homes of our co-inhabitants.

Ultimately, to live in harmony with our neighbors on this planet, we must expand our concept of home. It must encompass not only the structure of the house but also the yard and garden, the surrounding site, the watershed and the entire bioregion. That way, in taking care of our home, in maintaining it and beautifying it, we will make life better not only for ourselves but also for the greater world of which we are an inseparable part.

Building the Natural Village: A Strategy for Repairing Cities

20

Mark Lakeman

Natural building has become a successful medium for bringing people together in order to accomplish common causes and projects. When strategically located in common spaces of urban neighborhoods, natural building can be a catalyst for urban transformation and social change. In urban and semi-urban areas, natural building can have a profound multiplier effect when local communities use it as a means of building community relationships in the form of physical places. This is especially true when the projects are located directly within the flow of daily life, where everyone in a community, no matter their political views or behaviors, can see and experience them. In fact, we are seeing that natural building can result in a functional commons of shared place and culture, so long missing from our cities and towns.

The spectrum of natural building techniques and processes exemplifies local and regional approaches to making shelter that are accessible, affordable, ecologically responsive and non-toxic. Unlike building practices in ancient societies that were more interdependent, the recent resurgence of natural building has often been taught and practiced in a one-shelter-at-a-time approach. Yet this approach doesn't necessarily add up to a greater whole— a community fabric of place that supports gathering, collaboration and ongoing cultural development. In order for that to happen, not only do shelters need to relate to each other but they also must help define public pathways and gathering places. Natural buildings must be the expressions of a participatory process in order for a natural community to emerge. Just as the organs of a living body add up to a whole biological life form, individual structures can express a larger evolving community. Places thus created contribute to a story of human mutuality and become emblematic of the community itself.

While there are now many examples of individual natural buildings, as well as village-scale projects in rural settings, only recently have such ideas arrived in the urban context. As of this writing, natural building processes and techniques have already radically transformed the city of Portland, Oregon.

Mark Lakeman *is a national leader in the development of sustainable public places. In the last decade, he has directed, facilitated or inspired designs for more than three hundred new community-generated public places in Portland, Oregon, alone. Through his leadership in Communitecture, Inc., and its various affiliates such as the City Repair Project, the Village Building Convergence and the Planet Repair Institute, he has also been instrumental in the development of dozens of participatory organizations and urban permaculture design projects across the US and Canada.*

In fact, the Portland Bureau of Transportation loves cob so much that solar-powered cob kiosk designs are now preapproved to be located anywhere and everywhere in Portland, without any fees having to be paid. Though our city had already developed a great deal of momentum since the 1960s, the gears of our creative activism really began to shift when natural building arrived in a big way. At first, it was only a small group of women who called themselves Sisters of Creation, building demonstration projects here and there. Then it jumped in scale with the arrival of the City Repair Project in the mid-1990s.

The urban natural building and village-making movement is now an extremely exciting and incredibly effective development in the toolkit of urban activism.

Natural building can be a means for installing community places where they are desperately needed, but have been absent for years. For many decades, American communities have been created as "developments," built by commercial interests and almost never by people for themselves. Innumerable aspects of the "ecology of place" are missing. Places to gather, co-create, share ideas, make decisions or simply to sit with each other. In fact, unlike the villages of our ancestors that were infused with places to gather, neighborhoods in the US have the lowest number of community gathering places of all first world nations. Extreme rates of violence are directly related to social isolation.

In our own work in Portland, where we have built hundreds of community gathering places using natural materials, we at City Repair have seen that natural building is the perfect means for installing new places that meet the need for gathering, while at the same time modeling the most sustainable and accessible practices conceivable. There may be no better way for people to rediscover their innate village behaviors of co-creation, listening and mutual support than to engage in natural building together. There has never been a better approach to shared intergenerational creative habitat building, with even children welcome on the job site. The essential culture of stewardship that arises via natural building also turns out to engender that same spirit in urban areas where people are lacking such cultural benefits. This also includes mentoring processes.

Natural building can also be an entry point for anyone to be able to experience a form of living

FIGURE 20.1. Creating a cob bench and kiosk at a Portland, Oregon, elementary school. [Credit: Joseph F. Kennedy]

democracy. Just as the Greek *demos* refers to a place-based unit of community, from the visioning-inception of a project through every aspect of its realization, natural building lends itself to an interactive, place-based experience of co-creation that exactly embodies the daily life of the demos. After all, democracy isn't meant to be merely an occasional exercise in decision-making. Rather, it must be a cultural experience that we inhabit on a daily basis. It turns out that participation and peace are integral to each other, and natural building may be the best way to bring them back together. As one very conservative man in Portland recently put it, "What good is freedom of assembly without a place to assemble?" No good at all. With the accessible, inclusive and affordable means that natural building offers us, we have ways to heal this dearth of gathering places at last.

So, as Portland communities have been building ecological community gathering places across our urban fabric, we have simultaneously been restoring the co-creative process that people used to inhabit as a way of life. It turns out that through natural building we can restore both processes and places that are essential to community health and well-being, and even facilitate the emergence of new ideas and solutions to entrenched community problems. This is because,

FIGURE 20.2. A community gathering spot, information kiosk and free mini-library built of stone, cob and recycled materials. [Credit: Mark Lakeman]

via the inherently accessible practices of natural building, all manner of people are able to form new relationships and a shared identity.

But why, one might ask, after all this time of building human communities, would we even need to realize such things or do such work? Why are true gathering places so absent in our midst? Why do we lack the culture of

stewardship that always emerges around places of social convergence? Wouldn't that culture be essential to a sustainable culture of interactive community? Well, here's a giant piece of the answer: the places where we live have never really been ours. Though we've been employed to build them, we never designed the communities nor the very homes we live in. In fact, in every country in the western hemisphere, most people live in a massive, gridded, colonial infrastructure that was designed from the beginning of westward expansion to organize conquered territory, convert ecologies into landscapes

of commodities, organize vast extraction processes and form the basis of urban centers that turn working populations into human resources.

That's right: though we as working people have built the landscapes where we live, we have built someone else's vision of spaces, not places—a world for sale but not a world for all. Though this mentality forms the very basis of our Western economy and has become "normal" for so many people, this fact may be the most unnatural aspect of it all. Luckily, the story is not over. As many of us in the sustainability movement already know, our

FIGURE 20.3. The Memorial Lifehouse, conceived as a place of remembrance for a bicyclist killed at this corner. Built of cob, stone and recycled materials, including tricycle wheels with stained glass for windows, a living roof and a solar powered light (note the solar panel attached to the bicycle wheel). [Credit: Joseph F. Kennedy]

FIGURE 20.4. Repainting Sunnyside Piazza: a residential intersection is re-imagined as a community plaza through the "Intersection Repair" process pioneered by City Repair in Portland, Oregon. [Credit: Joseph F. Kennedy]

communities can, should and must reclaim our own local realities in order to begin to address and transform our compounding problems into solutions. A huge part of this work is already underway in the redesign and retrofit of cities and neighborhoods. Is this possible? Absolutely! Come to Portland and see for yourself! There are natural building projects all across the city. In the form of large and small buildings, open pavilions and outdoor classrooms, community kiosks and benches, they are located in public intersections, schools, institutions and commercial settings in every quadrant.

The forms that these projects take include an astonishing spectrum: information stations, creative outdoor installations that tell stories while being metaphors, small-scale constructions that embody gigantic principles and ideas, self-service poetry stations, cob saunas, sacred places, newspaper dispensers, solar-powered interactive tea-stations, many self-service libraries (the very first in the world in fact) and so many more. But the real impact is less in the physical reality of the buildings than in the fact that whole communities have been reconnected in the process of inspiring, designing, funding and building each one of them!

RESOURCES

Books
- Bohl, Charles C. *Placemaking: Developing Town Centers, Main Streets and Urban Villages*, Urban Land Institute, 2002. An excellent overview of strategies to make such communities livable and sustainable.
- Borrup, Tom. *The Creative Community Builder's Handbook*, Fieldstone Alliance, 2006. Nuts and bolts information on how to make creative projects happen.
- Chiras, Dan. *Superbia!*, New Society Publishers, 2003. A wonderful collection of real-world strategies for humanizing our communities.
- City Repair. *The City Repair Project's Placemaking Guidebook*, The City Repair Project, 2006. All of City Repair's hard-won knowledge is here, together with their inspiring story.
- Engwicht, David. *Reclaiming Our Cities and Towns*, New Catalyst Books, 2007. A compelling case for creative traffic-calming strategies to create better cities for pedestrians.
- Project for Public Spaces. *How to Turn a Place Around: A Handbook for Creating Successful Communities*, Project for Public Spaces, 2000. A brief but important text that should be on the desk of every city planner in America.
- Rudofsky, Bernard. *Streets for People*, Doubleday, 1969. A classic text on the importance of the streets as an integral part of the public realm.

- Schwarzman, Mat and Keith Knight. *Beginner's Guide to Community-Based Arts*, New Village Press, 2005. A uniquely illustrated training manual for grassroots social change based on ten pioneering community arts projects.
- Walljasper, Jay. *The Great Neighborhood Book*, New Society Publishers, 2007. A great series of case studies about successful community projects from around the United States.

Organizations
- Centre for Creative Communities: **creativecommunities.org.uk**
- City Repair: **cityrepair.org**
- Congress for the New Urbanism: **cnu.org**
- Context Sensitive Solutions: **contextsensitivesolutions.org**
- Creative Communities: **creative-communities.com**
- Culture Shapes Community: **cultureshapescommunity.org**
- Partners for Livable Communities: **livable.com**
- Project for Public Places: **pps.org**
- **Waterfire.org**

Because this exemplary work has met and exceeded civic goals to build community relations, engage children and make streets safer, it is now legal to repurpose and give streetscapes new diverse uses everywhere across Portland. Similar processes of adaptation and transition have also begun in more than 40 other cities in North America. In Portland, however, the process isn't limited to installations in the streets. It also includes public places built in private locations so that people are encouraged to transcend the lines that divide their perceptions and interests. In short, people are excited, have great momentum and are building community everywhere that they can.

Now, with all of the local and regional partnerships that have emerged, and all of the projects that have been implemented, in Portland natural building has

FIGURE 20.5. Neighborhood residents create a mobile cob bench during an ephemeral place-making event in Santa Rosa, California. [Credit: Joseph F. Kennedy]

become a household word. Site by site, each natural building initiative has left a footprint on the path to a better world, and all together we seem to have transformed our city into a dance hall for ecological community and social change. With by far the most and most varied community-built public place initiatives in the US, Portland has been able to shift its own destiny, and we who live here hope that the cities, towns and villages of the world will soon be ready to dance with us. Kind of like making cob.

PART THREE

Natural Building Materials and Techniques

Don't be afraid of being called "unmodern."
Changes in the old methods of construction are only allowed
if they can claim to bring improvement; otherwise stick with the old ways.
Because the truth, even if hundreds of years old, has more inner connection
than the falsehood that walks beside us.

« Adolf Loos, 1913 »

Natural Building Materials: An Overview

21

JOSEPH F. KENNEDY

Natural building has emerged as a response to an increasing concern for our built environment. Natural materials are an alternative to the toxic substances that have led to widespread environmental illness. Those seeking to simplify their lives can build their own homes with community help and local, inexpensive materials. Those who recognize the environmental, social and economic costs of our current ways of construction believe that natural building provides part of the solution to the complex worldwide problem of sustainable living.

While interest in natural building has surged in the industrialized West, in traditional communities, many ancient roots have been lost in favor of capital- and energy-intensive industrial building methods. In the name of progress, crucial cultural and technological riches continue to be abandoned. Ironically, some builders in industrialized countries are now turning to these very cultures for solutions to their building problems. It is to be hoped that a resurgence of interest and research into vernacular building systems will increase respect for these timeless solutions in their native lands.

Most natural builders would agree that a "natural" material is one closest to the state in which it is found in nature. Although natural builders and designers prefer using these materials to create the bulk of their structures, they frequently combine them with "non-natural" materials such as metal roofing, glass, concrete and waterproof membranes. The choice of what materials to use in a particular situation depends on such factors as ecological impact, cost, availability and workability.

FIGURE 21.1. Using techniques we still do not entirely understand, the Inca civilization built walls and buildings using immense stones, so carefully fitted that one cannot slip a thin knife between them anywhere. [Credit: Michael G. Smith]

JOSEPH F. KENNEDY *is an architectural designer, writer and peripatetic scholar of natural building and ecological design.*

Some materials, even though they are natural, may not be available locally, appropriate for the desired use, durable, aesthetically pleasing or easy to assemble. Local availability is the most important factor in deciding which materials to build with. It is also important to know how these materials are harvested and to determine whether using them has a disturbing effect on the local ecosystem.

Here are some of the materials most commonly used by natural builders. Most are natural materials, but some commonly used manufactured materials are listed as well.

Earth

Earth construction has been practiced for thousands of years in many regional styles, and still shelters more than a third of the world's population. Although widely available, versatile and highly workable, earth is not as strong as some other materials, especially in tension, and is vulnerable to damage from water and earthquakes.

Earth is composed (in decreasing order of particle size) of stones, gravel, sand, silt and clay. The best earth for building contains 20 to 30 percent clay and 70 to 80 percent sand. Soils vary enormously from site to site, and sometimes even within the space of a few feet. Before using an unfamiliar soil, a builder must perform a series of tests to determine whether that soil is suitable and, if so, what mix proportions are ideal. Earth that has too little clay tends to form weak building components, while earth with excessive clay tends to crack severely as it dries. Native soils are often mixed with sand and/or fibers such as straw to increase their strength and reduce cracking. Depending on the application, sometimes gravel and stones must be sifted out.

Stone

Stone is the mineral bedrock of the planet and comes in endless varieties. It is used in building for its strength, beauty and longevity. Stone is also an excellent source of thermal mass. Igneous stone is formed by the cooling of liquid magma. Some igneous stones (pumice and scoria) contain air bubbles, which make them good insulators.

Sedimentary stone is formed by the cementing together of mineral particles resulting from erosion by wind or water. Sedimentary stone is layered, which allows it to be split into flat pieces

FIGURE 21.2. Sifting clay-rich soil through a fine screen to make cob.
[Credit: Valentina Mendez Marquez]

that are easy to stack into walls. Some sedimentary stones, such as slate, can even be used to make thin overlapping roof tiles and durable floors. Metamorphic stone is igneous or sedimentary stone that has been altered by heat and pressure.

The best stone for building is angular, with parallel flat sides. Round stones are not recommended for structural purposes. Stone can be used as found or shaped with tools. Stone makes an excellent foundation, supporting and protecting less durable materials such as wood and earth.

Gravel

Gravel is composed of small stones. It is useful for filling drainage trenches and rubble trench foundations, as it is strong in compression yet lets water flow through. Gravel is often used as a drainage layer under earthen floors. It can also be used to fill bags, which are then stacked into walls. This type of gravel bag foundation helps keep water from reaching materials like adobe or straw bales that can easily be damaged by moisture.

Sand

Sand is small gravel. It is an essential ingredient (mixed with clay soil and, often, fibers in var-ious proportions) in cob, adobe, rammed earth, compressed earth blocks, as well as lime and earth mortars and plasters. Angular sand is best for most purposes. Sand gathered from riverbanks is sometimes fairly angular, but the harvesting process can be very destructive to the aquatic ecosystem.

The most angular sands are produced by an industrial process of crushing stone (or, in some cases, recycled concrete). Rounded sand found in riverbeds or beaches tends to form a weaker, more crumbly material. "Well-graded" sand with many different-sized grains is best for structural purposes, as the small grains lock into the spaces between the larger ones, forming a hard, stable matrix. For finish plasters and floors, the degree of smoothness you can achieve is directly related to the fineness of the sand grains.

Clay

Clay results from the chemical weathering of the mineral feldspar. It is composed of small flat plates that stick well to themselves, and to other materials, when activated by water. Clay is the essential binding ingredient in any earthen building system. To find soil with a high clay content, notice if the soil cracks as it dries, or if it is difficult to dig and clumps together.

There are other simple tests that you can learn from most books on earthen construction.

FIGURE 21.3. Sand of different colors and aggregate sizes. Sand provides compressive strength in concrete, adobe, cob, earth plasters, lime plasters and other earth-based techniques. [Credit: Catherine Wanek]

Expansive clays shrink considerably as they dry, requiring the addition of a great deal of sand or fiber to prevent cracking, while non-expansive clays are more stable. Clays occur naturally in many different colors, from the common browns, reds and yellows to the more unusual white, green and purple.

Brick

Bricks are made from clay that is formed into blocks, dried and then fired (baked) in a kiln. The higher the temperature they are fired at, the harder they become. Bricks come in many shapes and sizes. They are commonly used in walls, floors, foundations and vaulted roofs. Other brick-shaped building elements are adobes, which are sun-dried mud bricks, and compressed earth blocks (CEBs), which are also unfired.

Tile

Similar to bricks, tiles are flat or curved thin elements made from fired clay. They are often glazed with a compound which, when fired, makes them waterproof. Glazed tiles are available in many different colors and are commonly used for decoration and waterproofing. Tiles are usually attached to a base material which is structurally strong (for example, stone, brick or concrete). They are often used on floors, waterproof walls and counters. On roofs they are laid in a shingled fashion to prevent water infiltration.

Sod

Sod is the interwoven roots of grasses and the soil they trap. It can be cut into bricks and stacked to form a wall, as was commonly done by the first European settlers on the American prairies. Sod can also be layered over a waterproof membrane to create a "living roof." In some places, the mineral subsoil is hard and stable enough that it can be cut and used like bricks, even without reinforcing roots. In central Mexico, this material is called *tepetate*.

Wood

Wood is strong in compression and especially in tension. It can be used for many purposes, including posts, beams, floors, roofs, windows, doors and furniture. It is an essential material for

FIGURE 21.4. Using a traditional drawknife to peel the bark from this freshly harvested tree. [Credit: Joseph F. Kennedy]

natural builders but must be used wisely to conserve forested regions. Logs cut into short lengths can be stacked like bricks in cordwood construction. Longer round poles can be used for posts, roof beams and rafters. Notching logs helps them to interlock to form the walls of log cabins. Logs can also be sawn into dimensional lumber, but appropriate trees are becoming harder to find, making such timber increasingly expensive. Indeed, all-wood construction is now unsustainable in many parts of the world because of the overharvesting of forests. Wood, however, remains one of the best ways of sequestering excess carbon from the atmosphere. In order to continue using this excellent material in the future, we need to concentrate on planting more trees and sustainably managing existing forests.

Bamboo

There are hundreds of species of bamboo which are native in many parts of the world, especially the tropics. The culms (stalks) of these giant grasses are used in construction. Bamboo is very strong in tension and compression, but is weak in bending. It grows very quickly and can be used as a substitute for wood in many cases. Strong bamboo construction requires special joinery techniques. Traditionally, bamboo is typically lashed together with natural fibers. A more recently developed joinery system relies on metal bolts and mortar surrounding the bolt inside the hollow culm.

Straw

Straw is the hollow-stemmed stalks of cereal grains such as rice, wheat, oats, barley, etc. It can be baled into large blocks and stacked to make walls. When mixed with earth, straw improves that material's tensile strength, resistance to cracking, insulation value and workability. It is used full length or chopped fine as an ingredient in cob, straw-clay and plasters. If the straw is particularly long and strong, it can also be used as a thatching material. Straw is vulnerable to rapid decomposition when wet. Before

FIGURE 21.5. Reeds have been lashed with rawhide to wooden rafters to faithfully recreate the 18th-century Spanish techniques used to build the Presidio in Santa Barbara. [Credit: Joseph F. Kennedy]

being used as a building material, it must be stored carefully to protect it from water.

Reeds

Reeds are hollow-stemmed water plants, similar in appearance to grasses. Because they are straight, long and shed water well, they are often used for thatching roofs. Reed thatch lasts longer than straw thatch because reeds are naturally rot-resistant.

Leaves

Leaves of plants have been used throughout history as a building material, mostly to shed rain or create shade. An example is the use of palm leaves for roof thatching in the tropics. Leaves tend to deteriorate quickly and require frequent replacement.

Hemp and Other Fibers

Hemp and other fiber-producing plants such as cotton, kenaf, flax and sawgrass are currently being investigated as potential building products. Cotton batting is now widely available in North America for insulation. Hemp particularly has several advantages, as it provides four times the usable fiber per acre as wood, grows in degraded soils and needs little chemical processing. Commonly used for numerous purposes before drug laws made its cultivation illegal in many countries, non-psychoactive hemp is being rediscovered as a source of fiber, edible seeds, oil and hurd (the pithy inner stalk left over after the fibers are removed). Hemp hurds can replace wood and petrochemicals in a variety of building applications, including pressed-board products and a strong, well-insulating mixture of hurds and lime called hempcrete. Hemp oil is a drying oil, like linseed oil, and can be used to seal earthen floors.

Paper

Paper is made of compressed plant fibers, usually from wood. Paper can be used as a wall material (as in Japanese shoji screens) or to cover other materials (wallpaper). A recently discovered use of recycled paper is to soak it in water and mix it vigorously to release the fibers, which are then combined with cement and sand, or with clay, to make lightweight blocks. This is called papercrete, fibrous cement or, mixed with clay, fidobe. Paper fibers can also make a good addition to earthen and lime plasters. Dry paper is

FIGURE 21.6. Athena and Bill Steen created these examples of how a variety of clays and fibers can be mixed together to make lightweight adobe blocks. Note the reed mat and burlap, which can be used as a support for plaster over wood or other materials. [Credit: Catherine Wanek]

shredded, treated with mold and flame-retardants (usually boric acid, which is fairly benign) and used as "cellulose" insulation in walls and roofs.

Cloth

Cloth is made by weaving natural or artificial fibers together into a continuous sheet. Cloth can be sewn into bags (used in earthbag construction), or used as roof coverings, ceiling treatments or to provide shade. A coarse-woven natural fabric called burlap is widely used as lath to make natural plasters adhere to slick surfaces such as wood or painted walls. Even coarser fiber fishnet material can be inlaid in earthen plasters to make them much stronger.

Manure

Manure from cows and horses is a common additive in earthen plasters around the world. It serves the same function as chopped straw, but with much less work in chopping and screening. Very fine plasters can be created using cow manure, because the cows' several stomachs break down the plant fibers into very fine pieces. If the manure is fresh, the cow's stomach enzymes may also act as a preservative and hardener in earth plasters. In Africa, fresh manure was traditionally spread to create a floor, which was then often sealed with ox blood. To maintain its fiber strength, manure must be used before it begins to compost. If it has dried out (but not yet begun to rot), manure can be soaked in water and beaten to release its fibers.

Organic Additives

A number of products derived from animals and plants have been used as additives to earthen and lime plasters. Properly used, they can improve hardness, workability and water resistance. Such additives include: eggs, milk, blood, urine, linseed and other

FIGURE 21.7. This traditional house in Japan demonstrates the harmonious juxtaposition of a number of natural building materials, including, wood bamboo, reed mats, earth plasters and clay tiles. [Credit: Joseph F. Kennedy]

oils, prickly pear cactus juice, starch, tallow, tree sap, wheat flour paste and molasses. Many of these substances are also used as binders in natural paints. Linseed and other drying oils (hemp and tung oil, principally) have an amazing ability to seal, harden and waterproof porous surfaces such as wood and earth.

Seashells

In some coastal areas, shells from mussels, clams and oysters have been used to build houses. They are mixed with lime and put in

FIGURE 21.8. Using an angled plumb stick to obtain the proper degree of slope in this cob wall. [Credit: Joseph F. Kennedy]

forms, which set up to create solid walls. The same shells can also be burned to create lime. In Northern Europe, waste shells from food production are being used below floors for insulation and drainage.

Lime

Lime is a traditional binding agent made from limestone or seashells that are burnt at high temperatures in a kiln, then crushed. The resulting powder is combined with water, causing a chemical reaction (slaking) and forming lime putty. Kept wet, lime putty can be stored indefinitely, and it improves with age. It was commonly used around the world in mortars and plasters before Portland cement replaced it during the 19th century. True lime putty is difficult to find in the US, and the inferior dried (mason's hydrated) lime is used instead.

Lime putty is also a by-product of acetylene gas production, and some natural builders are obtaining high-quality putty in this way. Lime is mixed with sand to create "breathing" plasters and mortar. It can also be used to make paint. Because it is less brittle and less environmentally damaging to produce than Portland cement, many natural builders are rediscovering lime.

Concrete

Concrete is made of sand, gravel, water, Portland cement and sometimes lime or fly ash, a by-product of coal burning. These ingredients are mixed thoroughly, then poured or sprayed into forms. The mixture solidifies and cures over time; forms can generally be removed within 24 hours. Concrete has high compressive strength and can be used in foundations, walls and many other applications. Concrete blocks serve similar functions, stacked in a cement mortar. When steel or other fibers (including synthetic fibers such as acrylic or even natural fibers like bamboo) are embedded, concrete can have enormous tensile strength as well. Ferrocement is a very thin but exceptionally strong construction of cement-sand plaster over wire mesh. It can be used to make sculptural roofs, water tanks and even boats.

However, the making of the cement in concrete is a highly energy-intensive and polluting process, and a major contributor of greenhouse gases. It can also be difficult to recycle, though some natural builders are finding uses for old concrete, such as for building foundations. Cement plaster or stucco is not recommended to cover walls made of materials like earth and straw that are subject to degradation from moisture. This is because, while cement allows liquid water to pass through (either through cracks or capillary action), it is relatively impermeable to water vapor, and so moisture frequently becomes trapped underneath the stucco.

Steel

Steel is iron that contains carbon, making it harder and more flexible. It is used to make metal roofs, structural elements and hardware. Because it has very high embodied energy, natural builders use it sparingly. However, it is very strong, and can be easily recycled, making it more ecological than some other manufactured materials.

FIGURE 21.9. Broken pieces of ceramic tile are pressed into the mortar of this adobe wall to provide an additional "key" for the initial layer of earth plaster. [Credit: Joseph F. Kennedy]

RESOURCES

Books
- Racusin, Jacob Deva and Ace McArleton. *The Natural Building Companion: A Comprehensive Guide to Integrative Design and Construction*, Chelsea Green Publishing, 2012. Contains a chapter on choosing materials.
- Snell, Clarke. *Building Green: A Complete How-To Guide to Alternative Building Methods*, Lark Crafts, revised edition, 2009. This encyclopedic book gives well-illustrated examples of a wide range of natural building techniques.
- Stulz, Roland and Kiran Mukerji. *Appropriate Building Materials: A Catalogue of Potential Solutions*, SKAT Publications, 1993. This book is an excellent catalog of many of the materials mentioned here, with many illustrations. It is conveniently keyed (wall materials, roofs, etc.) for easy reference.
- van Lengen, Johan. *The Barefoot Architect*, Shelter Publications, 2007. This book, originally published in Spanish, is a simple, comprehensive and well-illustrated discussion of a wide range of natural building techniques.
- Woolley, Tom, Sam Kimmens, et al. *Green Building Handbook: A Guide to Building Products and Their Impact on the Environment, Vols. 1 and 2*, Routledge, 1997, 2000. An excellent overview from a European perspective.

Periodicals
- Environmental Building News: **buildinggreen.com**. This excellent monthly newsletter, targeted toward professional designer-builders, contains frequent updates on environmental building products and systems. One can also subscribe to their online database.

Glass

Glass is quartz sand, limestone and additional minerals heated until molten. It is then cast, blown, rolled or spun into a variety of building products including glass blocks, window glass and fiberglass insulation. While its manufacture is high in embodied energy, it is easily recyclable and its physical properties of light transmission are impossible to duplicate with non-industrial materials. Some natural builders use recycled glass windows and bottles in creative ways.

Recycled and Repurposed Materials

In an effort to lessen waste, some builders and manufacturers are reusing materials that would otherwise end up as trash. Bottles and cans can be used like bricks. Large cans may be flattened to make roofing shingles. Old plastic bottles are ground up and mixed with sawdust to make artificial "lumber." Many natural builders prefer to salvage materials such as bricks and lumber from old structures or other sources rather than buying new materials. Windows, doors and other fixtures can be refurbished and reused, saving valuable architectural heritage and cutting down on waste.

Conclusion

The use of natural building materials in construction has a bright future. Increasingly, innovative systems such as cob and earthbag construction are becoming code-approved and are joining more established systems such as rammed earth, adobe and straw bale construction. As techniques evolve and more builders, architects and developers employ them, structures that meet human needs while assisting in the regeneration of the planet will become more common. While many challenges still lie ahead, this is a hopeful and exciting time to be part of the quest to create a sustainable human culture.

Foundations for Natural Buildings

22

Michael G. Smith

It is often said that natural buildings appear to grow right out of the ground. While it's true that the materials from which they are built may be harvested from the site, and their form and appearance may mimic the natural landscape, the relationship between any building and the earth beneath it is always more complex than meets the eye. Even a tree (which does in fact grow out of the ground) needs a specialized root system to support its trunk; in some species, the root system is bigger than the tree we see. In a similar way, the below-ground parts of a building are often among its most important and expensive systems.

Foundation Functions

"Foundation" is the general term used to describe the lower structure of a building that comes in contact with the ground. A foundation may serve any or all of the following important functions.

Support

One of the main purposes of a foundation is to spread the load of the structure above it. In the same way that your foot is wider than your ankle, the bottom of a foundation (called, logically enough, the "footing") is often wider than the wall above. This stabilizes the wall and reduces the likelihood that the ground beneath the structure will settle unevenly. Strong, wide footings are especially important in post-and-beam buildings like traditional timber frames, where all of the weight of the roof and wall structure bears on a few small and widely spaced points.

Reinforcement

The part of the building that meets the ground is most vul-nerable when the ground moves, whether as a result of a sudden, catastrophic earthquake or landslide, of expansion and contraction due to wet-dry or freeze-thaw cycles or of slow slippage and settling over years or centuries. In seismically active regions, or those subject to high winds, it's important to tie the base of a building together with a continuous structure capable of resisting bending and twisting forces. It is crucial to make sure that the walls (and roof) are all well connected to the foundation so that the building can best resist seismic or wind forces. This is often done with bolts, straps, welded wire or other mechanical means of tying one part of the building to another.

Protection from Water

Most kinds of walls can be damaged by excessive moisture. This

Michael G. Smith *likes to experiment with low-tech, natural building systems. He teaches workshops and provides consulting and design services, especially to owner-builders:* **strawclaywood.com.**

is especially true if they are built of natural materials like wood, earth and straw. Foundations serve to protect the walls and the interior of the building from moisture in the soil. Some foundations (often called "stemwalls" or "plinths") extend well above ground level to protect the walls from wind-driven rain and from splashing roof runoff. In rainy climates, foundations for earth and straw structures should generally extend from 12–18 in. (30–40 cm) above ground level.

Drainage

Good site drainage is very important in natural building. Especially in rainy climates and on sites with poorly drained (high-clay content) soils, great care must be taken to prevent the moisture in the soil from migrating into the building. In modern conventional building, this is achieved by using highly processed waterproofing materials including concrete, plastics, tar and other sealants. If we wish to reduce the use of industrial materials for environmental, health and/or economic reasons, the only reliable replacement is good drainage.

Site drainage can be enhanced in a number of ways. The ground immediately around the building should be regraded as necessary so that surface runoff flows away from, rather than toward, the foundation. Uphill from the building, ditches can be dug to catch surface and subsurface runoff and carry it around or away from the building. A deep drainage ditch close to the building, backfilled with gravel and often with a perforated drain tile at the bottom, is called a curtain drain or French drain. Curtain drains are a good idea on poorly drained sites and in rainy climates, especially if any part of the inside floor will be lower than the exterior ground level (below grade), or made of earth.

Drainage can be combined with the load-bearing function of the foundation (see "Rubble Trench Foundations," p. 160). Rubble trenches are popular with natural builders because they provide excellent protection from ground moisture and frost heave while minimizing the use of concrete. They may also reduce earthquake damage by allowing the building to slide around a bit when the ground moves, dissipating the violent forces before they are transferred to the structure.

Even when a rubble trench is used, there is generally some kind of above-grade foundation to hold the building together and elevate the bottoms of the walls. There are many materials and construction systems to choose from. Your choice will depend on what you can gather or acquire locally; what you know how to build; and how strongly you value natural materials, proven performance and engineering rigor.

Foundation Materials
Concrete

Concrete is a combination of sand, gravel, water and Portland cement—an artificial compound made by baking lime, clay and other chemicals together at a very high temperature. Nearly all foundations for conventional modern buildings are made of concrete in one of its several forms, whether as a monolithic pour, concrete block masonry or various kinds of recycled foam and concrete units. Poured concrete reinforced with steel rebar is most common, due to its great strength, flexibility of form and ability to withstand earthquakes. Many natural builders prefer to minimize the amount of concrete in their buildings because of its high embodied energy, the environmental costs of its manufacture and disposal issues.

One way to reduce the use of new concrete is to build a foundation out of recycled concrete chunks. The easiest chunks to use are broken-up slabs and sidewalks, sometimes called urbanite because they are such an available resource in cities. In Eugene, Oregon, Rob Bolman received a building permit for a straw bale house with a foundation made of stacked urbanite with a cement-sand mortar and a poured concrete bond beam on top.

Various products are available commercially that combine concrete with recycled plastic foam for insulation. One such product is RASTRA, a foam-block system into which steel is inserted and concrete poured. This reduces the amount of concrete used, eliminates the step of building forms and improves the energy performance of the foundation.

When used in combination with natural materials, concrete can cause problems by wicking or trapping moisture. Straw bales particularly should never be placed directly on concrete because of the danger of moisture buildup on top of the foundation. Usually a pair of wooden "sleepers" is set atop a concrete foundation to create a "toe-up" that keeps the bales away from moisture in the concrete.

Stone

All around the world, for thousands of years, stone has been the material of choice for foundations. Its advantages are obvious. Stones are heavy, strong, extremely resistant to weather and readily available in many areas. Traditional stone foundations are

FIGURE 22.1. An urbanite foundation for a cob house, made of broken pieces of concrete sidewalk with a cement-sand mortar. Urbanite's flat shapes and regular thickness make it easy to stack in stable courses, and it is readily available in urban areas, often for free. "Dinosaur spines" projecting upwards from the middle of the stem wall will help lock the cob walls to the foundation. [Credit: Eric Hoel]

built either with or without mortar. The mortar is made of sand bound together with clay, lime and/or Portland cement.

An unreinforced stone masonry foundation is held together primarily by gravity. In severe earthquakes, these foundations can crack and crumble. To make them stronger, steel reinforcing can be embedded in liberal amounts of cement mortar between courses of stone. Another strategy is to cast a concrete bond beam above and/or below the masonry part of the foundation to tie it all together.

One of the disadvantages for owner-builders is the amount of skill and time required for stone masonry. These vary widely, depending on the type of stone you have to work with. Sedimentary stones like sandstone, which break naturally along flat planes, are much easier to build with than harder, irregularly shaped stones. Round river stones, although beautiful, are very difficult to stack solidly and require lots of mortar. One technique promoted by early owner-builder movement leaders, including Helen and Scott Nearing and Ken Kern, is the slip-form method, in which concrete is poured between stones that have been placed inside a temporary wooden form.

Wood

Foundations can be made of wood in either of two ways. The more

FIGURE 22.2. This small cob building in Oregon has a dry-stacked stone foundation. Stone stacked without mortar is one of the most ecological ways to build a foundation, but it can be vulnerable to intrusion by water and small animals, and to damage from earthquakes. [Credit: Michael G. Smith]

common option is to raise the entire building on wooden posts, as is often done in the hot, humid tropics. This has the advantage of getting the main structure away from the wet, heat-retaining earth and into the cooling breezes higher up, and of making the invasion of pests like termites easier to see and to control. Modern buildings are sometimes set on post-and-pier foundations, in which the wooden posts are either placed on concrete footings to spread the load or are replaced entirely with concrete or steel. Post foundations are most suitable for lightweight, wooden buildings. The weight of many of the thermal mass wall systems featured in this book makes a post-and-pier system impractical. Great care must be used in seismically active regions to engineer a post foundation that will resist earthquakes.

The other way to use wood in foundations is to build with heavy beams on grade. This brings the building in direct contact with the earth, which is more appropriate for passive solar designs. Wood has the advantage over stone masonry of being easier to shape and to fasten together. The major issues are the capacity of the wooden members to withstand

FIGURE 22.3. Novel building solutions often arise out of the desire to use locally available materials. At Emerald Earth Sanctuary in Northern California, there is no stone suitable for building, but there is an abundance of trees, including rot-resistant redwood. This foundation for a light straw-clay wall is made of site-milled redwood boards bolted onto either side of the structural posts, with the cavity between filled with lava rock for insulation and drainage. The drainage layer extends below the stemwall to help protect the walls and the earthen floor from water. [Credit: Michael G. Smith]

FIGURE 22.4. Bags filled with compacted soil or gravel can make a quick and versatile foundation system, especially well-suited to straw bale and cob walls. The polypropylene bag material degrades rapidly in the sun, so the bags must be protected with plaster. Here, earthbags double as both retaining wall and a foundation for straw bale walls. [Credit: Catherine Wanek]

the loads placed on them and to resist rot.

One inexpensive solution that's been used in several straw bale structures is to place used railroad ties, which are impregnated with creosote as a preservative, onto a bed of gravel for drainage. Unfortunately, creosote can off-gas into the air and leach harmful chemicals into the soil. I have also used salvaged redwood beams, which are naturally rot-resistant, on top of a rubble trench.

Rubble Trench Foundations

by Rob Tom

When water freezes, it expands volumetrically by 9 percent and in so doing, exerts a force of 150 tons per square inch (2,100 millipascals). When that water is found in poorly draining soils, nature, as usual, chooses the path of least resistance and dissipates much of the force by popping things up and out of the earth—much like what happens when one squeezes on a bar of soap. If a mere house, whose footings may only be carrying a few tons per linear foot, happens to be buried in that earth above the frost line, then it too gets heaved upward. As houses aren't usually dynamically balanced assemblages, there's no assurance that the bathroom will get heaved the same distance as the kids' bedroom. Speculation as to where the randomly displaced elements will fall when the earth thaws again presents odds that would delight any bookie.

A good solution to the freeze-thaw problem is the rubble trench foundation, which, as the name suggests, consists of a trench dug down to a depth below the frost line. The trench is then filled with clean stone ballast in which drainage tile or perforated pipe has been embedded to ensure positive drainage. The compacted stones bear solidly against each other and effectively transmit building loads to the supporting earth below. Furthermore, the voids between adjacent stones provide space for any water that may collect to freely expand, without detrimental consequences to the structure. Rubble trench foundations work in most soils whose bearing capacity exceeds 2,000 pounds per square foot (95 kilopascals).

Before digging the trench, topsoil should be peeled away (and saved for grading and landscaping) in the area of the building footprint to create a level building site. After laying out the foundation in the usual fashion, a line denoting the center of the wall is marked onto the earth (using garden lime, brightly colored stones, etc.). As the trench is dug, that line is kept in the center. The general rule is that footings are at least twice the width of the wall thickness. However, since thick natural walls such as straw bale and cob include a lot of structurally redundant width, the footing width can be reduced in this case if the soil-bearing capacity is adequate.

The shallowest part of the trench (the high point) will be dug to below the frost line and then sloped from there to one or more outlet trenches at the lowest parts of the building footprint. The outlet trenches leading away from the building are run out to daylight or to a dry well and sloped at least one-eighth-inch per foot (one centimeter per meter) of horizontal run. Take care to ensure that the bottoms of the trenches are flat, free of loose debris and properly sloped to the outlets.

The bottoms of the trenches are filled with a few inches of washed stone to provide a firm bed for a 4 in. (10 cm) perforated drainage pipe. Then the trench is filled with washed stone (1½ in.

Earthbags

Building with earthbags is a system for building using woven polypropylene bags filled with rammed earth. Although this technique was developed for constructing self-supporting domes and vaults, it has been adapted as a very easy-to-build, inexpensive foundation system.

In rainy climates, the bags should be placed atop a rubble trench; the earth inside can be replaced with gravel, in effect creating an above-ground rubble trench.

[38 mm]) is a nice size for shoveling, but larger random sizes are okay, too), compacting at every vertical foot or so it as it is filled. In sloppy, oversized excavations, in an attempt to minimize the amount of stone rubble required, larger stones can be laid up in the manner of dry-stacked walls where the sides of the excavation should have been (it's easier than it sounds). Then use smaller, irregularly shaped stone to fill in between. The drainage pipe only requires a foot or so of stone around it. To prevent fine soil particles from washing down and plugging the drainage media, a filter of landscape fabric, asphalt-impregnated felt, reclaimed woven polypropylene lumber tarps or burlap should be laid over the stone before backfilling. The sidewalls of the trench would benefit from the use of a filter membrane, as well, to prevent clogging of the voids by loose dirt washed into the trench by the movement of sub-surface groundwater and burrowing animals. The outlet end of the drain tile should be capped with stout, corrosion-resistant mesh to keep critters out.

ROB TOM is a builder who now spends most of his days as an architect.

FIGURE 22.5. The bottom of a rubble trench should slope downhill "to daylight." Sometimes this requires extending the trenches and the drainage pipe far from the building. [Credit: Mark Mazziotti]

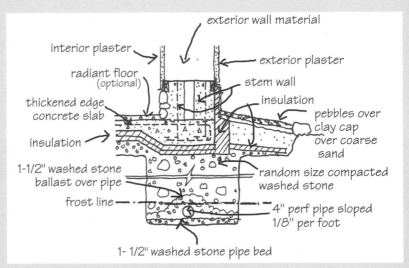

FIGURE 22.6. Rubble trench foundation for a cold climate region. [Credit: Joseph F. Kennedy]

interior plaster

exterior wall material

radiant floor (optional)

exterior plaster

thickened edge concrete slab

stem wall

insulation

insulation

pebbles over clay cap over coarse sand

1-1/2" washed stone ballast over pipe

random size compacted washed stone

frost line

4" perf pipe sloped 1/8" per foot

1-1/2" washed stone pipe bed

Often, strands of barbed wire are used between courses of bags as a type of "Velcro mortar."

Cob can be built directly onto earthbag foundations. To improve the connection and keep the cob from sliding off during an earthquake, stout wooden stakes are pounded into the top course of bags. Straw bales can also be placed directly on the bags. After the first course or two of bales are in place, sharpened rebar pins can be driven down through them and all the way through the bag foundation, helping to hold the layers of bags together. This approach is most appropriate in dry climates.

In rainy climates, I prefer to install an additional drainage layer between straw bales and polypropylene bags, to prevent the possibility of condensation buildup on the water-resistant bag surface. One way to achieve this is to build a wooden frame the width of the bales and fill it with pea gravel or pumice. In post and beam wall systems, the posts can either sit on a wooden beam that rests on and is pinned into the earthbags, or they can rest on separate footers placed to one side of the bag foundation.

The biggest concern with earthbag foundations is their durability. Polypropylene degrades rapidly when exposed to sunlight. It is a matter of some debate how effective plaster is at preserving bags long-term. This is particularly important when the bags are filled not with rammed earth but with gravel, making the bags permanently structural. One possible solution is to surround the bags with a thin, reinforced concrete shell that will retain the material even if the bags degrade to the point of failure.

Rammed Tires

The concept of reusing car tires filled with rammed earth as a foundation is similar to the use of earthbags. Again, whole buildings can be made this way (see "Earthships: An Ecocentric Model," p. 289). Stacked rammed tires can create a stable, earthquake-resistant base for various wall systems. Like earthbags, they lend themselves to curved, organic wall shapes. The large diameter of the tires can present an interesting design challenge when the wall above is much narrower. One solution is to sculpt indoor or outdoor benches at the base of the wall.

RESOURCES

Periodicals
• *The Last Straw: The International Journal of Straw Bale and Natural Building*: **thelaststraw.org**. Issue #16, Fall 1996 is devoted to discussing the many different foundation systems possible for straw bale (and natural building in general), ranging from the cheap and simple to the elaborate and expensive.

Stone Masonry

23

Michael G. Smith

If I ask you to think of an ancient building, chances are the structure that appears in your mind's eye is constructed of stone. Stone masonry is, indeed, one of the oldest and most ubiquitous building systems on Earth, but its dominance of ancient sites is more the result of its unequaled durability than of anything else. The intricately fitted defensive walls of Machu Picchu, the soaring cathedrals of Western Europe and the engineering feats of Roman aqueducts, Egyptian pyramids and British stone circles all inspire us with awe. The signature characteristics of strength, solidity, heaviness and durability give stone structures a reassuring timelessness.

In modern industrial society,

stone masonry is no longer common; it has been largely superseded by concrete and other manufactured materials. In that process, some ancient techniques for transporting and shaping stones have been forgotten. Yet for the contemporary natural builder, stone can still be both

viable and practical. Stone is a particularly good option for those interested in reducing or eliminating the use of Portland cement from their buildings, for environmental or health reasons.

Stone makes excellent foundations for other wall systems; durable, waterproof floors for

Michael G. Smith *learned stone masonry while building foundations for cob buildings. He offers trainings in many natural building techniques, as well as consulting and design services:* strawclaywood.com.

FIGURE 23.1. The Inca civilization may have seen the most skilled stonemasons of all time. The stones in this wall in Cuzco, Peru, fit together so tightly that one cannot insert a piece of paper between them, yet some of them weigh many tons. Very heavy stones with a lot of surface contact produce enough frictional resistance to withstand earthquakes. [Credit: Michael G. Smith]

indoor or outdoor spaces; massive, heat-retaining fireplaces and chimneys; cool, moisture-resistant basements and root cellars; and even whole houses, for the especially dedicated. As with many other natural building techniques, stone construction can be very inexpensive if the materials are locally available and if the builder is amply supplied with time and/or volunteer help.

Stone masonry also presents the owner-builder with plenty of challenges. Foremost among these is the sheer weight of the material, which can be a strain on your back, your vehicle and other tools. The quantity of stone required for most projects is far more than most novices would predict. Shaping and working stone is an art, involving both skill and luck; some types of stone are more cooperative than others.

From an engineering perspective, unreinforced stone masonry is vulnerable to damage from earthquakes. Stone is also a very poor insulator. But with care, practice and good planning, all of these limitations can be overcome. The best advice for a would-be stonemason is to start small.

Safety is of paramount importance when building with stone. Stones are both heavy and hard,

providing ample opportunities for injury. Be very careful when lifting; use proper body mechanics and get help if the stone is beyond your safe weight limit. Always wear safety equipment: leather gloves and boots when moving stones; gloves when handling cement or lime mortar; eye protection when cutting or shaping stone.

Selecting Stone

The first consideration for every stone builder is where to acquire the material. There are many options, ranging from having the stone delivered by truck from a quarry to scouting around your own backyard with a digging bar and a wheelbarrow. Before you go out hunting, you need some idea of what you are looking for. The kind and quality of stone you need depends on what you intend to do with it.

There are many different techniques for building with stone. A solid wall, built either with or without mortar, is suitable for a foundation or a load-bearing wall and requires the most precise fit among the stones. Since it is built up of horizontal courses, each stone should have two relatively flat "faces"—the top and the bottom. It's nice if there is a third attractive face at approximately

right angles to the other two, to expose on the wall's surface. Construction will be much easier if there are many stones of about the same thickness top to bottom.

A boulder wall is made of more irregular or rounded stones. It's harder to create a stable wall using this technique. For the beginning mason, a more reasonable option might be a slip-form wall, in which stones are placed in a re-

FIGURE 23.2. The Mediterranean island of Sardinia is home to some 7,000 *nuraghi* dating from the Bronze Age (between 1900 and 730 BCE). These mysterious towers, some of which stand up to 60 ft. (20 m) high, were built of enormous boulders, shaped and stacked without mortar. [Credit: Joseph. F. Kennedy]

movable form with plenty of concrete mortar packed or poured between them. Round river rocks, which are very difficult to stack into a solid wall, can be successfully used this way.

A flagstone floor can be made from any stones that are relatively flat and thin. In fact, only one flat face is really necessary, since a rounded or irregular bottom can be dug into the ground or buried in mortar. To build a stone "veneer" over a wall of brick, concrete block, poured concrete or even wood, you will need stones that are all about the same thickness.

Stones for any building project should be hard and sound, as opposed to crumbly and fractured. A range of different sizes is good, although none should be so heavy that it is impossible to maneuver into place. Small, flat, wedge-shaped "chinkers" are very useful for stabilizing larger stones.

Where to Get Stones

Since stones are so heavy and their transport can be expensive, the logical place to build with stone is where stones are abundant. Start by looking around the building site. If surface stones are not plentiful or are eroded and fractured, try looking just below the surface.

A heavy digging bar is an excellent tool for probing beneath the soil and for levering stones up to the surface. A large contractor's wheelbarrow can comfortably transport stones of up to several hundred pounds. Lay the wheelbarrow on its side, roll a large stone into it and then push the wheelbarrow upright.

For carrying stones uphill or over uneven ground, a good alternative is to make a simple carrying cradle out of wire fencing. By sliding strong poles through the wire, you can make a litter that can be carried by four people or even more.

If you need to transport rock from outside the immediate neighborhood, a pickup truck is practically indispensable. If you are lucky enough to live in an area

FIGURE 23.3. In the hands of a craftsman, all stones can be useful. A variety of stones and lime mortar were used to build both walls and window frames in this 1880s New Zealand house. Note the clear courses despite the irregularly shaped stones. [Credit: Catherine Wanek]

with a long history of agriculture or stone building, then you may be able to recycle previously used stones. In the old days, fieldstones were often stacked into fencerows or thrown into piles to get them out of the way of the plow; these may be considered a nuisance by the present landowner. Similarly, abandoned cellars, demolition sites and excavations for new construction sometimes yield prime building materials.

Another good place to look for building stones is in road cuts.

Where a road has been blasted through a hillside, stones often slide down to litter the shoulder. Be careful not to further destabilize the bank or roadbed in your zeal for material. Seashores, creek beds and riverbanks can also be sensitively harvested (though make sure that such activities are legal in your area).

If you need to purchase your stone, try to find the most local source, as transportation will likely cost more than the stone itself. Always go see the stone before you order, to make sure

that it will be suitable for your purposes—it could be too big or too small, too crumbly or too irregular in shape.

It's easy to underestimate the amount of stone you will need. Even a modest-sized stone wall or foundation will swallow up astounding quantities of material. Calculate the volume of the wall, and then add 50 percent to that figure when assembling your rock pile. Some of the stones will be unusable because they are cracked, irregular or simply the wrong size or shape to fit. If you are shaping your stones, some will get broken in the process. Others will lose a percentage of their volume under your hammer and chisel.

Shaping Stones

Most stones can be cut or shaped with some degree of success. Soft sedimentary rocks, such as sandstone and slate, are fairly easy to split into flat planes along the "grain." Hard igneous rocks, such as granite and basalt, are the most difficult to shape. Other types fall somewhere in between.

The most important tool for shaping stone is a stone hammer. A long-handled 8 lb. (3.6 kg) sledgehammer is useful for breaking large stones into smaller pieces. Smaller hammers

FIGURE 23.4. A road-building crew at work near Machu Picchu in Peru. With enough persistence, human power and hand tools can shape and move even this extremely hard granite. [Credit: Michael G. Smith]

come in various weights, between 1½–4 lb. (0.7–1.8 kg). These can be used alone for cutting by repeatedly striking the stone with the square edge of the hammer's face. For more precision, use a heavy cold chisel or brick chisel. A mason's hammer combines hammer and chisel into a single implement.

In theory, if enough force from enough blows is directed along a single plane through a stone, then the stone will eventually break along that plane. The practice is somewhat less predictable, especially for the beginner.

The stone is likely to break along any preexisting cracks or faults. Any chips or pebbles caught underneath the stone when it is struck can redirect the force. It's easiest to cut a stone along a visible crack, or to remove a corner or weak protrusion. Several of the books listed in "Resources" contain detailed instructions on shaping stone.

Building Techniques

Just as there are multiple ways to build an earthen wall, so there are many ways to build with stone. Here I will focus on two

of these options: the solid wall, which can be constructed with or without mortar, and the slip-formed wall.

The Solid Wall

In a solid stone wall, all of the weight is transferred directly from stone to stone, from the top of the wall down to the bottom. A solid wall may be built with or without mortar; the construction sequence is practically identical either way. The purpose of the mortar, if used, is not to cement the stones together but merely to keep them from shifting and to

FIGURE 23.5. A historic chateau in France, being reconstructed to repair damage done by bombing during World War II. Some of the carved cornerstones and lintels bear dates from Roman times, and may have been reused in multiple buildings. [Credit: Catherine Wanek]

prevent the passage of air, water and small creatures.

There are many options for mortar mixes. The simplest is a mixture of sand and clay. This works fine in dry locations but is susceptible to erosion if exposed to weather. Another traditional mortar mix is made of lime putty and sand (see "Working with Lime," p. 347). Modern masons often use a mortar of Portland cement and sand. Lime is a good addition to this mixture, as it slows down setting, making the mix workable over a longer time period; it also reduces the mortar's brittleness.

A solid wall is built in an orderly sequence. Start with the most visible face. Line up a few stones to form a pleasant-looking row, with a fairly smooth face and an even, level top. It will be very helpful to have a lot of the stones of the same height. If you are using mortar, then remove each stone one by one after the row is in place, put a bed of mortar below it and then tap the stone down into the mortar. Then move to the other side of the wall and repeat the process, building a second row of stones the same height as the first. Don't worry if there is a space between the two rows; this can be filled in with mortar and small stones.

Continue on along the wall until you have completed the first course. If the wall is longer than a few feet, it may not be possible to make this first course all the same height. You can have steps in it periodically where the level changes, but the fewer of these

the better. Fill in all the cracks between stones with mortar, pushing it into place with a mason's trowel.

When the first course is complete, begin the second. Fit a row of stones in place, then remove them one at a time to place the

FIGURE 23.6. As this slate-roofed building in Wales demonstrates, stone can be used for every part of a building, from foundation and floors to chimney and roof. [Credit: Catherine Wanek]

mortar. Tap each stone down into the mortar until it touches the stone below it. Actually, it should touch at least two stones. The principal rule of the solid wall is the "running bond." The joint between every two neighboring stones should be bridged by the stone above it. This is why it is so important for the top of each course to be fairly even. Wherever a step occurs in the top of one course, start the next course with a stone that brings the lower level up even with the upper level. In the next course up, a stone will bridge that gap to reestablish the running bond. When you stand back for a look, the vertical joints should be discontinuous, zigzagging up the face of the wall.

There is an equally important overlap that won't be visible. You've bound each face of the wall together by bridging all the joints. But you must also bridge the two faces with long stones that run through the entire width of the wall. These are called "tie stones" or "bonding units." The more bonding units that are used, the stronger the wall will be.

A solid wall built in this fashion will be very strong in compression but not so strong in tension. Because it is made out of discrete units that are held together mostly by gravity and friction, a big earthquake can bring the whole thing down. There are several ways to reinforce a solid wall to make this less likely. You can pour "bond beams" of concrete reinforced with steel both beneath the base and on top of the wall. In high walls, you might even want one or more bond beams partway up. These can be poured between rows of narrow stones to make them invisible.

The Slip-Formed Wall

The slip-formed wall requires less care and skill than does a solid wall and depends less on the shape and strength of the stones. It is basically a concrete wall, with a substantial amount of the concrete displaced by stones that are visible on one or both faces of the wall. Although this technique demands less of the stone, both in quality and quantity, a slip-form wall requires large amounts of concrete and wood for forms which can raise the cost of materials considerably.

Slip-form walls are more difficult to make beautiful; the concrete tends to show in large, uneven joints and to stain the stones, unless great care is used

---

RESOURCES

Books

• Kern, Ken, Steve Magers and Lou Penfield. *The Owner Builder's Guide to Stone Masonry*, Owner Builder Publications, 1976. Look for this very readable and well-illustrated classic in used bookstores or online. Introduces three different building techniques: traditional laid masonry, stone "facing" over other wall systems and formed masonry.

• Long, Charles. *The Backyard Stonebuilder*, Warwick Publishing, 1996. An entertaining, accessible and non-intimidating introduction to stone masonry for the hobbyist, including detailed instructions for many small outdoor projects.

• McRaven, Charles. *Building with Stone*, Storey Publishing, 1989. An excellent beginner's guide to stone building, both dry and mortared. Contains instructions for many projects, including a fireplace, root cellar, bridge, dam, flagstone floor and even a stone house.

• Nearing, Helen and Scott Nearing. *Living the Good Life*, Shocken Books, 1990. Among countless other pearls of homesteading wisdom, these back-to-the-land pioneers describe in detail their system for building a slip-form stone house.

to clean them off almost immediately. However, slip-forms can be a good option for unskilled masons working with poor-quality stone. It's easy to add steel reinforcing to make the wall stronger and more earthquake resistant. Furthermore, insulation can be either added in the middle of the wall or attached to the interior face, helping to solve one of the most significant problems with stone as a primary wall material.

Since their invention in the 1840s, many different forming systems have been developed, ranging from simple bulky constructions of lumber and plywood to more complex but lightweight forms of pipe and welded steel. Some forms are built in short sections, which must be moved laterally along the wall; others extend the full length of the wall.

Most forms allow only a foot or two (30 to 60 cm) of height to be built at a time. After that, the concrete is allowed to set, anywhere from an hour (if quick-setting additives are used) to two days, before the forms are removed and raised into place for the next section of wall. Cement mortar can either be set between the stones as they are placed into the form or poured in afterward. In the latter case, the joints must be "pointed" with more mortar after the forms are removed.

Among the best-known proponents of slip-form masonry are Helen and Scott Nearing, who left the world of urban academia in the 1930s to live a life dedicated to simplicity and social justice. Their classic book, *Living the Good Life* (Shocken Books, 1970), is an eloquent testament to the role stone building can play in the creation of a more sane and harmonious society.

Adobe Building

PAUL G. MCHENRY

24

Earth buildings in many forms are found in most parts of the world, with various degrees of sophistication. They range from mud-covered brush shelters to magnificent palaces in the Middle East to luxury homes in Santa Fe, New Mexico. The choice of earth building method is dictated by climate, as well as by tradition developed by trial and error through the centuries.

Frequently, through cultural influence, various styles are found side by side. Earth-building techniques from ancient peoples on every continent are well documented in the reports of explorers and archeologists. What may come as a surprise is that at least a third of the world's people still live in earth homes today. Earth buildings are even found in wet climates.

A useful principle in building with earth is to keep it simple. A good shelter can be built with a minimum of skilled labor and tools or even with no tools at all. Modern efforts to mechanize, standardize and improve earthen building may lead to unnecessary complexity and other problems.

Adobe bricks are blocks made of earth and water that are dried in the sun. Sizes vary widely, mostly determined by historic tradition. After the bricks have been cast, it may take a week or more for them to be dry enough to handle. A larger and thicker brick will tend to crack more and will take longer to dry. Heavy rain can damage the bricks as they are drying, so brick making must be done in a period when the possibility of rain is low.

Bricks can be made in a number of ways, depending on site, climate and tools available. The simplest way is with a single mold. Mud is mixed and placed in the molds by hand on a smooth surface. The mold is removed and the bricks allowed to dry sufficiently to stand on edge, after which they are trimmed and allowed to dry completely before they're stacked or used. The whole process takes about one week in most favorable dry climates.

The brick-making process can be expedited with the use of shovels, wheelbarrows, multiple forms, front-end loaders and concrete or plaster mixers. Another option is the use of a hydraulic pressing machine that can create a large number of bricks (compressed earth blocks)—up to 4,000 per day. This type of

PAUL G. ("BUZZ") MCHENRY (1924–2002) was an architect and builder specializing in adobe construction. He taught in the architecture department at the University of New Mexico, and founded the Earth Architecture Center International, Ltd. in 1994 and the Earth Building Foundation in 1998. The author of Adobe and Rammed Earth Buildings: Design and Construction and Adobe: Build It Yourself, McHenry researched innovations in earth building and ecological design.

production has many advantages but requires a large capital investment (see "Compressed Earth Blocks," p. 195).

Once they are dry, adobe bricks are stacked to make walls. The bricks are cemented together with a mud mortar made up of water and screened soil taken from the same sources as the soil used to make the bricks. Although early buildings in the southwestern US were sometimes placed directly on the ground, adobe walls should be built on a foundation of concrete or stone to protect them from moisture damage. Frames for windows and doors are set in place as the wall goes up.

Soils

Contrary to popular belief, most soils will make suitable building bricks. Adobe soils contain a mixture of clay, silt and sand or aggregate, with the respective percentages being relatively flexible to create a strong brick. Clay provides the waterproofing and is the glue that holds the aggregate together. Bricks have been made that have no clay, but they are prone to rapid erosion. Too much clay in a soil will cause cracks as the bricks dry.

Many natural soils have too high a clay content and must be modified with a tempering

FIGURE 24.1. Taos Pueblo, the oldest continually inhabited settlement in North America, is made largely of adobe. [Credit: Mark Mazziotti]

FIGURE 24.2. A single-family home made from stabilized adobe blocks in New Zealand. [Credit: Catherine Wanek]

agent of sand or straw. (In the book of Exodus in the Bible, the need for straw to make bricks is mentioned; this supports the tradition that adding straw is necessary when the clay percentage is too high.) However, most good adobes will have a proportion of approximately 50 percent clay and silt, and 50 percent sand and gravel. The resulting brick should be dry, hard and free of major cracks.

The rate of erosion of mud surfaces from rain is much slower than might be expected. Historic examples in the southwestern United States indicate an erosion rate for vertical wall surfaces of perhaps 1 in. (2.5 cm) in 20 years, in an area with average rainfall of 25 in. (64 cm) per year. Unprotected horizontal surfaces, such as tops of walls, will erode much faster.

Energy, Ecology and Insulation

Energy and ecology go hand in hand. An often-overlooked feature of energy consumption is the cost of producing our primary building materials—their embodied energy. An adobe brick made by hand on the building site uses no fuel except the builder's sweat and the solar energy to dry the brick. Earth building holds answers to many of today's concerns about energy and ecology.

Tests indicate that adobe has the capacity to absorb, store and release heat, making use of solar energy and damping ambient temperature swings. These tests found that the interior wall temperature of a 10 in. thick (25 cm thick) adobe wall on the south side of a building was the average

FIGURE 24.3. Making small adobe bricks using a wooden slip form. The cured but not yet dry adobe bricks are stacked to enable good ventilation and even drying. [Credit: Michael G. Smith]

outdoor temperature through the previous week. Interior wall temperature varied only by two or three degrees in any 24-hour period, while outside air temperatures varied from 60°F to 90°F (15°C to 32°C). At midday, with outdoor temperatures in the 90s (30s), the interior temperatures, at 75°F (24° C), felt cool. At night, when the exterior temperature was 60°F (15° C), the interior temperature, still at 75°F (24°C), felt warm. Other tests on 24 in. (60 cm) walls had the same results, but the interior temperatures only varied by one or two degrees. This is called the "thermal flywheel effect."

The insulation value of adobe, however, is quite low, and if the building needs to be heated continually, the walls will lose heat unless additional insulation is supplied. The flywheel effect is most effective in areas with highly variable ambient temperatures.

Historic Use

Prehistoric peoples everywhere used earth and other natural materials for building. When traders and invaders later arrived, they adapted the materials they found in use locally to the architectural styles of their countries of origin. Adobe was the most widely used form in most of the southwestern United States and northern Mexico. It did not always follow the local architectural style of Pueblo or American Territorial; adobe bricks were also used in place of fired brick in Victorian-style buildings.

When the railroads arrived, offering economical transportation of manufactured goods,

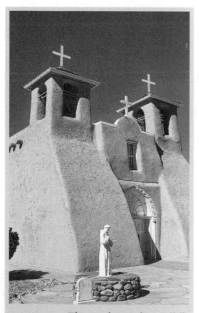

FIGURE 24.4. The sculptural possibilities of adobe are demonstrated by the famous San Francisco de Asis Mission Church in Ranchos de Taos, New Mexico. [Credit: Joseph F. Kennedy]

FIGURE 24.5. In Abiquiu, New Mexico, students prepare to build a vault of small adobe bricks, examples of which can be seen stacked on the walls built of traditional adobe blocks. [Credit: Kurt Gardella]

those who could afford them began using more modern materials. But in difficult economic times, people always returned to earthen buildings to meet their needs. If funds were scarce, then churches, schools, public buildings and homes were built with adobe. Governments found this useful as well. When the New Mexico State Fairground in Albuquerque needed buildings in the late 1930s, money was scarce and there was massive unemployment. As material was available onsite, what better way to meet both needs than to build with adobe?

During the Great Depression, the Farm Home Administration and other government agencies sponsored another program to assist farmers who had been broken by the drought. They obtained land in the Rio Grande River valley, portioned it off into various sized plots and sent tools and supervisors to build simple adobe homes. This allowed motivated farmers to build new lives for themselves. Of the 40 or more homes built during this program, all but 2 are still occupied by satisfied owners.

Challenges to Current and Future Use

Adobe construction in New Mexico has a split image. On the one hand, a person with few resources can build a snug shelter with the materials under his feet, using only his hands. On the other, a wealthy person can build an adobe palace, paying top dollar. Adobe is now thought of in New Mexico as a luxury material that only the wealthy can afford.

Today, the primary enemies of building with earth are ignorance and building regulations. Prior to World War II, most people in the Southwest were familiar

FIGURE 24.6. Earth and/or lime plasters are preferred for adobe construction as they can allow moisture to escape, as demonstrated by this recreation of the Presidio in Santa Barbara, California. Cement plasters can trap water within adobe walls, which may lead to catastrophic damage over time. [Credit: Joseph F. Kennedy]

with adobe construction. After World War II, when professionals went back to school and work, earth building got lost among the new materials. As a result, we now have an entire generation of professional engineers, architects and building officials who are unfamiliar with this type of construction. The only people familiar with the material are those in developing nations and a small number of professionals who specialize in natural building. Even people in developing nations are rapidly losing their earth building skills.

Building regulations were frequently written by people who had no knowledge of adobe. Some current building regulations place such limitations on its use that the cost becomes prohibitive. The answer to this is education. Three things need to be done:

1. Change building codes to recognize the centuries of earth building experience and tradition.
2. Establish community and higher-education programs that provide real, hands-on experience. Use these programs to train more trainers.
3. Build full-scale demonstration projects that people can walk into and experience.

RESOURCES

Books

• Byrne, Michael. *The New Adobe Home*, Gibbs Smith, 2009. A beautifully illustrated overview of recent adobe residences.

• Gray, Virginia and Alan Macrae, and Wayne McCall (photographer). *Mud, Space, and Spirit: Handmade Adobes*, Capra Press, Santa Barbara, 1976. Takes you inside beautifully sculpted, owner-built adobe homes.

• McHenry, Jr., Paul. *Adobe and Rammed Earth Buildings: Design and Construction*, University of Arizona Press, 1984. Includes history, engineering and overview of construction techniques, including soil testing, windows and doors and plastering options.

• McHenry, Jr., Paul. *Adobe: Build It Yourself*, University of Arizona Press, 1985. A thorough and readable introduction to many aspects of adobe construction.

• Norton, John. *Building with Earth*, Intermediate Technology Publications, 1997. A good, brief introduction to the general principles of earth building, including testing soils and adobe blocks. Contains instructions on building adobe vaults and domes.

• Sanchez, Laura. *Adobe Houses for Today: Flexible Plans for Your Adobe Home*, Sunstone Press, rev. ed., 2008. A good resource for current designers in adobe.

• Schroeder, Lisa and Vince Ogletree. *Adobe Homes for All Climates*, Chelsea Green, 2010. A recent book with many useful construction details for the modern adobe home.

• Tibbets, Joseph. *The Earthbuilder's Encyclopedia*, Southwest Solaradobe School, 1989. Useful pictorial reference to materials, tools, techniques and details of adobe and other earth building systems. Out of print but available as CD-Rom from **adobebuilder.com**.

Organization

• The Earthbuilders' Guild (TEG), is an organization dedicated to the betterment and advancement of earthen homes and commercial buildings: **theearthbuildersguild.com**.

High-Fiber Adobes

by Michael G. Smith

Some naturally occurring clay soils contain ideal proportions of clay and aggregates (silt, sand and gravel) to make strong adobe blocks with no further additions except for water. The ideal clay content is around 25 percent by volume, but adobes can be made with as little as 5 percent clay. Some types of clay are more adhesive than others, and some are more expansive (meaning they take on more water when wet and therefore shrink more as they dry), so there is no set recipe. Once the clay percentage goes higher than about 30 percent, the resulting shrinkage as the block dries may lead to large cracks that weaken the wall. A common solution to this problem is to add sand to the mud, reducing the clay percentage and subsequent shrinkage to within acceptable parameters.

A more traditional approach is to add fiber. In most areas where adobe was used historically, locally available fiber such as straw, horse manure or pine needles was mixed into the mud before it was formed into blocks. Fiber doesn't prevent the mud from shrinking as it dries, the way sand does. What it does is distribute the shrinkage so that instead of a wide crack running most of the way through a block, you get hundreds of tiny short cracks, bridged with fiber, that are generally too small to see and don't weaken the block. Fiber-reinforced adobes are stronger in tension than mud bricks with no fiber.

The amount of straw in traditional adobes is quite low—usually no more than 5 percent by volume. Recently, however, natural builders on several continents have discovered that there are advantages to adding much more straw to their mud bricks. With a sticky high-clay soil, the percentage of straw can be raised to 70 percent by volume or even higher. The resulting blocks are much lighter than traditional adobes, and presumably much better insulating, since insulation value is inversely related to density.

In 2012, Hana Mori Böttger and Michael Rizza of the University of San Francisco conducted tests in collaboration with natural builder Massey Burke to compare the compressive and tensile strengths of high-fiber cob mixes with regular cob. (Since the samples were

FIGURE 24.7. In Ciudad Obregon, the center of a grain-growing region in northern Mexico, the use of high-fiber adobes has become commonplace. These large blocks will be used to create insulating ceilings. [Credit: Catherine Wanek]

formed into small blocks for testing, they were essentially adobes.) A mixture of two parts chopped straw to one part soaked clay soil by volume yielded blocks with a density of 64 lb./sq. in. (440 kilopascals) compared with 95 lb./sq. in. (650 kilopascals) for a standard cob mix. The light blocks were found to have a much higher modulus of rupture than the heavy ones, with only a slightly reduced compressive strength. (Modulus of rupture is a measure of tensile strength that indicates a material's resistance to failure when loaded as a beam.) Although preliminary, these tests indicate that high-fiber adobe and cob can likely be used structurally in the same ways as conventional mixes.

One of the earliest applications of this technology was on the 5,000 sq. ft. (460 m²) office of Fundación de Apoyo Infantíl (Save The Children) in Ciudad Obregon, Sonora, Mexico. The building was designed in 1995 by Athena Steen of the Canelo Project in Arizona, following years of collaboration between the two organizations to introduce straw bale building to the region (see "Builders without Borders," p. 421). Although straw bales were used for the building's

FIGURE 24.8. Janell Kapoor of Kleiwerks demonstrates adobe making at Earthaven Ecovillage in North Carolina. She combines mud and straw on a tarp, a technique borrowed from cob builders. [Credit: Mark Mazziotti]

exterior walls, the team wanted a narrower wall system for interior partitions.

Adobe construction is familiar in the local culture, and the addition of a high straw content to prevent cracking and to make the blocks lighter and more weather resistant was readily accepted by local builders. With less thermal mass than traditional adobes, straw-clay blocks also have less tendency to absorb and retain heat in the very hot summer weather. Along with straw bales, the use of these blocks has since taken off in the region.

One common fear about adding straw to the mix is that it could attract termites or ants. This may be a legitimate concern in some areas. In fact, some of the early straw-clay block structures in Ciudad Obregon suffered from termite damage. In most places, high-fiber blocks can be protected from pests and moisture by a combination of an insect-proof foundation that elevates the blocks away from the ground and an appropriate plaster, just like straw bales.

Where straw is locally available and inexpensive, the biggest reason not to use a high-fiber mix may be that it complicates the mixing process. Traditionally, adobe was

FIGURE 24.9. This Nubian vault is being built of small high-fiber adobes. Straw-rich blocks have many advantages when used overhead: less weight to lift and handle; better insulation; more resistance to seismic forces; and less likelihood of injury in the case of collapse. [Credit: Michael G. Smith]

often mixed simply by digging a hole in the ground, adding water and stirring the mud by treading in it. A small amount of fiber can easily be incorporated this way, but large amounts tangle into clumps and the mixture becomes uneven. Mixing on a tarp, as many cob builders do, improves the situation. The tarp is used to roll the mix over before stomping it flat again and again, which produces thorough mixing even with stiff, fibrous mixes. Mixing this way can be an enjoyable aerobic workout...or an exhausting chore.

Massey Burke came up with an easy way to make high-fiber adobe mixes, which she calls "lasagna mixing." First, clay soil is loaded into plastic buckets, covered with water and, if time permits, left to soak until soft. Then the mud is mixed with an electric drill with a paint- or mortar-mixing attachment until it reaches the consistency of chocolate pudding or runny peanut butter. A layer of straw is placed in the bottom of a large wheelbarrow, followed by a layer of mud (about equal in volume to the straw), then more straw, more mud and so on. (This is the "lasagna.")

The mix can be left to sit for a few minutes and wheeled into place near the adobe forms. To fill the forms, reach down to the bottom of the wheelbarrow and grab a large lump of straw-rich mud. Pulling from the bottom in this way tends to combine the ingredients well enough that little or no mixing is necessary.

High-fiber mixes can also be made in a mortar mixer; a regular cement mixer doesn't work well. Vital Systems, a natural building company in Northern California headed by Timothy Kennedy, discovered an agricultural implement capable of mixing large batches of straw-rich mud. Dubbed the "cobasaurus," the machine consists of three corkscrew-like augurs that turn horizontally inside a large hopper, driven by a tractor PTO. This mixer was designed to mix grass and grains for livestock feed, but can easily produce up to 5 cu. yd. (4 m³) at a time of straw-rich cob or earthen plaster. The augurs chop the straw as they turn, so the longer the machine is left running, the finer the mix becomes.

When using other mixing techniques, it can be very helpful to chop the straw first, especially if the straw is particularly long or stiff, or the adobe forms are small. This is done most efficiently with a motorized wood chipper or a leaf mulcher; but there are many other methods. A mud mix with chopped straw fills the forms more evenly, and there is less likelihood of large voids in the blocks.

Jorge Belanko, a natural builder in Argentina, makes straw-clay blocks that are considerably lighter even than most high-fiber adobes. His blocks are made in special forms with inserts that slide out to release the block from the mold. He uses a very light mix, perhaps five percent clay by volume, similar to light straw-clay. The blocks have cylindrical air spaces in the middle to increase their insulation value even further (for more details, see "Natural Building Thrives in Argentina," p. 413).

In recent years, high-fiber adobes have been used on many innovative projects in several countries. Once builders hear about the concept and work out a viable mixing method, they are likely to be converted, since these lightweight adobes offer so many advantages over heavy earth blocks.

MICHAEL G. SMITH loves learning about even more things that can be done with clay and straw. He teaches workshops and provides consulting and design services, especially to owner-builders: **strawclaywood.com**.

RESOURCES

Videos

• *Mud, Hands, a House* (*El Barro, las Manos, la Casa*). 2007, 116 minutes. An excellent how-to DVD which teaches many of the basic techniques of natural building and features Jorge Belanko's straw-clay blocks. Spanish with English subtitles. Available from **handprintpress.com/mud-hands-a-house.**

A Brief History of Cob Building

25

MICHAEL G. SMITH

Because of its versatility and widespread availability, earth has been used as a construction material on every continent and in every age. Cob is one of the oldest building materials on the planet—indeed, the first freestanding human dwellings were probably built of mud, or wattle and daub. About 10,000 years ago, the residents of Jericho were using oval hand-formed, sun-dried bricks (adobes), and even today, it's estimated that one-third of the world's population lives in earthen dwellings.

"Cob," the English term for mud building, uses no forms, no bricks and no wooden framework. Similar forms of mud building are common throughout Northern Europe, the Ukraine, the Middle East and the Arabian Peninsula, India, China, the Sahel and equatorial Africa and the American Southwest. I focus here on the English cob tradition because of its historical relevance to the European and North American natural building revival.

Exactly when and how cob building first arose in England remains uncertain, but it is known that cob houses were being built there by the 13th century. Cob houses became the norm in many parts of Britain by the 15th century and stayed that way until industrialization and cheap transportation made brick popular in the late 1800s.

Cob was particularly common in southwestern England and Wales, where the subsoil was a sandy clay, and other building materials, like stone and wood,

FIGURE 25.1. The walls of traditional cob homes in Britain ranged from three feet thick to occasionally nearly twice that, as shown by this doorway in an old Devon home. These extra-thick walls produced a stable interior temperature despite the cool, damp climate. [Credit: Catherine Wanek]

MICHAEL G. SMITH *was a co-director of the Cob Cottage Company from 1993 to 1998. He is the author of* The Cobber's Companion: How to Build Your Own Earthen Home *and co-author of* The Hand-Sculpted House: A Practical and Philosophical Guide to Building a Cob Cottage. *He teaches workshops on cob and many other natural building techniques:* **strawclaywood.com.**

were scarce. English cob was made of clay-based subsoil mixed with straw, water and sometimes sand or crushed shale or flint. The percentage of clay in the mix ranged from 3 percent to 20 percent. It was mixed either by people shoveling and stomping, or by heavy animals such as oxen trampling it.

The stiff mud mixture was usually shoveled with a cob fork onto a stone foundation and trodden into place by workmen on the walls. In a single day, a course or "lift" of cob—anywhere from 6 in. to 3 ft. (15 cm to 1 m) in height but averaging 18 in. (45 cm)—would be placed on the wall. It would be left to dry for as long as two weeks before the next lift was added. Sometimes additional straw was trodden into the top of each layer.

As they dried, the walls were trimmed back substantially with a paring iron—commonly to between 20–36 in. (50–90 cm) thick—leaving them straight and plumb. In this way, cob walls were built as high as 23 ft. (7 m), though they were usually much less. Frames for doors and windows were built in as the wall grew.

Many cob cottages were built by poor tenant farmers and laborers who often worked co-operatively. A team of a few men, working together one day a week, could complete a house in one season. A cottage begun in the spring would receive its thatch roof and interior whitewash in the fall, and its inhabitants would move inside before winter. Often they waited until the following year to plaster the outside with lime-sand stucco so that the walls would have ample time to dry. Cob barns and other outbuildings were sometimes left unplastered.

But cob buildings were not reserved solely for humble peasants. Many townhouses and large manors, built of cob before fired brick became readily available, survive in excellent condition today. An estimated 20,000 cob homes and as many outbuildings remain in use in the county of Devon alone. It was common for well-built cob homes to go for a hundred years without needing repair.

British settlers to other parts of the world carried the technique of cob with them. Early colonists of New Zealand found that the clay soil and tussock grass common on the South Island made excellent cob and constructed at least 8,000 houses there, of which several hundred survive today.

Cob was less popular in Australia, where mud bricks and rammed earth were the preferred earth building techniques, but a few cob buildings survive in New South Wales, Queensland and the vicinity of Melbourne. Cob buildings in North America dating from the same era are few and far between but include a church in Toronto, a house built in 1836 in Penfield, New York, as well as some recently discovered cob houses in Brooklyn, New York.

The English Cob Revival

By the late 1800s, cob building in England, considered primitive and backward, was declining in popularity. In recent decades, however, public attitudes have slowly evolved and traditional cob cottages with their thatched roofs are now valued as historical and picturesque.

As there was virtually no new cob construction in England between World War I and the 1980s, traditional builders took much of their specialized knowledge with them to the grave. But enough information survived to allow a cob building revival in the 1990s that was fueled largely by historical interest and the real estate value of historic cob homes.

In the final decades of the 20th century, many long-neglected cob homes needed repair, causing a resurgence of interest in traditional building techniques. People involved in the restoration of ancient cob buildings became the greatest advocates for the reintroduction of cob as a contemporary building technique.

The first new construction project of the English cob revival was a bus shelter built by restorationist Alfred Howard in 1978 in the village of Down St. Mary. Since then, there has been a slow increase of new cob built in England, especially in Devon. In 1994, Kevin McCabe built a two-story, four-bedroom cob house, the first new cob residence to be built in England in perhaps 70 years. McCabe has since built nearly a dozen new homes and additions and won many awards. In 2001, he completed a 3-story cob house for his family, with 5,000 sq. ft. (450 m²) of living space. In a departure from the traditional architecture of the region, the house was oval in plan, with rounded interior spaces and a spiral staircase. After a fire, the original thatched roof was replaced with slate.

Not content with this impressive accomplishment, in 2010 the McCabes began construction of what Kevin calls "the largest cob house in the world." Actually a complex of buildings including a 3-story main house, a guest annex, workshop and garage, Dingle Dell consists of a quarter mile (400 m) of cob walls weighing a total of 2,000 tons. The walls of the main house are up to 33 in. (10 m) high, and the barn features load-bearing cob pillars. The house was designed to meet PassiveHaus Gold standards and to exceed Sustainable Homes Level 6, the UK's highest rating for energy efficiency. To meet these standards, McCabe took the controversial step of cladding the outside of the house with polystyrene insulation. (Some natural builders have expressed concern that foam covering the entire exterior surface of the house will compromise the vapor permeability of the cob walls and lead to moisture problems over time.) Even before its completion, the project had attracted a great deal of attention from the national press and been featured on a popular television series, *Grand Designs*.

The building technique of these revivalists closely resembles that of their ancestors. They mix Devon's sandy clay subsoil with water and straw (and sometimes sand or "shillet"—a fine gravel of crushed shale) and fork the mixture onto the wall, treading it in place. Walls are generally from 2–3 ft. (60–100 cm) thick, applied

FIGURE 25.2. This two-story cob home in Cornwall, the southwestern-most part of England, was built in 2012 by Adam Weismann and Katy Bryce of Clayworks. The roof is made from reed thatch and the foundation from local stone. The design, materials and building techniques all closely resemble traditional cob houses of the region. [Credit: Ray Main]

in lifts up to 18 in. (45 cm) high. The machine age has, however, altered the traditional process in significant ways: McCabe and others use a tractor or excavator rather than oxen for mixing cob; sometimes the machine is used to load the cob onto the wall as well. But once the cob is on the wall, the old ways take precedence as the cob is trodden in place by foot and beaten into shape with a large wooden paddle.

A new generation of earthen builders is now emerging in England, producing both public art installations and practical shel-

FIGURE 25.3. Linda Smiley of Cob Cottage Company in the kitchen of her cob home. [Credit: Michael G. Smith]

ters using this ancient technique. Adam Weismann and Katy Bryce of Clayworks, for example, have built a number of high-profile cob buildings, including a two-story cob home and a small thatched cottage for the Prince of Wales.

The Development of "Oregon Cob"

Concurrent with the renewed interest in cob in England, there was a parallel revival in the United States, led by the Cob Cottage Company in western Oregon. With less access to traditional knowledge, the building system that has arisen here is sufficiently distinct from British cob that it merits a separate name: "Oregon cob."

By 1989, Cob Cottage Company founders Ianto Evans and Linda Smiley recognized the need for inexpensive, healthy, bioregional housing. Ianto grew up surrounded by cob in Wales and later took part in earthen construction in Africa and Latin America. Experimenting with earthen building in rainy western Oregon, Ianto and Linda chose British cob as a model because of its demonstrated durability in a cold, wet climate.

When starting their first cob structure, Ianto and Linda were unable to locate anybody with

first-hand experience. They relied entirely on their explorations of existing cob structures in Britain and a very sparse literature on the subject, much of it inaccurate and contradictory. The system they developed involved making loaves of stiff mud, called "cobs" (cob itself is an Old English word for loaf). The system has advantages: the mix can be made at some distance from the wall and easily transported by tossing the cobs from person to person as with a bucket brigade. As construction progresses, cobs can be thrown to a builder much higher on the wall than a pitchfork can be raised.

Most Oregon cob builders have shifted to a building technique we call Gaab cob, which combines the control of hand-worked loaves with the speed of traditional trodden cob. Larger chunks of cob mix, stiff but still sticky and workable, are lifted onto the wall. By using either one's fingers or a wooden tool called a cobber's thumb, the new material is married firmly to the wall beneath. The result is a strongly bonded, monolithic wall that should be considerably more resistant to earthquakes and other shear forces than traditional cob.

Another way in which Oregon cob differs from traditional cob is in the attention given to the quality of ingredients and to the proportions of the mix. Whereas cob builders in previous centuries had to use whatever soil was on hand with little or no amendment, we can now cheaply import as much sand or clay as is necessary to make the hardest, most stable mixture. Furthermore, whereas grain straw was formerly a valuable resource for animal bedding, thatching and the like, it is now an underutilized waste product available in huge quantities for little cost. Oregon cob is

characterized by both a high proportion of coarse sand and lots of long, strong straw, which helps strengthen the earthen mass. Since soils vary so much from site to site, mix proportions should always be carefully tested before a wall is built.

Oregon cob is commonly mixed by foot on a tarp. Wet or dry clay soil and sand are mixed by rolling the tarp back and forth; then water is added. Builders dance on the mix to forcibly combine the clay and sand particles. Straw is added slowly as the

dancing continues, and the tarp is rolled back and forth. Although the tarp method works well for many owner-builders, there is often a desire for increased mixing speed on large or contract-built projects. Many people have had good results with commercial mortar mixers and some have used rototillers to mix cob. A tractor or backhoe can rapidly mix very large batches, though quality control can be a challenge.

Better ingredients, more precise proportions and thorough mixing allow the construction

FIGURE 25.4. When mixing cob on a tarp, clay, sand and water are first combined and mixed to a dough-like consistency before straw is added. [Credit Michael G. Smith]

FIGURE 25.5. Cob is most easily trimmed to make surfaces plumb and even at the "leather-hard" stage, when it is firm but not yet dry. [Credit: Joseph F. Kennedy]

of stronger, narrower and more sculptural walls. Exterior walls of Oregon cob are typically between 12–20 in. (30–48 cm) thick; non-load-bearing partitions taper to as little as 4 in. (10 cm) but are more commonly 8 in. (20 cm).

Most Oregon cob buildings have curved walls, niches and nooks and arched windows and doorways. By adding extra straw in the needed direction, the Cob Cottage Company has developed a system for corbelling arches, vaults and projecting shelves beyond the capability of traditional cob.

One quality which attracts many artists and owner-builders to cob is its extreme fluidity of form. Hand-formed from pliable mud, a cob cottage literally becomes a living sculpture. Cob combines nicely with other natural materials including stone, roundwood and straw bales. Because of its capacity to stick to almost anything and to fill awkward gaps left by other materials, cob has been dubbed the duct tape of natural building. It is frequently combined with straw bales and other natural wall systems to create "hybrid homes" (see "Hybrid Homes: Combining Natural Materials for Energy Efficiency," p. 81). It is also a favorite for public art and placemaking projects in which communities come together to hand-sculpt beautiful and functional works of art (see "Building the Natural Village: A Strategy for Repairing Cities" p. 137).

Cob is one of the simplest and cheapest building techniques imaginable, making it particularly appealing to first-time builders. Since it requires no machinery, little training and few tools, cob building is accessible to almost everyone, including children and those with limited financial resources, provided they can secure a building site. Many new cob buildings are created by community efforts similar to an old-time barn raising. In North America, the technique has become especially popular amongst people wishing to build their own homes very inexpensively, often without official permission. This makes it challenging to estimate how many

FIGURE 25.6. Hilda Dawe's cob home in British Columbia, Canada, designed and built by Cobworks, demonstrates the sculptural potential of Oregon cob. [Credit: Catherine Wanek]

new cob homes have been built in the last two decades.

Current Events

Since the Cob Cottage Company offered its first workshop in 1993, the technique has taken off in unexpected directions. Thousands of people have been trained in cob construction, many of whom have gone on to teach workshops of their own in other countries and settings. Modern cob buildings have appeared in Canada, New Zealand, Australia, Mexico, Nicaragua, Costa Rica, Argentina, Ecuador, France, Spain, Italy, Denmark, Finland, Romania, Armenia, South Africa, India and Thailand—that I know of. Dozens of individuals and small organizations offer cob trainings around North America, with the greatest concentration in the Pacific Northwest, followed by the Southeast, southwestern US and southwestern Canada.

Cob building techniques continue to evolve, with new developments in mix ingredients and proportions, mixing speed and building efficiency. One recent adaptation is high-fiber cob with very high straw content but little or no sand. In addition to eliminating one of the ingredients and sometimes saving work and expense, this lightweight cob partially addresses one of traditional cob's major disadvantages, its poor insulation value (see "High-Fiber Adobes," p. 177). Another innovation with the same purpose is "bale-cob," a system for building with straw bales stiffened and contained by cob.

The future of cob is difficult to predict. Due in part to the wide variability of soils from site to site, which complicates

FIGURE 25.7. Cob's sculptural and thermal mass properties make it an excellent choice for heat-retaining hearths and other interior elements in any natural home. This fireplace was handcrafted by Vital Systems, Timothy Kennedy's natural building crew. [Credit: Catherine Wanek]

mix testing and engineering, and also to the amount of labor required for manual mixing and building and the extended drying time necessary in cool climates, cob has yet to make it into the mainstream of building practices either in North America or the UK. While cob homes have been built with official building permission in the US, Canada, England, Ireland and New Zealand, the development and adoption of building codes for cob has been slow. The Cob Research Institute, a non-profit based in California, is currently assembling code and testing information from around the world in the hopes of writing a code for cob.

Despite these obstacles, in combination with other natural building materials, cob provides a real solution to many of the economic, social and environmental problems associated with the modern building industry. Cob's sculptural beauty and its accessibility to owner-builders with minimal resources and training ensure that this ancient technique will continue to be practiced, improved and celebrated far into the future.

RESOURCES

Books

• Bee, Becky. *The Cob Builder's Handbook: You Can Hand-Sculpt Your Own Home*, Groundworks, 1997. A clearly written step-by-step guidebook, including everything from design to plasters.

• Evans, Ianto, Michael G. Smith and Linda Smiley. *The Hand-Sculpted House: A Practical and Philosophical Guide to Building a Cob Cottage*, Chelsea Green, 2002. The most comprehensive book on cob construction, with extensive supplementary material on natural building philosophy, site considerations and designing a compact, comfortable cottage.

• Norton, John. *Building with Earth*, Intermediate Technology Publications, 1997. A good, brief introduction to general principles of earth building.

• Snell, Clark and Tim Callahan. *Building Green: A Complete How-to Guide to Alternative Building Methods: Earth Plaster, Straw Bale, Cordwood, Cob, Living Roofs*. Sterling Publishing Company, 2009. Contains excellent photos of the cob mixing process, as well as great information on other building techniques.

• Weismann, Adam and Katy Bryce. *Building with Cob, A Step-by-Step Guide*, Green Books, 2006. A UK-oriented cob building guide with good information on mechanical mixing.

Videos

• *Building with Earth: Oregon's Cob Cottage Company*, Inner Growth Videos, 1995. A brief, entertaining introduction to the "whys" and "hows" of cob. Available from the Cob Cottage Company: **cobcottage.com**.

• *First Earth: Uncompromising Ecological Architecture*, **davidsheen.com/firstearth**. A sprawling documentary about the cob building movement.

Organizations

• Cob Cottage Company: **cobcottage.com**. Workshops, consulting, mail-order books and videos, networking and information on cob and other natural building systems.

• Cob Research Institute: **cobcode.org**. Spearheading the effort to develop a building code for cob.

• Devon Earth Builders Association: **devonearthbuilding.com**. Dedicated to the research, promotion and revival of traditional cob building in Devon. You can also find links to cob specialists in the UK on their site.

Websites

• Cob Workshops: **cobworkshops.org**. Most complete and up-to-date international listing of cob workshops.

Rammed Earth: From Pisé to PISE 26

SCOTT GROMETER

People often overlook earth building in the search for environmentally, economically and socially sustainable building technologies. They associate the term "earth building" with primitive materials and techniques, limited to the most arid of climates. They imagine that earthen structures built elsewhere would necessarily be dirty, damp, cold and unlikely to survive the ravages of rain, freezing temperatures or earthquakes.

A handful of dedicated architects, engineers and builders, however, are working to quell this resistance to earthen walls as they investigate new ways of applying modern technology to an ancient form of construction. The myths are slowly giving way. Statistics show that earth-walled structures can, and frequently do, outper-

SCOTT GROMETER *has a degree in fine arts with an emphasis in architecture, and hands-on experience in French pisé.*

form conventional wood-frame and concrete-walled buildings in aspects of comfort, efficiency, safety and longevity.

While much of North American earth building is still executed in adobe, particularly in the more arid southwestern states, the greatest advances have come in

the age-old technique of rammed earth, or *pisé de terre*. Pisé differs from adobe brick in both composition and technique. Adobes—unbaked mud bricks—are typically a clay, sand and straw mix which require a lengthy drying time before they can be mortared in courses to form walls. The

FIGURE 26.1. The majority of the 3,000-year-old, over 4,000-mile-long "Great Wall of China" was constructed of earth, hand-tamped by hundreds of thousands of workers. In later centuries, the rammed earth walls were faced with fired brick, for greater longevity. [Credit: Catherine Wanek]

189

bricks are usually of a relatively low crush strength, and if left exposed, are subject to erosion.

On the other hand, rammed earth involves a carefully measured amount of pure mineral earth—with its constituent components of clay, sand and aggregate—mixed with a small amount of water and sometimes Portland cement, and compacted into wall forms. After completion, the forms can be removed and reused. As the resulting rock-hard monolith cures, it takes on a greater crush strength than adobe. It is also less susceptible to erosion. Eliminating the extra steps of forming, drying, transporting and laying up bricks gives rammed earth the edge over adobe in labor costs.

Pisé is already a proven building material in a variety of regions, climates and architectural styles. For more than 6,000 years, and in virtually every region of the world, rammed earth has been employed for structures great and small. Portions of China's 3,000-year-old Great Wall were constructed of rammed earth, as were many of the archeological remains of the Middle East and Africa. Introduced in Europe by the Romans, one finds rammed earth structures from Italy to England. In some regions of France, particularly the Rhône Valley, virtually every historic structure is *pisé de terre*.

French and German immigrants of the late 1700s and early 1800s brought the pisé technique to America. Large stately

FIGURE 26.2. A contemporary solar rammed earth condo in a neighbourhood development near Lyon, France, constructed entirely from rammed earth and compressed earth blocks, called "Domain de la Terre." These sturdy and comfortable homes are in high demand. [CREDIT: Catherine Wanek]

homes done in pisé, many still in use, ranged throughout New York, New Jersey, Pennsylvania and Washington, DC. By the mid-1850s, pisé had spread to the South, and then throughout the Midwest during the westward expansion. The US government became interested in rammed earth, publishing a Department of Agriculture bulletin titled "Rammed Earth Walls for Buildings" as early as 1926. Earth building seemed destined to flourish. But the end of WWII brought a dramatic increase in housing demand, and with it a shift to the American tract home, built of lightweight, easily transportable and seemingly inexhaustible materials. Pisé slipped into obscurity.

Then in the 1970s, during the energy crisis, the concept of earth building resurfaced. In Western Australia, where there was a shortage of timber and an abundance of termites, designers and contractors already familiar with conventional masonry techniques were quick to accept the reintroduction of rammed earth. Giles Honen, who spurred the Western Australian movement, established the firm Stabilized Earth Structures. With ten affiliate companies employing his techniques, production increased to nearly 200 buildings per year.

In France, graduate students from the architectural school at Grenoble established CRATerre (the International Center for Earth Construction). Inspired by a rich history of French earth building, this group set out to study and adapt earth building techniques to modern applications. CRAterre gained international recognition in the early 1980s by sponsoring an architectural competition for the entirely new earth village of Le Domaine de la Terre, near Lyon. The success of this project prompted plans for the International Raw Earth Institute, a resource and educational center for the applications of earth architecture.

Meanwhile, in North America, rammed earth was being used primarily as an alternative to adobe in the American Southwest. The advent of stabilized rammed earth, with the addition of a small amount (usually ten percent) of Portland cement to the earth mixture, yielded higher strength walls with a lower rate of moisture transfer. More advanced forming systems were developed, and power equipment helped speed up the placement process.

In 1978 in Northern California, an industrial engineer named David Easton formed the design/build and consulting firm Rammed Earth Works. For over three decades, Easton has tirelessly pushed the frontier of rammed earth into wider application and greater public acceptance. Situated in a seismically active and climatically diverse region, Rammed Earth Works has pioneered a variety of new techniques and amendments to the materials. Their reinforced structures have been approved by building departments with even

FIGURE 26.3. A modern rammed earth crew utilizes pneumatic tampers and steel form work to compress the clay, sand and cement mixture. In the foreground, a cut-off piece of PVC pipe is placed in the corner so that the finished rammed earth wall will have a rounded corner. [Credit: David Shaw]

the most stringent seismic engineering requirements, and many have been exposed to repeated earthquake loading. Easton has designed and built homes ranging in climate from the Sierra Nevada mountains to the rain forest of the Northern California Coast.

After years of labor-intensive work in stabilized rammed earth, Easton recognized that if the material was to enjoy truly widespread application, a system would have to evolve to speed the process and make it more palatable to the existing construction industry. Inspired by the gunnite-shooting technology of swimming pool builders, Easton developed a new technique coined PISE (for pneumatically impacted stabilized earth). In this method, compaction is attained by spraying the earth mixture horizontally against a rigid, one-walled form. This differs from conventional rammed earth, in which the soil is manually tamped or rammed downwards in-between forms.

The process to construct a PISE wall is as follows. Pour a concrete footing and slab and allow it to cure. Then, using plywood (or other suitable rigid material), erect a form wall to form the inside perimeter of the walls. Attach displacement boxes to the forms to leave openings for doors and windows. Install a wall-high steel reinforcing grid, and set electrical conduit and hardware in place. Then blow the mix against the form to the desired thickness, and finish the outside surface with a hand float.

The resulting exterior surface is not unlike stucco, and apart from a clear sealant, no other treatment is necessary. Plastering of the smooth interior walls is also optional. As with rammed earth, the roof system is the choice of the designer. Because the technique yields considerable labor and time savings over conventional rammed earth, and because it utilizes the services of conventional building trades, Easton is optimistic about widespread acceptance.

Earth construction in its myriad forms would seem to offer obvious and immediate environmental advantages that extend to all earth building techniques—adobe, cob, etc. The industry cites the following statistics for a typical earth-walled structure over conventional stick frame: per unit

FIGURE 26.4. Soledad Canyon Earth Builders uses locally sourced crusher fines with three percent Portland cement as a "stabilizer." The cement is dry mixed with the crusher fines, before water is added. Soil mixtures are tested for compressive strength before being used in the construction of a home. [Credit: David Shaw]

timber consumption reduced by up to 50 percent; reduced energy consumption for heating and cooling through effective use of thermal mass (wall thickness typically ranges from 18–24 in. [45–60 cm]); virtual elimination of toxic substances found in wall coatings, construction adhesives and wood preservatives. The less obvious but perhaps most significant benefit of pisé, adobe and cob are their longevity. As centuries-old structures throughout the world attest, a properly designed and built earth home is likely to be standing long after most wood-framed structures are in landfills.

Earth building requires a number of special design considerations. Finding suitable earth for building is important for a quality finished product. If not available onsite, soil needs to be imported. Rock quarries are often a good source since tailings are available inexpensively and are often of ideal composition. The color of the material is also important. Because the addition of a cement stabilizer can alter the appearance, potential soil mixtures should be tested by ramming or shooting a small test wall.

The choice of method, either rammed earth or PISE, will most likely be influenced by site conditions. Small lots with tight setbacks or sites on steep hillsides may not be appropriate for conventional rammed earth, which needs room for mixing and tractor loading of the material into the forms. The PISE method, on the other hand, has been successfully applied in dense urban settings and on steep terrain.

Rammed earth and PISE structures require "a good hat and a good pair of boots." Sufficient roof overhangs and adequate footings will ensure a dry, comfortable structure. The concern is not that the walls will wash away, but rather that they might become saturated due to excessive exposure. Porosity tests show stabilized rammed earth to be comparable to concrete block, so this point need not be a cause for alarm. For ease of construction and seismic concerns, low-aspect-ratio structures are preferred, though many successful multi-story structures have been built. Because forming is an integral part of rammed

FIGURE 26.5. Inside a Swiss hospital solarium, this rammed earth wall absorbs both heat and moisture, contributing to a healthy indoor climate, while displaying an array of colors and architectural possibilities. [Credit: Catherine Wanek]

earth construction, designs that are modular are most efficient to build. Reusing different sized forms throughout the project can reduce labor, costs and waste.

Style considerations are more guidelines than restrictions. Earth building is not limited to prototypical antiquities nor to traditional or period designs. Contemporary examples are being constructed in diverse parts of the world. More recent experiments in color mixing or banding of different color layers have led to some interesting art forms.

The construction costs of rammed earth and PISE vary. At present, the square-foot cost of the PISE technique is roughly comparable to that of custom wood-frame construction. Labor is the major expense, so as more builders enter the field and the process is streamlined, increasing economies of scale will likely result in a net reduction of cost. Those in the industry point out that actual construction costs do not reflect the more significant long-term savings of reduced energy consumption, low maintenance and long life.

RESOURCES

Books
• Easton, David. *The Rammed Earth House*, 2nd ed., Chelsea Green, 2007. A thorough guide to rammed earth, including traditional, mechanized and PISE. Good chapters on design and landscape issues.
• Houben, Hugo and Hubert Guillaud. *Earth Construction: A Comprehensive Guide.* Intermediate Technology Publications, 1994. This detailed, well-illustrated technical guide to many forms of earth building contains good information on low-cost, low-tech rammed earth, with or without stabilization.
• Jaquin, Paul and Charles Augarde. *Earth Building: History, Science and Conservation*, BRE Press, 2012. Presents a wide-ranging view of earth construction including adobe, cob and rammed earth, a history of earth building, principles from soil mechanics and preservation techniques.
• King, Bruce. *Buildings of Earth and Straw: Structural Design for Rammed Earth and Straw-Bale Architecture*, Ecological Design Press, 1996. An engineering approach to rammed earth.
• Norton, John. *Building with Earth*, Intermediate Technology Publications, 1997. A good, brief introduction to general principles of earth building, including testing soils.
• Walker, Peter. *Rammed Earth: Design and Construction Guidelines*, IHS BRE Press, 2010. Promotes the use of unstabilized rammed earth walls for new construction in the UK.

Organizations
• CRAterre: **craterre.org**. Professional school of earth architecture, engineering and construction, especially for developing actions. Maison Levrat, Parc Fallavier, France.
• Rammed Earth Works: **rammedearthworks.com**. David Easton's design/build firm; also offers consultation, referrals and workshops. Napa, California.
• SIREWALL, Inc.: **sirewall.com**. Founder Meror Krayenhoff's company offers consulting, training and construction support for this proprietary system of stabilized insulated rammed earth (SIRE) earth walls. Salt Spring Island, British Columbia, Canada.
• Soledad Canyon Earth Builders: **rammed-earth-homes.com**. Design/build company for rammed earth and adobe homes in the US Southwest. Las Cruces, New Mexico.

Website
• Historic Rammed Earth: **historicrammedearth.co.uk**

Compressed Earth Blocks 27

HUBERT GUILLAUD

Compressed earth blocks (CEBs) are a relatively recent evolution of molded earth blocks, better known as adobes. However, the idea of compacting earth to improve the strength of the material is an old one. Archeologists have found wooden pestles used by the Anglo-Saxons in Europe to compact earth in molds. This technique is generally called rammed earth or pisé.

The very first earth block press was derived from a wine press in France at the beginning of the 19th century by François Cointeraux (1730–1840), an architect and entrepreneur from the city of Lyon. Thanks to a number of enthusiastic disciples and the network of scientific societies that had sprung up across Europe during the Enlightenment, Cointeraux's ideas spread widely, most notably in Germany, where pressed blocks were used both in rural and urban architecture. The technique spread all the way from England to Italy, but for a long time remained in the shadow of a stronger interest in pisé.

Only at the start of the 20th century were the first modern mechanical presses created. These presses had heavy lids that would come down forcefully into the mold, and later also pistons connected to a mobile mold bottom, which would further compress the block by pushing upward into the mold after the lid was closed. The baked earth and sand-lime brick industries had already been using similar presses, some of which were later motorized.

CEBs became widely used only after the Cinva Ram was invented in Colombia in 1952. Developed by engineer Raul Ramirez at the CINVA (Centro Interamericano de Vivienda y Planeamiento) research center, this small manual press was made under license and sold all around the world. It was also widely copied, so that a variety of manual presses came into being, followed in the 1970s and '80s by motorized presses and eventually by larger units designed for industrial production.

Over this time, a market for the production and use of

HUBERT GUILLAUD *is a professor in the School of Architecture of Grenoble, France, and scientific director of the CRAterre-ENSAG research laboratory of the Architecture, Environment and Construction Cultures Unit, which is based there. He is the chairman of the UNESCO Chair "Earthen architecture, building cultures and sustainable development," an international network of 41 academic entities in 21 countries. As an expert for UNESCO's World Heritage Centre, he has been involved in the conservation of historical earth building sites in Oman and Iran. He has also worked on various development projects valorizing the use of local materials and building cultures in developing countries. He is the author of numerous scientific publications.*

CEBs has also developed. This emerging market was strongly supported by an investment in scientific research carried out by CRAterre (the International Center for Earth Construction at the School of Architecture of Grenoble, France) in particular. CRAterre published a large body of literature in the eighties and nineties, including production manuals, testing procedures and production norms, leading to the creation of a French building code for CEBs.

At the same time, CRAterre began a large-scale pilot project on the French island of Mayotte, between northern Madagascar and mainland East Africa. This was in response to a request made by the local Public Works Author-

ity and the Real Estate Society of Mayotte. An initial project of eight CEB housing units for expatriate state employees jump-started the construction of numerous public buildings including primary schools, middle and high schools and governmental offices. These were followed by twenty thousand more housing units built between 1981 and 2000. Mayotte is still the most significant example of CEBs applied to social housing at such a large scale.

A Promising Technology

How CEBs are produced varies depending on whether they are produced at the local craftsman level using manual or semi-mechanized presses, or at the

industrial level, which uses the same organizational systems as the baked brick industry. Manual presses are generally small and portable and can handle only the processes of compression and de-molding. Motorized production units may be either portable or stationary, and are sometimes automated to handle materials preparation and block unloading in addition to compression and demolding.

Typically, average resistance in dry compressive strength is around 725 lb./sq. in. (50 kg/cm² or 5 millipascals) and can reach, in ideal conditions of production and with cement stabilization, up to 1,740 lb./sq. in. (12 millipascals or 120 kg/cm²) (Houben and Guillaud, 1994). With cement stabilization, and under ideal conditions of production, CEBs can be produced at any time of year, as long as special measures are taken to protect the production and storage sites from rain and extreme heat.

The most common dimensions are nominally 12×6×4 in. (30×15×10 cm). These dimensions, being modular, allow many different stacking and bonding patterns in the wall. A block of this size may weigh between 14–18 lbs (6.5–8 kg), depending whether the press is manual or

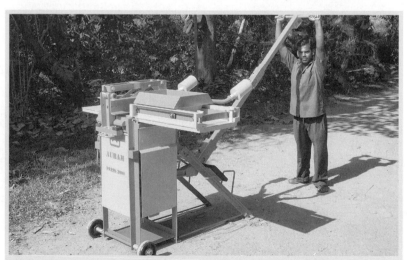

FIGURE 27.1. The hand-operated Auram Press 3000 developed by the Auroville Earth Institute in India. [Credit: Serge Maïni]

hydraulic. If the blocks are much heavier than this, their weight could slow down the rate of construction.

On today's market, there are four major types of blocks, depending on the kind of press. Solid blocks are usually rectangular, but may also be cubic or hexagonal. Their uses are very diverse, including walls, floors, paving and roofs. Hollow blocks have cavities that displace between 5 percent and as much as 30 percent of the volume. This hollowness can improve both the adhesion of mortar and the handling of the blocks by reducing their weight. Honeycomb blocks with multiple small cavities offer the advantage of being light, but require sophisticated molds as well as higher compacting pressures. Interlocking blocks fit together like Lego blocks without the need for mortar, but also require sophisticated molds and high compacting pressures.

The preferred soil type is high in sand, low in clay (15–30 percent by volume). Any stones over ¾ in. (20 mm) should be sifted out. In order to improve their water resistance, CEBs are often stabilized by the addition of small quantities of lime or Portland cement. Unstabilized CEB structures are typically protected by wide roof overhangs and by coating the outside of the walls with a lime distemper or stabilized earth plaster, but when stabilized they are very resistant to weathering. When adding cement, the recommended proportion is 6 to 8 percent by volume. Beyond this, the cost of the blocks goes up without significantly increasing their quality.

The optimal moisture content of soil used for making CEBs is between 10 to 12 percent. Depending on the scale of production, soil, stabilizer and water can either be combined by hand (by moving and turning the pile with a shovel two or three times) or with a rotating mechanical mixer. The mix is then poured into the molds and compressed. Cement-stabilized blocks cure over a minimum of 9 days, with 28 days being the optimum. CEBs coming out of the presses are stored in stacks with alternate layers being laid on their short and long sides, no more than a dozen layers high, with a slight air gap between each block. These piles are covered with a plastic film, which favors a damp cure.

Once properly cured, CEBs are assembled into walls using standard bricklaying and masonry

FIGURE 27.2. Compressed earth blocks curing in the sun. Dennilton, South Africa. [Credit: NextAid]

techniques. The mortar may be a simple slurry made of the same soil mix as the blocks themselves, spread or brushed very thinly between the blocks for bonding. Cement-sand mortar may also be used for higher strength, or when construction during freeze-thaw cycles causes stability concerns. The main issue to avoid is an inconsistent bond between the mortar and the CEBs.

The Ecological Advantage

Unlike fired bricks, which are traditionally baked in wood-fired furnaces, the production of CEBs does not contribute to deforestation. Making CEBs does not emit toxic polluting fumes as do bricks fired using wood, tires or oil, as is practiced in several countries. This material doesn't depend on the use of non-renewable energy resources in either production or actual construction. Any energy consumed for the transportation of materials can be significantly reduced by using earth from the construction site itself or its near vicinity. Earth displaced by highway construction and other public works projects could be used as well.

Another advantage of using earth as a building material is that, unlike sand and gravel, which are often obtained from quarries and rivers, it is less destructive to natural environments (though care must still be taken to responsibly source the earth utilized). Compared to other building systems, including fired brick, concrete and adobe, the production of CEBs requires minimal use of water, an increasingly scarce resource critical to humans, animals and plants alike. Unstabilized CEBs do not generate any industrial or

FIGURE 27.3. CEB house under construction in the Philippines. [Credit: CRAterre]

chemical waste and, at the end of the building's useful lifetime, will be almost fully reabsorbed by nature.

The Financial Advantage

The production of CEBs remains a very light industry, using mainly manual presses or mobile motorized presses. The low level of investment makes compressed earth block infrastructure very cost-effective. Applied in a decentralized way, this technology can create jobs at every level of the production and construction chain. CEBs are also well adapted to production and construction by owner-builders.

Because it requires neither a large investment in infrastructure nor a massive use of energy, CEB technology can help to reduce the costs of construction businesses and to balance the expenditures of the construction industry as a whole. These effects are especially relevant for developing countries that have to import foreign capital and energy sources.

The Technical Advantage

Like other earthen building techniques, CEBs have physical properties that regulate temperature and humidity and support good bioclimatic functioning of the building. In appropriate climates, their good thermal mass stores and then releases solar energy, thereby moderating

FIGURE 27.4. Construction of a school covered by groined CEB vaults in Auroville, India. [Credit: Serge Maïni]

FIGURE 27.5. A three-story building constructed at Auroville of CEBs and ferrocement. [Credit: Serge Maïni]

FIGURE 27.6. This dwelling by architect Dario Angulo in Colombia combines CEBs with wood, bamboo, tile and other natural materials to elegant effect. Note the judicious use of concrete to create a structural bond beam in this seismically active country. [Credit: Dario Angulo]

interior temperature fluctuations. Compaction increases the density of the blocks, which significantly improves their compressive strength, as well as their resistance to erosion by water, which can cause great damage to other kinds of earthen walls.

A single mechanical press can produce from 800 to over 5,000 blocks per day, enough to build a 1,200 sq. ft. (110 m²) house. The highest performance machines can produce from 8,000 to 17,000 or more blocks per day. The production rate is limited more by the ability to get material into the machine, than by the machine itself. The choice manufacturers make is often between the greater financial investment in purchasing a high-performance machine versus creating jobs with less costly presses and more manpower.

CEBs are much appreciated by masons for their regular shapes, sharp edges and consistent dimensions. They come in dimensions that allow them to be used in weight-bearing walls, in partitions and as infill for wood-framed structures. They can also be made into special shapes such as preformed lintels and non-rectangular elements for arches, vaults and domes. These qualities allow the construction of truly beautiful works of masonry, especially when the blocks are left visible and unplastered.

The Future of Building with Earth

Because of their strength, beauty and consistency, CEBs can easily satisfy the needs of today's architects, engineers and builders. In many parts of the world (especially in developing countries), this material represents a real technological improvement and has won over many author-ities and builders. Thanks to the ever-expanding body of scientific and technical information and in-depth university curricula and professional trainings, there is a solid future for CEBs in construction around the world.

The quality of the blocks (and the resulting buildings) depends on the care used in selecting and preparing the earth and on the right choice of production tools. To guarantee safety and quality control, a specific set of rules must be followed both in the design and in the actual building process. Architects' and builders' skills must be guaranteed by equally specific professional training. This training already exists and is offered by several institutions and associations. A post-master course is offered at the National Superior School of Architecture of Grenoble and many other universities in the world (see also "Building with Earth in Auroville," p. 441).

The lack of official building codes published by authorized

RESOURCES

Books
- Boubeker, Sid and Hugo Houben. *Compressed Earth Blocks: Standards*, Centre for the Development of Industry & CRAterre-EAG, 1998.
- Guillaud, Hubert, Thierry Joffroy and Pascal Odul. *Compressed Earth Blocks. Vol. 2: Manual of Design and Construction*, Eschborn: Deutsches Zentrum für Entwicklungstechnologien—GATE, 1995.
- Houben, Hugo and Hubert Guillaud, *Earth Construction: A Comprehensive Guide*, Intermediate Technology Publications, 1994.
- Houben, Hugo, Vincent Rigassi and Philippe Garnier. *Compressed Earth Blocks: Production Equipment*, Centre for the Development of Industry & CRAterre-EAG. 1994.
- Mäini, Serge, Alexandre Douline and Sylvain Arnoux. *The Production and Use of Compressed Earth Blocks: A Training Manual for Technicians and Entrepreneurs*, CRAterre-EAG & AV-BC, 1992.
- Mesbah, Ali, Jean-Claude Morel, Hugo Houben et al. *Compressed Earth Blocks: Testing Procedures*, Centre for the Development of Enterprise, ENTPE & CRAterre-EAG, 2000.
- Norton, John, *Building with Earth: A Handbook*, Intermediate Technology Publications, 1986.
- Rigassi, Vincent. *Compressed Earth Blocks. Vol. 1: Manual of Production*, Eschborn: Deutsches Zentrum für Entwicklungstechnologien—GATE, 1995.

Videos
- *Sustainable Building Technologies: Compressed Earth Blocks.* Building Advisory Service and Information Network (BASIN), DesignWrite Productions, CRAterre, et al. Rugby: DesignWrite Productions. 1994.

Organizations
- Auroville Earth Institute: **earth-auroville.com**. Research publications and information on earth building for development, especially with compressed earth blocks. Auroshilpam, Auroville, India.
- Centre de la Construction et du Logement de Cacavelli: **ccltogo.tg.refer.org**. Production of blocks, technical assistance, training. Lomé, Togo.
- CRAterre: **craterre.org**. Professional school of earth architecture, engineering and construction.
- Tierratec: **tierratec.com**. Design, production, technical assistance and training. Bogotá, Colombia.

bodies—though being progressively developed—still represents a handicap to greater acceptance of CEB technology. However, the processes necessary for quality control in production and construction have been codified and could be translated overnight into building codes anywhere on Earth. All this normalization process requires is the political will of public authorities and building control institutions, sadly still lagging behind in France at a time when many other countries (including Switzerland, Germany, the US and Australia) are establishing their own norms and specifications. It is to be hoped that such pioneering attitudes will keep spreading across borders. Pressure from the general public and from the building community in particular will certainly lead to greater official acceptance in the near future.

It has taken most of the last 50 years for Earth to recover its status as a building material. This change occurred thanks to the counterculture movement of the 1960s followed by the search for less energy-consuming solutions brought about by the energy crises of 1973 and 1979, which encouraged interest in bioclimatic architecture, and finally to the paradigm of sustainable development. Due to their label of "modernity," CEBs undoubtedly played a crucial role in this wider movement to return raw earth building practices to the consciousness of the construction world. As to the future of earthen building and design, the possibilities are as endless as the human imagination.

(*Translated from the French by* Jan Erkelens.)

Building with Earthbags

JOSEPH F. KENNEDY AND KELLY HART

Earthbag construction has emerged over the past couple of decades as an important technique in the natural building movement. Sandbags have, of course, been used for many decades by military forces to create bunkers and other structures and for temporary walls by archeologists. In recent years, however, the earthbag technique has been improved in order to create more permanent structures.

In 1976, Gernot Minke at the Research Laboratory for Experimental Building at Kassel Polytechnic College in Germany began to investigate the question of how natural building materials like sand and gravel could be used for building houses without the use of binders. He filled fabric bags with pumice, because it weighs less and has better thermal insulating properties than ordinary sand and gravel. His first successful experiments were with corbelled domes, but he later also made vertical walled structures using long pumiced-filled tubes of material lashed together with bamboo poles.

Later, Persian architect Nader Khalili, with his students and associates, built a number of prototype structures at his school and research center, the California Institute of Earth Art and Architecture (CalEarth) in Hesperia, California. Khalili's experiments with earthbags emerged out of an exploration of how to build structures on the moon and Mars.

His vision was to create domed and vaulted buildings of site-woven sacks filled with lunar soil in order to save the immense costs of rocketing building materials from the Earth. Joseph Kennedy was working with Khalili at the time, and helped build the initial lunar prototype structures using flood control sacks obtained from the local fire station. Now run by Khalili's children, CalEarth continues to promote earthbag building globally.

Earthbag building is essentially rammed earth in a flexible form. It is literally dirt cheap, as it uses locally available site soil and polypropylene or burlap sacks, which often can be obtained free or at low cost. Khalili eventually chose to work with long tubes of the same bag material, calling this technique "superadobe." Whether in bag or tube form, earthbag building demands few

JOSEPH F. KENNEDY *is a designer, writer and peripatetic scholar of natural building and ecological design. A former student of Nader Khalili, he teaches earthbag construction as well as other natural building techniques.*

KELLY HART *is a video producer, builder and founder of* greenhomebuilding.com, earthbagbuilding.com *and* dreamgreenhomes.com *and shares* naturalbuildingblog.com *with Dr. Owen Geiger.*

skills, is easy to learn and can go up extremely quickly, much faster than any other manual earth-building technique.

Earthbag construction is adaptable to a wide range of site conditions and available fill materials. When built properly, earthbag structures—especially domes—are extremely strong, as shown by International Council of Building Officials (ICBO) testing at CalEarth. While some structures have proven resistant to earthquakes, fires and floods, additional testing is necessary to determine the most appropriate detailing for these situations. As the bags themselves are light-weight and easily transported, they are useful for remote locations and for emergency shelter.

Materials and Tools

One essential material for building with earthbags is, of course, the bags themselves, which are commonly made of polypropylene. Woven polypropylene sacks come in a variety of sizes for grain, feed and flood control and also come in tube form. Burlap sacks have also been used but are not as durable and are often more expensive. Joseph Kennedy used custom-sewn burlap bags for an art piece in Prague by Nobuho Nagasawa in 1993. A recent inno-

vation by Brazilian engineer Fernando Pacheco is the use of long tubes of raschel mesh, made out of synthetic acrylic fabric, for a technique he calls "hyperadobe."

The other essential material is the fill, which may include sand, clay, pumice and/or gravel. While the ideal mixture would be a standard adobe mix of sand and clay, pretty much any subsoil can be used. Steve Kemble and Carol Escott have used decomposed coral in the Bahamas with excellent results. The fill can be either damp or dry, but moistening it and then tamping it in the bags creates a more stable structure.

The most important consideration for bag choice is the kind of fill. The weaker the fill material, the stronger the bags must be. In some cases (as with gravel for a foundation course), it is recommended to use double bags, with one inside the other. It is essential to keep the bags covered when work on the wall is not in progress, and they should be plastered as soon as possible to protect them from deterioration due to ultraviolet solar radiation.

Additional materials include barbed wire, used to keep the bags from slipping and for tensile strength (especially with domes),

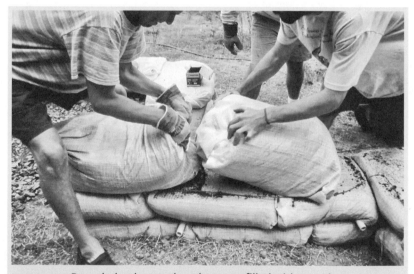

FIGURE 28.1. Recycled polypropylene bags are filled with gravel as a non-wicking foundation for a straw bale structure. Note the barbed wire to keep the bags from slipping and to add additional tensile strength to the wall. The small plastic tubes are used as "chase" to thread straps, wire or twine to tie together the foundation, straw bale walls and roof plate to counter seismic or other loads. [Credit: Kate Lundquist]

and regular wire or polypropylene twine, used to tie the bags together and to provide anchors for plaster lath. For extremely strong structures, cement can be added to the fill to create soil-cement. Old nails, fencing staples or wire are often used to pin bags closed, create new shapes and keep barbed wire in place.

The necessary tools are readily available or easily constructed. The basics are a shovel, wheelbarrow and tamper. It is convenient to make a simple funnel to hold the bag open while it is being filled, and this can be done by simply cutting the bottom off a plastic bucket of the right size. Longer tube-shaped bags can be filled by inserting a tube of cardboard or PVC.

A tamper is used to compact the bags once they are in place. Tampers are often made of welded steel or wood. A serviceable homemade tamper can be made from a large yogurt container filled with concrete attached to a stout staff. A large coffee can is handy for tossing soil up to those working higher on the wall.

The Building Process

The process of building with earthbags is quite simple. The site is first prepared; often a rubble trench foundation is used as a base for the bags. In wet climates or on sites with poorly drained soils, the use of a French drain is advised. Material removed during excavation can be saved to fill the bags, setting aside topsoil and organic materials for other uses.

The fill material is then prepared by removing large rocks and sticks from the subsoil. For short non-structural walls, the soil can be used dry, but for structural purposes, the fill is evenly moistened and left overnight. The material should be just damp enough to compact well, but not so wet that water oozes out during compaction. In moist climates, the first couple of layers of bags are filled with gravel to preclude vertical wicking of water into the wall.

The bags can be filled in several ways. They can be partially filled on the ground using a funnel or a homemade stand, or with one person holding the

FIGURE 28.2. Tamping earth-filled tubes in Dennilton, South Africa. The tubes are allowed to go long at the corners for additional structural stability. [Credit: Joseph F. Kennedy]

FIGURE 28.3. Tubular earthbags utilized to create a self-supporting dome structure at CalEarth, Hesperia, California. [Credit: Joseph F. Kennedy]

bag open while another fills it, then moved into position and filled completely. It is preferable to finish filling bags in place in order to avoid having to pick up and move the heavy bag. Large bags can be filled in place from a wheelbarrow.

Bags high up on the wall can be filled with shovels or cans. Tubular bags can be filled from both ends by placing soil in one end, then picking up the end of the tube and shifting the soil to the middle of the bag. To avoid straining your back, tubes should be no longer than 20 ft. long (6 m). Another technique is to gather the tubular bag around a 1–2 ft. (0.3–0.6 m) length of pipe that holds the bag open and allows the bag to be let out gradually as it is filled. A mechanical pump can make filling extremely fast and easy.

Before the bags are filled (unless they have already been sewn to create a rectangular bottom), the corners are poked in, squaring the bag ends. This process produces a more uniform wall surface, minimizing the use of plaster. The first bag in a row is usually pinned securely, and subsequent bags are folded closed and laid down with the folded end butted up to the factory-sewn end of the previous bag—much easier than sewing each bag closed. In

order to get a secure fold, it is important not to overfill the bag. Bags can be stitched closed if need be, but usually it is sufficient to fold the bag under and tamp it in place.

Once a row of bags is laid, they are checked for plumb and proper placement, adjusted and then gently pressed into place by standing on them. The tamper is used for final compaction, usually after a complete row has been placed. It is important to lay the bags in a running bond as with bricks: the joints of the previous row are covered by the bags of the next row.

After each course of bags has been placed and tamped, two strands of barbed wire are stretched along the bags and temporarily held in place with weights or secured with nails. The barbed wire should be of the four-prong variety, which digs into the bag material better than two-pronged barbs. A convenient tool to help place bags properly without catching on the barbs is a metal slider (like a large cookie sheet) that can be pulled out once the bags are correctly positioned. It is easy at this point to place short pieces of wire or twine across the bags with the

FIGURE 28.4. Completed earthbag building with cement plaster, Dennilton, South Africa. [Credit: Joseph F. Kennedy]

ends hanging over either side of the wall; these can be used later to secure plaster mesh or lath. Sticks laid between bags can also be useful to key the plaster.

Structural Considerations

Different structural issues arise depending on how the bags are used. When bags are used as foundations for other wall systems, for instance, they should be filled with gravel or concrete rubble to at least a foot above grade, with the top course level to receive the wall material (straw bales, adobe, wood, etc.).

Retaining walls can be built with bags, but it is important to provide drainage behind the wall and to make sure that the bags are properly secured against slipping. Stability is improved by leaning the wall against the bank ("battering"), and compacting the tops of the bags such that each slopes back toward the earth bank.

Openings for windows or doors can be spanned by a lintel of concrete, wood or metal, which must be strong enough to bear considerable weight from above. A common way to make openings for windows and doors is to build an arch over a temporary form. Gothic and catenary arch shapes have been found to be much more stable than hemispherical Roman arches.

When building arches, it is crucial to fill the bags in place, and to tamp them into wedge shapes, which will not slip when the form is removed. One drawback is that glazing these arched shapes often demands custom windows. Small vaults for door openings (like the entrance of an igloo) have been built with earthbags, but larger vaults are probably not practical due to the need for excessive formwork and the difficulty of tamping in such situations.

Earthbags can be used to make domed structures. A rotating guide makes this simple. The only really practical dome has a pointed or catenary shape and is built on a round base with supporting buttress. Hemispherical domes are extremely challenging without additional formwork and are not advised.

Kelly Hart built an oval dome but encountered structural problems that required additional support. It is important to lay the bags in flat rings (corbelling) in order to prevent slippage in the upper rings. Over small spans, earthbags can be easily used to create free-form domes and arch shapes without forms or guides.

FIGURE 28.5. A unique earthbag system that utilizes plastered sand-filled bags laid between structural frames. Cape Town, South Africa. [Credit: Joseph F. Kennedy]

A direction worth pursuing is to make domes using bags filled with a straw-clay mixture (as was done with the roof of the first Cal-Earth dome) or pumice or vermiculite, in order to reduce weight and improve insulation.

Plastering

It is important to plaster a structure built with polypropylene bags as soon as possible, as their worst enemy is sunlight. The structure can even be protected with a scratch coat as it is being built. Sometimes, when bags are filled with concrete or soil cement, the bag material can then

FIGURE 28.6. A visitor indicates the "truth window" in an earthbag structure in Saudi Arabia. The burlap bags used for this building are generally not advised as they more easily degrade over time, potentially impacting structural integrity. [Credit: Meshaal Abanomia]

RESOURCES

Books

• Elizabeth, Lynne and Cassandra Adams, eds. *Alternative Construction: Contemporary Natural Building Methods*, John Wiley and Sons, 2005. Includes a thorough introductory article on earthbag construction.
• Geiger, Dr. Owen. *Earthbag Building Guide: Vertical Walls Step-by-Step.* This builder's guide provides simple, clear explanations of each step of construction, from earthbag foundations to complete information on tools and supplies, as well as tips, tricks and advanced earthbag techniques. Available as PDF download at **earthbagbuilding.com**.
• Hunter, Kaki and Donald Kiffmeyer. *Earthbag Building: The Tools, Tricks and Techniques*, New Society Publishers, 2004. This is a comprehensive guide to all the tools, tricks and techniques for building with bags filled with earth. This profusely illustrated guide first discusses the many merits of earthbag construction and then leads the reader through the key elements of an earthbag building.
• Khalili, Nader. *Emergency Sandbag Shelter*, Cal Earth

Press, 2011. Shows how to use sandbags and barbed wire—the materials of war—for peaceful purposes. Earthbags can shelter millions of people around the globe as a temporary as well as permanent housing solution.
• Ostrow, Judy and Karen Leffler. *The House That Jill Built: A Woman's Guide to Home Building*, Gibbs Smith, 2005. One of the featured stories tell of Allison Kennedy, a woman who built an earthbag house all by herself after her boyfriend left her.
• Wojciechowska, Paulina. *Building with Earth: A Guide to Flexible Form Earthbag Construction*, Chelsea Green, 2001. This book teaches the basics of earthbag construction: how to design and build rounded forms, including arches, vaults, domes and apses; shows a method for building essentially "tree-free" structures from foundation to roof; and explains how to combine earthbags with conventional and ecological building techniques. Now out of print, it is well worth finding a used copy.

be removed from the sides to expose the fill material or to aid in adherence of plaster.

Earthen plasters are commonly used on earthbag structures, but they can be problematic where there is no roof overhang to keep rain off. Except in the driest areas, where earthen plaster could be possible, domes should be covered with a cement- or lime-based plaster. When using lime/sand or cement/sand plasters, metal lath can be tied to the bags to improve adhesion.

Kelly Hart's intriguing house in Colorado utilized papercrete (paper pulp mixed with sand and cement) as a plaster, although this was eventually covered with a traditional stucco to keep it from eroding in key areas. As all these techniques are experimental, plastering and waterproofing

RESOURCES

DVDs
• Geiger, Owen. *Basic Earthbag Building: A Step-by-Step Guide*, 2011. This is a comprehensive DVD created by Owen Geiger. The first part provides clear, simple explanations of each step of construction, and the second part documents the construction of a cool pantry, which uses the same basic steps as most any other earthbag structure.
• Hart, Kelly. *Building with Bags: How We Made Our Experimental Earthbag/Papercrete House*, 2000. Kelly wanted to build an environmentally sensitive and aesthetically pleasing home at a moderate price. He chose to create earthbag domes covered with papercrete. This candid DVD documents details of the construction, insights gained and the ups and downs (literally!) of the building process.

Organizations
• AuwaEarth: **auwaearth.com**. They facilitate workshops in various techniques such as earth building, energy and water conservation and ecological sanitation. Newcastle, Australia.
• CalEarth: **calearth.org**. Research and teaching center where many of the advances in earthbag construction have been made. Hesperia, California.
• Earth, Hands & Houses: **earthhandsandhouses .org**. Ecological design, alternative and conventional building and construction methods, consultation and workshops, with a special interest in supporting, reestablishing and furthering ecological building methods among indigenous people. Provides consulting and workshops on earthbag construction and other natural building techniques.

• Earthbaghouse: **earthbaghouse.com**. Conducts workshops and does natural building contracting. Austin, Texas.
• Earthen Hand Natural Building: **earthenhand.com**. Conducts workshops around the world in earthbag building techniques. Portland, Oregon.
• Permastructure: **permastructure.com.au**. Their aim is to make earthbag technology a recognized and accessible building method within Australia, through workshops and education.
• Phangan Earthworks: **phanganearthworks.com**. Conducts earthbag workshops, mostly in Thailand.
• Soma Earth: **somaearth.com**. Conducts many different kinds of workshops in Canada, including earthbag. Udora, Ontario, Canada.
• Superadobe del Sur: **superadobedelsur.blogspot .com**. Conducts earthbag building workshops in South America.
• Starseed Creative: **guidingstarcreations.blogspot .com**; Conducts earthbag workshops around the world. Portland, Oregon.
• Ulew Atitlan: **ulewatitlan.com**. Teaches ancient building techniques combined with the latest earthbag construction. Santiago Atitlan, Solola, Guatemala.
• United Earth Builders: **unitedearthbuilders.com**. This is a collective of natural builders who are dedicated to education and designing and building natural structures through workshops and construction. Joshua Tree, California.

Website
• **Earthbagbuilding.com**. Profiles exciting earthbag projects around the world.

is a subject that requires much additional research.

International Acceptance

Since the mid 1990s, when Nader Khalili popularized the concept of building with earthbags, there has been a steady increase in their use around the world. CalEarth has been responsible for many projects, including a school in Nepal and emergency shelters in Pakistan and Haiti after their respective earthquakes. Dedicated builders and teachers have helped spread the technology throughout Japan, India, Thailand, the Philippines, Jordan, Uganda, South Africa, Brazil, Argentina, Chile, Bolivia, Mexico, Australia, New Zealand and across Europe. There are now at least a dozen organizations conducting earthbag workshops around the world (see "Resources").

During the early years at CalEarth, Khalili established a relationship with the local building department in Hesperia, California, an area where earthquakes are naturally a great danger. In 1993, live-load tests to simulate seismic, snow and wind loads were performed on a number of domed earthbag

FIGURE 28.7. A sod-covered earthbag dome by Doni Kiffmeyer and Kaki Hunter, Moab, Utah. [Credit: Catherine Wanek]

structures at CalEarth and these exceeded code requirements by 200 percent.

In 1995, dynamic and static load tests were performed on several prototypes for a planned Hesperia Museum and Nature Center to be constructed using Khalili's superadobe concepts with both dome and vault shapes. All of these tests exceeded ICBO and City of Hesperia requirements. Despite these and other positive test results, no building codes for earthbags have yet been adopted.

The lack of codes creates a hurdle for builders in many areas, but it has not stopped committed pioneers from building earthbag homes in many countries. The advantages of earthbags are obvious: they can be extremely durable, resisting wind, flood, fire, earthquake and even bullets! We expect that with continuing global climate and economic changes, earthbag building will only become more popular as time goes on.

This shepherd's shelter in Sardinia is made entirely of a single material: stones gathered from the surrounding countryside. Its roof resembles a catenary dome, one of the strongest shapes for enclosing space using masonry. Stone walls without mortar are called "dry stacked." [Credit: Joseph F. Kennedy]

This historic stone millhouse in eastern France was constructed using lime-sand mortar. Structural stone walls are generally built in horizontal courses, like bricks. Each stone bridges the joint between the stones below, forming a "running bond" to hold the wall together. [Credit: Catherine Wanek]

Many of the stones in this farmhouse in Brittany, France, have been painstakingly shaped. Different kinds of stone were used for the door arches and window lintels, the main wall, and the slate roof. [Credit: Catherine Wanek]

STONE: Traditional peoples and today's natural builders share a relatively small number of primary construction materials: stone, earth, wood, straw and other plant fibers top the list. Even though the variety of building materials has been vastly increased by the addition of industrially manufactured products, stone is still the most durable building material in use today.

The Church of the Good Shepherd, in Tekapo, New Zealand, was built in 1935 from stones collected on the nearby shore of Lake Tekapo. All the stones were left in their natural state. It takes great skill and artistry to combine such irregularly shaped stone into a strong wall. The slate roof was added later. [Credit: Catherine Wanek]

The word adobe traces back at least 4,000 years to an Egyptian term for "mud brick." Clay-rich mud is mixed with fiber (such as straw, dry grass, or animal manure) and placed in a wooden mold to form a brick. When dry, these blocks can be stacked to form a wall, with mud mortar between. The entrance of this hotel in Arfoud, Morocco reveals the adobes from which the walls are built. [Credit: Janine Björnson]

The city of Shibam in South Yemen is known for some of the tallest mud buildings in the world. Sometimes called "the Manhattan of the Desert," Shibam is home to 500 tower houses, made primarily out of adobe blocks and reaching up to eight stories high. Most of these buildings originate from the 16th century, but require periodic maintenance to repair damage done by rain. [Credit: Danny Gordon]

EARTH: Earthen building techniques have developed in nearly every climate and region. There are three major ways to construct load-bearing walls out of earth: adobe, cob and rammed earth, each of which has many variations.

The Spanish carried adobe building to the New World, where it flourished in many areas, including the Southwestern US. The San Francisco de Asis Mission Church, completed in 1816 in Ranchos de Taos, New Mexico, is a fine example of the adobe architecture that has become emblematic of the region. The walls are up to ten feet thick (three meters), keeping the inside of the church cool even on hot summer days. [Credit: Joseph F. Kennedy]

"In-situ adobe" originated in New Zealand. These earthen blocks containing paper pulp and Portland cement are cast in place on the wall. The forms are quickly removed and the blocks slump slightly before they set, which gives them their organic appearance. The foreground arch in Dahj Sumner's home is made of pre-dried adobes. [Credit: Catherine Wanek]

Cob is endemic to many parts of the world, including rainy Britain. Clay soil, usually containing gravel and sand, is mixed with straw and water to the consistency of stiff dough. The mixture is then placed on the wall and allowed to dry in place. High stone foundations and reed-thatched roofs help protect the walls of these historic cob houses in Devon, England, from water damage. [Credit: Catherine Wanek]

Rammed earth involves compacting slightly moist earth into a strong form, which is then removed. The technique has been known for millennia, from China to North Africa. The Roman Empire spread the concept around northern Europe, where it has been in use ever since. This historic rammed earth house near Lyon, France, typifies the elegance of the technique. [Credit: Catherine Wanek]

Earthbag construction is also called "super-adobe" and "flexible-form rammed earth." Bags or tubes, usually made of woven plastic fabric, are filled with damp soil and compacted. Earthbags are commonly used to make vaults and domes, like this one at Cal-Earth (California Institute of Earth Art and Architecture) where the technique was popularized. [Credit: Misha Rauchwerger]

Compressed earth blocks (CEBs) combine attributes of rammed earth and adobe. They are often made using human-powered machines and have been promoted in many developing countries, especially in Africa. This CEB vault at the Auroville Earth Institute in Southern India demonstrates the amazing strength of the material. [Credit: Serge Maini]

By the Middle Ages, complex systems of timber framing had developed in forested regions around the world, notably in Japan and northern Europe. Where two beams and a post come together at the base of this historic Norwegian building, now preserved at the Maihaugen Open Air Museum near Lillehammer, each member was carefully carved to fit tightly with the others. Impeccably crafted frames like this one have lasted close to a thousand years. [Credit: Catherine Wanek]

Robert Laporte built this workshop in Santa Fe, New Mexico, using locally milled timbers for the frame and straw-clay with clay plaster for the wall enclosure. A timber frame provides a strong structure that can be enclosed using nearly any natural wall system. [Credit: Catherine Wanek]

WOOD is one of the most versatile of all natural building materials; it can be used to make any part of a house, from floors and framing to walls and roof coverings. Concerned for the health of the forests, many of today's natural builders prefer to take advantage of wood's unique structural properties—especially its high tensile strength—by using it primarily for structural elements such as roof framing.

Hand-crafted wooden double doors provide an elegant finishing touch to this hybrid natural building at the Lama Foundation in New Mexico. The surrounding wall is made of cordwood masonry, a wall system consisting of short lengths of wood embedded in a mortar matrix. [Credit: Catherine Wanek]

Welsh furniture maker David Hughes constructed this whimsical workshop for himself from local wood and reed thatch. For the timber frame, he used curvy oak logs rejected by conventional builders. Note the wooden pegs holding the gate joinery together. [Credit: Catherine Wanek]

Bamboo tools, utensils, and buildings are an important part of life for half the world's population. This pavilion in China is built almost entirely of bamboo and was constructed using traditional pegged joinery. [Credit: Catherine Wanek]

The global resurgence in bamboo construction was spearheaded by Colombian Architect Simón Vélez. Vélez developed new joinery techniques that make bamboo suitable for modern structural applications and has pioneered the use of bamboo for trusses, some of which span up to 66 feet (20 meters.) The architecture building at La Gran Colombia University in Bogotá was inspired by Vélez's designs. [Credit: Darrel DeBoer]

Split bamboo is very pliable yet strong in tension, allowing it to be woven or bent into curved forms. Bamboo splits can also be bundled and lashed to make very strong structural elements such as the curved beam shown here. This house in Bali was designed and built by Oren Hardy and Jörg Stamm. [Credit: Jörg Stamm]

BAMBOO encompasses a large diversity of plants in the grass family, native everywhere from the hot tropics to the Himalaya mountains. Some tropical timber bamboos can grow as much as 100 feet tall (30 m) and 6 to 8 inches (15–20 cm) in diameter. A culm or stalk of bamboo reaches its full height in a single growing season of several weeks, and is ready to harvest in 3 to 5 years. This makes bamboo a more rapidly-renewable resource than most trees.

Manufactured bamboo building products such as laminated flooring, combined with recent testing and code development, are helping bamboo move into the mainstream, even in parts of the world where it has been little known. This home by Bamboo Living in Hawaii features code compliant bamboo structural elements as well as bamboo surface treatments. [Credit: Bamboo Living]

The mechanical hay baler became widely available at the end of the 19th century, and the first uses of bales for construction followed soon after. In the Sandhill region of Nebraska, where there were very few trees and the sandy soil was unsuitable for building, settlers stacked bales of hay or straw to make well-insulated walls. The Pilgrim Holiness Church in Arthur, Nebraska, was built in 1928 out of baled rye straw. [Credit: Catherine Wanek]

STRAW is the stalks of cereal grains including wheat, oats and rice. Traditionally, straw has been used in many ways, including as reinforcement in earthen wall systems such as adobe, cob, and wattle and daub. The massive expansion of grain production since the middle of the 20th Century has made straw abundant and inexpensive almost worldwide. Today, straw bale construction is one of the most popular of natural building techniques, largely due to straw's excellent insulation properties.

Straw bale construction is appropriate for almost every climate, including where winters are very cold. Well-detailed bale walls help keep Carol Elston's Bayfield home cozy during Colorado's snowy winters. The thickness of the walls creates opportunities for deep interior window shelves and window seats. [Credit: Catherine Wanek]

Straw bale walls can be load-bearing ("Nebraska style"), in which case they directly support the weight of the roof, or they can be used as infill within a post and beam framework. The bale in this picture has been notched to fit around a structural post. Bales can be quickly stacked by groups of volunteers with little training. [Credit: Catherine Wanek]

The high insulation value of straw bale walls, combined with passive solar design, solar collectors, thermal mass storage and a variety of other energy and water efficiency measures, earned this Northern California straw bale farmhouse, designed by Daniel Smith and Associates, a Platinum certification from LEED for Homes. [Credit: Russell Abraham]

This off grid straw bale home in central California, built by owner Linda Drew with many helping hands, combines whimsical curves with a very practical passive solar design. Completed in 2001, it was the first permitted straw bale home in California to use natural earth and lime plasters inside and out. The bale walls were raised during a two-day workshop led by the architects, Kelly Lerner and Pete Gang. [Credit: Catherine Wanek]

Athena Steen designed this 5,000 square foot (460 square meter) office for Fundación de Apoyo Infantíl Sonora (Save the Children) in Ciudad Obregón, Mexico. This innovative building combines straw bale exterior walls with interior partitions of high-fiber adobe blocks containing much more straw than traditional adobes. All of the finishes are natural and the building was constructed almost entirely without power tools. [Credit: Catherine Wanek]

Students at an EcoNest workshop pack straw-clay into wooden forms that have been temporarily attached to the building's framing. The mixture is made by lightly coating loose straw with clay slip, or clay dissolved in water. Note that the tops of the wall cavities have been left open to make filling the walls easier; once all of the straw-clay has been installed, the top plates will be attached and the roof will be framed. [Credit: Robert Laporte]

This Japanese-inspired EcoNest, designed and built by the wife-husband architect/builder team of Paula Baker-Laporte and Robert Laporte near Santa Fe, New Mexico, combines timber frame construction with straw-clay walls and clay plaster. Although the walls are typically much thinner than straw bales, straw-clay can provide good insulation for moderately cold climates. [Credit: Laurie Dickson]

THATCH: A special use of straw and other plant stalks is as a roofing material. Around the world, reeds, grasses, grain stalks, and palm leaves have all been used to make beautiful and effective roofs. Thatched roofs are among the few types of roofs that can be made entirely from natural materials.

A roof being thatched in South Africa. Many bundles of reeds are laid down in thick overlapping layers. Each bundle is tied to the wooden purlins below. Later, the ends of the reeds will be beaten into a smooth surface so that water will run off quickly. [Credit: Joseph F. Kennedy]

Thatching has been honed to a fine art in Northern Europe, where the practice is still common. Shown here are the tools and materials needed for a reed thatch roof, which can last 40 years or longer even in the harsh climate of Denmark. [Credit: Catherine Wanek]

Thatch may be the only roofing option that provides waterproofing and insulation with a single material. Thatch roofs easily match the curved wall shapes common to many natural buildings. This round, load-bearing straw bale home in Monaghan County was one of the first to be given planning permission in Ireland. [Credit: Joseph F. Kennedy]

Palm leaves, though less durable than reeds, are commonly used for roofing throughout the rainy tropics. This reconstructed *hale* at the Limahuli Tropical Botanical Garden on Kauai, Hawaii, overlooks taro-producing terraces supported by lava rock retaining walls, which capture creek water for irrigation. [Credit: Catherine Wanek]

HYBRID NATURAL HOMES combine multiple wall systems in a single building. By taking advantage of the complementary properties of different natural materials, hybrid homes can have superior thermal performance and more interesting designs.

Steen Møller's house near Sønder Felding, Denmark combines walls of straw bale, baled flax, rammed earth, compressed earth block, and cordwood masonry with a reed thatch roof, round pole framing and decorative wattle and daub elements. The home is kept cozy through a combination of passive solar heating and a Finnish masonry stove. [Credit: Catherine Wanek]

Visitors enjoy the south-facing patio at Steen Møller's owner-built hybrid natural home. A rammed earth Trombe wall collects solar heat even during Denmark's long cloudy winters. [Credit: Catherine Wanek]

Inside Steen Møller's home, this decorative log-end wall separates two rooms. The builder chose a variety of different local woods for visual interest, and mortared them together with cob made from local clay. [Credit: Catherine Wanek]

In Pagosa Springs, Colorado, Sudeep Biddle and Rosalind Wu hired Kelly Ray Mathews to design and build their natural home. Surrounded by the excellent insulation of straw bale walls, the cob bench and earthen floors store heat from both the sun and the wood stove to keep the interior temperature stable. Earthen finishes also moderate humidity, helping to create a healthy living climate. [Credit: Catherine Wanek]

On a winter morning, sunlight slants through the south- and east-facing windows and doors of Mark and Kristin Sullivan's home in Capitola, California. This straw bale home produces nearly all the energy it needs with a photovoltaic array and a solar water heater mounted on the roof. [Credit: Catherine Wanek]

The ancient pueblo builders of Mesa Verde, Colorado understood passive solar design principles perfectly. Sited in a south-facing cave, this 200-room housing complex is shaded from the scorching summer sun by the overhanging stone. In the winter, heat from the low-angled sun is absorbed and stored in the stone and earth walls and floors. The circular, underground "kivas" in the foreground are earth-coupled, keeping them comfortable year round.
[Credit: Catherine Wanek]

THERMAL STRATEGIES: In industrialized nations, far more energy is spent on heating and cooling than in the manufacture of building materials and the construction of houses. An environmentally sensitive design will reduce heating and cooling needs and other energy usage in the home. Fortunately, a set of simple and well-tested design tools is available, including passive heating, cooling, and lighting strategies.

The Real Goods store in Hopland, California is a model of passive solar efficiency, using about one sixth the energy of a conventional commercial building of the same size. Straw bale walls with thick earthen plaster supply insulation and thermal mass, while south facing windows provide solar heating and ventilation. East-facing clerestory windows bring natural light deep into the 5,000 square foot (460 square meter) space, which is diffused in intensity by the white panels. [Credit: Catherine Wanek]

Efficient heating in a cold climate requires excellent insulation combined with good detailing to prevent air leakage. The walls of Urs Braun and Christiane Dubuis' retreat in the Swiss Alps, designed by Werner Schmidt, are made from load-bearing jumbo bales 4 feet (1.25 meters) thick. The floor and roof are also insulated with straw bales. The large south-facing windows are shaded by a wide roof overhang and motorized retractable shades. [Credit: Catherine Wanek]

This troglodyte or "cave dweller" home is carved into the soft limestone strata of the Loire Valley in France. As many ancient peoples knew, earth-coupling a dwelling by sinking it into the ground or mounding earth over it will increase comfort while reducing heating and cooling demands, since the home is protected from both hot and cold air and heat-stealing winds. [Credit: Catherine Wanek]

The Ridge Winery near Healdsburg, California was at the time of its construction the largest straw bale building in the United States. Wishing to replicate the thermal properties of the caves where wine was traditionally stored, the owners chose straw bale walls with thick earthen and lime plasters for thermal mass and moisture management. The south-facing entrance is protected from overheating with a vine-supporting trellis. [Credit: Joseph F. Kennedy]

This innovative home was built by traditional timber-framer Gunter Herbst in the former East Germany. Herbst made the walls from a variation of 'light clay,' combining shredded Styrofoam packaging with clay slip and packing the mixture into temporary forms. More common versions of light clay use straw or wood chips. The thermal properties of light clay vary depending on the mix proportions and the amount of tamping. [Credit: Catherine Wanek]

Cordwood walls like these at Earthwood Building School in New York also combine properties of insulation and thermal mass. The mortar joints on the faces of the wall provide mass, and the cavity in between is usually filled with sawdust insulation. Living or "green" roofs are another application of thermal mass, helping protect buildings from the hot summer sun. [Credit: Rob Roy]

Susie Harrington designed her home in Moab, Utah, borrowing not only its materials but its form from the surrounding landscape. Natural stone and earth finishes complement the straw bale walls while the undulating roof mimics the shapes of surrounding hills. The curved retaining walls are made of plastered earthbags. [Credit: Catherine Wanek]

SCULPTURAL DESIGNS: Using irregular materials such as earth, stone, and unmilled wood allows natural builders to sculpt uniquely artistic buildings. The most inspirational buildings result from synergistic collaborations between the designer and builder, the site, and the materials at hand.

This solar sanctuary was designed and built by Mark Lakeman and Joseph Kennedy in a Portland, Oregon backyard. The sound-blocking properties of earthen walls and roof make this a peaceful retreat from the noise of the city. [Credit: Joseph F. Kennedy]

Sometimes simple forms are the most pleasing. Peter Gina's straw bale home near Aspen, Colorado features this oval view window. [Credit: Catherine Wanek]

Rounded cob walls and a curved log roof beam embrace the second floor of Misha Rauchwerger's cottage. Located in California's Sierra Nevada foothills, this was the first cob building to be permitted (retroactively) in a seismic zone in the United States. [Credit: Misha Rauchwerger]

Massey Burke designed and built this cluster of small cabins at a private retreat in coastal Northern California. The curvaceous living roofs were inspired by the nearby ocean swells. The walls are framed with locally-harvested round poles, infilled with woodchip-clay, and plastered with earth from the site. [Credit: Massey Burke]

On the south wall of one of the cabins, Burke built this light mural of cob and salvaged bottles. The curved beam above it is a home-made glue-lam constructed of many thin redwood boards laminated with wood glue and screws. [Credit: Massey Burke]

Native American sculptor Roxanne Swentzell's Tower Gallery in Pojoaque Pueblo, New Mexico, was built using traditional adobe techniques. The artist's sister, Athena Steen, and her husband Bill, supervised the fine clay plaster finish work. [Credit: Catherine Wanek]

The non-profit ReBuilding Center in Portland, Oregon diverts 4.5 million pounds of building materials from landfills each year and sells them at low cost. The remodeling and expansion of their facilities was an opportunity to demonstrate the use of both recycled and natural materials. Dozens of volunteers helped build this sculptural cob entrance. [Credit: Mark Lakeman]

Women building an HIV/AIDS hospice in the Northwest Province of South Africa apply plaster made of a locally-harvested burgundy clay mixed with sand and fine fiber. The hand-finished texture resists weathering better than a very smooth clay plaster would, since it forces water running down the surface to slow down. [Credit: Joseph F. Kennedy]

Sara and Sven Johnston finished the interior of their straw bale home in Geraldine, New Zealand, with these colorful clay plasters. Thick earthen plasters like these protect bales from humidity, fire, and pests. Note the "truth window" at right, where the straw is visible. [Credit: Catherine Wanek]

CLAY PLASTERS:
Clay finishes are well suited to most natural wall systems. When correctly formulated, clay plasters are beautiful, easy to apply, and fairly durable in dry conditions.

Parishioners in Ranchos de Taos, New Mexico sift clay soil for the annual ritual of replastering their beloved San Francisco de Asis Mission Church. A half-inch thick (1 cm-thick) layer of clay, chopped straw, and water will repair most damage done to the structure by seasonal rains. Later, a thin *alis*, made of the same clay without straw, will be brushed on and polished smooth with sheepskins. [Credit: Nigel Fusella]

Katy Bryce and Adam Weisman of Clayworks have installed their clay plaster products in dozens of restaurants, including this one in London. Clayworks is one of several companies in both Europe and the U.S. that formulate and sell pre-mixed high-performance clay plasters. [Credit: Nando's]

These buildings on the Greek island of Santorini have been built of local stone, plastered and whitewashed with lime. White walls and roofs help deflect the heat of the Mediterranean sun. [Credit: Joseph F. Kennedy]

LIME: Builder's lime is made from burned limestone that has been slaked in water. This process has historically been done artisanally in small batches, as shown at archeological sites from Japan to the Yucatán. Today, lime putty and powdered slaked lime are available as industrial products. Lime has high embodied energy and should be used sparingly, but it is uniquely suited to protect earthen and straw walls from water damage.

Lime plasters should be maintained by the periodic application of whitewash, a thin paint made of lime and water. In addition to brightening and smoothing the plaster surface, the lime solution gets into cracks, where it eventually hardens, sealing and repairing the crack. [Credit: Joseph F. Kennedy]

At a Natural Building Colloquium in Oregon, Sukita Crimmel experiments with the age-old art of *fresco*, painting mineral pigments onto wet lime plaster over a cob sculpture. As it calcifies, the lime bonds chemically with the pigment, creating brilliant surfaces whose colors will never fade. [Credit: Michael G. Smith]

Tadelakt is a special type of lime plaster, sealed with olive oil soap and burnished with super-smooth stones. Originally developed in Morocco for sealing the insides of water tanks, *tadelakt* provides a uniquely waterproof coating suitable for tubs, sinks and showers, as shown in this Moroccan bathroom. [Credit: Janine Björnson]

New Mexican potter Felipe Ortega follows the ancient custom of hand-harvesting local clay and shaping and firing it into sparkling earthenware. He used the same mica-rich clay for the *alis*, or clay paint, inside his adobe home. [Credit: Catherine Wanek]

Carole Crews has adapted the traditional technique of *alis* to a wide range of clays and applications, adding flour paste to increase durability and water-resistance. This hand-sculpted earthen figure greets visitors to her adobe dome house near Taos, New Mexico. [Credit: Janine Björnson]

NATURAL PAINTS provide the finishing touch on many natural homes. Why buy synthetic paint when you can make your own durable, non-toxic paint from simple ingredients such as clay, flour, milk, pigments, and lime?

When making finishes from found clay, testing is essential for good results. Here Bill Steen checks the color and other characteristics of many clay samples collected in and around Ciudad Obregón, Mexico. [Credit: Catherine Wanek]

The streets and walls of Chefchaouen, Morocco, are painted blue with a tinted whitewash or lime paint. Originally, the blue pigment came from ground seashells, but synthetic pigments are used today, allowing for deeper color. [Credit: Janine Björnson]

Digging In for Comfort

KELLY HART

29

Think of all the animals that dig into the ground to find refuge, comfort and security. Their ancestors discovered millennia ago that the earth could provide all of that, free for the digging. We humans have done this too, at times, but, preferring to follow the trend of building on the surface, we've largely forgotten the benefits of going underground.

What animals instinctively know is that the earth can shelter them from extremes of temperature from wind, sun and snow. If you dig several feet into the ground, you will discover that the temperature does not vary much there, year round. In fact, even at the high elevation in Colorado where I live, the earth five feet under the surface constantly stays around 50°F (10°C). I'm sure you have experienced the delicious coolness of a basement room on a scorching summer day. Perhaps you've gone into that same basement in mid-winter and been surprised how warm it felt. This is the moderating effect of the earth's thermal mass at work.

Of course, most of us would not be comfortable in a house kept at 50°F (10°C), so we would need to bring the temperature up maybe 20°F (11°C) to relax at home. Compare that with say the 70°F (39°C) increase necessary to be comfortable in a

KELLY HART *has been involved in media most of his life, initially working as a professional photographer and then branching into cinematography and animation. He has produced many film, video and DVD programs related to his interests in sustainable architecture, cultural education and animal behavior. He is the founder of* green homebuilding.com, earthbagbuilding.com *and* dreamgreenhomes .com *and is currently writing a series of books about green home building.*

FIGURE 29.1. These traditional cave dwellings, known as *Yao Dong*, were carved into the silty soil of China's Loess Plateau to keep their inhabitants comfortable during cold winters and hot summers. [Credit: Liu Yang]

conventional home when it's 0°F (-18°C) outside. It would take over three times as much energy to stay warm if you have not taken advantage of the earth for shelter. And on a hot day, it works in the other direction, with above-ground buildings requiring tremendous air-conditioning energy to stay cool, while those dug into the earth need minimal resources to remain comfortable.

Many people think that an earth-sheltered house must be dark, dank, dirty and doubtful as a pleasant abode. They are wrong. There are many ways to introduce light, views and an airy feeling into an earth-bermed house. I'm not suggesting that we live in a hole in the ground, although even that can be pleasant if the hole is big enough to provide an atrium/central courtyard. More commonly, an earth-sheltered house is dug into a hillside, ideally one that faces more or less south (in northern latitudes). Then the windows for solar heating are naturally at ground level, and much of the rest of the house can be surrounded with earth. Even on flat land, soil can be pushed up around the sides of the house to provide protection.

When building an earth-sheltered house, it is important to pay attention to certain details.

If your site has a high water table, drainage must be integrated into the design, as well as grading, swales or other strategies for re-directing surface runoff. As with the rest of the house, the walls that are in contact with the earth need to be well insulated, or else the soil will continually suck the warmth out of the house. Also, these walls need to be strong enough to withstand the pressure of that earth, and waterproof to keep out the moisture. Reinforced concrete has often been used to build subsurface walls, and this works well, but it is not the most environmentally friendly way to do it.

Mike Oeler, author of *The $50 and Up Underground House Book*, suggests using heavy timbers to frame the structure, with boards to form the walls and plastic sheeting to waterproof it. He has lived in such a structure in Idaho for quite a few years and is still happily advocating this approach.

My wife Rosana and I built our own earth-sheltered home at nearly 8,000 ft. (2,400 m) elevation in Colorado using earthbag construction. First we carved a flat building pad into the southern face of a large sand dune. Then we stacked up polypropylene bags filled with either sand or scoria, which is a

FIGURE 29.2. In the foreground is the vaulted entry to Kelly and Rosana Hart's earthbag house. Further back, you can see the earth-bermed north side of the house, including the underground pantry dome. [Credit: Kelly Hart]

naturally occurring lightweight volcanic rock. The lower bags that are filled with sand are insulated from the outside with scoria. We covered all of this with a double layer of 6 mil polyethylene film before backfilling with earth. Between each course of bags are two strands of four-point barbed wire. The wall itself has a convex curve set against the earth to withstand the pressure of the surrounding soil. The beauty of this is in the simplicity of construction and the fact that it uses very little industrial material.

Our passive solar house consists of a large elliptical dome with its long axis facing south (containing the living room/kitchen/dining areas) connected to a smaller circular bedroom dome by a long passageway that serves several other functions (greenhouse/bathroom/utility room). All of these spaces gather heat during sunny days, store that heat in the adobe and flagstone floors, as well as in the bags full of sand, and then gently radiate the heat at night to help keep the home warm. This simple system does so well at keeping the house comfortable that often, even on very cold nights, there is no need for supplemental heat.

Another advantage of digging in is that it makes it easy to create an adjacent walk-in cool pantry that is also bermed into the soil. We did this with our earthbag house and were treated to the luxury of having abundant space for storing all kinds of food supplies right next to the kitchen. This pantry never freezes nor gets very warm, staying between about 36°F (2°C) and 60°F (15.5°C) all year-round. And it costs nothing to maintain this temperature!

I have visited several other houses that take advantage of the earth for shelter. Mark Jacobi and Christine Canaly built their house several years ago, and originally lived in a nearly totally bermed room at the lowest level,

FIGURE 29.3. "Earthships," a building system developed by Michael Reynolds in Taos, New Mexico, are U-shaped structures made primarily of earth-filled tires, open to the sun on the south side and dug into a hill or covered with earth on the north side. [Credit: Catherine Wanek]

This room was built with "Foam-form" insulated blocks that were filled with rebar and cement, and then tarred on the outside and covered with Q-bond adhesive on the inside. Mark finds it very soothing to be in that room. The surrounding earth keeps it snug, cozy and quiet. Mark points out that digging in allows for a lower profile, which is not as much of an intrusion on the landscape. And it saves fuel costs.

Alan London and Julie Kove's passive-solar house was two years in the making. The house is set into a south-facing sand dune that was notched all the way through, so that the garage/entrance is on the north side. The exterior walls were formed with RASTRA foam-insulated concrete blocks, which were filled with rebar and cement. A Bituthene self-adhesive waterproof membrane was applied to the blocks below grade, and then blue-board rigid foam insulation set in place before backfilling. This is one of the best passive solar designs I've seen; I'm sure they are comfortable.

These people have happily dug into the earth for shelter. They know what the wild animals know: Mother Earth provides for our needs.

RESOURCES

Books

• Baggs, Sydney et al. *Australian Earth-Covered and Green Roof Buildings*, UNSW Press, 2005. The authors are among Australia's leading authorities in earth-covered and green-roof building design and construction.
• Campbell, Stu. *The Underground House Book*, Garden Way, 1990. Although this book is many years out of print, it is worth trying to find a used copy, as the information, backed by the design expertise of Don Metz, is still good.
• Oehler, Mike. *The $50 and Up Underground House Book*, 6th ed., Mole Publishing, 1997. A quirky but valuable book on how to build a truly "dirt cheap" house.
• Roy, Rob. *Earth-Sheltered Houses: How to Build an Affordable Underground House*, New Society Publishers, 2006. This very readable book guides the designer/builder through all the necessary considerations, including structure, waterproofing, insulation and drainage.
• Wells, Malcolm. *The Earth-Sheltered House: An Architect's Sketchbook*, 2nd ed., Chelsea Green Publishing, 2009. A witty and profusely illustrated treatise on the subject of underground houses.

Cordwood Masonry: An Overview

30

ROB ROY

Cordwood masonry is a technique by which building walls are constructed of short logs—sometimes called "log ends"—laid up transversely, much as a rank of firewood is stacked. The walls consist of an inner and outer mortar joint, with an insulated space between. The log ends are structural, tying the two mortar matrices together. With a continuous history of over 250 years, cordwood masonry has enjoyed a slow but steady growth in popularity since its "rebirth" in the mid-1970s. Green builders are gradually becoming aware of cordwood's compelling "5-E" advantages: economy, ease of construction, energy efficiency, aesthetics and environmental harmony.

ROB ROY *is director of Earthwood Building School, which he cofounded with his wife Jaki in 1980. He has written and edited several books on cordwood masonry, including* Cordwood Building: The State of the Art *(New Society Publishers, 2003).* **cordwood masonry.com**

Economy

Because cordwood masonry can make use of wood unsuitable for milling, the cost of structural wall materials can be extremely low in forested bioregions. When cob mortar is used, the materials cost can be next to nothing if both wood and suitable earth are available onsite. As the log ends are typically 8–24 in. (20–60 cm) in length, suitable pieces can be derived from fire- or disease-killed wood, logging slash, driftwood, sawmill scrap or even pieces left over from log cabin manufacturers and furniture makers. Insulation cost is also low, as lime-treated sawdust is the typical insulation of choice. My wife Jaki and I insulated our 2,000 sq. ft. (183 m²) Earthwood house for US$75 worth of sawdust, delivered.

Ease of Construction

Children, grandmothers and beavers can (and all do) build cordwood masonry buildings. If you can stack wood, you can build a cordwood home. The heaviest lift in the wall-making process

FIGURE 30.1. In upstate New York, Rob and Jaki Roy have created an attractive compound of green-roofed cordwood structures, gardens and monolithic stones that they call Earthwood. [Credit: Rob Roy]

might be a 20 lb (9 kg) log end or, perhaps, a window frame.

Energy Efficiency

Cordwood masonry combines insulation and thermal mass in a wonderful way. The key, surprisingly, is that the thermal characteristics of the insulated mortar matrix are superior to the wooden portion. Mortar makes up about 40 percent of the total wall area, the log ends about 60 percent. Insulation values of wood, on end grain, range from approximately R-0.5 to R-1.0 per inch, with dense hardwoods toward the bottom of the list and light and airy woods, such as Northern white cedar, at the top. Our 16 in. white cedar cordwood walls at Earthwood have an R-value of about R-19. In Manitoba, Professor Kris Dick, PE, has tested a 24 in. wall with sensors and derived an R-35 value.

But insulation is only part of the story. Equally important is the great thermal mass of both the log ends and the mortar joints. The entire mass of the inner mortar joint is correctly placed on the warm side of the insulation for winter heat storage and summer cooling. Thus, thanks to this wonderful juxtaposition of insulation and mass, cordwood homes can stay a steady comfortable temperature, summer and winter.

Aesthetics

Jaki and I were first drawn to cordwood masonry by its appearance, which combines the warmth of wood with the texture of fine stone masonry. And all sorts of special design features, including shelves, patterns and "bottle-ends," can be incorporated into a cordwood wall. Some cordwood homes are sculptural works of art. And the work is fun!

Environmental Harmony

Cordwood masonry makes good use of indigenous and recycled materials: wood, sand, sawdust, even bottles. Although we have had good long-term success with Portland cement-based mortar mixes, some natural builders may object to the environmental impact of cement. The pros and cons of this argument are too numerous to list here, but those who cannot or will not use Portland cement will be glad to know that a cordwood wall can also be built with cob instead of a cement mortar. When such a home finally

FIGURE 30.2. A "MIM-stick" helps the builder judge the width of the three components of the mortar joint. MIM stands for Mortar-Insulation-Mortar. This one, for a 12 in. (30 cm) cordwood wall, shows the width of the 4 in. (10 cm) inner mortar joint, the 4 in. of the sawdust insulation and the 4 in. outer mortar joint. [Credit: Jaki Roy]

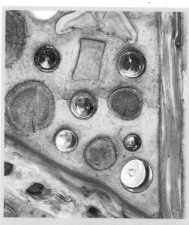

FIGURE 30.3. Bottles and cordwood create a uniquely decorative wall. [Credit: Rob Roy]

gives up the ghost—after hundreds of years if it is built right—it will recede gracefully into the landscape whence it came.

Three Building Styles

Cordwood masonry houses come in three distinct styles, along with various hybrids of these styles. They are (1) cordwood infill within a post-and-beam frame; (2) stackwall (or built-up) corners, with regular cordwood masonry between the corners and (3) curved-wall or round houses, such as Earthwood. With the first style, the timber frame supports the load, but in the other styles, the cordwood masonry itself is load-bearing.

The stackwall corners method involves building up the corners first with regular units (called "quoins"), such as six-by-six timbers or quartered logs. The quoins are crisscrossed on alternate courses; the technique evolved from a similar stacking method used to support the ends of firewood ranks. After stackwall corners are built up, say, three feet (one meter), a mason's line is stretched from corner to corner and the sidewalls are built in the usual way. A typical 8 ft. high (2.4 m) wall can be built in three lifts by this method.

However, I must admit that I am not a big stackwall corner fan. A strong timber frame actually uses less milled lumber, while allowing early roof installation for umbrella protection of the cordwood walls during construction. As for load-bearing round structures, well, we live in one and we love it. But work would have progressed faster and easier had we built within a 16-sided (virtually round) post-and-beam frame. In seismic zones, a wood-framed structure is an absolute necessity.

The Four Most Frequently Asked Questions

Doesn't the wood rot? No. Rot is caused by fungi that literally digest the wood. Fungi need air, food and moist conditions to propagate. With cordwood masonry, which breathes along end grain, the wall may get wet in a driving rainstorm, but it very quickly dries out again, and fungi cannot get a foothold. The Mecikalski Store in Jennings, Wisconsin, (now a museum) was built in 1899, and the log ends are still in excellent condition. Many cordwood walls built in the middle of the 19th century in Wisconsin, Canada and Sweden are also still in good condition.

To avoid rot, follow four simple rules: (1) Use only sound wood with the bark removed. (2) Do not allow two log ends to touch each other, as this traps moisture. (3) Use a good overhang of at least 16 in. (40 cm) all around the building. And (4) keep the cordwood at least 8 in. (20 cm) clear of the ground, supported by

FIGURE 30.4. This octangular structural framework is infilled with cordwood and mortar. This sturdy structure also supports a living roof, which in the winter will sport an insulating cap of snow. [Credit: Rob Roy]

What kind of wood should be used? Short answer: use what you've got. If there is a choice, though, go with the lighter, airier woods, such as white cedar, spruce, loblolly pine or poplar (quaking aspen), rather than the harder denser species like oak, maple or Southern pine. The lighter woods have better insulation value, and perhaps more importantly, they are more stable, with less tendency to shrink or expand. With the preferred woods, it is good to air dry them in single ranks, covered, for a full year before using them in a wall.

With denser woods, there is a danger of wood expansion if the log ends are seasoned too long: over-seasoned wood will absorb moisture and re-expand, creating cracks in the wall and possible structural (expansion) damage. So just cut them to length, remove the bark, split them if desired and dry them for only a few weeks before use. They will probably shrink in the wall, but they will do that anyway, even if you dry them for a year. Wood shrinkage is a temporary cosmetic problem, not structural, and after a year or two, the shrinkage gaps (if they occur) can be filled with

clear caulk, less noticeable than trying to match the mortar color.

Are round or split log ends best? You can use rounds, splits or a mixture. Just maintain a consistency of texture and style. Rounds absorb less moisture from the mortar through their edges (the cambium layer), but you can season your wood faster by splitting it. If you split the wood, make a variety of sizes and shapes. It is difficult to keep a constant thickness of mortar joint, for example, with all quartered log ends. Over the years, Jaki and I have come to prefer working with rounds, from 2 in. up to 16 in. (5–40 cm) in diameter. But our main house, Earthwood, is mostly built of old split-cedar fence rails, and has worked very well for us. A few large rounds are mixed in as design features. Which style looks better is a value judgment. Do what *you* like.

What is the best mortar mix? A full discussion of mortar mixes is not possible here, but I will share a mix that has stood the test of time at Earthwood for over 30 years: 9 parts sharp sand, 3 parts soaked sawdust, 3 parts lime, 2 parts Portland cement. The sand should be fine, not coarse, to retain plasticity and

to allow good smooth "pointing" (also called "grouting"). The sawdust is used to retard the set of the mortar, thus reducing mortar shrinkage and cracking. To accomplish this, the sawdust must be of the light and airy variety, and is passed through a ½ in. (1.25 cm) screen to remove bark and chunks of wood. The sawdust is then soaked overnight in an open vessel such as a 55-gallon drum, and introduced wet into the mix. The cement is for strength, and lime is used to make the mix more plastic (workable). Use Type S builder's (or mason's) lime, not agricultural lime, intended for lawn and garden use; it will not calcify.

Lime-putty mortar is another option and has pros and cons and cautions too numerous to list in this short article. See *Continental Cordwood Conference Collected Papers*, 2005 and 2011, for good articles on the subject.

Hardwood sawdust does not seem to work as a mortar additive, and the worst thing you can do is to put *dry* sawdust into the mix, as this accelerates rather than retards the mortar set. If the right kind of sawdust cannot be obtained locally, it is better to go with a commercially available cement retarder such as Daratard-17 (W.R. Grace and Co.) or Plastiment (Sika Corporation). Typically, three ounces of retarder is used in a wheelbarrow load of mortar. Leave out the sawdust and add an extra shovelful of sand to replace the missing bulk.

Jaki and I always mix in a wheelbarrow for quality control and worksite harmony. With a powered mixer, it is all too easy to overwater the mix. And you're at the mercy of the loud and vexatious "infernal frustration" engine. Plus, you still have to carry the mortar to the wall with…a wheelbarrow! Add just enough water to make a good stiff mix. We use a "snowball test." Throw a snowball-sized ball three feet in the air (one meter in Canada). It should not splatter when you catch it (too wet) nor should it crumble apart (too dry). Only with the right consistency can you juggle two or three snowballs. In masonry parlance, you want stiff—yet plastic—"stone" mortar, not the thinner mortar used for brickwork.

Pointing

Pointing or smoothing the mortar, on both interior and exterior surfaces, is a very important part of cordwood building and can take 10 to 20 percent of the total building time. We use an old non-serrated butter knife as a pointing tool, with its last inch bent about 15 degrees. Here's why pointing is important:

- Smooth stainless-steel finish pointing beautifies the wall by accenting the masonry units, the log-ends, like fine stone masonry.
- The pointing tightens up the friction bond between wood and mortar.
- Smooth mortar repels water on the exterior and diminishes dust gathering on the interior.
- Finally, by pushing the mortar back from the ends of the logs, creating say a ¼ in. (0.5 cm) recess, you create a place to apply any needed remedial action in case the wood shrinks or the mortar cracks. Log chinking products like Log Jam (Sashco Industries) work well in this instance.

FIGURE 30.5. Pointing the mortar joint—here with a butter knife—is a very important part of the cordwood building process. Pointing maximizes the friction bond between the log ends and the mortar, beautifies the wall, helps repel water on the exterior; and lessens dust and cobweb buildup on the interior. [Credit: Jaki Roy]

FIGURE 30.6. Cordwood walls can also be mortared with mud (a clay/sand/fiber mixture). This is more eco-friendly, and typically less expensive, than cement mortar. And there is no danger in applying and pointing the mortar with bare hands. [Credit: Michael Smith]

Cobwood

Over the past 20 years, several people around the world have used cob instead of cement mortar. The results are encouraging. Tony Wrench in Wales has been living in his cordwood and cob round house for many years. (See thatroundhouse.info.) In late 2000, Jaki and I collaborated on cobwood building with Ianto Evans and Linda Smiley of the Cob Cottage Company, both at Earthwood and at the Natural Building Colloquium in Kingston, New Mexico. We have learned that we can substitute straw-rich cob for the mortar, and found that the cob points quite well with our regular pointing knives.

Another option is to apply a "finish cob" (without the straw reinforcing) to a recessed cob joint later on, in order to obtain a smoother grout. An ecological advantage of cob is that no Portland cement is used; walls can be built entirely of indigenous materials. From a cob builder's perspective, the cordwood saves one heckuva lot of cob mixing. The insulated space should still be retained for energy efficiency, particularly in the north, and this further reduces cob mixing. Cobwood building may very well be a return to the cordwood masonry of a thousand years ago, when the use of clay as a binder was much more likely than the use of lime mortars. Cordwood masonry may simply be coming full circle.

RESOURCES

Books

• Flatau, Richard. *Cordwood Construction: Best Practices*, Cordwood Construction Resources, 2012. This self-published compendium details "best practices" methods of cordwood masonry and its relationship to foundations, electrical considerations, energy codes and more.

• Flatau, Richard, Becky Flatau et. al., eds. *Continental Cordwood Conference Collected Papers, 2005 and 2011*. These papers from the most recent Cordwood Conferences, with 50 articles between them, contain the latest developments in the field, including lime putty and paper-enhanced mortars, "wraparound" log ends and dozens of case studies. Available from Earthwood Building School.

• Flatau, Richard, Alan Stankevitz, Rob Roy and Dr. Kris Dick, PE, eds., *Cordwood and the Code: A Building Permit Guide*. Here's documentation for your building inspector, covering R-values and fire-resistance of a cordwood wall, compression strength, cordwood in a seismic 3 zone, REScheck (energy) analysis and more. Available from Earthwood Building School.

• Roy, Rob. *Cordwood Building: The State of the Art*, New Society Publishers, 2003. This comprehensive volume collects the experiences of 25 of the world's leading cordwood masons, from the early pioneers right up to modern visionaries writing about paper-enhanced mortar, cobwood and more.

DVDs

• *The Complete Cordwood DVD with Rob and Jaki Roy*. This 3.25-hour DVD combines *Cordwood Masonry Techniques*, a how-to introduction showing every step of the wall building process, with *Cordwood Homes*, a tour of seven cordwood houses, featuring interviews with owner-builders.

• The books and DVD listed above are all available from Earthwood Building School.

Websites

• daycreek.com: an excellent long-standing forum on all things cordwood, plus books, workshop listings and other resources.

• greenhomebuilding.com includes a Q & A cordwood column by Rob Roy.

Organization

• Earthwood Building School: cordwoodmasonry. com. Offers workshops and consulting on cordwood masonry, earth-sheltered construction and "timber framing for the rest of us." West Chazy, New York.

Straw Bale Building: Lessons Learned

31

CATHERINE WANEK

A wonderful irony about straw bale advocates is that they often started out as complete skeptics: "Doesn't it rot? Doesn't it burn? What about the Big Bad Wolf?" We converts who have heard this before have learned to answer patiently. After all, it was only a couple of decades ago that modern-day pioneers seeking affordable, ecological, healthy housing built the first code-approved straw bale homes. Since then, straw bale houses have been built all across the USA and all over the world. And we've observed many doubters converted to passionate natural builders by the amazing potential of the humble bale.

Individually, a stalk of straw seems fragile, but hundreds together, compressed and baled, make a sturdy building block. Stack a bunch of these blocks together, and walls can go up in a hurry—especially if you enlist your family and friends to help. Roof and plaster it, and you have a super-insulated, healthy house. The concept is simple and intuitive.

A straw bale home not only feels good, but you can feel good about it—straw is commonly underutilized, either composted or burned as an agricultural waste product. The "staff" of the "staff of life," straw is available wherever grain is grown. Baled and stacked like giant bricks to form a thick wall, bales offer super insulation from the heat or cold or noise outside, providing a quiet, comfortable living space with modest lifetime energy requirements. The thick finish plaster on interior walls also provides a significant amount of the thermal mass required for effective solar design, enhancing energy efficiency and human comfort.

Replacing stick-frame walls with bales can reduce the amount of timber needed in a modern home, reducing demand on forest resources. Should a building fire get started, lab tests and experience have shown that wooden studs and trim will burn readily and foam insulations ignite at low temperatures, releasing poisonous fumes. But straw bales, compressed and sealed with plaster, are starved of oxygen and resist combustion. If they do catch on fire, they merely smolder, allowing precious time for occupants to exit and for help to arrive. Conventional construction codes require a 30-minute fire rating. Plastered straw bale walls

CATHERINE WANEK *is the author/photographer of* The Hybrid House: Designing with Sun, Wind, Water and Earth *and* The New Strawbale Home, *and producer of* The Straw Bale Solution *and the* Building with Straw *series of videos. She spent five years managing and editing* The Last Straw Journal: The International Journal of Straw Bale and Natural Building. *In 1992, the inspiring process of building a straw bale greenhouse during a weekend workshop changed her life.*

have been tested and certified at 1-hour, 90 minute and 2-hour fire ratings.

Unlike manufactured insulation materials such as fiberglass and foam, straw is natural and non-toxic, and very low in embodied energy—the energy required to process and deliver a material to a building site. Building with bales also has the potential to reduce global warming gases by significantly reducing fossil fuel consumption for heating and cooling. Preliminary studies in China, where homes are typically heated with coal, indicate that each straw bale home built there, over a projected 30-year life (and they should last much longer), will reduce the amount of carbon entering the atmosphere by 150 tons (136 metric tons). That's huge.

Good Design and Detailing

To live up to their promise, straw bale building systems must be understood and optimized. Up to the present, most straw bale buildings have been custom designs, built one at a time by construction workers learning as they go. As more builders gain experience with bale building, and efficient designs and standard details are developed, economies of scale will reduce costs and

some problems associated with inexperience.

While straw bale building is a fairly forgiving methodology, every kind of building shares critical common failure points that require careful attention. Moisture is the greatest cause of building failure for all types of construction; steel studs can rust inside a wall, concrete and synthetic stucco can develop severe mold problems and wet wood can rot or be attacked by termites. Similarly, moisture intrusion from a leaking roof, through cracks around windows and plumbing leaks, have led to problems in straw bale buildings. So has wind-driven rain finding its way through flaws in cement stucco. The solution is a climate-specific

design, good craftsmanship and attention to detail.

Successful straw bale buildings in places like Alabama, Florida, Texas and Haiti have shown that airborne humidity need not be an insurmountable problem. Straw bales have a greater ability to buffer (absorb and then release) moisture than many conventional building materials. A proper air barrier and attention to the vapor permeability of the plasters is important. Choose plasters with adequate permeability, and eschew elastomeric coatings and paints, so as to not trap moisture inside the wall. In rainy coastal climates, builders often protect the plastered bale assembly with a ventilated rain screen, such as wooden shiplap

FIGURE 31.1. Pioneers who settled in the sandhills of western Nebraska found themselves in rolling hills with few trees and sandy soils. From the material at hand—bales of prairie grass—they built themselves sturdy homes. Some of these historic homes still stand today, proving the viability of plastered straw bale construction. [Credit: Courtesy Matts Myhrmann]

siding on the exterior, to keep wind-driven rain from saturating the plaster.

Whenever possible, build with bales with under 10 percent moisture content, which can be tested with a standard hay moisture meter. If a straw bale attains 24 percent moisture content for an extended time, it may begin to decay. Wet bales can also lead to insect infestations, which will likely disappear if the bales can dry out. Conversely, kept perfectly dry, straw can remain inert for centuries, even millennia. (Straw found in the pyramids of Egypt has been carbon dated to nearly 7,000 years old!)

A well-designed roof and foundation (the proverbial "good hat and shoes") will prevent most problems with moisture in bale structures. Raising straw bales 6–12 in. (15–30 cm) above grade, depending on climate, and installing a moisture barrier or a capillary break between the stem wall and first course of bales, should prevent moisture wicking up from the ground. It's also wise to create a "toe-up" to raise the bales above the final floor level, in case of interior flooding from a plumbing problem.

A roof design that incorporates wide eaves (20 in. to 3 ft.) [0.5 to 1 m] is also highly recom-

mended. Not only will it shed rain and snow away from bale walls, but it will protect earthen plasters from erosion and cement stucco from becoming water saturated. Wide overhangs help provide solar shading in summer; wide eaves, portals and porches offer living/storage space useful in any season. Flat roofs and parapet walls, commonly called "Santa Fe style," are not recommended. Unless their detailing and maintenance is impeccable, they will eventually leak, causing moisture problems in your home, no matter what your walls are made from.

Good window detailing is also critical to avoid moisture infiltra-

tion; follow the "best practice" in your region. In a straw bale wall, windows may be set all the way to the outside of an opening, leaving a bale-wide shelf or window seat on the inside; this eliminates any horizontal bale surfaces which must be protected from the weather. When windows are set inside the width of the bale wall, the exterior ledges should be sloped outward to allow moisture to drain. Also, proper flashing is essential, especially at the inside corners of the windowsill. In every climate, flashing and moisture management above windows, and a "drip edge" at the outside edge of the windowsill is good construction practice. Window

FIGURE 31.2. The wide eaves of this steel-frame structure in rainy northern California shed precipitation far away from the stuccoed straw bale walls. [Credit: Catherine Wanek]

maintenance is also important, as rain may find its way in through cracks that develop over time.

Structural Options

Load-Bearing Wall Systems

The first straw bale homes, built on the Nebraska prairie over a hundred years ago, relied on the bales themselves to support the weight of the roof (as well as other loads like snow and wind). This load-bearing capacity has been confirmed by modern laboratory tests, and many building codes will now give permits for this type of structural wall system.

A load-bearing bale structure requires a stiff and strong bond beam (also known as a top plate, ring beam or roof-bearing assembly). Typically made of wood, the bond beam receives the roof loads and transfers them down evenly so that all of the walls bear equal weight. The straw bales are laid like bricks (without mortar), butted tightly together in a running bond, with full bales overlapping the cracks between the bales below. The weight of the roof will compress the bale walls to some degree, depending on how dense the bales are already. The orientation of the bale, whether it is laid flat or on edge, also affects how much the straw will compress (an on-edge bale compresses less). As it turns out, when a wall is in compression, it is stronger.

A load-bearing wall should be somewhat compressed (either by waiting while roof loads compress the bales, or pre-compressing by various methods) before the plaster is applied. The plaster skins stiffen the wall and hold the bales in compression. The larger the structure, the more tricky a pure load-bearing design can be; challenges include compressing all of the walls equally and getting the roof on before the rains come. Thus a modest-sized single-story rectangular building lends itself best to load-bearing design. Structural bale wall systems typically use less wood, and can often be erected faster, as they avoid the complex interface between bales and a separate structural system.

Non-structural

Larger, more complicated floor plans generally require a post and beam structure to support the roof, with bales used to infill the walls. One big advantage of this method is the possibility of raising the roof before the bales arrive onsite. This provides a place to store bales out of the weather and virtually guarantees no wet bales—something that has proven to be a nightmare to many unprepared builders.

Be sure to think through how your structure and the bales will

FIGURE 31.3. Plastered straw bales are strong enough to support the weight of a typical roof, along with the loads of wind and snow. In this load-bearing bale wall, the bale orientation varies, yet the bales, compressed by the bond beam, still support the roof loads. With a plaster finish, the bales will perform much like a stressed-skin wall system. [Credit: Catherine Wanek]

interact while designing your building. Ideally the lengths and heights of all of the walls should be multiples of bale dimensions; minimizing the need for notching, and custom bales will pay off in ease and speed of construction. One common approach is to wrap the bale walls around the outside, leaving the posts exposed inside. This results in a continuous insulating envelope and an interior framework that is easy to tie into.

Hybrid Structural Systems

Combining the structural capabilities of compressed bales and wooden posts is also possible.

Wherever doors and windows are located, they are attached to a wooden frame called a "rough buck." If these rough bucks extend from floor to ceiling, and are attached to the bond beam, they become part of the structure. This system uses very little additional wood to create a very strong structure that can support a two-story dwelling. One advantage of this simple system is that the bales can overlap in the corners, locking the walls together.

Another hybrid system that is very simple and very strong utilizes threaded metal rods on both sides of the bale wall, inserted through both the sill plate and the top plate, where they are attached with bolts. The bolts are tightened to aid compression of the bales. The rods hold the bales in alignment and are later encased in plaster. A variation of this "corset" system is the use of bamboo or saplings on either side of the wall, tied with twine, cinching the bales together. In both of these hybrid straw bale wall systems, it is common to use bales on edge.

Earthquake Resistance

The relatively low density of a bale wall system gives it a kind of shock-absorber quality.

FIGURE 31.4. Straw bales are most often used as "infill" insulation within a structure of wood, steel or adobe. They may be notched around posts, or the bale wall may stand to the inside or outside of structural members, as shown here. [Credit: Catherine Wanek]

FIGURE 31.5. Sometimes called a "buck and beam" system, this two-story hybrid design utilizes door and window framework (called "rough bucks") to support a continuous beam around the structure, to which the roof is attached, both with fasteners and strong strapping. At the same time, the straw bale walls overlap and interlock at the corners of the building. Roof loads are transferred equally around the structure by the continuous beam, and are carried partially by door and window bucks and partially by straw bales. [Credit: Catherine Wanek]

Laboratory testing has shown that a well-built bale wall system can endure a very sizeable seismic event. While the straw bale building codes in California require welded wire mesh embedded in the plaster and diagonal bracing to stiffen the structure, a low-tech alternative developed by engineer Darcey Donovan for seismically safe buildings in Pakistan proved effective in laboratory shake-table tests (see "PAKSBAB: Seismically-Safe Straw Bale Buildings in Pakistan," p. 403). Key elements include strong connections between the walls, the floors and the ceiling/roof structure, so that the building holds together as a single unit. A lightweight roof is also a plus.

Plasters and Stucco Finishes

Finish plasters serve multiple functions. Plasters add structural strength to the bale wall, dramatically increasing compression strength, wind resistance and racking shear strength; a plastered bale wall is considered a "stressed-skin panel." Protecting the bales from wind and rain, plasters also seal out birds and rodents that would otherwise find them to be an attractive cozy home, just like humans do. Common choices for finishes include earth-, gypsum-, lime- and cement-based plasters.

It's important to plaster both sides of a straw bale wall for fire resistance. Straw bales that are unplastered will support a fire in many circumstances. For example, if an interior wall were "furred out" with studs to attach drywall without plastering it first, the resulting air space could act as a chimney in case of a fire. A well-sealed bale wall is also critical for energy efficiency, as even minor gaps allow air to filter through the porous bale, reducing its effective insulating ability, or R-value.

Plasters must not freeze before they have cured, and all plaster will shrink as it dries, leaving a gap where it meets framing (see "Natural Building for Cold Climates," p. 73). Straw bales are potentially vulnerable to mold growth from moisture introduced into the building as interior plasters are applied. To prevent excessive humidity levels indoors, it's imperative to open windows, and even use fans, to vent this moisture vapor out of the building. Plan to plaster in the dry season, and before winter.

Permeability (sometimes called "breatheability") is the capacity of a material to allow moisture vapor to move through it. Canadian testing has confirmed that plasters on straw bale walls should have some degree of permeability, so that any water vapor that finds its way into a wall can exit harmlessly. An impermeable

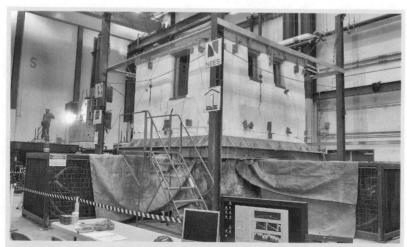

FIGURE 31.6. Tested on a University of Nevada "shake table," a low-tech straw bale building system developed by Pakistan Straw-bale and Appropriate Building (PAKSBAB) withstood twice the seismic acceleration of the Northridge, California, earthquake. [Credit: Darcey Donovan]

plaster will cause water vapor to condense into liquid moisture inside the wall, setting the stage for potential mold growth.

Conventional builders and local building codes often specify a plastic membrane under the siding, usually referred to as the WRB (water-resistive barrier). This layer is generically called "house wrap," and sometimes mistakenly called the "air barrier." While house wrap may be useful in some construction methods, it is dangerous and destructive in a straw bale wall. We must avoid anything that will prevent the plaster from "keying in" or bonding to the bales, reducing the wall's structural strength Also, as water vapor released inside the building migrates to the colder exterior through the straw bale wall, it will tend to condense on the inside of the membrane. This moisture will dry out very slowly, and when the temperature warms, it can produce conditions ripe for fungal growth.

An air barrier is useful for every kind of construction. This is a continuous surface that prevents the flow of air (but not moisture) from inside to outside, and vice versa. A good air barrier improves the thermal efficiency and moisture properties of the wall. Building science has shown

that plaster can perform very well as the air barrier, provided that it is well detailed at the floor, ceiling and around all the doors, windows and other penetrations.

As expected, cement-based stucco is the strongest plaster, and also the least permeable. It cures quickly, through a chemical reaction, and dries to a hard, brittle finish that is prone to cracking, especially if it dries too quickly or if too much water is used in the mix. Adding lime to cement aids the workability and permeability of the mix. In a study by Canadian building scientist John Straub, the ratio of 1/1/5 cement/lime/sand tested as an adequately perme able plaster. Natural builders use cement sparingly, as it is high in embodied energy.

Like the manufacture of Portland cement, lime burning also occurs at very high temperatures and releases carbon dioxide into the atmosphere. Unlike cement, lime gradually reabsorbs CO_2 from the atmosphere as it cures. Lime finishes are significantly more permeable than cement stucco, and cracks are somewhat self-healing through the periodic application of limewash. Lime is hygroscopic, that is, it can absorb large amounts of moisture safely, and lime is anti-fungal and anti-bacterial (until fully cured), so it's appropriate wherever germs are a concern (see "Working with Lime," p. 347).

Earthen plasters, made from a mix of clay, sand and fiber, can be accurately called "dirt cheap,"

FIGURE 31.7. Even if you plan to finish a straw bale wall with a protective wood siding, it is essential to plaster it first. A continuous coat of clay plaster on both sides seals the bales against air, pests and humidity. Designer/builder Matthias Boehnisch, Windeck, Germany. [Credit: Catherine Wanek]

as some of the raw materials can often be harvested from the subsoil beneath a building site. They are the most permeable of plasters, and have the great advantage of being hygroscopic and hydrophilic, which means that they will naturally wick moisture away from a straw bale wall, protecting it from moisture intrusion. Judging from historic dwellings throughout Europe, it appears that clay actually has a long-term preservative effect on adjacent materials. And contemporary studies indicate that clay plasters help maintain a constant and healthful relative humidity within an enclosed space. Praised

FIGURE 31.8. While functioning to manage moisture and clean the air, interior clay plasters like these in Linda Drew's straw bale home also allow unlimited variety and creativity. [Credit: Catherine Wanek]

for absorbing odors and softening sounds, plasters of earth are also renowned for their beauty.

Comfort Control

Straw bale buildings are known for their thick walls and high insulation value. Once completely plastered, the bales are sealed, and the tiny air pockets in the straw create effective insulation. A straw bale wall, 20 to 40 in. wide is often referred to as "R-enough." While the exact R-value will vary from building to building, a straw bale wall gives enough insulation to provide comfort in almost all climates. Depending on climate, solar orientation and design can fulfill some or all of a building's winter heating needs, with thermal mass materials such as masonry or earthen floors and earthen plasters to absorb and store this heat. A thick coat of clay plaster on the inside will also aid in moisture management and, combined with adequate ventilation, help keep the air clean.

Without ceiling insulation, a straw bale house is like a thermos bottle without a lid. Since warm air rises, more heat loss and gain occurs through the roof than through the walls. Whatever insulation you choose in the roof cavities, air infiltration will significantly compromise its perfor-

mance and your comfort, so take care to seal any cracks, especially the joint where the walls join the ceiling, and around any ceiling penetrations. Moisture barriers in the ceiling and/or roof are recommended in some climates. It's usually wise to follow local codes.

Bales are rarely used as roof insulation in the US, but there has been much experimentation in Europe and Mongolia. It can work well, but the bales must be thoroughly plastered, as a fire-retardant and to deter rodents from taking up residence. Also, the combined weight of the bales and plaster will require a very strong structure to support it. Lighter-weight insulations commonly used include cotton and wool batts and blown in cellulose (see "Natural Insulation," p. 321).

Codes

The first straw bale codes were adopted in 1994, by the cities of Napa, California, and Tucson, Arizona, and the state of New Mexico. With each passing year, straw bale construction has been included in more state and regional building codes. Most countries throughout Europe, plus Canada, New Zealand and Australia, all have code-permitted straw bale buildings. In 2013, straw bale building was approved as an appendix of the 2015 International Residential Code (IRC) for one- and two-family dwellings. As a US code adopted in nearly every jurisdiction in the United States (and as a model for some other countries), acceptance into the IRC paves the way for routine permitting nationwide.

Codes have been both a blessing and a curse for straw bale designers and builders. Code approval has been essential for gaining acceptance with lenders and insurance companies. Yet, within just a few years of their adoption, the new codes are often perceived as inflexible and restrictive, hindering new, improved bale building methodologies. New codes in general are mandating more insulation, reflecting our society's growing awareness of the need for increasing energy efficiency. In this context, straw bale building offers a green alternative to conventional construction methods, and, for many, a stepping stone toward natural building and greater sustainability.

Trends

Experimentation with plastered bale wall systems continues unabated. It seems that on each home that is built, someone comes up with a new, more effective or faster solution. As more building professionals become aware of plastered straw bale walls, the field of building science has increasingly been applied to these systems, offering an awareness of detailing that can make any building perform even better (see "Natural Building for Cold Climates," p. 73).

The "Passivhaus" (Passive House) is a concept for energy-saving buildings developed in Darmstadt, Germany. The evolving Passivhaus standard is currently being adopted and applied throughout Europe and the US. It offers strict standards for insulation, airtightness and solar orientation that reduce energy use by 90 percent or more, compared to code minimums. Straw bale architects and builders have successfully risen to the Passivhaus challenge by paying close attention to areas of potential air leakage, proving that well-detailed straw bale buildings can stack up against high-tech manufactured materials.

Many high-profile commercial buildings have also been built using straw bales, including schools, businesses and even a post office. In 2013, an eight-story social housing building was constructed in Saint Die, France, using prefabricated straw bale panels in a very contemporary design, which worked to solve the potential rain exposure issues with straw bales in tall buildings.

FIGURE 31.9. The challenging energy standards of the German "Passivhaus" concept have been achieved by straw bale architects and builders both in Europe and the United States. This super-energy-efficient home in Wienerherberg, Austria, designed for Angelika Rutard by architect Winfried Schmelz, employs modular straw bale wall panels, finished with a wooden rain screen. [Credit: Catherine Wanek]

Other smaller-scale panelized straw bale wall systems are being used effectively in Canada and Australia. Straw bale author and teacher Chris Magwood developed a very low-tech panelized straw bale system in response to unpredictable weather. These small-scale plastered bale panels can be preassembled and plastered inside a shop, then rapidly erected onsite with little concern for weather. John Glassford of Huff & Puff Constructions in Australia also developed a panelized bale wall system similar to concrete tilt-up systems, in which he can use either a regular small bale or a jumbo bale measuring 4 ft. wide by 8 ft. long by 3 ft. high (2.4 by 0.9 m).

Swiss architect/builder Werner Schmidt has developed another structural wall system utilizing jumbo bales. In the laboratory, he has measured their amazing strength and insulation value—R-128! His solar-designed homes have little need for conventional HVAC systems. Typically, residents use their backup heating system (usually a wood stove) very occasionally, and for ventilation they just open a window. Schmidt favors clay plasters throughout the interior and lime plasters on the exterior, and usually incorporates prefabricated straw bale floor and ceiling panels.

At the same time, responding to the marketplace and human needs, other builders continue working to develop small, simple, affordable straw bale home designs. These have taken many shapes and forms, using straw bales in all configurations—laid flat, on edge, on end, even sliced in half. Experiments with straw bale vaults have had mixed results: the inexpensive bale is used for both wall and ceiling insulation and can provide its own structure. Disadvantages include difficulties in roofing and/or making the bales watertight. A number of initiatives in developing countries where straw is an untapped resource have introduced low-cost, high-performance buildings.

Retrofitting existing buildings with straw bale insulation also shows great promise. Although a quality job requires much planning and attention to detail, wrapping a sound but inefficient building with bales can make a huge difference in energy bills, comfort and aesthetics. A Tucson, Arizona, retrofit by straw bale pioneers Matts Myhrman and Judy Knox transformed a hot, homely concrete block home into a well-insulated work of art. In many situations, the choice to retrofit can extend the life of a building by reducing the energy drain of poor design (see "Re-

FIGURE 31.10. In the Swiss Alps, where winter snow can pile up to 33 ft. (10 m) high, jumbo straw bales plastered with lime outside and clay inside support the considerable roof loads, plus snow loads. Due to the high insulation value of the four-foot-thick walls, residents can rely almost entirely on solar heating through the cold, but sunny, winters. [Credit: Werner Schmidt]

modeling with Natural Materials," p. 91).

A Straw Bale Future?

Given our rapidly expanding world population and the mounting evidence of global warming, many visionaries are embracing straw bale construction as a housing solution that minimizes the use of fossil fuels and sequesters carbon. Currently the United States has more straw bale buildings than any other country, estimated at more than 10,000. Rather than leading the rest of the world toward resource exhaustion, innovative US owners and

RESOURCES

Books

• Jones, Barbara. *Building with Straw Bales: A Practical Guide for the UK and Ireland*, 2nd ed., Green Books, 2014. Up-to-date how-to design and building guide from the most experienced straw bale builder in England, emphasizing low-tech, cost-effective construction. Offers value to both novice and veteran.

• Lacinski, Paul and Michel Bergeron. *Serious Straw Bale: A Construction Guide for All Climates*, Chelsea Green, 2000. This excellent how-to guide focuses particularly on good detailing for cold and wet climates.

• Magwood, Chris, Peter Mack and Tina Therrien, *More Straw Bale Building: How to Plan, Design, and Build with Straw*, New Society Publishers, 2005. Clear, step-by-step guide on permitting, budgeting, designing and drawing up plans, plus the building process. Extremely useful even if you hire a contractor to build for you.

• Myhrman, Matts and S.O. MacDonald. *Build It with Bales: A Step-by-Step Guide to Straw-Bale Construction Volume 2*, Out On Bale, 1996. A profusely illustrated guide to all phases of construction, from planning through plastering. Excellent low-tech ideas and options. Find a free download at **dcat.net** and **thelaststraw.org**.

• Steen, Athena Swentzell and Bill Steen. *Small Straw Bale*, Gibbs Smith, 2004. A survey of small homes and simple buildings that inspire with their simplicity and beauty.

• Wanek, Catherine. *The New Strawbale Home*, Gibbs Smith, 2003. A color-photo-filled book of 40 homes in varying climates across the US and Canada, that showcases a wide range of floor plans and aesthetic possibilities of building with bales.

Periodicals

• *The Last Straw Journal: The International Journal of Straw Bale and Natural Building*: **thelaststraw.org**. The number one go-to resource for current straw bale information, this quarterly journal is available as pdf download and in print in full color. TLS is up to date on the international natural building movement, human resources and technical developments. *The Last Straw Journal* CD-Rom includes the first 40 issues.

DVDs

• *Building with Straw, Vol. 1: A Straw-Bale Workshop, Vol. 2: A Straw-Bale Home Tour and Vol. 3: Straw-Bale Code Testing*, Black Range Films, 1994: **strawbalecentral.com/st_bale.html#vol1**. From the early days of the straw bale revival, my humble videos are now available on DVD. They chronicle the building of my straw bale greenhouse, showcase ten of the very first straw bale homes in the early 1990s, from owner-built to code-approved Santa Fe style, and the very first lab tests on moisture, wind, fire and compression strength. Running time: three hours. Other, more recent, DVDs also exist, too numerous to mention.

Workshops, Training and Gatherings

• StrawWorks: **strawworks.co.uk**. Straw Works is based in Todmorden (UK) and works Europe-wide, offering architectural design and planning, consultancy on straw bale projects and building regulations and training in straw bale building and natural plastering.

• Endeavor Center: **endeavourcentre.com**; **endeavourcentre.org**. Chris Magwood's Canadian educational organization offers in-depth, hands-on training on actual construction projects, including some of the greenest homes in Canada. As of publication, they are planning to add an online Sustainable Design program by January 2015.

builders have begun to set an example of resource conservation, as more and more Americans choose to build their homes with bales—and boast about it.

The good feelings that emerge when people work together to help each other seem to be the strongest magnet attracting people to straw bale and natural building. Working, laughing and sweating together is a visceral reminder of our interdependence, and this connects us with those around us in an essential way. That is when building with bales becomes more than a methodology for a resource-efficient future; it becomes a doorway into a compassionate human community that holds out a hand to their neighbors in need.

RESOURCES

Organizations
• California Straw Builders Association (CASBA): **strawbuilding.org**. Leading regional straw building organization in the US. Holds a spring conference and fall gathering.
• The Canelo Project: **caneloproject.com**. Athena and Bill Steen's non-profit educational organization offers consulting, internships and workshops using natural materials to create hand-crafted buildings at their center in south-central Arizona. Elgin, Arizona.
• Ecological Building Network (EBN): **ecobuildnet work.org**. NGO founded by engineer Bruce King, an engineer working on making better buildings from ecological building materials. Excellent resource for technical information and code testing research on straw bale, adobe, rammed earth building and much more. He organizes interesting conferences and is a consulting engineer for appropriate technology and straw bale projects at **bruce-king.com**. San Rafael, California, USA.
• The German National Organization of Straw Bale Building (FASBA) has championed straw bale construction through laboratory testing, demonstrations and advocacy. Their website is in both German and English: **fasba.de**.
• Le Campillions, the French Straw Bale Network: **compaillons.eu**.
• The Straw Bale Association of Texas (SBAT): **design buildlive.org**. This group has evolved into an organization, Design-Build-Live, based in San Antonio, Texas, which offers presentations, workshops and networking.
• Spanish Straw Bale Network: **casasdepaja.org**. Spanish language informational network, including listserve and resources.

Websites
• ASRi, *The Straw Bale Alternative Solutions Resource*: **asri .ca/shop**. A resource for designers, engineers, builders and building officials working with straw bales in British Columbia and elsewhere in Canada. Detailed, comprehensive and peer-reviewed information to assist in applying for building permits. (PDF version, 52 pages.)
• CREST Straw-bale Listserve. An e-mail discussion group with lively and often useful discussion on mostly technical aspects of bale building. To subscribe, type "subscribe strawbale" in the first line of an email message to: majordomo@crest.org.
• European SB Listserve: **amper.ped.muni.cz/mailman /listinfo/strawbale**. Discussions, announcements, enquiries, etc., about building with straw bales in Europe (in English).
• Global Straw Building Network (GSBN) Archives. Professional straw bale network discussions, archived at **Greenbuilder.com**. Invitation only, but archives are available to all. To use your standard search engines to search GSBN try searching, for example, on "GSBN Foundations" and you get: google.com/search?q=GS BN+Foundations. In other words, just preface your search term or phrase with "GSBN." Your results will depend on how well you pick your search terms.
• Strawbale Registry: **sbregistry.sustainablesources .com**. Source of existing straw bale homes with location, lender and insurance information.

Building With Hemp

32

Tom Woolley

Over the last decade, "hemp-crete" or hemp-lime construction has evolved from a marginal activity, largely unknown in the United Kingdom, into a mainstream building methodology. In fact, hemp-lime has become the UK's predominant natural building technique, outnumbering straw bale and cob buildings tenfold. Why? Hempcrete is, for many, the most accessible, affordable and easy-to-understand method of achieving energy-efficient and environmentally responsible buildings.

The advantage offered by hempcrete over other natural building techniques is that mainstream builders find it simple to apply in relatively conventional buildings. It is possible to teach a competent builder how to work with hempcrete in just a few hours, as it is similar to forming concrete or spraying stucco. Hemp and lime together form a natural, environmentally friendly composite that can be incorporated into almost any kind of building.

Hempcrete has already been used in many large-scale commercial projects and public sector-funded schemes. This means that hemp-lime has great potential to reduce the environmental impact of buildings even when the actors involved have not completely signed on to green ideals. Much remains to be done, however, in terms of perfecting this unique composite material and creating greater awareness and usage within the construction industry.

An Alternative Approach to Wood-Frame Construction

Conventional wood-frame buildings consist of stick/balloon frames sheathed with boards on the exterior and plasterboard (drywall) on the interior. The resulting cavity is filled with insulation, typically mineral wool, glass fiber or petrochemical-based foams. Wooden siding or masonry cladding is then added to the outside surface for weather protection. To achieve the high levels of airtightness required for energy efficiency, plastic membranes with taped joints line the walls. The whole buildup is quite complex and involves several different trades, requiring a great deal of care and quality control.

While it is common to choose wood framing for "low-energy"

Formerly a Professor of Architecture at Queens University, Belfast, **Tom Woolley,** *PhD, now works as a freelance educator and environmental consultant for Rachel Bevan Architects in Northern Ireland. He has published widely on community participation, housing and green architecture. Tom is editor of the* Green Building Handbook *and author of* Natural Building *(Crowood Press) and* Hemp and Lime Construction *(BRE/IHS Press). His most recent book,* Low Impact Building, *was published by Wiley Blackwell in February 2013.* **bevanarchitects.com**

buildings, this modern conventional approach rarely achieves the standards predicted. Research in the UK has shown that despite claims of zero carbon for many low-energy retrofits, they rarely achieve even 33 percent of the predicted energy efficiency targets.* The poor performance of these so-called low-energy buildings, including overheating, is frequently blamed on bad building methods, such as thermal bridging, but it can also be argued that it is due to the poor performance of lightweight synthetic petrochemical insulation materials, and plastic membranes.

Hempcrete is also commonly used within a wood-framed structure, but the hemp-lime mixture is cast around or inside the frame, providing a solid, massive and airtight wall. Hempcrete walls can be stuccoed on the outside with a lime render and either plastered or left "as is" internally. There is no need for plastic membranes, tape or paint.

Hemp-lime may also be sprayed rather than cast. In this case, the solid wall can simply be rendered inside and out, or the exterior can be protected with a rain screen cladding such as brick, masonry, timber boards or cladding panels.

Thermal Performance and Other Advantages

Apart from its simple buildability, hempcrete has many other advantages. The hemp-lime matrix hardens into a robust, durable and vandal-proof wall, much stronger than lightweight forms of construction. It is also extremely fire-resistant, achieving much better than one-hour fire-resistance in tests at the UK Building Research Establishment. Hempcrete walls have good sound absorbency, providing excellent acoustic properties as long as the wood-frame detailing and internal finishes are appropriate.

Hemp-lime is more ecological than conventional construction as it eliminates the use of synthetic petrochemical-based insulation, plastic membranes and toxic foam fillers. There are no toxic chemicals in hempcrete. Lime has been used for centuries to protect timber from rot, so untreated timber can and should be used.

The excellent thermal performance of hempcrete results from its combination of insulation— the short particles of the hemp hurd—with the thermal mass of the lime binder. A solid wall with qualities of both insulation and mass buffers diurnal temperature swings, while minimizing opportunities for air infiltration.

FIGURE 32.1. A hempcrete wall under construction showing the structural timber frame. When plastered, this assembly is insulating and airtight.
[Credit: Miles Yallop Limecrete Co., UK]

* affinitysutton.com/media/364652
/futurefit-quick-links-PDF-1.pdf
(Dec 14 2013)

A 12 in. thick wall (30 cm) will give a theoretical "u" value of about 0.20 (R-25) at a density of 6.2–6.9 lb./cu. ft. (100–110 kg/m³). Better insulation can be achieved by reducing density or using thicker walls. In practice, hemp-lime is much more effective than simple conductivity calculations indicate, because of its thermal mass effects.

Hemp-lime is hygroscopic (able to absorb moisture from the air) and vapor-permeable, so it is able to buffer moisture and maintain an excellent relative humidity in buildings, while reducing risks of condensation. Also, lime is a natural biocide, killing both bacteria and fungus. Conventional synthetic materials do not have this capacity, and thus risks of condensation and mold growth are much higher. Hemp-lime has even been used in specialized museum buildings to preserve artifacts under ideal thermal and moisture conditions.

Using the Correct Hemp Material

The question is often asked, "Why use hemp instead of ordinary straw, wood fiber, etc.?" The answer is very simple: other cellulose materials mixed with lime and water will lead to a soggy mess, whereas hemp is tough and binds into a strong composite.

FIGURE 32.2. Detail of temporary plywood forms used to cast hempcrete for the Hemp Cottage, Crossgar, Northern Ireland. [Credit: Rachel Bevan Architects]

The hemp consists of "shiv" or "hurd" chopped from the woody core of the dried hemp plant. The fiber is stripped from the hemp plant using special decortication machinery (though this is still done by hand in China), and is a valuable product that can be used in many ways. The size of shiv particles can vary from ½–1 in. (12.5–25 mm); larger pieces should be avoided. It is important that very little fiber is left in with the shiv, and it should also be relatively dust-free.

Some people suggest that it is more ecological to use the whole of the hemp plant, without stripping off the fiber. This is a mistaken approach, as the fiber is much more valuable for a thousand other uses such as textiles, paper, rope, quilt insulation,

FIGURE 32.3. Bags of hemp shiv produced by Hempflax in northern Holland. [Credit: Tom Woolley]

bioplastics, etc. Also the fiber retains much more water than the shiv, which creates fewer air pockets in the final composite, thereby decreasing insulation value. Hempcrete with a high proportion of fiber does not dry out fully, so building this way can be a disastrous mistake.

As long as clean, dry, short and fiber-free hemp shiv is used, it can be sourced from anywhere. There is no need to use a proprietary hemp product. Hemp is bulky so it would be better if it could be sourced locally, but sadly there are very few hemp processing factories at present. While it seems romantic to grow hemp locally, stripping and chopping hemp by hand is very hard work, so it is better to buy it from a hemp-processing factory. As it is light and relatively inexpensive, many builders currently use hemp imported from other countries.

Getting the Lime Binder Right

Nearly 20 years of research and experimentation have resulted in a good technical understanding of the right kind of lime binder to use with hemp. Best practice involves a blend of both hydraulic and hydrated lime with some pozzolanic and other additives, sometimes including a small amount of Portland cement, which aids a quicker set and ensures proper management of the competition between the hemp and lime for the water in the mix. In hemp-lime renders, sand can also be added.

Proprietary lime binders such as Tradical, Vicat Prompt and Batichanvre are available in the market in Europe, and new products are under development. Most bags of specialized lime binders cost up to four times the price of a bag of ordinary Portland cement, but make the job of getting the correct mix much simpler. Critics say that because they contain cement, these products are less ecological, but generally the proportion of cement is quite small (less than ten percent of the binder). It acts like a catalyst to help the lime set faster.

It is possible to mix up your own blend, but it is much harder to ensure consistency unless great care is taken. Mixing hemp with Portland cement, rather than lime, results in a denser mix with less insulation value. Mixing hemp with earth also results in a dense composite (although we have recently made some progress with clay-rich subsoil to produce lighter hemp-adobe blocks). These may be useful in warmer countries where insulation is not so critical.

Mixing and Placing Hemp-Lime

The hemp and lime must be mixed in the correct proportions, though this will vary depending on whether a denser or lighter composite is required. Increasing the amount of lime binder in the mix reduces the thermal performance but increases the strength. In France, where hemp-lime is commonly used as roof insulation, the density is often substantially reduced by doubling the proportion of hemp shiv in the mix.

The correct amount of water must be added to the mix to ensure there is a proper set of the lime binder, but not so much that the mix is slow to dry out.

As hemp can absorb as much as ten times its own weight in water, it can deprive the lime of the water it needs to set and carbonate. This has led to suggestions that the hemp should be soaked first, but this is quite wrong. It is important to use as little water as is necessary to ensure that no dry powdery lime residue is left. Normally it is best to use a horizontal paddle mixer rather than a conventional cement mixer. Experienced hemp-lime builders can see at once whether they have got the mix right—too much lime or water will create too dense or sloppy a mix with poor insulation or setting properties.

Cast hempcrete is usually poured into forms that are about 30–40 in. (80–100 cm) high. Within 12 hours, the material is strong enough to cast the next lift. If the material is to be sprayed rather than cast, a whole wall section can be built in one process. After a few days, it is dry enough to resist damage, and within four to eight weeks, it is dry enough to be plastered or stuccoed.

It is important not to cast hemp-lime in very cold weather, so there are seasonal limitations in countries with cold winters. Freezing will damage lime, and the wall may not set properly.

Hemp-Lime for Flooring, Roofing and Renovation

Hempcrete can be used not only for walls but also in floors and roofs. Hempcrete floors require great care to ensure they dry out fully before floor finishes such as tile, set in lime mortar, are used. When cast as ceiling insulation, the roof construction will need to be stronger than normal to support the weight of the hempcrete. Thus it is often easier and simpler to use lightweight natural materials such as hemp-fiber, wood-fiber, cellulose or sheep's wool insulation to insulate the roof.

A key use of hempcrete is as a retrofit solution for insulating

FIGURE 32.4. Hempcrete being sprayed onto a permanent shuttering board by the Limecrete Company, UK, to create a prefabricated panel. [Credit: Tom Woolley]

existing buildings. Applying lightweight foam and fiber insulations to masonry walls can be very problematic and ineffective, whereas hemp-lime can be cast or plastered onto a wide range of old walls, both externally and internally. Historic building organizations in the UK have approved the use of hempcrete, either plastered on or cast in layers from 1.6–4 in. (4–10 cm) thick. Hemp-lime works with the existing thermal mass and gives insulation results better than expected. It is likely that hempcrete will be widely used in this way in the future.

Hemp-lime plasters and renders have been used on straw-bale and other natural buildings.

Hemp-lime and hemp/earth can also be made into blocks and there are even some commercially available. While these may be useful in some situations, hempcrete blocks are not a very efficient use of the material. This is because the resulting wall is much weaker, depending on mortar joints and the render system to hold the blocks together, and losing the benefit of a solid airtight wall. Casting or spraying hemp-lime like concrete is a much better and more cost-effective use.

Carbon Footprint, Cost and Warranties

Skeptics often challenge hemp-lime construction in terms of its embodied energy, as the burning of lime is seen as contributing to global warming. While the energy used to create lime is significantly less than Portland cement manufacturing, many regions do not have local lime production, so transport fuel can add to hempcrete CO_2 emissions. On the other hand, hempcrete may be carbon neutral or even carbon negative. The CO_2 absorbed by the growing of hemp can be seen to offset the lime production. One hectare of hemp absorbs between 10 and 15 tons of CO_2 during its growth; thus CO_2 is actually sequestered into the fabric of the building.

Hemp and lime are relatively inexpensive to produce. When constructing a house with hempcrete walls, the cost of the hemp-lime materials can be less than five to ten percent of the total capital cost. Of course labor, shuttering (forming) and framing materials have also to be factored in, but these are required in any form of construction. Currently some of the proprietary hemp-lime materials are overpriced as the manufacturers attempt to recover all their development costs and exploit the ecological niche nature of the material. But as more suppliers of hemp and lime enter the market, costs

FIGURE 32.5. A hemp-lime apartment building called Tomorrow's Garden City in Letchworth, England. This was featured in two prime-time TV programs. Houses built here used Tradical Hempcrete with Baumit render. [Credit: Tom Woolley]

will fall. Unfortunately, many people considering hemp-lime construction make a simplistic comparison between a bag of cement and a proprietary bag of lime binder, then complain that it is too expensive and start looking for cheaper alternatives.

Most owners and developers require guarantees, warranties, insurance and certification for building materials and methods. In the UK, this has largely been answered by Local Authority Building Control (LABC), which provided approval for hemp-lime at an early stage in its development. Obtaining insurance for hemp-lime buildings does not seem to have been a significant problem to date. However the investment costs in obtaining certification and carrying out testing are substantial, and further work is required.

Potential Problems

As hempcrete has gained popularity, a few rogue companies in Europe have misled customers with poor technical advice, and this has led to a handful of badly built hemp-lime buildings. Apart from encouraging people to use the whole of the hemp plant with a high proportion of fiber as referred to above, poor quality lime binders adulterated with soil have been supplied. As hemp-lime becomes even more widely adopted, it will be necessary to establish clear and rigorous technical standards for hemp-lime construction in building codes.

Hempcrete must be allowed to dry out fully before the building is closed in. There has been some negative propaganda about

Hemp and Agriculture

Growing hemp is not difficult, and it is relatively easy to source a wide range of seed. Harvesting hemp is a specialized activity as the plant is very tough and can wreck normal harvesters. A field of one hectare can grow enough hemp to provide shiv for a moderately sized house.

A common critique is that hemp takes up valuable food crop growing land, and that if everyone switched to erecting buildings with hemp, there would be no land left for food. This is a fallacious proposition, as even if all new houses were built with hemp-lime, this would still require less than ten percent of arable land in most developed countries.

Hemp is also a valuable food crop, often grown for seed, much desired in health food shops. Edible oil can also be extracted from the seed. So growing hemp is adding to, not detracting from, food production. Hemp fiber is used for clothing, rope making and many other uses including the interiors of luxury cars. There is even talk of hemp "plastics" being used for the interiors of Airbus planes.

Growing hemp is usually done in rotation with cereal and potato crops, as the hemp plant helps to clear the ground of weeds. No pesticides are needed, and fertilizer is not essential. Hemp growing does not normally require irrigation, except in semi-arid regions, and it may even be grown in areas where sewage is spread, as it cleans up the ground. Thus hemp is a positive part of healthy agronomy.

Surprisingly the drug association has not had too much negative impact on the adoption of hemp-lime construction in the UK. The growing of non-psychoactive hemp is still controlled or even illegal in some countries (including the US), but as the benefits of hemp fiber become recognized, there should be little difficulty in obtaining hemp shiv.

hemp-lime not drying out properly, but where this has occurred, it is the result of poor construction practice, using the wrong materials, casting hemp-lime during very cold weather or using non-breathable permanent shuttering or impermeable plaster and paint finishes.

While there are those who think that a material that sets or dries instantly is necessary in modern construction, in reality most buildings need time to cure and dry out, and the benefits of hemp-lime outweigh any small delays to allow proper drying time. While the casting of hemplime may appear to be labor-intensive, it does not slow up the building process. Indeed, in a demonstration project in Letchworth, England, where half the houses were built with hempcrete and the other with a dry wood-fiber insulation system, the hempcrete went as quickly as the wood fiber.

Examples of Hemp Buildings

There are now so many hempcrete buildings around the world that it is impossible to provide a database. They are found all over Europe as well as South Africa, the US, Australia, New Zealand and Canada. Hemp-lime workshops have taken place in the last few years in Spain, Switzerland, Poland, Holland, Denmark and Sweden.

Hemp-lime buildings in the UK can now be counted in the thousands. Houses include one-off private houses and low-cost social housing. Many of them exhibit other innovative energy and ecological features as well as the use of hemp.

In the UK, the Labour Gov-

FIGURE 32.6. Drumalla House social housing in Carnlough, Northern Ireland—one of many hempcrete housing projects in the United Kingdom. [Credit: Oaklee Housing Association]

FIGURE 32.7. Cheshire Oaks Superstore with hemp-lime prefabricated walls, perhaps the largest store ever built in the UK. Marks & Spencer's make great claims as to its progress towards a carbon-neutral policy for its buildings. [Credit: Tom Woolley]

ernment under Prime Minister Gordon Brown set up a special Renewable House Programme to encourage the construction of social housing with renewable insulation and construction materials. Eleven projects led to the construction of over 200 houses, most of which were constructed with hemp and lime.

A number of large wine and food warehouses have been constructed with hemp-lime. Educational buildings built with hempcrete walls include the Wales Institute for Sustainable Education (WISE) at the Centre for Alternative Technology and a six-story building at Bradford University. Newcastle University plans to construct a £60 ($102) million student housing project with hemp-lime modular units.

The retail clothing and food company Marks and Spencer's (M&S) used 230 prefabricated hempcrete (Hemclad) panels in a £22 ($37) million superstore outside Chester, Cheshire Oaks. The Hemclad panels saved 360 tonnes of embodied CO_2, and operational energy for the store is claimed by M&S to be 30 percent lower than similar conventionally built stores.

The Future of Hempcrete?

After a rapid expansion of hemp-lime in the UK, there have been some recent setbacks. The large Hemp Technology processing factory in the UK closed in 2013, and a factory in Wales making sheep's wool and hemp insulation was relocated. However, new companies

RESOURCES

Books

• Amziane, Sofiane and Laurent Arnaud, eds. *Bio-aggregate-based Building Materials Applications to Hemp Concretes*, Wiley, 2013. A highly technical collection of academic scientific studies translated from the French, covering structural, hygrothermal, acoustic and environmental characteristics of hemp-lime.

• Bevan, Rachel and Tom Woolley. *Hemp Lime Construction: A Guide to Building with Hemp Lime Composites*, IHS/BRE Press, 2008. An early technical guide to hemp-lime, much of which still remains valid.

• Sparrow, Alex and Will Stanwix. *The Hempcrete Book: Designing and Building with Hemp Lime*, Green Books, 2014. A new book which looks at the buildability issues of hempcrete with many case study examples and construction details.

• Woolley, Tom. *Low Impact Building Housing Using Renewable Materials*, Wiley Blackwell, 2013. Case studies of hemp-lime and other UK ecological projects with an in-depth discussion of policy and theory issues.

Organizations

• Construire en Chanvre: **construction-chanvre.asso.fr**. The French organization setting standards and good practice guidance for hemp-lime construction

• Hemp Technologies Global: **hemp-technologies.com**. New Zealand business promoting hemp construction.

• Ecocentrycy: **ekocentrycy.pl**. Ecological centre in Poland, supporting hemp construction.

• Rachel Bevan Architects: **bevanarchitects.com**.

• Example of hemp house with videos showing hempcrete construction: **irishcottagesdown.com/cottages/downpatrick/hempcottage**

• Modece Architects: **modece.com**. Pioneers of hemp-lime in the UK.

• The Limecrete Company: **limecrete.co.uk**. Hemp-lime construction company.

• Hemp-Lime Construct: **hemp-limeconstruct.co.uk**. Hemp-lime construction company.

• Lhoist: **lhoist.co.uk/tradical/construction.html**. A leading supplier of lime, dolomite and minerals.

• St. Astier: **stastier.co.uk**. Pure and natural hydraulic limes.

• Vicat Group: **vicat.com/en/Vicat-Group/News-from-the-Group/Vicat-introduces-its-100-natural-hemp-solutions**

• UK Building Limes Forum: **buildinglimesforum.org.uk**.

have entered the market making lime binders or supplying hemp, and it seems likely there will be a period of change as market forces have their effect on the supply chain.

Ecological construction methods still remain fairly marginal in the UK and other countries, and many advocates of low-carbon construction continue to promote toxic petrochemical-based insulation materials in preference to environmentally responsible alternatives. The success of the many hempcrete buildings that are providing energy-efficient and durable performance speaks for itself, however, and this will ensure a strong future for hemp-lime as a building material.

Building with Hemp Bales
by Chris Magwood

In 1998, the Canadian government legalized industrial hemp as an agricultural crop, allowing the return of what had been a prominent crop until the 1920s. Indeed, the region of Ontario where I live once supported a large hemp crop, used to make rope for the ship-building yards on Lake Ontario.

A neighbour of mine, whose grandfather had grown hemp, began planting the seeds of feral plants that had survived many decades of eradication attempts. He was growing hemp for seed production, and as is common with other seed and cereal grains, his straw was a by-product with little or no commercial value to him. When he harvested his first crop, he gave me a call to see if I'd be interested in using his hemp bales in my straw bale construction business. After inspecting them, I was very excited by the quality of the bales.

Hemp plants grow very tall (8–12 ft. typically), and because the stalks are very tough, they tend to remain whole within the bale, meaning that each "straw" is folded and crisscrossed many times across the bale. Each time the straw is folded during the baling process, it breaks open without snapping completely, and each break releases the fiber in the plant so that the surface of a hemp bale is a mixture of voids and fiber. Structural testing on straw bale walls has shown that the strength of bale walls comes from a strong bond between plaster and bale, and from the effect of the plaster skins being "tied" across the junction between bales. Hemp bales excel in these regards.

Once we started building with the bales, another advantage became obvious. Compared to ordinary straw, there is much less compression and distortion of the bales due to the thickness and ruggedness of the hemp stalks.

As with all things, there is a trade-off for these desirable qualities. Hemp bales proved very difficult to cut or trim. No lancelot wheel, chainsaw, bale saw or any other device we have tried is

FIGURE 32.8. The structural columns for this community performance space in Madoc, Ontario, Canada, are formed from large round hemp bales.
[Credit: Chris Magwood]

capable of making a good clean cut in a hemp bale. The strength of the fibers makes cutting difficult, and once a cut is started, the fibers frequently entangle the most powerful electric motors and ensnare the sharpest blades. We took to shaping window openings by retying smaller bales with the desired shape. It worked, but it was more time consuming than cutting other types of straw.

In addition to working with the local hemp farmer to make good building bales, I was intrigued by hempcrete. There was little information available at the time, but I knew that it involved mixing chopped hemp with lime. Armed with that much knowledge, the farmer and I embarked on a series of experiments with different "grinds" of hemp and mixtures of lime. We eventually arrived at a mix that was remarkably similar to what was being developed at the same time in the UK and Europe. Using the same kind of slip-forming system being

commercialized in these places, I made my first hempcrete walls.

While both the use of hemp straw bales and chopped hemp for hempcrete were great additions to my building practice, they have both been off the palette for a few years now. While there was an initial flurry of interest in hemp in Ontario, no commercial processing was developed for either the seed or the stalks, and as a result many of the pioneer hemp farmers were not able to make a living growing hemp. The farmer I was working with quit growing hemp in 2009, as did many others.

However, before the fledgling hemp industry folded (though I expect it will rise again), we were able to make a remarkable hemp-based building in Madoc, Ontario. The Arts Centre Hastings was designed to be an indoor/outdoor performing arts center built from as many locally sourced materials as possible. With the hemp farm just minutes away from the building site, hemp materials played a huge role in the building.

The octagonal performance space was formed using structural columns made from large round bales of hemp. The straight walls between the columns are small "square" bales of hemp. Hempcrete was used as a footing material,

FIGURE 32.9. Standard-size hemp bales are used to infill between the round bale structural columns. Chopped hemp was also incorporated into the plasters, and into the hempcrete used in the walls and foundation. [Credit: Chris Magwood]

As with so many natural building materials, hemp is a very viable and promising prospect. It wouldn't take much to develop the growing, processing and mixing technologies needed to make it an affordable and important part of a more sustainable building practice. For now, the likes of the Arts Centre Hastings building is unlikely to be reproduced until the advantages of industrial hemp as a crop enjoy more widespread support. I look forward to its return to my menu of natural building options!

FIGURE 32.10. Inside, the round hemp bale columns are darkened with additional coats of linseed oil on the clay/hemp plaster. The ceiling in the performance space is hemp canvas to help with the acoustics. Local compressed earth blocks are used for the wainscot. The performer room, seen through the doorway, features cobwood walls and an earthen floor. [Credit: Chris Magwood]

CHRIS MAGWOOD is obsessed with making beautiful and efficient buildings without wrecking the whole darn planet in the attempt. He is a founding director of The Endeavour Centre, a not-for-profit sustainable building school in Peterborough, Ontario, Canada, where he is also a lead instructor in the full-time Sustainable New Construction program. Chris is the author, most recently, of *Making Better Buildings: A Comparative Guide to Sustainable Construction*, as well as *More Straw Bale Building* and *Straw Bale Details*. **endeavourcentre.org**; **chrismagwood.ca.**

sub-floor insulation and wall insulation for one of the wings of the building. Another wing is insulated with light-clay/straw, using hemp straw. The entire building is plastered with an earthen plaster made from site soil with chopped hemp as the fiber. It is a very harmonious blend of materials, and makes good use of all the desirable qualities of the hemp plant, while avoiding most of the drawbacks.

RESOURCES

Books
- Fine, Doug. *Hemp Bound: Dispatches from the Front Lines of the Next Agricultural Revolution*, Chelsea Green Publishing, 2014.

Light-Clay: An Introduction to German Clay Building Techniques

33

FRANK ANDRESEN

Clay is an excellent building material, found in most places in the world. It is affordable and recyclable. Being an excellent heat and moisture absorber, it regulates indoor temperature and humidity variations. Mixed with fibers, it provides insulation, while preserving the fibers from insects, mice and fire. It absorbs odors and lends itself to architectural creativity.

Building with clay has a long tradition in Germany and other European countries. Half-timbered houses from the 12th century, framed with wood and infilled with a mixture of clay and straw, still exist. This traditional technique, known as wattle and daub, is still used in the preservation of historic buildings. Oak stakes are installed vertically or horizontally into the frame, woven with thin willow whips (wattle), and plastered with a heavy mixture of clay and straw (daub). When the daub is dry, it is plastered with a mix of lime, sand and animal hair. Finally, the surface is painted with limewash (see "Wattle and Daub," p. 253).

Several other historical techniques are still practiced in Germany. *Lehmwickelstaken* consists of oak stakes wrapped with a mix of straw fibers and clay paste and is mainly used as a ceiling infill. *Lehmwellerbau*, a technique similar to cob that was already established by the Middle Ages, involves straw-clay loosely stacked with a pitchfork and then compressed with a tamper. After a couple of days drying time, the wall is shaved with a triangular spade and the next layer is added.

As modern building materials became common in the second half of the 20th century, many of the medieval half-timbered buildings were renovated, and the clay infill was replaced with modern materials. Within a few years, these buildings began to show signs of decay and structural problems brought about by a combination of moisture infiltration and a lack of flexibility in the new materials. Research began to show that the best way to preserve old buildings was to replace the new infill with the traditional materials that had proven themselves over the centuries.

By the early 1960s, traditional building in Germany had almost died out, but much like the revival of timber framing in North America, a small group of builders began to relearn the craft. The increased environmental consciousness of the '80s led to a revival of traditional building systems throughout Europe. Clay construction techniques once again began to be studied as a viable building alternative, and

FRANK ANDRESEN *has been involved in professional clay building in Germany since the early 1980s. He has taught and applied both traditional and modern techniques in Europe and America for both historical and new buildings.*

many technical advances took place, especially in Germany and France.

Because clay building requires relatively simple tools and technical know-how, it has found increased popularity among owner-builders. Clay building

FIGURE 33.1. Two ways to make a straw-clay wall. The wall on the left was made of straw coated with clay slip and tamped into a form temporarily attached to the wall framing. To maximize insulation, the mix for the wall on the right was kept very light, with a minimum of clay slip added to the straw. This mixture was packed by hand into the wall cavity and is contained by wooden lath, which will stay permanently in place. Both walls will later receive two coats of earthen plaster. [Credit: Catherine Wanek]

companies have also been established, specializing in a variety of building techniques using commonly available equipment and pre-mixed, delivered raw materials.

The term "light-clay" refers to the mixing of liquid clay with large quantities of light materials such as straw, wood chips, cork or minerals. One of the recent refinements has been the development of straw light-clay, a mixture of liquid clay slip and large quantities of straw. [Note: In the United States, this technique is commonly called "straw-clay" or "slipstraw."—Editors] More straw added to the clay will result in a lighter mixture, with correspond-

ingly higher insulation values, while less straw creates a heavier wall. Mixtures range between 20–75 lb./cu. ft. (300–1,200 kg/m³). To get a very light mixture, the use of soil with a high clay content is necessary. Medium-heavy (between 40–50 lb./cu. ft. [650–800 kg/m³]) mixtures are most realistic for practical work on the building site.

The straw-clay mix is tossed together, then covered with a tarp for a day or two before the mixture is placed into a form and tamped. To preserve insulation qualities, it is important that the tamping not be too hard. After filling and tamping a section, the form boards can be removed

FIGURE 33.2. Seeds in the straw sprout as the wall dries. This is a wonderful example of synergy when working with nature. The sprouts help the wall to dry out. Once the walls are dry enough to plaster, the sprouts will die. Their roots will help bind the wall, while the dead sprouts create extra tooth for anchoring the plaster. [Credit: EcoNest Co]

Straw-Clay Nomenclature

by Michael G. Smith

After the devastation of World War II, German builders looking to reconstruct with inexpensive, available materials developed a new variation on the age-old theme of earthen infill for timber structures. Lighter and more insulating than traditional wattle and daub and similar systems, the new technique was called *Leichtlehmbau*, which translates as "light earth building."

Robert Laporte, a timber framer then living in Iowa, went to Germany in 1990 to study *Leichtlehmbau* as a natural enclosure system for healthy homes. Along with Frank Andresen and other visiting German experts, Laporte introduced the technique to many builders in North America, calling it "straw light-clay" or "light straw-clay." Over the years, this somewhat awkward translation has been shortened to both "straw clay" and "clay/straw." The same technique is also called "slipstraw," both in reference to the clay slip used in the process and the "slip-forms" the material is usually packed into.

Around the same time Laporte was in Germany, a computer engineer named Gary Zuker was building himself a house in Austin, Texas. Zuker had studied historical accounts of medieval European buildings, and initially called his wall system "cob," although it was actually closer to the German *Lehmwellerbau*, containing much more straw than traditional English cob.

Today, heavier mixtures of straw and clay that can be used for plastering and to sculpt walls without the need for forms are variously called "heavy straw clay," "straw-clay mud," "supercob," or "strob." Over time, the confusing diversity of terms in current usage in English will probably become simplified and standardized. Heavy or light, varying mixtures of straw and clay are among the most versatile and widely used materials in the toolkit of contemporary natural builders.

RESOURCES

Books
• Baker-Laporte, Paula and Robert Laporte. *EcoNest: Creating Sustainable Sanctuaries of Clay, Straw and Timber*, Gibbs Smith, 2005. Inspirational photos and case studies from North America's premier straw-clay building team.
• Elizabeth, Lynne and Cassandra Adams, eds. *Alternative Construction: Contemporary Natural Building Methods*, John Wiley and Sons, 2000. Contains a chapter on light-clay by Frank Andresen and Robert Laporte.
• Minke, Gernot. *Building with Earth*, 3rd ed., Birkhaeuser, 2012. Wide-ranging book from one of the world's leading experts on contemporary earthen building systems. Contains a chapter on various types of light-clay, with plenty of test data and other practical details.
• Racusin, Jacob Deva and Ace McArleton. *The Natural Building Companion: A Comprehensive Guide to Integrative Design and Construction*, Chelsea Green, 2012. Includes an instructive chapter on straw-clay and woodchip-clay walls, especially for cold and wet climates.

Organizations
• Econest Building Company: **econesthomes.com**. Robert Laporte and Paula Baker-Laporte offer workshops on straw light-clay as well as timber framing and professional design/build services.
• Fox Maple School of Traditional Building: **foxmaple.com**. Workshops in timber framing and traditional enclosure techniques, including straw-clay.

immediately and moved up for the next section. This technique, known as slip-forming, can be used for both exterior and interior walls, as well as for ceilings. Although dependent on water content, outside temperature and wind conditions, final drying time for a 12 in. thick (30 cm thick) wall is approximately 12 weeks during the warm season (making sure that both sides of the infill are exposed to the air while drying). Hence builders in northern climates must be prepared to start early in the year.

The use of wood chips instead of straw as an aggregate in light-clay mixtures increased in popularity in the 1990s. The drying time, shrinkage behavior and (most importantly) labor intensity are reduced when using wood chips. The size of the chips ranges from coarse sawdust to chunks up to 2 in. (5 cm) in diameter, depending on the chipper. The chips can be dry or green, but they should be bark-free, as bark decomposes rapidly. Wood light-clay [Note: called woodchip-clay or slip-and-chip in the US—Editors] is made of about four parts wood to one part clay slip. These ingredients can be mixed easily and quickly using a mortar mixer or even a cement mixer, then poured or shoveled into the formwork. Hardly any tamping is required.

A variety of forming systems can be used with wood light-clay. When reed mat forms are used as an infrastructure, studs should be no wider than 12–16 in. (30–40 cm) on center. By using wooden laths or bamboo as a light framework to cage the infill, these distances can be nearly doubled. Because the infill is anchored to the laths or matting, the whole wall is stiffer and shrinkage is virtually nil.

Temporary plywood forms

FIGURE 33.3. This woodchip-clay wall in Belarus will be covered with wooden siding for weather protection. The "rainscreen siding" will be attached to the furring strips, with a ventilated air space between the siding and the clay wall. [Credit: Catherine Wanek]

FIGURE 33.4. These 12 in. thick walls (30.5 cm) are tamped by walking in them. A tamper fashioned from a 2×6 is used to tamp corners. Note the reinforced plywood slipforms and the "Larsen truss" framing that allows the straw-clay insulation to run continuously through the middle of the wall. [Credit: EcoNest Co.]

can also be used to build walls that require no mats or lath. In this case, horizontal or vertical reinforcing such as saplings or small-dimension lumber should be placed in the middle of the wall about every 16 in. to add lateral strength. Many types of plaster can then be easily applied, making sure exposed framing is covered. The insulation value for a 12 in. (30 cm) wall with plaster can be up to R-25, depending on the quality of the wood chips and clay and the density of packing.

Besides being a strong and efficient building material,

FIGURE 33.5. Straw light-clay provides good insulation, making it appropriate even in cold climates. This small house built by EcoNest Co. awaits its exterior plaster. [Credit: Michael G. Smith]

FIGURE 33.6. A home under construction by Gunter Herbst in Germany. The frame is a combination of newly milled wood and salvaged timbers from old *fachwerk* buildings. The infill is made of Styrofoam mixed with clay, showing that light-clay can be made out of just about any light material. [Credit: Catherine Wanek]

light-clay reduces the use of wood in construction. The raw materials—clay, straw and wood chips—are available at very little cost. In many places, clay is available from the ground in large quantities, making transportation unnecessary. The mixing of the materials requires much less energy than the burning of bricks or the production of cement or synthetic foams. While the installation of light-clay is labor-intensive, the low cost of the raw materials can make it cost competitive with some modern building systems.

It is also possible to make bricks, blocks or panels with clay and fiber, which can then be used in a pre-dried state. With these dry materials, the range of construction techniques is even greater and the construction season can be extended. Light-clay bricks can even be used as a ceiling infill between beams. [Note: An early earthbag dome at CalEarth utilized bags filled with straw-clay to create a light-weight domed roof.—Editors] As required, these elements can be made either light or heavy and can be cut quite easily with a band or handsaw. Some producers in Europe hope to reduce costs by automating production, enabling them to price clay bricks and other natural products competitively with modern building materials.

An industrial prefabricated

Mechanizing Straw-Clay Production

by Alfred von Bachmayr

My first experience with light-clay straw was at a workshop in which the straw and clay had to be mixed by hand with pitchforks. I remember thinking that I loved the finished product, but I discounted the viability of the material due to the high labor requirement.

Having grown up on a farm where my father was always creating machines out of items from the junk pile, my mind went to work on a mixing device that could be easily made out of materials obtainable anywhere. I first tried a conventional cement mixer but found it too small and awkward to process significant amounts of material. I then created a tumbler out of a 55 gal. (250 L) drum, which replicated a cement mixer; even though the volume was greater, the problem of limited batch size remained. I started thinking about a rotating tube with the raw materials being fed in one end and the mixed product coming out the other.

After welding two 55 gal. (250 L) drums together to form a tube, I attached a driving belt to turn the tube to an HP electric motor. The raw material was fed in the upper end of the tube in sequence (straw, water, clay) and mixed as it tumbled down the tube. By adjusting its pitch, I could control the rate at which the materials went through the tube. A series of tines welded inside the tube helped mix the material more thoroughly by lifting it at each rotation up the side of the drum and dropping it when the tines approached vertical.

This device allows the ratio of clay to straw to be adjusted as desired. For walls where high insulation values are desired, the material can be mixed at a dry weight of approximately 35 lb/ft³ (560 kg/m³). Where more mass is desired, a higher percentage of clay is used, and the mix can be made to weigh 50–75 lb/ft³ (800–1,200 kg/m³). To optimize the thermal performance of a building, the lighter mix is used in north and west walls, while the heavier mix is used on the south and east, and in interior walls.

My mixer design continues to evolve. In order to produce even

dry board was developed in Germany in the 1990s. *Lehmbauplatte* is a clay panel board that is burlap coated and reinforced with plant fiber. Clay paste is applied to jute net fabric, then two to five or more layers of reed mats are laid crosswise with alternate layers of clay paste. Finally, it is covered with another layer of burlap and transported to a drying station. Material tests with this board have shown excellent fireproofing, soundproofing, deforma-

tion and diffusion values. The *Lehmbauplatte* can be used as a permanent form, combined with blown-in cellulose, or used as a ceiling and insulation board. It can be screwed, nailed and sawed.

All clay construction must be properly protected from the weather with appropriate construction details. Large overhangs are helpful. Lime plaster will protect the clay on exterior walls; paint, clapboards or shingles can also be used.

Get advice when necessary. Involve friends and family. Then, besides building a healthy home, you can save money, too. Working with clay is labor-intensive and requires patience, but you will be using materials from your own property—clay, wood, stone, straw, reed and other fibers—instead of forking your money over to industry or the bank in return for artificial, potentially toxic products.

more material, I developed a larger tumbler, 36 in. (90 cm) in diameter and 10 ft. (3 m) long. It is made of a tractor tire rim split in half, with corrugated metal roofing attached to create the tube. It is turned with a gear motor at about 30 revolutions per minute, and the whole device is mounted on a trailer that can be pulled to construction sites. This large device can produce enough mixed light-clay to keep a large crew busy compacting it in forms. The next evolution will involve a more automated feeding of the raw materials to the rotating drum and better delivery of the mixed material to the walls for compaction.

FIGURE 33.7. Alfred adds straw, clay and water into one end of his mixer as it turns. Out of the other end comes mixed straw-clay, ready to be packed into a wall. [Credit: Catherine Wanek]

Alfred von Bachmayr (1948–2013)

by Catherine Wanek

My friend Alfred von Bachmayr passed away from a rare cancer on August 4, 2013, at his home in Tesuque, New Mexico. I miss him, and wish to honor his memory with a short tribute to his many contributions to human beings in need, and to his cleverness as a natural builder.

Alfred von Bachmayr cared about people and the planet. An award-winning architect, he designed and built low-cost, energy-efficient and sustainable buildings using straw bales, straw-clay, pumicecrete, adobe, earthen plasters, rainwater catchment, alternative waste disposal systems and solar electricity. He also came up with low-tech ideas to make natural building easier, simpler and more affordable. He invented the straw-clay tumbler described above and developed the "pallet truss," a structural solution for supporting roofs where wood is scarce and pallets are readily available (see "Evolving a Village Vernacular in Missouri," p. 453).

Alfred was one of about 20 straw bale advocates who met at the Black Range Lodge in 1999 to discuss how we might use straw bale building knowledge to help during the war in Kosovo. By the end of the day, we had founded Builders Without Borders (BWB), which was conceived as a network of ecological builders and other volunteers dedicated to teaching and promoting natural building materials and methods as a solution to affordable, comfortable housing (see "Builders Without Borders," p. 421). Through BWB, Alfred was integral in designing and building a straw bale hogan with the National Indian Youth Leadership Project near Laguna Pueblo, an ecological compound for Catholic sisters in Chaparral, New Mexico, and a straw bale house for a family whose house had burned down in Anapra, Mexico. Anapra is a sprawl of pallet houses without city infrastructure, across the border from relatively prosperous El Paso, Texas.

This initial project evolved into a long-term relationship with the Anapra community, during which Alfred founded World Hands Project to continue the work, forging a partnership with a local priest and developing relationships with local builders. Alfred listened more than talked, and developed designs that worked with locally available building materials and skills. He located a nearby source of free clay to replace cement (which was unaffordable), and shifted from straw bale buildings to straw-clay infill inside pallet walls covered with pallet roofs, which were easier for local builders and families to construct.

During the last decade, Alfred worked closer to home, consulting with the Picuris Pueblo on a greenhouse design and helping the nearby Tesuque Pueblo to design and build a straw bale Seed Bank and develop their proposed Community Plan of 2013. He also helped restore an old adobe building into the Esperanza Shelter, a wonderful, warm space for kids from battered families. Alfred's community service included many years as *mayordomo* of the *acequia* (the neighborhood irrigation system) in Tesuque.

Alfred will be remembered as a creative tinkerer and a hardworking, practical person. He loved people and nature, grew a bountiful garden, lived an active and joyful life and had many friends.

Wattle and Daub

34

JOSEPH F. KENNEDY

Wattle and daub consists of a framework of thin, flexible sticks (also known as "withies") woven around wooden staves and then covered with clay-rich plaster. It is perhaps the most ancient earth building technique, developed when an enterprising human first daubed mud upon a branch shelter to make it more weatherproof. Wattle and daub (also known as rab and dab, *bajareque* in Central America and *quincha* in South America) was historically used throughout Europe, the Middle East, parts of Asia, North and Central America and in Africa.

In medieval Europe, wattle and daub was used as infill in "half-timbered" oak-framed houses. Usually, three oak staves were set vertically in each panel of the frame, with one end of each stave set into a pre-made hole in the top member of the frame

JOSEPH F. KENNEDY *is a designer who enjoys weaving twigs and plastering them with mud.*

and the other end into a slot in the bottom member of the frame. Then green twigs—usually of a flexible hardwood like ash, maple, hazel or willow—would be woven horizontally between them.

A green twig can be twisted at the point needed to create a curve when weaving the wattle. Twisting releases the wood fibers, thus allowing the twig to be wrapped around a stave without breaking

the twig. The wattle was sometimes left unplastered where ventilation was needed. Over time, this technique evolved into the lath-and-plaster walls that were common in the US and Canada up until the 1950s.

In Africa and Central America, thin horizontal poles were lashed on either side of vertical posts, creating a cavity that was filled with mud and stones. The

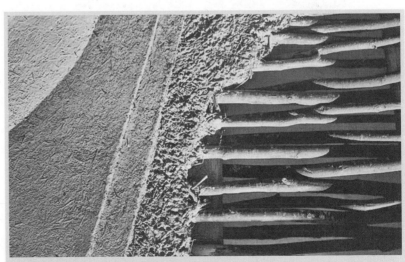

FIGURE 34.1. Detail of plaster layers on a wattle-and-daub panel. [Credit: Joseph F. Kennedy]

framework was then plastered on both sides, or sometimes just the inside. In Japan, whole narrow culms of bamboo or split larger stalks were used as wattle. In the Mississippean cultures of the Central US, researchers conjecture that grass or reeds were used to make woven panels.

There are a number of closely related techniques that also allow the construction of thin, non-load-bearing walls from clay, straw and sticks. Central European immigrants to Argentina brought with them a traditional technique called *Lehmwickelstacken* in German and *chorrizo* in Spanish. In this system, a straight stick was wrapped with clay-covered reeds or straw to form a long cylindrical "sausage." These sausages could then be stacked between wall framing members or slotted between rafters to make a ceiling. Some natural builders today make baguette-shaped "wattles" out of long straw and clay slip, then weave these around vertical staves. A quick natural wall covering can be made by screwing or stapling reed fencing material, available in many hardware stores, to a stud frame and covering that with earthen plaster.

However they are built, wattle panels are usually covered with an earthen daub. In Europe, daub traditionally consisted of clay, cow dung, chopped straw and/or horsehair. A high clay

FIGURE 34.2. Bamboo lath between timber frame walls supports mud daub in this Japanese structure. [Credit: Tom Lander]

content is necessary to make the daub adhere to the wattle, while fibers prevent excessive cracking. Pebbles can be pressed into the plaster to provide extra weather protection. To make the wall even more weather-resistant, it was often coated with lime-sand plaster. A mixture of paper pulp and Portland cement to replace the daub has led to good results. It is important to fill in any cracks that may develop between the frame and the wattle-and-daub panel after drying, to reduce unwanted air infiltration.

FIGURE 34.4. Plastering a traditional Tswana-style building at Tlholego, South Africa. [Credit: Joseph F. Kennedy]

FIGURE 34.3. Cutaway view of a European wattle-and-daub panel, showing (from left) oak staff, woven hardwood wattle and mud daub inside a timber frame. [Credit: Joseph Kennedy]

FIGURE 34.5. Thatched wattle-and-daub "rondavels" under construction in South Africa. [Credit: Mark Mazziotti]

Wattle and daub is fun and easy to build but is only appropriate where a large number of straight wattles can be ecologically obtained. The art of coppicing developed in many places where wattle and daub was traditional. Coppicing entails cutting down a suitable tree such as a willow or hazel, which then sprouts numerous thin shoots from the stump. These straight, flexible shoots are allowed to grow to the desired thickness and then cut for wattle, basketry or other purposes. In heavily wooded areas, small saplings can be effectively harvested for wattle. Other alternatives include using flexible timber off-cuts, bamboo or even recycled plastic or metal.

Because of the thinness of the panels (generally 3–6 in. [7.5–15 cm]), and their relatively poor insulation value, wattle-and-daub walls are not the best choice for exterior walls of buildings that will be heated or cooled. Yet thin, strong wattle-and-daub walls work well in temperate climates, for interior walls and partitions and for unheated outbuildings and sheds. To increase thermal efficiency, two wattle "forms" can be built, leaving a cavity between them which is then insulated with straw-clay or other natural insulation (see "Regenerative Building: An Ecological Approach," p. 131). The infinite flexibility of this simple system lends itself to creative application with a wide variety of other natural building techniques. And it is so much fun!

RESOURCES

Books
• Houben, Hugo and Hubert Guillard. *Earth Construction: A Comprehensive Guide*, Intermediate Technology Publications, 1994. This detailed, well-illustrated technical guide to many forms of earthen building contains a brief discussion of wattle and daub.

• Norton, John. *Building with Earth*, Intermediate Technology Publications, 1997. A good, brief introduction to the principles of earth building, including a brief discussion of wattle and daub.
• Sunshine, Paula. *Wattle and Daub*, Shire Publications, 2008. This small illustrated book is an overview of the topic, including step-by-step instructions.

The Evolution of Timber Framing 35

STEVE CHAPPELL

Timber framing has a long and rich history as one of the most adaptable natural building systems on the planet. Every forested region of the world has developed a form of timber framing as a simple way to create a structural framework. The early examples relied on crude joinery, often lashed together with rope. As systems evolved, sophisticated joinery techniques developed and, with them, the ability to create more complex designs. By the end of the Middle Ages, timber framing had evolved to a high level, combining structure with art, as evidenced by the great cathedrals of Europe and the pagodas of Asia.

Medieval homes and farmhouses, from England to Japan, share a striking similarity. In fact, the *minka* farmhouses of medieval Japan are so much like the farmhouses built in Germany during the same period that one might believe the same builder built them. In nearly every example, from Europe throughout Asia, the wall enclosure was constructed of clay mixed with cellulose fiber, usually straw, in some version of wattle and daub. Roofs were usually of thatch or stone. This system remained with few modifications throughout Europe and Asia into the 19th century. It became the common mode of house construction in nearly all northern cultures for more than a thousand years. The remarkable thing is that a great number of these dwellings are still in use to this day.

Timber framing was nothing less than a revolution in building, equaling even that of steel and concrete, which revolutionized our building environment at the beginning of the 20th century. One of the revolutionary aspects

FIGURE 35.1. This 15th-century French timber frame church with wattle-and-daub infill demonstrates that oak timbers, infilled with natural materials, can last for centuries.
[Credit: Steve Chappell]

STEVE CHAPPELL *is a master timber framer and author. He founded and runs the Fox Maple School of Traditional Building in Maine:* **foxmaple.com.**

was the fact that a structural framework of timbers allowed for great flexibility in how a building was enclosed. Prior to the advent of timber framing, wall systems *were* the structural system. The wall and roof systems that developed to enclose timber frames were both quick and easy to make and easy to repair. The materials, primarily straw and clay, reeds and stone, were also readily available—most often directly from the building site or the farmer's waste products, but never more than a day's cart ride away.

FIGURE 35.2. Non-slipping scarf joints in a Japanese timber frame. [Credit: Tom Lander]

Timber Frame vs. Post and Beam

The terms "timber frame" and "post and beam" are often used interchangeably. However, as construction language has evolved over the past generation or two, the two terms have come to define different structural systems. Post and beam is a structural engineering term that simply means the supporting of a horizontal member (beam) by a column (post). To say that a 200-year-old Maine barn is post and beam is correct. It would also be correct to say that a modern pole barn, using no joinery, but fastened with steel plates, is post and beam. But, to call the modern pole barn a timber frame would be incorrect. The term timber frame, as it is used today, implies a timber structure that is connected using nothing but joinery—mortise and tenon, secured with wooden pegs.

Craftsmanship

If we look at all aspects of traditional building systems, one thing above all stands out: craftsmanship. The minka builders of medieval Japan would search for the most crooked logs for the principal members of their frames because the challenges these irregular members presented would stand as a testament to their abilities as artists and craftsmen. Successful builders attracted more apprentices, who were then trained to follow the master's example.

Throughout a student's long apprenticeship, as great an emphasis was put on developing their skills as a fine craftsman, as the understanding of structure and design; these went hand in hand. If a structure were to stand for many generations, then no corners could be cut. The 800-year-old timber-framed stave churches of Scandinavia stand to this day for two simple reasons: (1) the frames were built based on a solid technical understanding of structural design; and (2) the carpenters who built them prized craftsmanship.

Pure structural forms can often be stark and uninspiring, but if you take a pure structural form, add an artistic element, execute it impeccably, such that you and your children will be inspired and proud, then respect toward it will be passed down to each succeeding generation. Buildings we respect are buildings we maintain. Without maintenance, no structure can survive more than a generation or two at the most.

The Earliest Timber Frames

The most common style of timber frame during the Middle Ages consisted of frameworks constructed by inclining two timbers, or blades (often made from one timber split in half lengthwise), to form an A-frame. These frameworks were called "crucks." The base of the early crucks commonly spanned 12–16 ft. (3.6–5 m), but spans up to 20 ft. (6 m) were possible. A typical house consisted of two or more crucks, spaced from 10–16 ft.

(3–5 m) apart, connected to each other by smaller logs or hewn timbers known as purlins. These were either lashed or set into notches on the cruck blades.

The earliest cruck-framed houses, known as "hovels," were buried or bermed with earth four or five feet above the sill plate. Above the earth level, reed thatch or stone was attached to the purlins. Impoverished peasants commonly built these dwellings; hence the term "living in a hovel" implies a substandard,

FIGURE 35.3. These full cruck bents of oak were constructed during a 2013 Fox Maple timber-framing workshop in Brittany, France. This was a very early style of bent framing first practiced in medieval Europe. [Credit: Steve Chappell]

FIGURE 35.4. Norway's Borgund Stave Church, built in 1180, is an early example of sophisticated technical ability coupled with a very high level of craftsmanship. [Credit: Steve Chappell]

impoverished existence. Crucks are commonly equated with European building systems, but a similar evolution took place in Asia during the same period in time.

As the form developed into the 13th century, cruck framing became extremely elegant, and was commonly used to construct community halls, chapels and even structural elements in the great cathedral roof frames. The essential design became the pattern for much more sophisticated roof framing systems; a good argument could be made that roof trusses as we know them today evolved from the cruck.

The early cruck builders relied on the earth as a buttress to prevent outward thrust and, ultimately, collapse. As knowledge of structural design developed, along with the development of better steel to make tools and the ever-increasing knowledge of joinery design and function, framing systems that could adequately resist the effects of thrust began to develop.

The earliest examples simply raised the cruck by placing it on top of two vertical posts connected by a horizontal tie beam. The feet of the cruck blades were joined directly into the tie beam to resist outward thrust. The earthen berm was no longer required for the structural integrity of the frame, and people could move above ground at last. This development became know as a bent frame, the common structural pattern for timber framing to this day.

FIGURE 35.5. The frame for the Fox Maple library was cut and assembled during a timber-framing workshop in spring 1996. This photo shows straw bale walls going up during a follow-up workshop led by Athena and Bill Steen. The wattle-and-daub wall at left and clay plastering were led by Frank Andresen. [Credit: Steve Chappell]

Modern Timber Frame Design

In using the term "modern," I include the period from 1400 to the present. Though timber framing may have had a down time in the US for nearly a century, the essential structural systems, methods and approach used by the common house builder in the 1850s and the modern timber framer in 2014 are the same as those used in the 15th century.

Of course, there are always shortcuts to take, by either simplifying or doing away with joinery. However, this would not be a timber frame by definition, but some sort of hybrid assemblage of

FIGURE 35.6. The library at Fox Maple follows the design of the medieval Japanese minka. This was not planned, but resulted from our decision to build the structure using only materials harvested within 50 miles of the site. It was only afterwards that I recognized its similarity to minkas, which were designed under the same constraint. [Credit: Steve Chappell]

Timber Frame Efficiency

In a typical timber frame, vertical support posts are spaced from 12–16 ft. (3.6–5 m) apart. A building 28 x 40 ft. (8.5 x 12 m) would require no more than 10 vertical posts. Assuming that a common timber dimension for a post is 7 x 10 in. (18 x 25 cm), and the wall height is 8 ft. (2.4 m), the board footage of wood required to build the structural wall support system for a 28 x 40 ft. timber frame would be less than 500 board feet (1.2 m³).

Using a conventional 2 x 4 framing system with studs at 16 in. on center, the same house would require nearly 2,500 board feet (6 m³) of wood. If 2 x 6's were used instead, which is normally the case due to insulation requirements, the board footage would increase to 3,400 board feet. This is more than seven times the amount of wood required for a structural timber-frame wall system. [Note: These figures include only the structural lumber used to hold the building up, not any wall or roof sheathing.—Editors]

By analyzing a number of different design models for a 2,000 sq. ft. (185 m²) house comparing stud frames to timber frames, consis-

tent ratios for the board footage of wood used per square foot of living area were determined. This averages were 8.1 board feet of wood per square foot of floor area for a stick frame, and 5.5 board feet per square foot for a timber frame. When comparing houses of different sizes, results showed that as the square footage of living area increased in a timber frame, the ratio of wood to living area decreased, while the ratio for a conventionally framed house remained relatively constant regardless of size.

timbers. While this may be a viable approach for some purposes, I will stick here to the pure system of timber framing using traditional mortise and tenon joinery.

While there are many regional differences in style and technique, the essential elements of traditional timber frames, east and west, are all based on the same basic structural principles: vertical posts supporting horizontal tie beams, rafters and connecting plates, to which the enclosure system is attached.

One of the distinct benefits of timber framing is that it acts as a structural skeleton, capable of carrying large clear-spans, thereby creating more open living areas. This also allows great flexibility in how the structure is enclosed because the wall enclosure system is not load-bearing. This is an advantage when approaching your local building department. Frames today can be designed to accommodate virtually any natural enclosure system, from straw bales or woodchip/clay to traditional wattle and daub—and also pass every local and international building code.

The most common form of timber framing relies on a rigid framework known as a "bent." A bent is a structural framework similar to a truss, made up at minimum of two posts, a tie beam and two rafters. The design of the frame will determine the type of joinery required, but there are only a handful of essential joints that make up the basic vocabulary of joinery.

At minimum, a frame requires two bents, spaced anywhere from 8–16 ft. (2.4–5 m) apart, making a frame with one bay. A typical house frame usually has three or four bents, making two or three bays. The traditional medieval European and colonial New England house frame commonly consisted of 4 bents, spaced 12–16 ft. (3.6–5 m) apart, with each bent spanning 24–28 ft. (7.2–8.5 m).

The bents are connected with secondary members—a top plate at the eave line, summer beams from tie beam to tie beam in the floor system and common purlins joined from rafter to rafter. The bent frames act as the principal structural element with the secondary connecting members supporting the floor and roof loads. Bents must be designed to support the combination of both live loads (the weight of external forces such as snow, furniture and people) and dead loads (the weight of the structural components).

The art and the joy of timber framing lie within the joinery. There are few things in life as satisfying as seeing—and hearing—a perfectly fitted joint go together. Understanding the basic structural principles of the timber-frame bent is essential, but to the builder, increasing their vocabulary of joinery, and learning to execute it to the highest level of quality and craftsmanship, are where the mystery and art of timber framing lies.

One of the best ways to develop natural patterns of building is to study the traditional building systems of the past. In so doing, we may also find that we gain a deeper understanding of the impact that fine craftsmanship has on our daily lives. Joined timber frames with straw/clay walls and thatch or slate roofs are as practical today as they were 500 years ago, and for the same reasons. They have proven to be one of the most sustainable and enduring structures of all time.

RESOURCES

See the end of the next chapter for a complete list of timber-framing resources.

The Art of Timber Framing

DEVIN SMITH

36

Wood is among the oldest and most useful of natural building materials. Most forested regions have one or more native tree species suitable for timber framing. Traditional choices in North America include many species of pine, hemlock, Douglas fir and various oaks.

It wasn't until the mid-19th century that sawmills made it practical to saw trees into the kinds of dimensional lumber common today. For most of history, wood was dimensioned on site and by hand. Smaller pieces, called scantlings, were often made by splitting along the grain in a process known as riving. Larger timbers were prepared by hewing, using a special tool

DEVIN SMITH *is a designer/builder and timber framer with a passion for all things green, currently plying his trade in southern Vermont. He lives comfortably with his wife and daughter in a timber frame house of his own creation.*

known as a broad axe to chop flat faces onto a log. In both cases, it was important to choose logs of the appropriate size and grain pattern so as to minimize labor.

Timbers that only needed to be flat on one face, such as joists or rafters, might even be left otherwise round to save time. The birth of the water-powered

sawmill quickly rendered riving more or less obsolete, though hewing continued to be practiced extensively for nearly a century. In part, this was because sawmills only had the capacity to produce timbers of a limited length—typically 20 ft. (6 m) or less. Though it has become something of a lost art, hewing remains a viable

FIGURE 36.1. Timbers can be milled onsite using a portable mill like this Wood-Mizer. This allows the utilization of onsite resources, reduces transportation cost and energy and allows waste products to be returned to the forest whence they came. [Credit: Devin Smith]

method of producing timbers, though perhaps one best reserved for remote locations or unusually long timbers.

In regions where forest products are a significant industry, timbers can often be sourced from a small sawmill that uses local logs. Some mills have the capacity to plane timbers square and to exact dimension. Though this is more expensive than purchasing rough-sawn timbers, it provides a more refined look and makes layout and cutting significantly easier.

Another option is to hire or rent a portable band-saw mill. These can be easily transported and set up onsite, allowing for the conversion of standing trees directly into usable timbers.

Good milling requires an experienced sawyer who is able to "read" the log to predict how internal stresses in the wood will affect the cut. High-quality logs, relatively free of knots and with straight grain, also make a big difference in the strength and stability of the finished frame.

Layout

No matter what the source, irregularities in timbers are inevitable, and are dealt with by using the appropriate layout system. In the days when all timbers were hand-hewn, every piece was assumed to be unique. Before cutting any joinery, timbers would be arranged in the shape of the frame, and their intersections would be scribed. This ancient method,

known as the scribe rule, could deal with almost any degree of irregularity including curved timbers like those used in cruck frames.

Scribe rule necessarily implies that pieces are not interchangeable in the frame, and therefore the mating ends of each joint would be labeled with a unique match mark. As much art as science, scribe rule framing requires both a trained eye and attention to detail. Though it remains a useful method for unique circumstances, this old-world technique was largely displaced by a new layout approach that developed in the Unites States around 1800. The new approach, known as the square rule, not only made layout easier, but also rendered pieces interchangeable.

Square rule is based on the assumption that an ideal timber—straight, true and square—exists inside of every irregular timber. Irregularities in timber dimensions matter most at the joints, and square rule deals with these irregularities by making adjustments in dimension at the joints. If all the posts in a frame were meant to be 8 in. (20 cm) wide, but instead varied from 7½–8½ in. (19–20.5 cm) wide, each would produce bents of different overall lengths unless some compensa-

FIGURE 36.2. It is important to make sure that joinery is executed accurately if a tight and sound frame is to result. The margin of error for a strong joint is less than ¹⁄₁₆ of an inch. [Credit: Steve Chappell]

tion were made. The innovation behind square rule was the idea of reducing the dimension of all timbers of a given type to a nominal size at the joint. In the previous example, all posts could be reduced to 7½ in. where the tie beams join, thus allowing all the tie beams to be cut to a common length.

The other key concept behind square rule is the reference face. Most timbers in a frame have one (or sometimes two) faces whose exact location is more important than the others. In the case of floor joists, for example, the tops must all be in the same plane or else the floor won't be flat. Thus the top of the joists becomes the reference face, and all layout is measured from (and square to) this face.

Joinery

At its core, timber framing is the craft of joining wood together by the shaping of interlocking wooden joints. Though timber frames can sometimes dazzle the observer with their seeming complexity, with just a few exceptions all joinery is variations on the mortise and tenon. The beauty of this simple and ancient joint is that it both positions timbers with respect to one another, and allows them to resist the forces of tension and shear that affect all structures. Learning to cut a mortise and tenon is the all-important first step in learning to timber frame.

Of the two parts of the joint, the tenon, or male end, is by far the easier to produce. By making a series of saw cuts, or kerfs, wood is removed from either side of a timber, leaving a "blade" of wood typically 1½ or 2 in. (3.8 or 5 cm) wide, and of varying length depending upon its place in the frame and the forces it will be asked to resist. To make this easier, special oversized circular saws are available, some with blades up to 20 in. (51 cm) across. These big timber saws also come in very handy for cutting timbers to length. However, even a typical 7¼-in. circular saw can be quite effective for cutting tenons, and sharp high-quality handsaws (antique American or Japanese of any vintage) also work well, provided time is not at a premium.

The mortise, on the other hand, cannot be sawn. Rather, a slot must be made perpendicular to the grain, a direction in which wood is quite resistant to being worked. The age-old solution is to drill a series of holes the width of the slot desired, and then to chop out the remaining wood with a very sharp chisel, preferably of the desired width. A heavy-duty half-inch (1.3 cm) drill and a self-feed auger have been used to cut many a mortise.

A more spartan option would be the antique predecessor to the

FIGURE 36.3. Paring a tenon with a framing chisel. Chisels must be kept very sharp in order to cut quickly and cleanly. [Credit: Michael G. Smith]

power drill, the boring machine, which continues to have its devotees. It is sort of a miniature drill press that the operator sits on and cranks by hand. A modern innovation is the chain mortiser, a specialized plunging chainsaw that cuts a square-sided mortise to begin with, thus eliminating nearly all of the tedious chisel work.

This, more than any other tool, has brought timber framing into the 21st century, allowing small independent builders to cut frames economically. It represents the single largest investment in many framers' toolkits, but pays for itself quickly for those who plan to cut frames more than once or twice. Despite these technological advances, mallets and chisels are by no means obsolete. A razor-sharp chisel and a skilled hand remain essential for making the slight adjustments necessary to achieve a proper fit.

FIGURE 36.4. A boring machine allows a framer to drill a hole perpendicular to the face of the timber using hand power. Two or more of these holes are bored to the desired depth, then squared up with a chisel to make a mortise. [Credit: Devin Smith]

FIGURE 36.5. The chain mortiser may be the most significant advancement in timber-framing technique of the last four centuries. [Credit: Devin Smith]

Tradition and Craft

Part of the unique appeal of timber framing in today's world is the sense of craft and tradition in which it is steeped. More than mere superficiality, craft is an integral part of what makes timber framing work. Timbers are massive not for effect, but because the myriad forces exerted by and on the building are concentrated into relatively few joints. And because wood is removed from the timbers at the joints, this is where the timbers are weakest. All joinery must be proportioned such that no member is weakened excessively. The would-be framer not only must understand the nature of the forces at play, but must execute the chosen joinery with skill, for the timbers themselves are helpless to resist these forces without well-crafted connections.

Tradition informs much of how joinery is chosen and executed. The vast majority of houses built today, whether timber framed or not, are in fact based upon traditional vernacular timber-frame forms such as the cape, colonial and saltbox. These types of houses were traditionally built in certain ways, utilizing particular bent arrangements, timber sizing and joinery. With 350 years of research and design behind them, these classic designs are surprisingly forgiving. Subtle variations abound, but essentially the elements of a durable traditional frame are more or less known without having to delve deeply into elaborate structural analysis. The further one strays from these basic forms, the greater must be one's understanding of the forces at play.

All vernacular American timber-frame forms share many common features. Naturally, they are all more or less cubical, or else built out of a series of connected cubes. Each of these cubes is constructed of a series of individual truss-like structures called bents. At the minimum, each bent is in turn made up of not less than two posts, a tie beam and two diagonal braces. Together, these elements provide a rigid framework that is capable of supporting a roof and floor, while resisting the various forces placed upon it by the elements—wind, snow, etc.—as well as by the weight of the building components themselves.

One of the primary concerns is the thrust generated by the roof's ceaseless urge to fall down and in the process push the walls outward. Bents are normally arranged perpendicular to the slope of the roof so as to provide the best resistance to this force. Typically, bents are spaced from 8–16 ft. (2.5–5 m) apart. Closer spacing is wasteful, while larger spans are limited by the strength-to-weight ratio of wood; at a span of much over 16 ft., wood can no longer effectively support its own weight.

Each bent is connected by secondary members, some of which are themselves diagonally braced. The exact arrangement of the secondary members varies, and relates mostly to the type of roof system being used. Broadly speaking, there are two general types of roof systems. The first uses many small, or "common" rafters on close centers. These require continuous support, so bents must be connected at the eave by stout secondary beams called top plates. If the common rafters are long, they may also be supported near their mid-span by equally stout principal purlins. This type of frame was often favored in the past because it could be raised by hand in many small manageable units.

The second system utilizes stout principal rafters that are incorporated directly into the structure of the bent. This system has found increasing favor in contemporary timber frames, because bents can be assembled in their entirety on the ground and raised up by a crane in short order. Because the principal rafters carry the roof load directly down to the rigid bent structure, bents often need only be connected by relatively small horizontal timbers, such as small common purlins that frame the remainder of the roof deck.

Frame Raising

The raising method and sequence is something to consider as the frame is being designed. It is important to visualize the raising process from start to finish, since it is quite possible to design a frame that cannot physically be assembled. Another pitfall to avoid is the piecemeal in situ method of assembly, an idea often

FIGURE 36.6. The foot of a principal rafter is set onto the top of its receiving post. All joints should be tested to make sure they fit prior to assembly. [Credit: Steve Chappell]

latched upon by beginners. It is far more efficient to preassemble units as large as possible, for tasks that would be simple on the ground are difficult and dangerous up in the air.

When the time arrives to raise the bents into position, many professional framers hire a crane. While expensive at roughly US$1,000 a day, a crane allows a frame to be raised safely by a two-person crew, and enables elaborate frame elements that would be prohibitively difficult to raise by hand.

Before the recent advent of the crane, frame raisings were huge community happenings featuring (in addition to a lot of grueling and dangerous work) music and dance and a tremendous amount of food and libations. Many people today choose to continue this tradition, and because timber frames are innately exciting and captivating, there usually isn't much trouble recruiting volunteers.

It is essential that one or two experienced people be on hand to orchestrate the process. Ground rules should be clarified beforehand, and each lift should be discussed in detail so that everyone works together without doubt or confusion. As old records reveal, deaths and severe injuries occurred at many raisings. While choosing not to break out the liquor before the frame is up (as was commonly done at historic raisings) will do much to improve safety, steps should be taken to safeguard against the inevitable hazards, including not only the obvious dangers of lifting such a heavy structure, but also the possibilities of falling people and objects.

There is no reason that a crane cannot also be used at a community raising. The bents may be raised by a crane, for example, while the secondary members are placed by hand. Another option is the use of site-built rigging in lieu of a crane. A-frames, gin poles and boom derricks are all relatively easy to construct, and can provide a good compromise between a crane raising and a pure hand raising.

Enclosure Systems

Another decision best made well before raising day, is how the frame is to be enclosed. Timber framing predates modern building materials, and is inherently better suited to being enclosed with more compatible materials. Sheet goods like plywood and drywall, for example, require

FIGURE 36.7. This four-bent frame uses king post trusses to create a clear span first-floor area. The bents span 30 ft., and the bay spacing is 16 ft., creating a 30 x 48 ft footprint. The bents are connected using top plates at eaves level, wall purlins and roof purlins. Note the crane being used to lift the heavy timbers into place. [Credit: Steve Chappell]

support every 16 or 24 in. (41 or 61 cm). Building a stud wall 16 in. on center within the frame is structurally redundant and wasteful.

Barns and outbuildings can be very quickly and efficiently enclosed using traditional methods, the most common of which is to apply vertical one-inch-thick (2.5 cm) boards, supporting them at their mid-span with a small horizontal nailer or two.

Houses, on the other hand, are trickier. Exterior walls typically need to provide not just a surface to keep the weather out, but an attractive interior finish, a place to run wiring and a space for insulation. Building science has also revealed the compelling need for a contiguous air barrier in all wall systems, at least those built in any climate requiring significant heating or cooling (see "Natural Building for Cold Climates," p. 73). Excessive heat loss or gain, poor occupant comfort and the potential for severe moisture damage are all likely when building pressure dynamics are not properly understood and applied. Fulfilling these various demands without creating lots of redundancy requires care and creativity.

Commercially, structural insulated panels (SIPs) made of foam and oriented strand board have dominated the market for decades. Their advantages include quick installation and high thermal efficiency owing to their airtightness and lack of thermal bridging. Many timber framers have been dissatisfied with the high embodied energy and pollution potential of SIPS, though, and alternatives are beginning to take hold.

The most promising enclosure systems mimic the best features of SIPs while replacing the materials with more appropriate ones. Insulation is best applied in a tight contiguous layer outboard of the frame, and the less wood needed to support interior and exterior finishes and provide service cavities, the better. Larsen truss walls filled with cellulose are one popular option. This system creates a deep insulation cavity with pairs of 2×2's tied together with plywood reinforcing webs, not unlike engineered I-joists, which can also be used to similar effect.

Another approach that is uniquely suited to timber frames is colloquially referred to as "wrap and strap." In this approach, one or more layers of sheet insulation are attached to the outside of the frame and secured with dimensional lumber strapping held on with long timber screws. A layer of one-inch-thick boards provides an attachment point for window and door frames—simple bucks are sufficient—as well as a nailing surface

FIGURE 36.8. If executed safely, a hand-raising can be an exhilarating finale to the slow and detailed work of cutting the frame. [Credit: Devin Smith]

for the interior finishes. Strapping (either vertical or horizontal) is placed on wide centers—as much as 4 ft. (1.2 m) apart—and so the system requires very little lumber. Reclaimed foam is widely available, much of it sourced from commercial buildings being dismantled.

A foam alternative worth considering is rigid mineral wool. While more expensive than most foam products, it arguably has significantly less environmental impact. It is also highly vapor permeable, making it more compatible with other natural building systems. Though less widely available, wood-, straw- and cork-based sheet insulation products can be used similarly.

Natural enclosure systems can also be good candidates. Straw bales, straw-clay and woodchip-clay have all been used successfully to enclose timber frames. Clay, straw and wood are a trio of natural materials that perform very well together, as is evidenced by the many ancient timber frames that survive today, most of which were enclosed with some combination of sticks, clay and straw. A well-built timber frame enclosed with natural walls makes a home for the ages.

RESOURCES

Books

• Benson, Tedd. *Building the Timber Frame House: The Revival of a Forgotten Craft*, Touchwood, 1981. Accessible introduction for the novice.
• Chappell, Steve. *A Timber Framer's Workshop: Joinery, Design & Construction of Traditional Timber Frames*, Fox Maple Press, 1998. An outstanding resource, not only for timber framers but for anyone who builds with wood. Excellent chapters on tools, structural considerations, comparing different wood species and builders' math and engineering, in addition to many different joinery details and framing and truss design.
• Chappell, Steve. *Advanced Timber Framing: Joinery, Design & Construction of Timber Frame Roof Systems*, Fox Maple Press, 2012. This book covers the history and design of compound mortise and tenon joinery. Over 900 color photos and CAD drawings illustrate the approach to designing compound joinery for any conceivable roof system.
• Sobon, Jack. *Build a Classic Timber-Framed House*, Garden Way, 1994. Good hands-on information on design, layout and basic-to-intermediate joinery.
• Sobon, Jack. *Historic American Timber Joinery*, Timber Framer's Guild Publishing, 2013. A detailed and inspirational visual tour through the variations of historic joinery. Created in partnership with the National Park Service, it is also available as a free download at: **ncptt** .nps.gov/blog/historic-american-timber-joinery-a -graphic-guide-i-tying-joints-tie-below-plate-2001-14
• Sobon, Jack and Roger Schroeder. *Timber Frame Construction: All About Post-and-Beam Building*, Garden Way, 1984. Good basics, including history, simple joinery and raising.

Organizations

• Fox Maple School of Traditional Building: **foxmaple** .com. Workshops in timber framing, thatching and traditional enclosure techniques, plus books and information. Brownfield, Maine.
• The Econest Building Company: **econesthomes.com**. Robert Laporte and crew offer workshops, consulting and design/build services, focusing on timber framing, straw light-clay infill, earthen plasters and floors. Ashland, Oregon.
• The Timber Framer's Guild of North America: **tfguild.org**. A professional organization and clearing house for all things timber framing. Share in the unique camaraderie that surrounds the craft. Events are frequent and invigorating. Online forums are open to non-members. *Timber Framing*, their quarterly journal, is exemplary and worth the cost of membership alone. Myriad books are published by and available only through the Guild.

Small-Diameter Roundwood: An Underused Building Material

37

OWEN GEIGER

Wood-frame construction is preferred in the US because of its speed and ease of construction, but unfortunately most of the dimensional lumber used is not sustainably harvested. The decimation of our old-growth forests for lumber means conventional framing wood gets more expensive at an alarming rate. At the same time, many US forests have been poorly managed and are now choked with small-diameter trees. Thinning these trees to reduce the increasing risk of forest fires is a Forest Service priority, and with an inexpensive firewood permit, anyone can obtain small-diameter wood for building a home. This material can thus enable many to build affordable homes, while improving forest health.

While building with poles can have its challenges (variability of size, taper and curvature from pole to pole and the detailing of connections), creative utilization of small-diameter wood can provide all of the lumber for a house. Using it has other advantages, including:

- The use of locally available wood reduces costs and dependence on lumber companies.
- Wood in the round is stronger than standard dimensional lumber of similar cross-sectional area and requires less processing. Smaller diameter trees can therefore be used, and fewer of them.
- Wood poles have a two-hour commercial fire rating, in contrast to dimensional and engineering lumber, which have a one-hour fire rating.

OWEN GEIGER *has two engineering degrees and a PhD in Social and Economic Development. His lifelong goal is to alleviate substandard housing by using natural building materials and sustainable building methods.*

FIGURE 37.1. The community house under construction at the Full Bloom community in Oregon. This building utilizes locally harvested Douglas fir poles for framing. [Credit: Michael G. Smith]

- Round-pole construction is aesthetically pleasing. The beauty of the wood is left exposed, honoring the source tree.
- Very few tools are required to build simple pole trusses and workers can be trained quickly.

The use of small-diameter wood creates local jobs and reduces reliance on industrial materials often shipped long distances. Jobs are created in four categories:

- Logging: Cutting, milling and delivering poles.
- Truss manufacturing: This could be a cooperative effort or an entrepreneurial cottage industry. Either way the quality will be higher and more consistent if specially trained workers build the trusses.
- Milling: Workers are needed to mill logs into purlins, studs, plates and joists. The simplest method uses a chainsaw and an inexpensive guide. Mass production methods with commercial-sized equipment are more efficient.
- Construction: Workers are needed to erect trusses, build walls, etc.

With the additional need to sequester carbon quickly in the coming years as a strategy to reduce global atmospheric carbon, tree growing should increase, and a sustainable harvest of small poles may likely be possible. With all the advantages of small-diameter wood, we should take a closer look at this resource that is often so near at hand.

RESOURCES

- Law, Ben. *Roundwood Timber Framing: Building Naturally Using Local Resources*, Permanent Publications, 2010. Inspirational and beautifully illustrated guide from a master of the craft.
- Seddon, Leigh. *Practical Pole Building Construction*, Williamson Publishing, 1985. A useful book for building barns and other types of outbuildings using poles.

FIGURE 37.3. This earthen house in Balstrop, Texas, utilizes wooden poles for the roof structure and railings. Note thatch above. [Credit: Catherine Wanek]

FIGURE 37.2. A traditional Hawaiian Hale house constructed of round-pole timber with lashed joints. Note woven palm front mats for the ceiling and palm thatch used for walls and roof. [Credit: Catherine Wanek]

Bamboo Construction

DARREL DEBOER

38

Many Americans see bamboo as invasive and at odds with our chosen landscapes, but in the southeastern US, bamboo once covered millions of acres—it *was* this place. Native to every continent except Europe, and with its use as a building material traced to 3500 BC, bamboo still strongly influences the lives of half the world's population in the form of tools, utensils, food and buildings. In Asia, hundreds of potential uses make bamboo not just desirable but a required element in every home.

A comprehensive system of growing, processing and (especially) understanding bamboo does not yet exist in the United States. And although there are already thousands of timber bamboos growing in the western and southern US, many Americans have never seen one. Yet, given the joinery system developed in Colombia over the last several decades, now is the ideal time for us to draw upon the proven methods of bamboo construction from Southeast Asia and South America.

In the United States, for the first time in our history, an unlimited, highly subsidized supply of structural-quality timber no longer exists. Bamboo can be a key element in creating large structures with minimal environmental impact. It allows

FIGURE 38.1. Using woven split bamboo as a wall covering for an indigenous dwelling in Colombia. [Credit: Shannyn Sollitt]

DARREL DEBOER *is an architect and furniture builder who became possessed by the idea of building with bamboo after seeing the structures of Colombian architect Simón Vélez. He was named one of the Top 10 Green Architects by Natural Home magazine and is co-author of Bamboo Building Essentials.*

affordable construction without highly industrialized, proprietary systems—wood, concrete and steel production are not needed—while taking some of the pressure off the forests. Bamboo structures can make a significant contribution to local self-reliance, and because of the speed and density of bamboo growth, a builder with access to a relatively small amount of land can be in full control of his or her source of construction materials.

We need to develop a bamboo culture—one that recognizes the value in the use of this plant. We will have many challenges along the way, including gaining access to inexpensive land that is not valued for other purposes; choosing appropriate species; allowing time for the bamboo to mature; understanding the aesthetic of working with cylindrical materials in a predominantly rectilinear society; learning to distinguish exceptional working stock; and developing a design approach that takes full advantage of both the strength and the beauty of timber bamboo.

Bamboo and Sustainability

Bamboo meets the basic criteria for a sustainable building material by being:

- **Renewable:** The *Phyllostachys* species—those most suitable for growing and building in the US, surviving temperatures as low as 0°F (−18°C)—will grow 10–12 in. (25–30 cm) a day once a grove is established. The record is 49 in. (124 cm) in a single day! Culms (the living stalks) achieve all of their growth in an initial six-week spurt, then spend the next three to five years replacing sugars and water with silica and cellulose, after which they are useful structurally. Once established, one-third of a mature grove can be sustainably harvested annually.

- **Plentiful:** Our current meager US supply of timber-quality bamboo could increase greatly within a decade with species selection appropriate to various microclimates and levels of water and nutrient availability. For now, strong tropical varieties are imported from Asia and South America, along with temperate varieties such as *Moso*. For microclimate information, see the websites listed in "Resources." In particular look at the American Bamboo Society's Species Source List at bamboo.org/FAQ.html.

- **Local:** Bamboo concentrates a large amount of fiber in a small land area, creating a rare situation in which a single person can be both the producer and consumer of a building material.

FIGURE 38.2. This small bamboo pavilion features concrete foundation piers for additional structural strength and to protect the bamboo from water damage. [Credit: Darrel DeBoer]

- **Waste-reducing:** As is nature's general practice, nothing goes to waste. At some times of the year, the leaves are a more nutritious animal feed than alfalfa, and bamboo compost serves to fertilize the next generation of plants. Any remaining scraps can be made into biochar to increase the fertility of agricultural soils—an effect that does not break down over time.

Bamboo production systems in Japan, Southeast Asia and Central and South America allow a small number of people to carry out the process from planting through utilization, with only minimal infrastructure and equipment. Every part of the plant has a use, and harvesting for that use at the appropriate time not only doesn't hurt the plant but encourages future vigor. Groves can be located to take advantage of the plant's unusual ability to quickly process water and nutrients left over from livestock farms, sewage treatment plants and industrial processes.

In contrast to most plants, the addition of fertilizer does not diminish the quality of bamboo poles, since energy is stored in the rhizomes for later release in the formation of the next year's culms. Meanwhile, those rhizomes are useful for securing topsoil and for erosion control. The plants use transpiration to create their own microclimate, cooling a grove (or a house located in a grove) by as much as 10–15°F (6–8°C).

Structural Properties

Standards have now been written for structural engineers to specify bamboo and for building departments to accept it. In Colombia, bamboo has been incorporated into the national code, although conservatively. No more than two-story buildings can be built, and the structural values assigned are very conservative. The International Code Council (which writes the codes for the US and several other countries) has an Acceptance Criteria for Structural Bamboo, while much of the rest of the world relies on

FIGURE 38.3. Jöerg Stamm's design for this jewelry showroom in Bali gets added strength by triangulating the rafters across each other.
[Credit: Darrel DeBoer]

ISO standards (see "Resources" below).

Bamboo is an extremely strong fiber, having twice the compressive strength of concrete and roughly the same strength-to-weight ratio of steel in tension. The strongest bamboo fibers have a greater shear resistance than structural woods, and they take much longer to come to ultimate failure. Unlike concrete and steel, bamboo does not fail catastrophically. Its hollow shape approximates the ideal shape of a beam, and testing has shown that the hollow cylinder has a strength factor of 1.9 over a solid pole of equivalent mass.

The useful life of a pole ranges from two years, if buried underground, to several hundred years, as seen in the rafters of traditional Japanese farmhouses. The natural flexibility of bamboo can create challenges in certain structural applications such as floor framing, but solutions have been developed using bamboo both in pole form and combined with binders to become a composite material. Bamboo finish flooring is now in common use throughout North America and Europe as a substitute for hardwood. This material is manufactured from thin bamboo strips glued and pressed together. It is very hard, stable and easy to install. Although marketed as an ecological building material, there are serious concerns about many aspects of the process of harvest and manufacture, from the common use of formaldehyde-based glues to deforestation of mountainous areas in China and Southeast Asia where bamboo is grown to the high energy cost of international shipping.

The fiber length of bamboo is several times greater than our structural softwoods. The laminated fibers of bamboo formed into board products have proven the most successful in gaining acceptance. Bamboo flooring is an easy substitute for hardwoods, while various other woven, split and glued variations of bamboo paneling and other products may be the future. Testing at Washington State University has led to building code approvals for panels and I-joists made by Bamcor (see "Resources" below). The 2013 Solar Decathlon entry by the University of Santa Clara was fabricated entirely of bamboo. The students tested several joinery techniques and assemblies, a great number of which could be made available for commercial use.

One of the best uses for this giant grass is as a roof truss. Successful experiments by Colombian architect Simón Vélez to achieve 66 ft. (20 m) spans and 30 ft. (9 m) cantilevers were conducted in areas not requiring inspection of structures. Now that these buildings exist, they stand as proof of what works and as models for future designs. Even one-quarter of Vélez's spans would be adequate for most of our needs.

Although bamboo is a bending and forgiving material, structural redundancy is a must in truss design. It is imperative that we over-

FIGURE 38.4. Hand-crafted bamboo gate of Satomi and Tom Lander, Kingston, New Mexico. [Credit: Catherine Wanek]

build; a structural failure at such an early stage of the introduction of bamboo architecture would be catastrophic. It is crucial to understand which members are in tension or compression and which points in a structure experience maximum shear and moment forces. Ambitious designers should do some small-scale work with bamboo to develop an understanding of the material, then find a structural engineer who can do the calculations for them.

There are two strategies for overcoming lateral forces in a bamboo structure. The first, represented by recently engineered Latin American structures, relies on the shear resistance provided by mortar on both the bamboo-lathed walls and the roof. The success of this approach was demonstrated in April 1991, when 20 houses constructed in Costa Rica for the National Bamboo Foundation survived a 7.5 Richter scale earthquake. The second approach takes advantage of the forgiveness of the traditional lashed, pinned or bolted joints found in both Asia and the Americas.

Even structures created with intuitive engineering and non-optimized joinery take great advantage of the broad elastic range of bamboo; a structure can deform and return to its original configuration once the load has been removed. It is difficult to cause failure of bamboo in pure compression or tension. Truss designs remove the bending forces and put all the weight along the axis of the pole in complete tension or compression. What was lacking until recently was a joint capable of making that smooth transition.

Joinery Design

Traditional joinery systems based on pegging and tying evolved to take advantage of the strong exterior fibers of the hollow bamboo tube. Lashed joinery has been used successfully for millennia since it allows some movement in the structure without failure of the connections. If natural fibers such as jute, hemp, rattan or split bamboo are used for lashing while still green, they tend to tighten around the joint. Unfortunately, the seasonal moisture changes in most of the US cause bamboo to expand and contract by as much as six percent across its diameter,

FIGURE 38.5. Bamboo building elements can be prefabricated, as demonstrated, by a low-cost modular bamboo system in Costa Rica. There, bamboo panels are made inside a workshop. They will be transported to the building site, erected within a structural bamboo framework, then plastered. [Credit: Catherine Wanek]

causing a slackening in tied joints, and not all joints remain accessible to be retightened as necessary over time.

More recent systems have been engineered to make joinery stronger and less labor-intensive. The joint of preference has become the one developed by Simón Vélez in Colombia. He uses a bolted connection with an understanding that the bolt alone concentrates too much force on the wall of the bamboo. Therefore, at the point where every bolt penetrates each bamboo culm, the void between the solid internal nodes is filled with solidifying mortar. Where members of a truss come together at angles and tension forces are anticipated, a steel strap is placed to bridge the pieces. It is important to design with redundant systems, capable of both tension and compression. Nevertheless, as Vélez told me, "I have never seen the bamboo fail; only the steel straps have failed under load testing." The bamboo can split and pull away from the mortar, but small stainless steel straps are easily available to prevent that in critical situations.

The Challenge

For those accustomed to framing with milled lumber, round bamboo can seem to be an awkward shape. It also doesn't have the forgiveness of wood when mistakes are made. As bamboo enters the Western building vocabulary, our initial tendency is to try to turn it into wood. For example, flooring milled from thin strips of bamboo becomes a simple substitution for wood. These changes require no training or shift in mindset. When using bamboo for structural framing "in

Checklist for Obtaining Construction-Quality Bamboo Poles

- Age: three- to five-year-old culms best, depending upon species
- Starch content: harvest at right time of year to minimize beetle/fungus attack
- Sufficiently preserved (through borax or other treatments) to avoid premature failure from insects and fungus
- Appropriate species for the intended use
- Sufficiently adapted to local humidity—especially for interior use
- Stored out of direct sun, preferably vertically
- In the running bamboo species, use the bottom five feet or so for other purposes, as it is usually crooked, with nodes too close together and with density characteristics different than the rest of the pole

Checklist for a Well-Designed Bamboo Structure

- Thorough static analysis to ensure that loads are distributed evenly among the joints and axially along the pole
- Slenderness ratio of less than 50
- Bolted joints with solid-filled internodes
- Dry poles that are still easily workable—about six weeks after harvest is ideal
- Find a way to obtain lateral strength; either create a shear panel consisting of a mortar bed over lath or avoid mortar altogether and design with many triangles
- Refer to the engineering formulas and testing criteria developed by Jules Janssen

the round," many practices common in wood construction have to be unlearned and replaced with a whole new approach to a very different material.

One thing that will help spread the acceptance of bamboo construction in the West is the development and adoption of appropriate building codes. In 2004, after a decade of effort, Jeffree Trudeau and David Sands of Bamboo Living achieved acceptance by the International Code Council (ICC) of bamboo as a structural material for use in construction. (ICC writes the building codes used in most jurisdictions in the US.) Bamboo Living has built over 300 homes and other structures in the US and other parts of the world that are fully engineered to meet the codes. Those buildings have ranged in size from 100 sq. ft. to over 5,000 sq. ft. (10–460 m²) and included a high school building built by the students themselves. Bamboo Living's buildings have withstood multiple hurricanes with winds up to 173 mph (278 kph). They continue to develop new materials and techniques for using bamboo in Western construction.

FIGURE 38.6. Curved bamboo poles used as bracing. [Credit: Darrel DeBoer]

FIGURE 38.7. Note the creative use of indigenous timber, structural bamboo and wrought iron supports in this plastered bamboo dwelling. [Credit: Darrel DeBoer]

The Revival of Bamboo Construction in Colombia

The traditional architecture of Colombia originally relied on the huge timber bamboo *Guadua angustifolia* for most construction in urban and rural areas. After fires ravaged bamboo structures in several Colombian cities a hundred years ago, however, the remaining buildings were covered with plaster, and people subsequently built with brick and concrete. While it leaves much to be desired thermally and its performance can be catastrophic in severe earthquakes, concrete won over the culture during the 20th century. However, in recent years, a few pioneering Colombian architects have worked to revive bamboo construction and to restore its lost status.

Some of the finest buildings of any type I've ever seen have been made of bamboo by Simón Vélez, Marcelo Villegas and their workers. This group has invented systems of joinery and preservation that have allowed bamboo structures to succeed in the modern engineered world. With the invention of the bolted/filled joint, the groundwork was laid for the current renaissance in bamboo construction. Vélez and Villegas built some very large, impressive buildings to demonstrate the effectiveness of their joinery system. Interest in bamboo

construction dramatically increased because of the positive performance of bamboo structures during the major earthquake in Colombia in January 1999. Near the earthquake's epicenter, 75 percent of the masonry buildings collapsed, while virtually all of the bamboo structures survived unscathed, including a tower with a bamboo roof structure located within a few thousand yards of the epicenter.

When I visited the *Guadua* bamboo region of Colombia several months before that earthquake, I was shocked to see how little was

being built of bamboo, except in the rural areas. Now there are perhaps 30 or 40 professionals designing with bamboo in the region. The wealthy now consider bamboo an acceptable building material and are allowing some interesting experimentation to go on. And where the wealthy lead, the masses will soon follow.

A committee led by Dr. Jules Janssen, under the mantle of the International Network of Bamboo and Rattan (INBAR), has put together a manual for the standardized testing needed to compare different

FIGURE 38.8. Following a series of large earthquakes in Central Colombia where bamboo performed much better than concrete structures, bamboo finally found a place in the national building code. This bamboo stable in Colombia features innovative concrete and metal pin joints.
[Credit: Darrel DeBoer]

bamboo species, to compare one person's testing with another's and to apply those numbers to engineering formulas. In Colombia this challenge has been met by the work of several universities and the Association of Seismic Engineers, who have put *Guadua angustifolia* through the whole range of tests. The development of the manual may make it possible for Colombia to export timber bamboo to the US, since the standard adopted here requires the same battery of tests. The Colombian Association of Seismic Engineering has published illustrated manuals that explain the best ways to build bamboo structures and how to avoid detailing mistakes. And for the first time in at least 500 years, there is code approval in Colombia for *bajareque*, a wall system similar to wattle and daub that uses wood or bamboo studs and flattened bamboo *esterilla* for lathing before plastering.

German bridge designer Jörg Stamm is pushing hardest at the limits of the material. Living in the bamboo region of Colombia, Stamm has built bamboo bridges with clear spans as long as 165 feet. He was initially aiming for spans half as great, but realized the possibilities when calculations showed they could work. Stamm has been very generous with his knowledge, writing a book that shares his five years of intense research on how to build bamboo bridges. Stamm feels strongly that the use of bamboo can save some of the large rainforest trees. His only limitation now seems to be the state of the Colombian economy as he searches for new projects.

FIGURE 38.9. Simón Vélez has taken bamboo architecture in new directions, showing that it is not (as is often perceived) a poor person's material. This bamboo pavilion features dramatic 30-foot (9-meter) overhangs.
[Credit: Darrel DeBoer]

RESOURCES

Books

• Bell, Michael. *The Gardeners' Guide to Growing Temperate Bamboos*, Timber Press, 2000. Good introduction to the running species.

• Cusack, Victor. *Bamboo World*, Kangaroo Press, 1999. How to grow and use tropical clumpers. The definitive work for regions where temperatures don't get below 15°F (−9°C).

• Dunkelberg, Maus et al. *IL31: Bamboo as a Building Material*, Karl Kramer Verlag, 1985. In-depth analysis of the possibilities of bamboo design and joinery. Doesn't predict the optimized joinery techniques now practiced in Colombia.

• Farelly, David. *The Book of Bamboo*, Sierra Club Books, 1984. Great stories and inspiration around the many uses for bamboo, but low in technical detail.

• Henrikson, Robert and David Greenberg. *Bamboo in Competition and Exhibition*, CreateSpace Independent Publishing Platform, 2011. Amazing examples of bamboo architecture.

• Hidalgo, Oscar. *Manual de Construcción con Bambú (Bamboo Construction Manual)*, National University of Colombia's Research Center for Bamboo and Wood (CIBAM), 1981. In Spanish, but so well illustrated that the intent is clear. Focus is on short-span, low-cost structures.

• Janssen, Jules. *Bamboo: A Grower & Builder's Reference Manual*, American Bamboo Society, Hawaii Chapter, 1997. See also his *Building with Bamboo*, Intermediate Technology Publications, 1995.

• Minke, Gernot. *Building With Bamboo*, Birkhauser, 2012. Examples of bamboo buildings in Europe, Japan and North America.

• Vélez, Simón, et al. *Grow Your Own House*, Vitra Design Museum, 2000. Slightly quirky narrative, leading to the construction of the amazing 20,000 sq. ft. (1,860 m²) ZERI pavilion for Expo 2000 in Hanover, Germany. If you can only get one book about bamboo construction, make it this one.

• Villegas, Marcelo. *New Bamboo: Architecture and Design*, Villegas Editores, 2003. The work of one of the most respected builders in bamboo.

Periodicals

• American Bamboo Society Newsletter: **bamboo.org** /wp/pnwc. Newsletter of the Pacific Northwest Chapter of the ABS. An exemplary newsletter dedicated to the promotion of bamboo.

• *The Temperate Bamboo Quarterly*. Detailed information for bamboo growers. Lots of articles on bamboo crafting as well as cultivation and construction. Out of print, but available as bound back issues from the publisher: **earthadvocatesresearchfarm.com/tbq**

Websites

• American Bamboo Society. Especially the Species Source List of all bamboos in cultivation in the US, with their sizes, temperature and shade tolerances: **bamboo.org**

• 1000 Things Bamboo: **bambus.de** (in German).

• Tradewinds Bamboo Nursery: **bamboodirect.com**. Best source of bamboo books in the US.

• 4Specs.com: **4specs.com/s/09/09649**. Bamboo flooring.

• Bamboo Living: **bambooliving.com**. Bamboo home builders. Hawaii.

• International Network for Bamboo and Rattan (INBAR): **inbar.int/publications**. A wide range of publications on bamboo and rattan-related topics.

• Building the ZERI pavilion: **zeri.org/pavilion/slideshow/pav_small/slideshow.asp**

• **bambus.rwth-aachen.de/eng/reports/zeri/englisch/referat-eng**

• Code approval in the US: **greenb.it/file_pdf/US_-_ACCEPTANCE_CRITERIA_FOR_STRUCTURAL_BAMBOO.pdf**

• DeBoer Architects: **deboerarchitects.com**. Darrel DeBoer's website with photographs, links and additional information on bamboo construction, See also: **BambooBuildingEssentials.com**—*Bamboo Building Essentials: The Eleven Basic Principles*.

• International Codes Council Acceptance Criteria for Structural Bamboo.

• Walk through several Velez buildings: **home.earthlink.net/~montecito/irongrass**

• Asociacion Colombiana De Engenieria Sismica (Colombian Association of Seismic Engineering): **asosismica.org.co/?idcategoria=1068&pag=2**. Publishes an illustrated instruction manual on building with bamboo.

Waste Not, Want Not: Building with Trash

39

JOSEPH F. KENNEDY

To manufacture our built culture, human society has extracted huge amounts of materials from the crust of the Earth. Materials manufactured now may persist for hundreds or thousands of years, and the improper disposal of many of these materials is negatively impacting our environment. To be responsible stewards of this planet, we must not only radically reduce the amount of waste we produce, but consider waste products such as plastic, paper, scrap wood, etc. as feedstocks for the ongoing needs of civilization.

An industrial ecology based on trash and other wastes could merge well with building systems that utilize natural materials like clay, lime, straw and wood. This hybrid approach would help clean up our mess, take pressure off of our ecosystems and make it easier to repair our world. Building with so-called refuse is a valid and useful addition to the family of natural building techniques. By sequestering these materials in our buildings (especially non-recyclable plastics), we can guarantee that they will not enter the ecosystem where they can wreak havoc with wildlife and future humans. We can take responsibility for our personal "garbage shed" by minimizing and creatively reusing materials to keep them from our lands and oceans.

Some trash is organic in nature (landscape trimmings, paper) while other garbage is synthetic (tires, concrete, plastic). All possibilities from the

JOSEPH F. KENNEDY *is an educator and designer inspired by the ingenuity of local builders around the world who have learned how to upcyle "waste" into building materials.*

FIGURE 39.1. Resourceful builders in informal settlements (such as here in the Cape Flats in South Africa) are adept at using scrap wood and other discarded materials to make dwellings. [Credit: Joseph F. Kennedy]

waste stream merit consideration except those materials that could negatively affect human and ecological health. Not all waste materials are appropriate for building, because of toxicity or biological hazard. An example is used engine oil. These must be dealt with separately and sequestered in safe places or destroyed.

When we look around for case studies, we can witness the ephemeral landscape of the Burning Man festival, where a huge (albeit temporary) city of architectonic and vehicular constructions made of reclaimed and recycled materials is erected and dismantled every year. In Portland, Oregon, the non-profit organization City Repair works with the community to catalyze wonderful community structures made of materials reclaimed from the waste stream (see "Building the Natural Village," p. 137).

We can also look to the billions of people who, out of necessity, currently address this issue in the world's informal settlements. In these communities, people build with whatever they can get. Some of the creative building solutions are very beautiful, but few are recognized as "architecture." However they may be considered, these shanty towns/favelas/colonias are important

laboratories exploring how to build (and how not to) with waste materials.

Numerous builders around the world have been inspired to create artistic and sustainable structures with a range of materials and techniques. These are opportunities for innovation, and synergistic solutions to building and ecological problems can emerge when an open-minded design approach is utilized, as you never know what kind of material you might be able to access (see "Natural Building Thrives in Argentina," p. 413). Many ways of converting trash to useful

building materials have been developed, though the information is sometimes scattered in obscure publications, or only practiced by local craftsmen. But images and ideas are very easy to come by with a simple Internet search, and there is a growing interest in the subject.

Plastic

Plastic is perhaps the most egregious of our waste products. Much of the plastic that makes its way to the ocean collects in more than five giant "gyres," where it causes an ongoing threat to wildlife. While we seek replacements

FIGURE 39.2. Plastic bottles can be effectively "upcycled" by filling them with sand, earth or plastic trash (for an insulating unit) and stacking them in mortar to create walls. [Credit: Valentina Mendez Marquez]

for plastic, in the meantime we must do all we can to remove it from the waste stream. This is best done on land before the plastic can reach the ocean.

An example of this is shown by the 4Walls International project on the Tijuana/San Diego border, where the Tijuana River meets the Pacific Ocean. This watershed is clogged with trash, which eventually makes its way to the shore. Plastic bottles and bags, wrappers, etc. make up a large part of this trash.

Enterprising folks comb the points where the trash tends to collect, picking up plastic bottles

FIGURE 39.3. Aluminum cans and bottles are used to create this out-building for an Earthship project in Taos, New Mexico. [Credit: Joseph F. Kennedy]

which are then stuffed with plastic bags and other trash. These bottles are laid up into thick walls using cement or earth mortar. Encasing the bottles in plaster effectively sequesters that material, minimizes the amount of concrete or earth needed, and results in a beautiful, thick, insulating wall. By incentivizing (through purchase) the collection of plastic bottles and bags to make lightweight building blocks, 4Walls has been able to help clean up the river and create inexpensive building blocks at the same time, all while creating a small local economic opportunity.

Similar systems have been used widely throughout Latin America, Africa and elsewhere. Sometimes, plastic bottles are filled with sand or soil to make a building unit. Plastic bottles have also been crushed and converted into an insulating wall core which is plastered over. Plastic trash has been used as vapor barriers, shredded as a strengthening fiber in earth blocks and simply stuffed into cavities as insulation. A wonderful use of plastic bottles is as a water-filled skylight bringing inexpensive daylight to those in darkness.

An exciting development to bring attention to the problem of oceanic gyre waste plastic has

been developed by two companies, Method and Envision Plastics. They have prototyped a system for making new bottles from material harvested from the oceanic plastic gyres (see savetheplastics.com). The big question that remains is the effective collection of this material from the gyre. There are a few visionary proposals for creating other products from the plastics in the gyres, but not a practical system yet.

Wood

Scrap wood is a common and important informal building material. An entire architecture has developed around wooden shipping pallets that are often discarded after initial use. Pallets have also been deconstructed into their board components, which can then be reconstructed into trusses (see "Evolving a Village Vernacular," p. 453). Scrap lumber can be glued together to form larger units, and can be creatively used for interior uses such as shelves, counters, ceiling/wall treatments, etc.

Paper and Cardboard

Paper and cardboard are already commonly recycled into fibrous form as cellulose insulation. These fibers can also be repulped and mixed with cement, lime or clay to make a lightweight building material (see "Paper-crete: Homes from Waste Paper," p. 293). Paper can also be used to create interior structures of *papier mâché* over wire or other armatures. It can also be used decoratively, pasted onto wall surfaces.

Cardboard boxes filled with straw have been used as light-weight ceiling panels in concrete roofs. Bales of cardboard can be stacked to form walls. Excess cardboard can be utilized in land-scapes as sheet mulch to greatly accelerate regeneration of de-graded landscapes. Wax-covered cardboard, otherwise impossible to recycle, has been used in baled form as a foundation material for straw bale walls, and could indeed be used for an entire wall system. Shigeru Ban, the winner of the 2014 Pritzker Prize for architecture, has used paper and cardboard extensively to create magnificent buildings in Japan and other countries.

Glass and Cans

Glass bottles have often been used as a decorative daylighting feature. Some charming early examples are still extant. Many natural builders have utilized bottles, especially in cob and cordwood buildings. Two bottles of the same size (or a jar over the neck of a bottle) are wrapped with a reflective material and taped shut, creating a unit which then can be placed transversely in a wall. Bottles can also be laid in sideways, with the opening buried inside the wall.

If the bottles are clear, more light can enter into the building. Some builders even put small electric lights inside the necks of bottles for dramatic effect at night. Bottles can be filled with water for additional thermal mass, but care must be taken to preclude leaking. Bottles have also been used for landscaping walls, mortared in either cob or cement. Cans can be utilized in a similar way to bottles, but the high value of recycling aluminum and other metals may preclude using them as a building material.

Cost-conscious cob builders frequently make windows by simply taking a used pane of glass and inserting it into a cob wall. This is an easy way to make a fixed window of any shape de-sired. One can often find used windows cheap or free at salvage yards, your local "re-store" and even dumps, including insulated

FIGURE 39.4. Making pallet trusses at a Builders Without Borders workshop. [Credit: Catherine Wanek]

double-pane units. Single-pane glass does not retain heat well so it is not recommended for exterior windows, but it could be utilized in a greenhouse or unheated outbuilding, or in an interior partition.

Tires

Tires have been famously used as earth-filled building units in the Earthship style of building developed by Michael Reynolds in New Mexico (see "Earthships: An Ecocentric Model," p. 289). Tires can also be used to make effective retaining walls in hilly areas. Tires have even been used cut up into roofing tiles. Many creative uses for tires, from sandals to door mats to cattle feed troughs to children's swings, can easily be found.

Agricultural Wastes

Straw is an essential component of many natural building systems, including straw bale, straw-clay and many earthen building techniques. Sequestering the straw of fast-growing fiber crops could be a good counter-strategy to rising atmospheric carbon dioxide levels. Rice hulls can be used as a lightweight additive to clay or cement, or as a fuel source, the ash of which can be added as a pozzolan to concrete, or buried in the

FIGURE 39.5. This famous artists' neighborhood in Buenos Aires, Argentina, is made entirely of scrap material. [Credit: Joseph F. Kennedy]

FIGURE 39.6. This bench in Portland, Oregon, is made of reused concrete, recycled stained glass and bicycle parts together with natural materials such as flagstone and cob. [Credit: Joseph F. Kennedy]

soil as biochar (charcoal). Charcoal has also been used in Chile as a lightweight roof insulation. Most organic material can also be composted to improve soils, so it should be removed from the waste stream whenever possible. The US federal government has published an exhaustive literature review of non-wood agricultural fibers used in construction—see "Resources" below.

Other Trash

Mylar-covered packaging, such as juice boxes and chip bags, can be used as reflective insulation. In African refugee camps, these waste products have been used to make the reflective mirrors for solar ovens. Anything that will not rot, including Styrofoam and hard plastics, can be utilized to displace concrete in foundations or in wall systems such as cob. Concrete chunks can be used like stone, or crushed and made into aggregate. Sheet metal scraps can be reconfigured into many useful items. Larger artifacts can be used creatively. Windshields can become windows, an old satellite dish a roof of a small shed. Rural Studio in Alabama has made an art form of the necessity of using a diversity of available materials.

We as a species must take responsibility for the materials we introduce to the landscape. We must reduce the ongoing generation of waste. As the adage says, the most effective strategy is to first reduce, then reuse, then finally recycle. Creative use of materials destined for the landfill or that are already polluting the commons is necessary, beneficial and economical. Building with waste increases adoption of "cradle to cradle" approaches as we close the loops in our human material ecology for greater planetary health and prosperity.

RESOURCES

Books and Articles

• Arango Design Foundation. *Refuse: Good Everyday Design from Reused and Recycled Materials*, Arango Design Foundation, 1996. A catalogue of innovative consumer products made from recycled materials.
• Architecture + Technology. "Reclaim: Remediate, Reuse, Recycle," *Architecture + Technology*, Issue 39–40, 2012. Innovative projects from around the world focused on reclamation in various ways.
• Bahmón, Alejandro and Maria Camila Sanjinés. *Rematerial: From Waste to Architecture*, W.W. Norton, 2008. A profusely illustrated and photographed range of architectural projects utilizing waste.
• Dean, Andrea Oppenheimer. *Rural Studio: Samuel Mockbee and an Architecture of Decency*, Princeton Architectural Press, 2002. An inspiring look at sophisticated architecture (made largely from trash) created by students working with and for local communities.
• Kahn, Lloyd. *Homework: Handbuilt Shelter*, Shelter Publications, 2004. Shows some fun examples from the communitarian era of the late sixties and early seventies.
• Peterson, Chris. *Building with Secondhand Stuff*, Cool Springs Press, 2011. A how-to manual focusing on reclaiming and then reusing building materials.
• Whitney, Sue and Ki Nissauer. *Junk Beautiful: Room by Room Makeover with Junkmarket Style*, Taunton Press, 2008. Great ideas for interiors using inexpensive used items.
• Youngquist, John et al. "Literature Review on Use of Nonwood Plant Fibers for Building Materials and Panels," United States Department of Agriculture, Forest Service, Forest Products Laboratory, General Technical Report FPL-GTR-80, 1994. Available at **fpl.fs.fed.us/documnts/fplgtr/fplgtr80.pdf**

Organizations
• 4Walls International: **4wallsintl.org**
• Earthship Biotecture: **earthship.com**
• Rural Studio: **ruralstudio.org**

Earthships: An Ecocentric Model

40

JACK EHRHARDT

The World Watch Institute estimates that if the rest of the world used natural resources at the rate we do in America, it would take two additional Earths to meet the global demand. With the Earth's population having almost tripled since 1950, it would seem that the real shortage of affordable housing has just begun. Sustainable building—using earthen and recycled materials and implementing principles of energy efficiency to take advantage of free, clean, renewable energy—will help to solve many of these problems.

The American wood-framed building system is being challenged by more ecocentric methods of construction. A modern home needs an interior temperature control system, a system providing clean water for consumption and common use and systems to manage both human waste and garbage—all of which have recyclable elements, if imaginatively conceived and intelligently executed.

Perhaps no other building designer has more radically interfaced all of these living systems than Michael Reynolds of Solar Survival Architecture. He started designing homes based on sustainable principles in Taos, New

JACK EHRHARDT *has been involved in the building industry for over 25 years.*

FIGURE 40.1. The angled windows of the Earthship welcome center in Taos, New Mexico, are designed to harvest the winter sun. [Credit: Catherine Wanek]

Mexico, more than 35 years ago. Now, over 1,000 homes around the world incorporate his "living building" systems. These homes, called Earthships, have built-in systems that take into account every human impact and need. They are designed to make a family feel as independent and free as if they were on a long voyage, only in this case the ship is their home, their voyage is on Earth and their goal is to live in balance with their environment.

My wife Sharon and I have lived in our 2,000 sq. ft. (185.8 m²) Earthship in northern Arizona for fifteen years. It could be described as a typical Earthship, but like all Earthships, it has certain unique features. Whether built on flat ground, dug down into the ground a couple of feet or built into a south-facing hillside, Earthships are buried in the earth on three sides. (Some people, like me, cheat a little and put some windows and a door on the east side, but doing so reduces energy efficiency.)

The building is oriented such that its long front faces south. This is part of the heating system, which uses solar gain through the windows to charge the thermal mass inside in order to heat our home in the winter (see "Designing with the Sun," p. 69). The

system works so well without any backup heat that even if it gets down to 16°F (−9°C) outside at night, when we get up in the morning it's 62°F (17°C) inside and quickly warms up with additional solar penetration. We have frequently commented to one another after coming home on a cold, windy night that it feels like a heater has been on.

The earth is retained by load-bearing walls constructed of "engineered rubber-encased adobe building blocks"—also known as used car and truck tires. Tires are used for the following reasons:

- They have an estimated half-life of 30,000 years.
- They are generally free.
- Once they have been filled with onsite dirt and compacted to 90 pounds, tires make the strongest walls I have worked with or studied.
- They do not outgas when covered with plaster. Studies based on leachate monitoring of old dumpsites have not shown traces of tire material. However, tires do outgas when piled in sunlight, which is another reason to build with them and cover them up. This solves the problem of how to recycle waste tires in an environmentally sound way.

- Tire walls covered with natural adobe or stucco are fire- and termite-proof. Tire walls have gone through fires, hurricanes and earthquakes and have remained standing.

When the first row of tires are laid directly on existing compacted ground and then filled with dirt and compacted, they form a spread footing. Subsequent courses are staggered, as in a block wall. The resulting thermal mass provides excellent cooling in the summer and warming in the winter. In addition, operable skylights at the

FIGURE 40.2. The walls of an Earthship are built from tires, rammed with dirt. [Credit: Catherine Wanek]

rear of the home draft warm air out in the summer.

An Earthship's passive solar design precludes the need for a forced-air HVAC unit, the most costly and energy consumptive appliance in many homes. Ninety-nine percent of Earthships use a solar and/or wind electrical system for independent power. One of the primary reasons that the solar energy market has not taken off like it should have is that it is not always economical to attach solar electric energy systems to conventional, inefficient buildings. They work best when integrated into a complete system of energy efficiency that uses all the free energy available.

Our Earthship's 650-watt power system cost US$4,500 and has never failed. As Sharon is typing this article on the computer for me (I'm still a pen and paper person), a clothes iron, a sewing machine, the DC refrigerator/freezer and our outdoor fountain are all operating at once. If energy-efficient building designs were universally adopted, families would be able to maintain their homes without the need for dangerous nuclear power or polluting coal- or oil-fired power plants.

Another design element of Earthships that promotes independence and responsibility involves water recycling. Roofs are designed to harvest rainwater and divert it to cisterns for storage. Pre-made tanks can be used, but cisterns made of tire walls are frequently built into the sides of Earthships. Water from the cisterns is brought into the home, filtered and used for all purposes, thereby reducing the huge infrastructure development usually required for water supply and the non-point pollution problems clean water is facing these days.

We recycle the greywater from our showers and sinks to irrigate gardens inside the front of the house. The organic vegetables and flowers are efficiently top watered, and the remaining water flows down to the deep roots of our fig tree and banana plants. Our "kitchen sink irrigation system," which has a sediment containment box to catch food particles, grows red peppers, broccoli and flowers. The size of the planters was calculated from the estimated amount of greywater use and the plants' projected absorption rate. Growing our own vegetables increases our self-sufficiency and reduces our dependence on mass agriculture and its poisonous pesticides and fertilizers.

Our toilets also use greywater. The Earthship's "blackwater" (human waste) system is especially efficient because a huge volume

FIGURE 40.3. This long-lasting metal roof harvests rain which is stored in a cistern for the use of residents, while the photovoltaic system harvests solar energy, to power their electrical needs. Note the ventilation ports on the right. [Credit: Catherine Wanek]

of greywater has already been removed from the waste stream, dramatically reducing the amount of blackwater to be treated. If you can't get yourself to use a modern composting toilet system, then this above-ground sealed system works the best.

Just as in greywater sealed systems, the blackwater goes to a sealed containment tank and then flows to second and third containment beds designed to keep the liquid out of the ground. Moisture-absorbing plants are grown in the second and third containers to draw out the liquids. Again, the size of the system is based on projected volume use. As almost everyone knows, water is a precious part of our environment and vital to all living things. Conservation measures keep our water safe to use and allow us to be in close contact with its life-giving processes.

FIGURE 40.4. In this advanced Earthship design, the greenhouse heat-generating space is separated from the rest of the building with windows. This allows residents to control how much warm moist air gets into their living space while still benefiting from the natural light. [Credit: Catherine Wanek]

The Earthship and similar designs personify a paradigm shift to a whole-systems approach to human sustainability. A sustainable society is defined as one that satisfies its needs without diminishing the prospects of future generations. Just as building codes are written to preserve the health and safety of the public, sustainable building is emerging as a responsible way for humanity to preserve the health and safety of the planet.

RESOURCES

Books

• Chiras, Daniel. *The Natural House: A Complete Guide to Healthy, Energy-Efficient, Environmental Homes*, Chelsea Green, 2000. Contains an excellent chapter on building with tires, as well as good information on energy independence.

• Hewitt, Mischa and Even Telfer. *Earthships in Europe*, IHS BRE Press (revised edition), 2012. A critical overview with recommendations for the application of the Earthship system in Europe.

• Reynolds, Michael. *Earthship, Vol. I: How to Build Your Own House; Vol. II: Systems and Components; Vol. III: Evolution Beyond Economics*, Solar Survival Press, 1993. The original references by the originator of the Earthship concept.

Organization

• Earthship Biotecture: **earthship.org**. Offers a wide range of services from design to construction.

Papercrete: Homes from Waste Paper

41

Barry J. Fuller

Papercrete is made from recycled paper, cardboard or other cellulose mixed with water and a binder like cement or clay. In areas of the world like the United States, waste paper is probably the best fibrous material to use. But there are many other natural cellulosic fibrous materials such as flax, hemp, jute, water hyacinth, palm fronds and pineapple leaf fiber. These can be used alone or mixed with paper in areas where waste paper is too expensive or not readily available.

Papercrete is lightweight and flexible, making it an ideal material for earthquake areas. It can be formed as blocks or panels, poured in place, conveyed by auger, pumped, sprayed, hurled, troweled or applied over a framework to make a roof or dome. Mix proportions can be adjusted for different applications. Variations in the amounts of fiber, cement, sand and clay change papercrete's compressive and tensile strength, insulation, thermal mass and sound attenuation.

When water evaporates from the mix, it leaves thousands of tiny air pockets. This is what makes the material lightweight and a good insulator. Depending on the mix proportions, papercrete has an R-value of about 2.0–3.0 per inch. Mixes without sand or clay are light in weight with higher insulating value but less compressive strength. But even mixes made with only paper, water and cement are more

Barry J. Fuller *is executive director of the Center for Alternative Building Studies (CABS), a non-profit organization which conducts research on building materials which do not deplete or pollute the environment. He is also manager of BetR-blok, LLC, a spin-off company commercializing papercrete. His website,* **LivingInPaper.com,** *is the most current, complete and accurate source of papercrete information available.*

FIGURE 41.1. This papercrete dome at Eve's Garden Bed and Breakfast was built by Clyde Curry in Marathon, Texas. [Credit: Clyde Curry]

than strong enough to support a roof. Papercrete is better suited for insulation than for thermal mass. But to build something with papercrete requiring mass, like a trombe wall, just add more cement, clay or sand to the mix. The clay and cement will increase the compressive strength of the mix as well the mass.

Papercrete walls can be built in many ways. Block walls are made by laying blocks in a running bond, like bricks. Many sizes of blocks have been used, dry stacked or with mortar. To increase their seismic resistance, papercrete block walls can be pinned together with rebar or bamboo in a similar manner to straw bale construction. The mortar can be a papercrete mix or conventional cement mortar. Cement mortar bonds better but compromises insulation by creating thermal bridges. It is also difficult to drill or cut.

Walls can also be poured in place, slip-formed or made with tilt-up panels, with or without reinforcement. All of these methods, done properly, can work well. And there is absolutely no waste. Cuttings, sawdust, spills and broken pieces can be returned to the mixer for reuse.

Papercrete is friendly to the unskilled builder—especially during the installation of plumbing and electrical systems. With careful planning, conduit or Romex wiring can be installed in the walls and roof as they are built. Otherwise, a chainsaw can be used to cut 3 in. (8 cm) deep grooves for Romex wiring. Outlets holes are made by drawing a line on the wall around the outlet box and using a skill saw set to maximum depth to overcut the outline. Then a chisel or screwdriver is used to pop out the center. If plumbing has to run through papercrete walls, holes can be drilled with hole saws or paddle bits. Any voids around plumbing holes can be filled with wet papercrete; the patches disappear when the final finish coat is applied.

Papercrete is an easy material for owner-builders to use, regardless of experience or physical strength. The light weight of the material makes it easier to load, move and transport. Best of all, it's easy to correct construction errors, which really helps those with no previous building experience. Beautiful papercrete homes have been built by inexperienced people in varying climates

FIGURE 41.2. Nine-year-old Elizabeth Kemp demonstrates that papercrete is lightweight. This is an enormous advantage for owner-builders. [Credit: Barry J. Fuller]

throughout the southwestern United States, in Northern California, Washington, Wisconsin, New York and in many other countries.

Fire

Papercrete does not burn with an open flame, but it does smolder slowly like charcoal. As an example, one small papercrete building containing very expensive tools became the target of a would-be arsonist. It burned so slowly that members of the local volunteer fire department were able to remove all the tools before applying water to the smoldering area.

Blocks can be made more fire-retardant by adding inorganic material to the mix or by dipping or spraying cured blocks with a boric solution: one cup of Borax soap + one cup of Boric acid in a gallon of water. Boric acid is a very mild acid used in eyewash.

The Center for Alternative Building Studies (CABS) performed a number of informal fire tests with papercrete blocks that had been sprayed or dipped in the boric solution. Dry treated blocks were placed in contact with a gas torch for varying periods. Just spraying a block delayed the onset of smoldering for up to two minutes. Some builders prefer to spray the boric solution only in areas where smoldering is most likely to occur—where electrical outlets or other fire hazards like fireplaces, stoves or dryers will be located.

If mortar with a high percentage of sand is used, each block will be encased in a fire-resistant box formed by mortar between the blocks, stucco on the exterior and plaster on the interior. This approach increases the number of heat conduction pathways (thermal bridges) so it should be used only in mild climates.

Water

Papercrete is hydrophilic, meaning it readily absorbs water. As long as it is able to dry out again, it will keep its shape and not be harmed by periodic wet-dry cycles. At the CABS research facility, piles of blocks and roof panels made from different papercrete mixes have been left outside for over ten years. They have been totally unaffected by exposure to the elements. Blocks have even been allowed to sit in snow piles for entire winters with no signs of deterioration. Papercrete seldom gets totally soaked because water absorption takes time. When the outside surface is totally wet, it cannot absorb any more water so it repels it—in effect waterproofing itself.

Papercrete can be water-proofed using DRYLOK, available at home supply stores. Several ponds and at least one swimming pool have been made from papercrete and sealed with DRYLOK. With some minor repairs, they have held water for years.

A papercrete home was once engulfed in flood waters. It stood in water over three feet deep for a number of days. It did not collapse and eventually dried out, requiring only minor repairs.

Mixes and Mixers

A standard mix recipe for a load-bearing papercrete wall is one 94 lb. bag (43 kg) of Portland cement, 85 lb. (39 kg) of paper pulp, 35 lb. (16 kg) of fly ash, 2.5 gal. (9.5 L) of sand and 150 gal. (568 L) of water. One mix made with this recipe renders about 17 blocks, 12 in. wide by 24 in. long by 4 in. thick (30 × 61 × 10 cm).

Mixes vary depending on the preference of the builder and the application, so be sure to do some tests first. A more fireproof material can be made by adding clay soil to the mix. For high thermal mass applications, the amount of fly ash can be doubled and an additional 180 lb. (82 kg) of clay soil added. Fly ash, a by-product of coal combustion, delays set time and adds cured strength, but it can be omitted if not available. Sand increases compressive strength and makes the mix slightly more fire retardant. But sand should be omitted if the builder intends to use a chainsaw to cut windows and doors after building the walls.

To start the mixing process, paper and water are first added together and pulped. Then the other ingredients such as Portland cement and sand are added. While it is possible to do this by hand or with simple tools like an electric drill with a mixing paddle, projects of any scale usually require a larger mixer. You may need to build your own or buy one left over from another papercrete project. There are a number of kinds of mixers, differentiated mainly by capacity and mobility. The tank volume can vary from 5 gal. (19 L) to 2,000 gal. (7571 L) tanks, and mixers can be towed or mounted on a truck bed or trailer.

A tow mixer is the most practical for most builders. It's made from the rear axle of a rear-drive vehicle, and is towed behind a car or truck. In rear-drive vehicles, the engine turns a drive shaft which is connected to a gearbox in the rear axle called a differential. The differential has right-angle gears which turn shafts to drive the rear wheels. The tow mixer reverses the function of the differential. When the mixer is towed by a car or truck, the wheels turn, rotating the differential. The differential is turned skyward and a tank (usually 200 gal. capacity) is mounted on the axle with the differential protruding through a hole in the bottom. A blade is attached to the differential where the drive shaft would otherwise be connected. The blade spins with such force that it easily tears apart newspapers and magazines—even small catalogs and books. Driving at 5 mph. (8 kph) for less than a mile (1.6 km) will pulp the paper and thoroughly mix everything in the tank.

To date, there are three types of mixers that have been made for larger batches of papercrete: truck-mounted, trailer-mounted and conventional rolling cement mixers. Truck-mounted mixers— 500 gal. (1,893 L) and more—start with a four-wheel drive vehicle, usually a flatbed truck, that can be rebuilt in such a way that the rear-wheel drive turns a blade in the mixing tank and the truck still operates as a two-wheel-drive vehicle. A very large 2,000-gal. (7,571-L) trailer-mounted mixer has been built by CABS. Its design is similar to a truck-mounted mixer, but it is much larger and

FIGURE 41.3. This tow mixer built by Barry J. Fuller easily tears apart newspapers and magazines—even small catalogs and books. The original wooden cover allowed too much papercrete to escape and was replaced by a plastic tarp, secured with a tie-down strap. [Credit: Barry J. Fuller]

the tank can be tipped to help remove the mix.

Conventional rolling cement mixers, the type seen on city streets every day, can be used to mix papercrete. These mixers do not have fast spinning blades and do not rotate quickly enough to break up paper, so shredded paper or hammer-milled paper must be used. Hammer-milled paper is *untreated* cellulose roof insulation, the type blown into the roof crawl space of many homes. (Cellulose roof insulation purchased from a building supply house is treated with moisture-resistant chemicals, so it does not work to make papercrete.) Shredded paper also works in a rolling cement mixer, but it takes a long time to reduce the shredded paper to pulp, so mixing takes a lot longer. There are challenges with both types of paper. Shredded paper has a huge volume-to-weight ratio so a very large amount of it has to be handled to reach a given weight. And it's messy. It flies all over the place. Hammer-milled paper is easier to work with because it comes in pressed bales, but it is very expensive when compared to recycled paper.

Forms

All papercrete starts out the same way—as a wet mix. Forms are needed to contain the mix until it has set enough to stand on its own. In warm dry weather, that can take as little as 15 minutes; then the forms can be removed to expose more surface area for faster drying. With the forms removed, the block, panel or other shape is still too soft to be moved, but the form is free to take the next batch of mix.

Forms can be built from just about anything, depending on the desired shape of the finished product. The most common materials are wood and sheet metal, alone or in combination.

Some people have poured or pumped papercrete into wall-height forms, like pouring a concrete basement wall. Pouring papercrete this way can be challenging. When the water separates from mix poured so deep, there is a great deal of shrinkage—up to 30 percent in height—so more mix must be repeatedly added to top off the forms. Because the forms stay in place until the entire height of the wall sets, most of the surface of the papercrete mix is cut off from the outside air. This extends drying time and prevents uniform water drainage, resulting in pockets, creases and voids. These issues can be addressed by adding drainage paths to the forms and vibrating the mix, but using slip forms is usually a better approach.

Slip forms are light movable forms, typically 8–10 ft. long, (2.4–3 m), which are temporarily placed on the wall, filled and then, as soon as the mix is set, "slipped" along the wall to be filled again. These forms are usually only 6–8 in. (15–20 cm) in height so the problems with tall forms are avoided. Slip forms can be built of wood or lightweight purlin steel very inexpensively. They can be sized as short or long as practical. Several sets of longer forms are necessary to accommodate the volume of mix in a standard tow mixer—about 170 gal. (644 L).

Sometimes forms aren't used at all; the mix is just augered, pumped or sprayed on some type of framework or mesh—often offset layers of chicken wire. Freeform animals, furniture and bowls have been made by manually patting papercrete onto wire forms or pressing it into containers like popcorn dishes.

Blocks

At first glance, papercrete blocks can seem primitive compared to the perfect dimensions of concrete blocks and bricks. As papercrete blocks dry, they shrink. The amount of shrinkage depends on the paper used. Newsprint shrinks the least. Mixed paper with a lot of glossy photos shrinks the most because the glossy surface is made with a kind of clay. The result is a block that may be quite misshapen, but is still very strong and functional. In reality, the irregular shape is of no consequence, and the surface irregularities actually allow one block to bond better to the adjacent block when mortared together with a wet layer of papercrete.

When a papercrete block wall is completed, it will never be perfectly smooth, no matter how much care is taken in laying the blocks. But this doesn't matter; being rough just helps the exterior stucco and interior finish adhere to the wall. Areas that protrude too much can be trimmed with the claw side of a hammer. Areas that are too concave are simply built up with papercrete plaster. In the end, applying outside stucco and interior plaster covers all the imperfections and produces a pleasing organic appearance.

Papercrete Roofs and Floors

Papercrete has been successfully used for both self-supporting roofs and for those supported by beams or rafters. Self-supporting roofs are domes and barrel vaults made only with papercrete blocks and mortar. The most common roof is the supported type. Beams or rafters are sized to support the wet weight of the roof—especially if the papercrete will be exposed to the elements.

Some unsealed papercrete roofs have been left exposed to the weather, which is fine if the roof system is strong enough to support the significant weight gain of absorbed rain. In some cases, papercrete roofs have been treated with elastomeric paint or other waterproofing material.

FIGURE 41.4. Eli Sutton built his house from papercrete blocks stacked and reinforced with rebar and cement mortar. In this photo, he is constructing a papercrete roof. When the blocks are all in place, a thick layer of papercrete, reinforced with rebar, will be poured on top. [Credit: Eli Sutton]

FIGURE 41.5. Domes and vaults are easy to construct from lightweight papercrete blocks. Tom Curry built this vaulted papercrete home, called Sunny Glen, in Alpine, Texas. [Credit: Tom Curry]

It's best to use waterproofing treatments that breathe so that any water finding its way under the waterproofing can eventually evaporate.

The key to using papercrete for floors is providing a solid base and a way for the water to escape. A 4–6 in. (10–15 cm) bed of ½–¾-in. (13–19 mm) gravel, tamped down on pre-tamped earth is a good base for a papercrete floor. It allows the water to

FIGURE 41.6. Kelly Hart used a standard papercrete mixture to plaster his earthbag dome house (see "Digging in for Comfort," p. 211) in arid Colorado. The papercrete was able to absorb all of the rain falling on the building without letting any of it drip through to the interior. [Credit: Kelly Hart]

quickly drain from the mix and after drying prevents moisture from wicking up from beneath the gravel into the floor. Papercrete floors will wear longer if more Portland cement is used in the mix, but many builders add a thin anti-abrasion or "wear" layer on top of the papercrete. Some use an adobe mix or an inch-thick layer of clay-paper, which can be sealed and stained, while others use floor tile. Thin set mortar bonds tile to a papercrete floor very well.

Finishes

Papercrete walls can be left unfinished, painted or plastered. Standard papercrete mix is best used to prepare the wall for finish, to make the wall more regular so that less finish plaster or stucco is needed. This initial coat fills voids between blocks and smooths out uneven areas in curves and arches. Chicken wire or stucco netting can be installed before this initial coat to minimize cracking and prevent the filler coat from delaminating around corners, windows and doors.

The final finish coat can be made from a variety of ingredients. Some builders use Portland cement and sand mixed 1:3 to make stucco and plaster topcoats. This is preferred for exteriors

because it is very durable and protects the papercrete from abrasion. Sometimes a color coat is added over the exterior finish or poured down the wall from the roof line to create beautiful marbled patterns. Or, latex paint mixed one part DRYLOK to three parts paint can be used to color and waterproof the walls and roof. [Note: Cement stucco and latex paint both create non-vapor-permeable surfaces, which can lead to condensation and moisture problems, especially in wet climates.—Editors]

Instead of Portland cement for an interior finish, I prefer Western 1 Kote Concentrate, a stucco base with fiberglass fibers. The recipe is 1.5 parts paper pulp: 1 part Western 1 Kote: 1 part sand. This mixture is much more like conventional plaster than normal papercrete and does not crack or delaminate. An even more abrasion-proof plaster can be made without the paper pulp.

Gypsum-based Plaster of Paris is another beautiful inside finish. It normally has to be mixed in small batches and applied quickly because it has a fast set time. Adding a small amount of citric acid or vinegar will delay set for up to several hours. Some people have used drywall mud and even clay as an interior finish. With these materials, some cracking may occur, but it adds to the organic look of the interior. A few people have used marble and Venetian-style plaster on the interior with stunning faux effects. White Portland cement and white sand, found at swimming pool suppliers, makes a very attractive finish which does not have to be painted.

When making papercrete stucco and plaster, the water and paper should be pulped without binders. Applying stucco and plaster takes time. Large quantities of pulp mixed with cement would set before it could be applied, so the Portland cement is added separately in small batches as it is needed.

The Future of Papercrete

It was thought that the emergence of the computer would lead to a paperless society, but that hasn't happened. In 2011, the US used more paper than in 1980. So it appears that there will be enough waste paper to support papercrete production for years to come.

Building with papercrete has a number of unforeseen benefits. Besides saving trees, using recycled paper provides a profit incentive to recycle in rural communities. Even a modest waste paper stream provides enough paper to start a cottage industry manufacturing this material, which creates new jobs and business opportunities. Keep-

ing waste paper out of landfills is an environmental bonus in itself.

The Center for Alternative Building Studies has been conducting research on papercrete for almost ten years. CABS research and development has produced an improved version of papercrete called BetR-blok. The new block is uniform and consistent in dimension, mass and strength. It is capable of being produced quickly and in great numbers. A prototype BetR-blok manufacturing system has been developed and is currently being automated. BetR-blok will soon be fully commercialized and ready for nationwide distribution.

RESOURCES

Websites
- greenhomebuilding.com. This site contains an enormous amount of hard-to-find information on many alternative building systems, including papercrete. You can ask questions of experts in most of the materials and techniques found in this book.
- livinginpaper.com. Barry Fuller's website with lots of free information, links and CDs for sale.
- papercrete.com. Downloadable papercrete resource guide for sale, along with hard-to-find information on other building techniques.

Roofs for Natural Buildings

42

JOSEPH F. KENNEDY

Just as a building needs a "good pair of boots" (a good foundation), it also needs a "good hat" (a good roof). Often the most complex part of a building, a roof must be designed and built to ensure weatherproofness, insulative qualities, sturdiness and aesthetic consistency.

A roof has to:

- **Protect against elements.** These include rain or snow, wind or excess light. A roof must be solid, strong and waterproof. The more severe the weather a roof must withstand, the stouter and steeper it should be to encourage drainage. Thus, steep roofs are traditional in places with lots of snow, and shallow roofs in dryer climates.

- **Prevent unwanted heat loss or gain.** Since hot air rises,

JOSEPH F. KENNEDY *is a designer, educator and perpetual student of building systems.*

most heat loss occurs through the roof of a building. Roofs in temperate and cold climates must therefore be well insulated. Insulation and radiant barriers are also important in hot, arid climates to avoid unwanted solar heat gain through the roof.

- **Withstand local climate and natural disaster conditions** such as hurricanes, earthquakes or high winds. This means the roof must be strongly constructed and well attached to the walls and foundation. Metal straps or hardware are usually used to connect the roof to the walls. When the walls are made of discrete units like straw bales, adobe bricks or compressed earth blocks, a bond beam on top of the wall is very important to create a continuous strong surface to hold up the roof load. In high-wind

FIGURE 42.1. A cascading series of clay tile roofs. Santa Barbara Mission, California. [Credit: Joseph F. Kennedy]

301

areas, the roof shape should be designed to shunt the wind away, and not catch it under too-wide overhangs (for example), causing damaging uplift forces.

- **Support its own weight and additional variable weights.** The weight of the roof itself is called a dead load. Weights that vary (snow, people) are called live loads. A roof must be designed to avoid collapse from the greatest imaginable loading a building may incur.

- **Shed water away from the walls.** This is achieved by overhangs, the parts of the roof that extend out beyond the edge of the wall. The greater the danger to the walls from weather, the bigger the overhang should be. Walls of earth and straw need a lot of protection in rainy climates. Roof overhangs should also be designed to block the summer sun yet allow the winter sun in (see "Designing with the Sun," p. 69).

- **Complement the aesthetic qualities of the building.** The shape and material of a roof is often the most dominant aesthetic feature of a building. Roof aesthetics should be carefully considered early in the design stage.

Roof Shapes

Roofs come in several basic shapes. Simple buildings usually use one or another of those described here. More complex structures may combine multiple

FIGURE 42.2. Roofs can be the dominant aesthetic feature of a building, as evidenced by this elaborate sculptural roof on a temple at the Palace Museum in Beijing, China. [Credit: Catherine Wanek]

roofs of different shapes. As complexity increases, so do construction time and cost.

Flat Roofs

Perhaps the easiest roof to build, a so-called flat roof has a single surface with no peaks or valleys. Flat roofs are actually slightly sloped to let the water drain. However, because they do not shed water quickly, and often have parapets that are difficult to waterproof, they are more likely to leak than steeper roofs, so they

FIGURE 42.3. A domed building built of corbelled earthen bricks in Turkey. [Credit: Catherine Wanek]

need to be absolutely waterproof and well maintained. They work best in areas that do not get much rain or snow.

Shed Roofs

Similar to flat roofs but with a steeper slope, shed roofs allow water and snowmelt to run off quickly. Choosing a shed roof can make for awkward walls, however, as the walls must be built to different heights, and two of the walls must be sloped.

Gable Roofs

A gable roof is composed of two flat surfaces that meet at an apex (ridge) and slope away from each other. One advantage of a gable roof is that it can provide extra space for living or storage under the roof without increasing wall height. A building with this type of roof is more easily expanded than some other styles.

In a gable roof, the ridge beam is held up by the end walls or by posts. Rafters are attached to the ridge beam, with the ends of the rafters resting on the side walls. In order to keep the rafters from pushing out the side walls, horizontal tensile members (either boards or cables) are used to connect the rafters. An option less frequently used is to add

buttressing on the outside of the building to counteract these lateral forces.

Trusses, which are triangulated structural components manufactured from small-dimension lumber, can be used instead of ridge beams and rafters. Because trusses are strong, yet relatively light, they are often used to cover large spans.

Hipped Roofs

Hipped roofs are sloped on all four sides, allowing the supporting walls to be all the same height. It is easy to build a bond beam across the level tops of the walls, making this a popular roof design for load-bearing straw bale and adobe structures. The rafters must be supported, as in a gable roof, to keep them from pushing the walls apart.

Domes and Vaults

Domes and vaults are roofing systems common in dryer parts of the world, especially Africa and the Middle East. Unlike the roofs mentioned thus far, which require materials with tensile strength (usually wood), domes and vaults can be made with materials such as bricks, concrete, stone and earth, that are strong in compression. A vault is a single-curvature roof and is best used to cover a rectangular room. A double-curvature dome can cover a square or round room.

Combinations of vaults and domes can be infinitely varied and extremely beautiful.

Earthen domes and vaults are not recommended for rainy climates, since they are difficult to waterproof and if the roof gets soaked it can collapse. Another reason to use domes and vaults only in the driest climates is because they do not shed water away from the walls. However, recent experiments with straw bale vaults and earthbag domes seem to offer great promise.

Roof Systems

Nearly all roofing systems have two main parts: the structural component that determines the shape and strength of the roof and the protective layer that covers and waterproofs the structure.

Roof Structure

Wood is still perhaps the most common material used to create roof structures, because it is easy to work, lightweight and strong in tension and compression. The long spans used in traditional framing can require lumber dimensions that are only achievable by milling large trees or by

laminating many smaller pieces of wood together into a "glue-lam." Engineered wood products and trusses constructed from small-dimensional lumber can reduce pressure on our forests and are often more convenient to use. Truss systems are already engineered, and the pre-manufacturing reduces the amount of labor necessary to install the roof. Trusses can also be constructed of recycled pallets (see "Evolving a Village Vernacular," p. 453).

Timber framing uses traditional wood-to-wood joinery techniques to create sophisticated integrated wall and roof structures. This option, while labor-intensive and therefore often expensive, can be viable in areas with sufficient wood resources (see "The Art of Timber Framing," p. 265).

Some natural builders are finding creative uses for abundant locally available timber that is unsuitable for milling. Homemade bentwood trusses can be made with flexible small-diameter trees, as has been demonstrated in Nova Scotia. Many builders in forested regions use round-pole timber, which allows smaller trees

FIGURE 42.4. Eco-shake roofing tiles being installed over a vapor barrier, Moab, Utah. [Credit: Catherine Wanek]

to be used for the same structural strength as a sawn timber from a larger tree (see "Small-Diameter Roundwood," p. 271). The whole trunks of beautifully curved trees can be used for unique custom roofs.

Bamboo: The largest plants in the grass family, bamboo grows very quickly and provides a strong renewable material for building, tools and utensils, as well as edible shoots. Common in the tropics, many species of bamboo grow in temperate climates as well. Strong and beautiful, bamboo has recently become popular with builders, especially for creating roof trusses. Bamboo can replace wood and steel in many other situations as well (see "Bamboo Construction," p. 273).

Metal: Though not recommended because of its high-embodied energy costs, metal structural members or trusses can be used, especially for long spans.

Waterproofing

Often a sheathing layer on top of the roof structure connects the structural elements, spreads loads and provides an attachment surface for the waterproofing and protective layers. Industrial materials such as plywood are commonly used for such sheathing, but many natural builders prefer to use natural boards, small-diameter saplings or bamboo. Non-toxic sheet products manufactured from straw and other agricultural wastes are also becoming more available.

The waterproofing layer is perhaps the most challenging aspect of natural roofs. Our ancestors used layers of natural materials like birch bark, reed thatch, slate and ceramic tiles. Today, these traditional methods tend to be expensive, labor-intensive and/or leaky. Most conventional construction relies on tar or asphalt, plastic or rubber products as waterproofing membranes. A less toxic natural alternative is much needed.

FIGURE 42.5. Thatching a performance space with grass in Dennilton, South Africa. [Credit: Joseph F. Kennedy]

Living Roofs: The living roof is really an update of the ancient sod roof of Europe. This type of roof has several advantages: it is beautiful, helps the house blend into its environment and provides sound dampening and climatic stabilization.

A living roof is heavy and needs a very strong supporting structure. The waterproofing membrane (usually durable synthetic rubber) needs to be applied very carefully, as it is very difficult to locate leaks once the growing medium is in place.

The growing medium can be cut sod, rolled turf, loose topsoil, compost or straw. It can be planted with ornamental or edible herbs and ground covers or allowed to grow naturally. In many climates, a living roof will need to be watered to stay green (see "Green Roofs with Sod, Turf or Straw," p. 309).

Thatch: The use of reeds, grasses or palm fronds as a roofing material is still common in Europe and many less industrialized countries. Thatch is one of the few roof systems that can be made entirely with natural materials. Thatched roofs, if well-built, can last up to 60 years or more and provide a beautiful complement to natural wall systems. Thatch "breathes," can be made from local materials and is highly insulating and extremely attractive. Many builders are exploring its use to replace methods that rely on manufactured materials (see "Thatching Comes to America," p. 313).

There are several downsides which limit the use of this

FIGURE 42.6. This roofscape in central Prague shows a combination of tile and metal roofing strategies. The valley where the houses meet can be particularly challenging to waterproof. [Credit: Catherine Wanek]

otherwise desirable technique. Thatching is a highly skilled and time-consuming craft, and very few professional thatchers are available in North America. Hence a thatched roof can be very expensive. If a thatched roof is not well built, it may leak and need to be replaced within a few years. Thatched roofs are vulnerable to fire, and they can also provide a home for undesirable pests. In many countries, thatching materials are increasingly rare and expensive.

Seaweed and Seashells: Seaweed is a unique roofing material similar to thatch. In Denmark, certain species of seaweed are harvested and placed on roofs to provide long-lasting protection. Mussel shells, obtained as waste from the seafood industry, are also being used on rooftops in Denmark, to protect membrane roofs and create a drainage layer.

Shakes and Shingles: Shakes are overlapping pieces of wood used to shed water and snow. They are created by splitting a rot-resistant log into thin pieces, using a mallet and froe. Shingles are similar but are sawn instead of split. Cedar and redwood shakes and shingles used to be very common in North America, but because they are made from old-growth trees, their use is no longer practical, except in certain rare circumstances. Although admittedly beautiful, a wood roof is also a potential fire hazard. A number of artificial shake and shingle products have been developed, made of concrete or recycled materials. These can be appropriate in certain circumstances.

Metal: Although it is not really a "natural" material, many natural builders choose metal for roofing. Relatively inexpensive compared to other systems, metal roofs are durable, long-lasting, easy to install and lightweight (allowing the underlying roof structure to be lighter as well). They can last 50 to 100 years in a dry climate and are easily reusable or recyclable. Metal roofs can be used to collect rainwater, a very important consideration in many dry regions and areas where groundwater is brackish or unavailable. Depending on the type of metal and its coating, this water may or may not be safe to drink. The mining of metal ore is, however, environmentally destructive, and the manufacture of metal is very energy-intensive. Still, the benefits of metal often outweigh the drawbacks.

FIGURE 42.7. This thatched roof in China, made from seaweed, could last 80 years or more. It is slowly being colonized by growing plants. [Credit: Catherine Wanek]

Other Roofing Materials: Other roofing materials exist; some are natural, some man-made. Slate (a flat, sheet-like stone) can be attached to the underlying roof structure with nails and overlapped like shingles. Ceramic tiles are common in many countries and can be an easy and beautiful roof option. Slate and tile can both be used to collect rainwater. Both are extremely heavy, however, and need a very strong roof structure to hold them up. Some people have experimented with cutting up old tires and using them like tiles for roofing. Asphalt shingles and rolled roofing, although readily available and easy to use, have a relatively short life and are extremely toxic to dispose of. They are therefore avoided by most natural builders.

RESOURCES

Books

• Chappell, Steve. *A Timber Framer's Workshop: Joinery, Design and Construction of Traditional Timber Frames*, Fox Maple Press, 1998. Good chapter on engineering, design and construction of timber-frame trusses.
• Clark, Sam. *The Real Goods Independent Builder: Designing and Building a House Your Own Way*, Chelsea Green, 1996. Contains helpful basic information for design and construction of conventional roofs.
• Gross, Marshall. *Roof Framing*, Craftsman Book Co., 2010. An excellent book covering the basics of conventional wood roof framing.
• Jenkins, Joe. *The Slate Roof Bible*, Joseph Jenkins, Inc., 2003. A passionate and entertaining book about this roofing system that can last up to 400 years.
• Roy, Rob. *The Complete Book of Cordwood Masonry Housebuilding: The Earthwood Method*, Sterling, New York, 1992. Contains an interesting chapter on Roy's method of earth roof construction.
• Steen, Athena Swentzell, Bill Steen, David Bainbridge and David Eisenberg. *The Straw Bale House*, Chelsea Green, 1994. Has a useful chapter on roof design and options.

Green Roofs with Sod, Turf or Straw

43

Paul Lacinski and Michel Bergeron
with John Swearingen

Natural builders frequently turn to green roofs for their beautiful aesthetics, particularly on buildings with organic forms and materials. You might also choose a living roof to help buffer the building from the heat of the summer sun, to grow flowers, herbs or other edibles, or simply to blend the house with its environment. Covering a roof with soil may be the most obvious way to replace the natural landscape removed by the imprint of a new house, and a living roof will last indefinitely if properly installed and maintained. Whether it evolves into a lovely rooftop garden or a long-lasting shaggy blanket is up to you.

Construction Techniques

Sod, turf and other living roofs don't differ much in the way they are built and are simple to construct. Build a low-pitched roof frame, cover it with a solid deck, stick on a waterproof membrane, and lay the organic material on top of the membrane. (Sod roofs can also be constructed with steeper pitches, providing that measures are taken to keep the soil from slipping off the roof.)

High-tech roofing membranes such as EPDM, Hypalon, neoprene, PVC and modified bitumen are the best choice for these low-pitched roofs. Single-sheet membranes have the advantage of being seamless, which reduces the possibility of leaks developing over time. In conventional construction, they are left exposed to weather. Although they all have a protective coating, membrane roofs will nevertheless slowly but surely degrade under ultraviolet

Paul Lacinski *is the author of* Serious Strawbale. *As a principal of Greenspace Collaborative, he designed and constructed natural buildings appropriate to the climate of the northeastern US. After many summers of camping at construction sites, Paul now stays at home in Hawley, Massachusetts. Along with his wife, Amy Klippenstein, he runs Sidehill Farm, an organic dairy and creamery in the foothills of the Berkshire Mountains: sidehillfarm.net.*

With a background in architecture and a degree in Industrial Design, **Michel Bergeron**'s *personal owner-builder, onsite experiences have led to professional consultancy, lectures and workshops in Canada, the US and Europe. In 1991, with Clôde de Guise and Francois Tanguay, he founded Archibio, a non-profit group promoting sustainable architecture. Now specializing in straw bale construction, Michel has contributed innovations like form-worked straw bale concrete stem walls, living roofs and an owner-built composting toilet.*

Award-winning designer **John Swearingen** *has extensive experience in residential and light commercial construction. John designed and built his first passive solar home in 1986 and has continued to work with sustainable, healthy materials, including straw bale, rammed earth and passive solar heating and cooling:* skillfulmeans.wordpress.com.

light exposure, and some will also erode over time from continuous heavy rains and ice buildups. Covering the membranes with a protective layer of soil and plants will considerably enhance their life expectancy.

It is a good idea to lay a drainage mat and/or volcanic rock (pumice or scoria) between the soil and the membrane to assure proper soil drainage and efficient runoff during heavy rains. Some drainage mats provide a protective covering for the membrane. This drainage layer below the soil helps retain moisture while discouraging root growth which could attack the membrane.

A thin coat of manure, compost, leaves or any other organic material is spread on the surface and either left to grow on its own or planted with edibles and flowers. Plants can be chosen to create safe habitats for challenged plants, insects, birds and small animals in the environment. The only maintenance required, besides the usual gardening work, is to add more straw periodically as the original layer decomposes.

In the 1990s, Archibio developed a living roof system using a substrate of second-quality straw bales on top of the waterproof membrane, laid side by side with the twine cut to loosen the straw. Archibio's straw bale concept originated with the use of a much lighter growing medium than soil, with enough volume for plant roots to stay healthy. However, in engineering the roof, the assumption has to be that the soil or straw will become thoroughly soaked, so the depth of the layer, rather than type of material, is the governing factor of weight, since water is usually heavier than soil. A lighter alternative to either soil or straw bales would be to lay down 4 in. thick (10 cm) flakes of straw. That wouldn't add more than 10 lb/sq. ft. (480 kiloPascals) to the whole structure and would still protect the membrane while offering the same natural look.

Soils and plants should be chosen for the specific climate, including the ability to withstand freezing where appropriate. Because the soil layer is relatively thin, soils that retain moisture and plants such as sedums that thrive with shallow roots are advantageous in dry conditions. When water is abundant, either through rain or irrigation, a wider range of plantings is allowable. Planting the roof in early spring allows the plant cover to get well established before the extremes of summer and winter take hold.

Advantages

The temperature-moderating effect created by 5–6 in. (12–15 cm) of soil and plants on the roof helps keep a house cooler in summer and somewhat warmer in winter, especially in climates with wide daily temperature swings. The plant layer provides nearly complete shade for the roof, and when the roof is irrigated, the soil

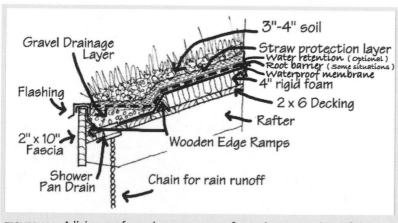

FIGURE 43.1. A living roof requires waterproof membranes and careful detailing. [Credit: Joseph F. Kennedy]

layer is further cooled by evaporation. Fourteen inches (35 cm) of decomposing straw will have a similar effect, while adding some insulation for a while.

While such roofs can be built in cold climates, the thermal benefits of a green roof in winter are minimal, since as soon as the material gets wet, it loses its insulation value. On the other hand, green roofs are excellent at holding snow on the roof and a layer of snow can add about R-1 per inch.

The wind and noise protection qualities of a living roof are also worth considering in specific environments. A city house built with straw bale walls and covered with an organic roof will be a peaceful retreat at any time of day, even in areas with dense traffic. Cities such as Portland, Oregon, have made it easier for building owners to install green roofs, as doing so reduces the demand on stormwater systems. Green roofs used widely in urban conditions could significantly improve the climate of cities, as well as providing huge amounts of new green space for recreation, agriculture and habitat for native species.

FIGURE 43.2. This layer of straw bales will gradually decompose and provide a growing medium for a living roof. The roof structure must be strong enough to support the loads of straw that will at some point become saturated with water. [Credit: Catherine Wanek]

FIGURE 43.3. This living roof at the Upland Hills Ecological Awareness Center near Detroit, Michigan, sports a growing medium of volcanic stone, with a thin layer of earth and straw planted with sedums, which will eventually grow to cover the entire roof. Plants may need to be watered while they are getting established, and in times of drought. [Credit: Catherine Wanek]

Disadvantages

The main drawback of building a green roof is the additional 50–60 lb./sq. ft. (2.4–2.9 kilo-Pascals) that the structure will have to support. This usually means larger rafters, spaced more closely together, than in a conventional roof. The added weight, in addition to any snow loading, might be too much for certain kinds of construction such as, for example, load-bearing straw bale walls. If, after investigation, the wall system is found not to be strong enough, the need to shore up the structure would obviously increase the building costs. That prospect should be cross-evaluated with the positive aspects of the roof. Usually gravity loads are easy to support, but restraining so much weight up top in heavy winds or an earthquake requires strong shear walls.

All the usual activities associated with gardening—weeding, watering, mulching, harvesting—will be required if your roof is going to look like any kind of a garden. The type of maintenance will depend on the degree of refinement you want in the appearance of the roof. Otherwise, you just need to keep the membrane covered by periodically adding more soil or organic material. Hardscrabble roofs that require hardly any maintenance can be created with minimal soil and many rocks, recreating dry, rocky habitats.

At worst, if no maintenance is done, the membrane might eventually become exposed. Generally it takes a long time for soil to blow off, as grasses and weeds will hold it in place. Most types of membranes used for roofing are UV-resistant and will last a decade or longer even uncovered.

FIGURE 43.4. High-tech or low-tech, urban or rural, a living roof makes use of our rooftops, offering both gardening potential and living space. And it gives a little bit of habitat back to nature. [Credit: Michel Bergeron]

RESOURCES

Books
• Peck, S. and M. Kuhn. *Design Guidelines for Green Roofs*, Canada Mortgage and Housing Corporation and the Ontario Association of Architects, 2003. Detailed overview of benefits and design and cost variables for commercial green roof installations. Available as free download.
• Snodgrass, Edmund C. et al. *Small Green Roofs: Low-Tech Options for Greener Living*, Timber Press, 2011. Profiles of ordinary homeowners who scaled green roofs down to the domestic level.
• Snodgrass, Edmund C. et al. *Green Roof Plants: A Resource and Planting Guide*, Timber Press, 2006.

A reliable reference devoted exclusively to the various species of drought-tolerant plants that are suitable for use on green roofs.
• Youngman, Angela. *Green Roofs: A Guide to Their Design and Installation*, Crowood Press, 2012. A guide to the process of designing and installing a green roof.

Organization
• Green Roofs for Healthy Cities: **greenroofs.org**. Dedicated to creating a green roof marketplace in North America. Includes news, upcoming events, FAQ, projects, public policies and research.

Thatching Comes to America

44

Deanne Bednar

A thatched roof provides creative scope to the builder and infinite charm to the dwelling. Warm in the winter and cool in the summer, a thatched roof offers a sustainable, insulating, non-polluting and durable alternative to asphalt shingles. Thatched roofs can be made from a wide variety of local plant materials, and the harvesting and application process offers a deep relationship with the natural environment and the seasons. They are a labor of love that brings delight and eventually can return gracefully to the circle of life. Thatching allows us to create a roof without ecological compromise while providing the beauty and soulful qualities so often found in hand-built indigenous structures throughout time.

Deanne Bednar *coordinated the Strawbale Studio program based near Oxford, Michigan, teaching natural building and sustainable living skills using primarily locally foraged natural materials. She has a Masters Degree in Social Ecology from Goddard College and began her adventure into natural building with a Cob Cottage class after retiring from teaching Art and Sustainable Futures at the middle school level. She loves to sculpt with earth and is also the illustrator of several books on natural building:* The Cobber's Companion: How to Build Your Own Earthen Home, The Hand-Sculpted House *and* The Natural Plaster Book.

FIGURE 44.1. The Strawbale Studio outside Oxford, Michigan, with thatched woodshed on the left. [Credit: Dana Lynn Driscoll]

As the natural building movement searches for roofing solutions, interest in thatching is growing worldwide. Several European-trained master thatchers practice their craft in the US on private homes, zoos and historic structures, and now there is also a growing grassroots exploration into thatched roofing in North America. My first encounter with thatch came in 1996 during a Natural Building Colloquium in California, where Flemming Abrahamsson, a master thatcher from Denmark, gave a delightful hands-on demonstration. Little did I know that a year later I would be collaborating with the Cob Cottage Company to bring Flemming to Michigan to teach thatching on the roof of the Strawbale Studio—an enchanting structure that I helped design and build. Out of that workshop grew a most incredible sculptured roof—and my ongoing love of the art of thatching.

Since then I have continued to harvest reed each winter and have overseen the thatching of a number of small buildings. My knowledge is rudimentary, yet like many in the natural building movement, I feel a calling to explore these traditional building methods, knowing that somehow our ancestors were able to do it, and surely we can learn, too. Master thatchers train for years, and I imagine they can outperform me in all ways. Yet with great patience and tenacity, I have experienced that it is possible for a person of my very basic training to create a simple small roof of adequate quality and great beauty. I continue to share these hands-on skills by offering workshops and internships, giving others the confidence to undertake their own projects.

There are many different thatching materials, techniques and styles that have been used throughout time and place. This is the Strawbale Studio story.

In July 1996, after returning from a cob building course, I came together with Fran Lee and Carolyn Koch to design an enchanting natural building for Fran on her rural land north of Detroit, Michigan. Buoyed by the vision of a building that would express the spirit of its place, the three of us walked out to the site and co-designed a 650-"round-foot" (61 m²) studio whose irregular and sculptural outlines are a response to the trees that surround its site. Stones for the foundation came from the land itself, while the straw bales were grown on a nearby farm and plastered with local earth to form the deep, sheltering walls. The sun shines through south-facing windows onto an earthen floor, and round timbers from local pine trees are visible inside the structure.

As we planned the project, we considered many different roof possibilities, but once we had imagined a thatch roof, we fell completely in love with the idea and there was no turning back. Bringing vision into reality was no simple matter, however. We couldn't just call a local thatcher, as one might do in England. After contacting several US thatchers who were gracious but cautious, we chose Flemming from Denmark who was willing to work with students up on the roof.

To prepare for the workshop, we needed reed—lots of reed. In fact, we needed to harvest four to five acres (1.6–2 ha) of plants in order to cover our 1,500 sq. ft. (140 m²) roof. *Phragmites communis/australis*, or common water reed, is considered one of the best of thatching materials. Well-constructed reed roofs are expected to last perhaps 50 to 75 years in Europe, with the ridge being replaced every 5 to 15 years. We knew that *Phragmites* grew in nearby private fields and in large state-owned marshes, as well as along the expressways, so we set about finding places to harvest.

Collecting and Storing Reed Bundles

Reeds are collected in the winter when they are dormant. In December 1997, with the permission of the St. Clair County Drain Commissioner and the Department of Natural Resources, we headed into the marshes of St. Clair County, about an hour east of our site. Finding reeds was not a problem: at first, every marsh appeared to be a vast resource, but we soon learned that the wild fields contained reed of varying ages, from one to several years old and in different stages of decomposition. The highest quality reed is straight, strong, bright colored, 5–8 ft. tall (1.5–2.4 m) and just one year old. Traditionally, reed fields are cut on a one- or two-year rotation, according to rain and weather conditions, to maintain optimum crops for thatching. It's great to harvest the same field every year or two because the reed will tend to be of higher quality and more uniform size. In wild fields, we harvest the reed, then separate it by length and bundle it.

The use of grain straw as a thatching material would also be worth considering. There are a number of old varieties of wheat (such as Maris Huntsman and Little Joss), rye and triticale that have the qualities required for thatching. Although grain straw has a shorter roof life than reed (20 to 25 versus 50 to 75 years), it is an economic crop that can be grown locally and harvested with a mechanical binder or by hand. Use of grain straw can also avoid the potential ecological problems associated with reed grass, which is highly invasive in Michigan and other parts of the US.

We harvested *Phragmites* using both hand and mechanical methods, averaging about two to three bundles per person per hour. (Each bundle has about 500 stems.) After our first attempts at harvesting, it became apparent that by ourselves we would not be able to get the 1,500 bundles of reed needed in time for the workshop, so we hired some local folks who were able to harvest 1,200 bundles for US$4.00 a bundle, using a gas-powered reciprocating pole hedge trimmer. This amount of reed covered only about half of the building, so we covered the rest of the roof with a tarp and went back to harvesting the following winter.

By then we had the confidence and experience to gather several hundred bundles by ourselves and with volunteers.

FIGURE 44.2. When harvesting *Phragmites* reed grass, cradles were used for measuring the diameter of the bundles. These harvesters were part of a winter internship program at the Strawbale Studio. [Credit: Deanne Bednar]

The gas trimmer was abandoned in favor of the safety and quiet, meditative qualities of the hand sickle. Yet again, we fell short of the number of bundles needed and went out a third winter to harvest the final amount needed to finish the roof. The grand total was 2,000 bundles! It is truly hard to imagine how much work and time it takes to harvest that much reed. The last few buildings I have been involved with have been in the 400–500 bundle range, which is a much more comfortable amount. There are also reaper binders available that could be an effective community tool for harvesting large amounts of reed in a short time.

Water reed is collected following several hard frosts, after the leaves fall and before new growth starts. It's really a lovely process to collect reed on a winter day when the stalks have dried to a bamboo-like hardness and wave their feathery plumes under an open sky. Here in Michigan, the appropriate time is December through March, with earlier being better because winter storms can damage the reed. Hopefully the ground is frozen, since reed often grows in areas that are wet or under water. Bundles are traditionally 8.5 in. (21 cm) in diameter and 4–8 ft. (1.2–2.4 m) long. Each

bundle of this size covers one square foot of roof. Tapered reeds are ideal, especially for thatching roof corners or eaves.

After cutting, the reed is cleaned, if necessary, to remove undesired weeds, bent stalks or remaining leaves. In our case, each bundle is tied with twine near the bottom and again in the middle, using a quick-release knot. Seed heads are cut off and the bundle is shortened to a length of about 5 ft. (1.5 m) for consistency in overlapping the rows like shingles. The bundle is tamped down to give it a flat end and is then ready for transporting to the site for storage.

Working the Roof

In mid-April 1998, two master thatchers from Denmark, Flemming Abrahamsson and Ole Hans, arrived at the Strawbale Studio. The roof had been constructed at a 45-degree angle with round-pole rafters and 2×2 purlins (battens) spaced at 1 ft. (0.3 m) intervals, with a 2×6 lift board at the bottom, which pushes the lower layer of reed up into compression and prevents it from sliding downward.

Modern thatchers often use an attachment technique that uses a battery drill, a long drill bit, stainless screws and wire.

I like the more traditional method using a homemade wooden thatching needle (instead of the drill and screws) and round-pole purlins hand-harvested from the land (instead of milled 2×2s). Thatching can easily tolerate the irregularities inherent in round foraged poles. The reed bundles are applied to the roof with the butt end downward, and held in place with long saplings (sways) ½–¾ in. (1.25–1.8 cm) in diameter which sandwich together and permanently hold each course of reed in place.

To thatch with a wooden needle, the person on the outside of the roof pushes the needle threaded with .040 gage stainless steel wire into the thatch, and a second person, on the interior, pulls the needle through to the inside and around the purlin, then pushes it back up through the roof to the person on the outside. The wire is cut, with the ends twisted over the sway, and tightened down with a ratchet to hold that row of reed tightly between the sway and the purlin. All parts of the roof can be accessed by using a combination of scaffolding around the building, full-length ladders, short thatching ladders with hooks and 4×4 beams attached by ropes to the purlins.

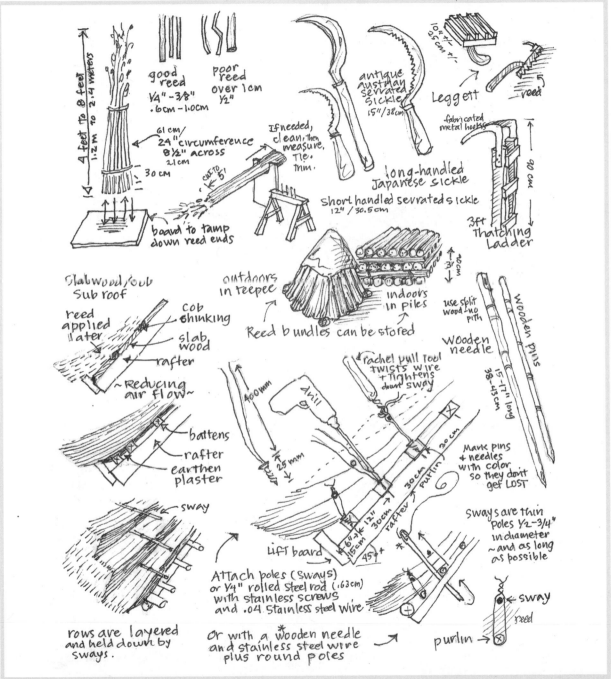

FIGURE 44.3. Some of the tools and techniques used for traditional and modern reed harvesting and thatching.
[Credit: Deanne Bednar]

During this process, the strings tying each bundle are cut, allowing the reed to blend together. The surface of the reed is tapped up or "dressed" at an angle with a leggett, a wooden paddle with indentations on its surface which push the reed up, creating an evenly shingled surface that water can quickly run off. The next overlapping row is applied on top, as with roof shingles, and it, too, is attached down, blended and feathered in. Ridge options range in materials and techniques. On the Strawbale Studio, we used a reed ridge, in what is called a "butt up" style. I have also used cattail stalks for a ridge, as well as a fabricated copper cap. [Note: Plastered ridges are common in South Africa and elsewhere.—Editors.]

It takes quite some time and experience to get a feel for the basic thatching process. Specific techniques are needed for the ridge, chimney area and roof valleys. As a first-time experiment, I would highly recommend thatching a very small building with a simple gable or hip roof, such as a doghouse or a garden or tool shed. This will allow some practice and familiarity with harvesting, construction and application.

Resistance to Rain, Heat Loss and Fire

A thatched roof is able to shed water effectively only when the following criteria are met. First, the roof needs to be steep, with a minimum angle of 45 or 50 degrees. Second, the reeds need to be of good quality—strong and straight—so that when they are properly applied and lying tight together, rainwater will quickly transfer from the end of one reed to the next without penetrating the roof more than about an inch (2.5 cm).

I have heard numerous insulation values quoted for a 12 in. thick (30 cm) thatched roof, in the range of R-22 to R-30 or more.

FIGURE 44.4. Cattail stalks and leaves, gathered in the fall, were used to create a protective ridge over the reed grass gable roof of the Oxford Kids Cottage. This decorative framework of sticks, wired to the purlins below, holds the cattails down. The Kids Cottage has a roof thatched with reed grass, and a ridge made of cattails. Note that the cattail leaves are folded over the ridge top of the roof and held into place with two rows of horizontal sticks that are wired down to the underlying purlin. Then an "X" made of sticks is slipped under, and wired to, the horizontal sticks. This attachment pattern is both decorative and practical. Cattails ridges will be replaced every few years as needed. [Credit: Deanne Bednar]

We do know that each reed is hollow with closed segments, that thousand of pockets of air exist between and within the stems that make up the roof, and that insulation is substantially increased when combined with a sub-roof that adds insulation and blocks air flow. My understanding is that the fire risk is similar to wood shakes, and can be reduced with applications of fire retardants every five to seven years. Inner air barriers significantly contribute to fire safety by reducing the flow of oxygen. In Denmark, Flemming uses rock wool mineral insulation for this air barrier. He also suggested the use of a slab-wood ceiling sealed up with cob.

Since building the Strawbale Studio, I have overseen and helped thatch several lovely structures, including the Kensington Kids' Cottage, located at the Farm Center in the Kensington Metropark outside Milford, Michigan. This project was well supported by the park, and offers the opportunity for thousands to see and walk through it each year. It has a copper cap which will eliminate the ridge replacements needed for ridges made of plant material. The Spiral Chamber is a small wattle-and-daub outbuilding, with an enchanting

FIGURE 44.5. Flemming Abrahamsson's architectural studio in Denmark, built of cob with a reed thatched roof. The thickness of the thatching provides good Insulation for cold winter climates. [Credit: Catherine Wanek]

FIGURE 44.6. Deanne Bednar thatching the roof of the Kensington Kids' Cottage, at Detroit's oldest and biggest metropark. Reed was collected by park staff and many volunteers. [Credit: Deanne Bednar]

conical roof. The Oxford Kids' Cottage features a ridge made of cattail attached by a decorative crossed pattern made of sticks. The Retreat Cabin, constructed during a Natural Cottage Project workshop, taught many participants the basics of thatching. The thatched woodshed shown in the first photo is an example of an easy project on which to practice.

It is December 2013 and I am looking forward to another season of harvesting reed, which I do each winter. As so many people have done throughout time, a small group of us will gather, dress warmly, pack some food and enjoy the process of hand harvesting. Ah!

Thatching is, from start to finish, an amazing process. It is a very time-intensive labor of love, and its beauty continues to bless the building it shelters and all those who experience it.

RESOURCES

Books
• Rural Development Commission. *The Thatchers' Craft*, 1981. The bible of English-style thatching. Available as a free online download at **hlcollege.ac.uk /Downloads/cp_thatch**
• Fearn, Jacqueline. *Thatch and Thatching*, Shire Books, 1978. Out of print, but available as a used book, this small resource is a satisfying overview, with lots of photos of different styles.
• Hall, Nicholas. *Thatching: A Handbook*, Intermediate Technology Publications, 1988. General thatching information, including clear sketches of various techniques.
• Sanders, Marjorie and Roger Angold. *Thatches and Thatching: A Handbook for Owners, Thatchers, and Conservators*, 2012. The National Society of Master Thatchers presents this excellent and broad resource including many technical charts on related issues.

Classes
Occasional thatching classes may be offered by:
• The Strawbale Studio, Oxford, Michigan: **strawbalestudio.org.**
• The Natural Cottage Project: **naturalcottageproject .com**

• Fox Maple School of Traditional Building, Brownfield, Maine: **foxmaple.com**
• Proyecto San Isidro, Tlaxcala, Mexico: **proyectosanisidro.com**
• Yestermorrow Design/Build School, Brattleboro, Vermont: **yestermorrow.org**

Master Thatchers
• Flemming Abrahamsson: **fornyetenergi.dk**
• William Cahill, Cincinnati, Ohio: **roofthatch.com.**
• Colin McGhee, Crozet, Virginia: **thatching.com.**
• International Thatching Society: **thatchers.eu**. Promotes the use of thatching on new buildings in Western Europe, South Africa and Japan, with a focus on fire protection and durability.
• National Society of Master Thatchers: **nsmtltd.co.uk**. Their website includes a searchable database of master thatchers in England.

Website
• **lowimpact.org/factsheet_thatching.htm**. Good online introduction to thatching with links to master thatchers and workshops in the UK, websites, books and other resources.

Natural Insulation

45

Joseph F. Kennedy and Michael G. Smith

Insulation is used to prevent heat from entering or exiting a building through the walls, roof and floor. Insulating materials trap air in small pockets, which reduce the transfer of heat. To save energy, architects and builders strive for an "insulated building envelope," so indoor temperatures can remain within the human comfort zone with the minimum of heating and cooling.

The effectiveness of insulation is indicated by its thermal resistance, or R-value, a measure of how well a material resists the passage of heat. The higher the R-value, the better the insulation. (Windows are measured in "u-value," also commonly used in Europe for all insulations. U-value is the inverse of R-value, so the lower the number, the better the insulation value.)

It is important to remember that R-values are tested under very strict laboratory conditions, and many factors influence the actual in situ thermal performance of insulation, including ambient temperature, moisture content, airtightness of the assembly and how completely the assembly has been filled with insulation. Also, air leaks greatly decrease the effectiveness of any insulation, an effect that is magnified in cold climates (see "Natural Building for Cold Climates," p. 73). Therefore, to be truly effective, a continuous air barrier must accompany all insulations.

The natural insulation materials with the greatest thermal effectiveness are wool, cellulose fibers, cork, vermiculite and cotton batts. These compare favorably with conventional fiberglass insulation, although no natural material can compete with modern foam boards on an R-value-per-inch basis.

Fibrous or loose insulation must be protected from animals, such as rodents, who like to use it for nesting material. Some organic insulation materials, such as loose straw and cellulose, are flammable and therefore should be carefully enclosed and treated with a fire retardant.

Insulation Materials

Different insulation materials are most suitable for different applications, and the choice of insulation can affect choice of building system, and vice versa.

Joseph F. Kennedy *loves being comfortable, and has become an advocate for proper installation of insulation as one of the easiest and best things one can do to improve energy, acoustic and thermal performance of buildings.*

Michael G. Smith *has found himself moving to progressively warmer climates over the years. He now lives near California's Central Valley, one of the biggest straw-producing areas in the country.*

Natural builders use the following materials as insulation.

Wool

Wool makes an excellent insulation and is one of the few natural materials that still insulates when wet. Wool batts have been produced commercially for some time in parts of Europe, New Zealand, Australia and Canada, and are just becoming available in the US. A more recent development is pelletized woolen insulation that is designed to be blown or packed into a wall or ceiling cavity.

Because these products can be expensive and in short supply, some natural builders make their own woolen insulation. This can be done either by washing and carding the wool and treating it with borax or Quassia chips to protect it from moths, or by stuffing raw wool into plastic garbage bags to keep the smell in and the moths out. Note that this technique may lead to in-cavity condensation in cold climates, or in hot, humid climates where air conditioning is used.

A worldwide surplus has made it difficult for US sheep farmers to sell their wool, so it is often available cheaply directly from the source. One danger to avoid is the organophosphate used in some sheep dips.

Straw

Straw can be an excellent insulator when fully sealed on all sides by a suitable air barrier—preferably a natural plaster. Plastered straw bale walls are highly insulating (R-29 to R-35, depending on wall thickness), and baled straw can also be used as roof insulation. However, straw bales are much heavier than most other insulation options, and the roof framing and ceiling structure must be designed accordingly. If the roof were ever to leak, the bales could absorb a great deal of water, increase their weight and become a hazard. Whenever bales are used for insulation, for walls or ceiling, they should be installed tight together, with the cracks carefully stuffed to avoid air leakage and heat loss.

Some builders have used loose straw, or flakes from straw bales, to insulate their roofs. Loose insulation of this kind can be a fire hazard and is also susceptible to damage from mold and rodents. Coating loose straw lightly with boric acid or clay slip may not be sufficient to fireproof it. However, straw and clay slip become much more resistant to all of these

FIGURE 45.1. Wool batts insulate the ceiling of Glenn and Karen Harley's straw bale home near Christchurch, New Zealand. [Credit: Catherine Wanek]

dangers when compressed. This straw-clay mixture can be made into insulating tiles or compacted directly into the ceiling cavity. Other natural fibers such as hemp, coir, flax, cotton and textile wastes could be used for insulation in ways similar to straw.

Cellulose

Cellulose insulation is a popular product; it is inexpensive, non-toxic and made from recycled newspapers and other paper products (romance novels are being used more often now that nobody is reading newspapers anymore). It is usually blown dry into the wall or roof cavity with a special machine. Borax makes it resistant to fire, mold and insects.

Due to its hygroscopic nature, cellulose can be very effective at handling incidental moisture events, but it is not suitable for wet-service locations such as below grade. In a horizontal application, such as an attic, "loose-fill" cellulose can be installed quite easily using equipment available from most rental agencies and allowed to settle naturally. In walls and sloped roof cavities, on the other hand, loose cellulose will settle over time, leaving an uninsulated area at the top of the cavity. There are two ways to prevent settling: the cellulose can either be "dense-packed" at high pressure to a minimum density of 3.5 lb./cu. ft., or it can be "damp sprayed" in place. Both of these techniques require higher-quality equipment and more training than loose-fill applications, so they are not generally appropriate for owner-builders.

Cotton

Recycled cotton in batt form has insulation values comparable to that of fiberglass insulation. Made from post-industrial denim and cotton fibers and available around the US, this insulation is treated with boric acid to discourage pests and retard fire and mold. It passes all ASTM tests, produces no chemical outgassing or airborne particulates and is produced with minimal energy inputs. One drawback to cotton, however, is that most conventional cotton growers use high levels of pesticides and herbicides to produce the crop.

Cork

Cork is the bark of the cork oak tree, *Quercus suber*, which grows primarily in Portugal and Spain. Responsible harvesting does not

FIGURE 45.2. To insulate effectively, straw bale walls must be stuffed (usually with uncoated straw towards the center of the wall and clay slip-coated straw towards the surfaces) and then plastered, with special attention to windows, doors and edges. [Credit: Janine Björnson]

damage the tree or reduce its lifespan; rather, sustainable cork production ensures an enduring cork oak forest ecology and working landscape on the Iberian Peninsula. Cork granules can be used for loose-fill insulation, and cork board products are dimensionally stable and useful for roofs, walls and floors. Although cork is produced from sustainably harvested forests by small firms, the high energy costs of shipping should be carefully considered when using it outside of Europe.

Expanded Minerals

Perlite and vermiculite are heat-expanded minerals that have very good insulating qualities. They can be more expensive than other options but are particularly good in areas that might be exposed to water or fire. These minerals are usually obtained from open-pit mines. Another option, currently available in Canada, is granules made of expanded recycled glass. Like perlite and vermiculite, these balls can be used as an aggregate mixed with clay, lime or cement to create insulating subfloors and stemwalls, for example.

Pumice and scoria are naturally occurring, porous igneous stones available in some parts of the US. They are sometimes used to make insulated concrete products called "pumicecrete." They can also be used in earthbags to build walls and domes, and as subfloor insulation.

Fiberglass

Fiberglass batting is currently the most commonly used insulation in conventional construction.

FIGURE 45.3. Cotton batt insulation made from recycled denim material is widely available in the United States. Here, Eric Hempstead installs Ultratouch cotton batts to insulate the roof of a demonstration ecohouse built by Builders Without Borders in Washington, DC. [Credit: Catherine Wanek]

FIGURE 45.4. At Emerald Earth Sanctuary in California, redwood bark left over from onsite lumber milling was run through a chipper-shredder. The resulting material—lightweight, rot-resistant and fire-resistant—was used as roof insulation. [Credit: Michael G. Smith]

Fiberglass is essentially glass heated to high temperatures and spun into fibers. It is typically avoided by natural builders because of its high embodied energy and potential toxicity, especially from formaldehyde resins commonly used as a binder. Small glass fibers may be carcinogenic if inhaled, and fiberglass creates a disposal problem when it reaches the end of its useful life. More recently, loose-fill fiberglass products have been formulated to reduce danger from contact and inhalation; they are made with acrylic binders rather than formaldehyde. Formaldehyde-free fiberglass batts are also increasingly available.

Insulating Foams and Boards

The very best insulation values can be obtained from foam products that are sprayed into a wall or roof cavity. Petroleum-derived isocyanate foam provides an air and moisture barrier as well as insulation. However, it is toxic, messy and difficult to install, making it unsuitable for DIY applications. This also places it on the expensive end of the insulation spectrum. Less toxic variations are now being made from soy and castor oil; although marketed as a "green" product, these require just as much fossil fuel to

produce as petroleum-based foam boards.

Because of a lack of alternatives, foam boards are often used for below-grade applications like foundation perimeter, sub-footing and sub-slab insulation. In moist situations, closed cell foams are generally necessary. These petroleum-based products are highly efficient insulators but are not biodegradable and contain high embodied energy. Ozone-depleting blowing agents are used in the manufacture of extruded polystyrene (XPS), so when rigid foam is used, high-density expanded polystyrene (EPS) is recommended. Rigid foam boards made from soybeans are now becoming available, although the soybean component replaces only a small percentage of the petrochemical use and is itself the product of petroleum-intensive agriculture.

More environmentally benign insulation boards have recently begun to appear on the market that do not outgas or deplete ozone and are resistant to water and fire. Probably the best option is "rock wool" or "stone wool," which is made of volcanic rock and metal slag, melted in a high-temperature furnace, spun into fibers and then bound with a carbon-based binder. Rock wool

is available in both board and batt forms and has much lower embodied energy than fiberglass or any other insulation board. A potential downside is that formaldehyde is used in the manufacture of rock wool boards.

Other newer alternatives include cellular glass and spun glass board and sheathing products. Although made of recycled glass, these products require very large amounts of energy to produce, making them a poor choice from the environmental standpoint.

Tough Choices

When trying to do the best thing for the environment, builders and designers are often faced with difficult choices about what kinds of insulation to use. On the one hand, good insulation is a critical part of energy-efficient design. On the other hand, many types of insulation require a lot of energy in their manufacture, and may have other negative impacts on human and environmental health. A good approach is to use the most natural, lowest-embodied-energy material that will do the job effectively. This choice will vary depending on climate and also on the part of the building in question.

Because walls can be thick and heavy and are comparatively easy to keep dry, they are the most appropriate part of a building to use relatively dense but cheap and low-impact insulation materials. Natural building has a lot of good options to offer for wall insulation. Some of the best insulating wall systems found in this book include straw bale, hempcrete, papercrete, light clay (straw-clay, woodchip-clay and mineral clay) and cordwood masonry.

A well-insulated roof is essential in both cold and hot climates. For safety and to reduce the amount of structural lumber needed, roof insulation should generally be lightweight; cotton or wool batts or loose-fill insulation such as cellulose, pelletized wool or rice hulls can be good choices. Roofs thatched with reeds or straw also provide their own built-in insulation.

Sub-grade applications such as in foundations and under floors are the most difficult places to find good natural options. The insulation value of concrete can be increased substantially by including light aggregates like perlite or expanded glass. Lightweight volcanic rocks such as pumice or scoria can work well where they are available, both as aggregate and as subfloor insulation. In other places, the choice will often be between using an industrial product and not insulating at all. As more environmentally benign products come on the market, this choice should become easier to make.

FIGURE 45.5. In Denmark, where mussel shells are available as waste from the seafood industry, they are used to provide insulation and drainage in a stemwall and under a floor. [Credit: Catherine Wanek]

RESOURCES

Books
• Racusin, Jacob Deva and Ace McArleton. *The Natural Building Companion: A Comprehensive Guide to Integrative Design and Construction*, Chelsea Green Publishing, 2012. Chapters on building science explain the relationship between heat, insulation and natural buildings, while other chapters describe insulating natural wall systems.
• Wilson, Alex and Mark Peipkorn. *Green Building Products*, New Society Publishers, 2009. The most comprehensive directory of green building products currently available.

Periodical
• *Environmental Building News:* **buildinggreen.com.** Unbiased reviews and analysis of new "environmental" building products helps the concerned reader differentiate between green and greenwashing.

Rice Hulls for Insulation

Catherine Wanek and Paul Olivier

46

Inventor and businessman Paul Olivier specializes in recycling automobile, industrial and municipal solid waste. Recognizing the treasure in our nation's trash, in 1996 Paul became intrigued with the idea of straw bale construction as using an agricultural waste product as a building material. He first built himself a home, and then a 3-story, 8,000 sq. ft. office building near Waxahachie, Texas, using straw bales as insulation.

Returning to his native Louisiana in 2000, Paul noticed another agricultural waste, prevalent in the southeastern United States—rice hulls. Paul learned that as rice is processed for sale, over a million metric tons of hulls are produced and discarded every year in the United States alone (and many more millions of tons everywhere else rice is grown).

Paul discovered that the rice hull, essentially the seed coating of the rice kernel, was high in silica and very resistant to decomposition. It also appeared to have good insulation potential. He commissioned a battery of tests on the humble rice hull, with amazing results. Examined for its R-value, mold resistance and fire and flame-spread potential, the rice hull proved excellent in all categories.

Paul proceeded to put theory into practice. He designed and built a house that utilized rice hulls for insulation in his hometown of Washington, Louisiana. Paul wanted his home to fit into the historic neighborhood, so he copied the traditional Acadian style and the floor plan of a regional museum. Beneath the historic exterior, the wood-thrifty structure consists of a lightweight framing system with 12 in. wide floor, wall and roof cavities filled with over 18 tons of rice hulls. The effect is a handsome, comfortable home, with miniscule energy bills. Rice hulls offer an ideal insulation for the house of the future in hot, humid climates, or any area where rice is grown.

Here's what Paul writes about his discovery:

When nature decided how to package a grain of rice, she wrapped this tiny bundle of nutrients with what is often referred to as a biogenic opal. The rice hull contains approximately

Paul Olivier, *PhD, is an inventor and industrial engineer. His wide-ranging projects have included automobile and industrial waste recycling centers; municipal solid waste separators; biopods for growing and harvesting black soldier fly larvae for livestock, fish and poultry feed; urine-diverting toilets; and gasifiers for converting rice hulls and other agricultural wastes to cooking gas and biochar. He is working with farmers in Vietnam to develop a humane, healthy and economical system for raising pigs, chickens, cows and fish. Paul believes that sustainability lies in the wise and efficient transformation of waste.*

20 percent opaline silica in combination with a large amount of the phenylpropanoid structural polymer called lignin.

Such a high percentage of silica is very unusual within nature, and this intimate blend of silica and lignin makes the rice hull not only resistant to water penetration and fungal decomposition, but also resistant to the best efforts of man to dispose of it. Since rice is grown on every continent except Antarctica, ranking second only to wheat in terms of worldwide area and production, and since the hull represents on average about 20 percent of the rough harvested weight of rice, our planet ends up with an abundance of this scaly residue.

The hull is a very tough and abrasive packaging material, consisting of two interlocking halves that encapsulate the space vacated by the milled grain. In proximity to myriad other hulls, it forms a thermal barrier that compares well with other high-performing insulating materials. Thermal resistance tests on whole rice hulls indicate R-values as high as 3.0 per inch.

Do rice hulls burn? Yes they do, but with difficulty. Since air cannot flow freely through a pile of rice hulls to provide the oxygen needed to sustain rapid combustion, they do not easily and cleanly combust. The bulk density of loose rice hulls is similar to that of baled straw, and anyone who has tried to burn a bale of straw understands the problem associated with the availability of oxygen. Rice husks are flame retarding and, at ordinary temperatures, self-extinguishing. A lighted match tossed onto a pile of rice husks will generally burn out without producing a self-sustaining flame in the husks.

Conventional cellulose insulation necessitates the addition of large quantities of flame and smolder retardants. The concentration of such retardant chemicals as boric acid, sodium borate, ammonium sulfate, aluminum sulfate, aluminum trihydrate and mono- or di-ammonium phosphate in conventional cellulose insulation may reach as high as 40 percent by weight. These chemicals are expensive to purchase and prepare, and the cellulosic fiber must undergo extensive preparation to receive them.

Nature employs several very effective strategies to protect the kernel of rice from the water and

FIGURE 46.1. Rice hulls have numerous potential uses, from insulation (whether loose-filled in wall cavities and ceilings, stuffed into bags or coated with clay slip and packed into forms), to fuel and animal bedding. [Credit: Paul Olivier]

high humidity generally associated with the cultivation and growth of this plant. Studies done on rice hulls indicate that the equilibrium moisture content of rice hulls is well below the moisture content needed to sustain the growth of fungi and mold.

Since the rice hull is hard and yet elastic, it resists settling and compression far better than shredded newspapers. The settling of cellulose insulation in a wall cavity can reduce its installed height by as much as 25 percent. Ordinarily, loose rice hulls have an angle of repose of about 35 degrees. But once firmly packed into a wall cavity, their tiny tips, edges and hairs interlock to achieve a negative angle of repose. Due to this peculiar bonding of rice hulls under mild pressure, they stabilize in a very uniform manner, and no further settling is possible.

Since rice hulls require no shredding, hammer-milling, fluffing, fiberizing, binding or stabilizing, they possess far less embodied energy than even cellulose insulation. In the southeastern US and California, where rice is grown and processed, they commonly sell for $5.00 per ton—virtually nothing. At this price, the material cost is a ridiculous two cents per cubic foot! The most significant cost associated with the utilization of the rice hull is its transport, which is roughly the same cost as straw bales.

To create a load-bearing structure, the hulls could be bagged, and these bags or sacks could be stacked in a manner similar to bales. I recently found two companies making a very durable particle board from rice hulls. Since the US generates less than 1.3 percent of the global production of rice, the rest of the world has a lot more to gain from this simple and unsophisticated use of such an abundant agricultural by-product.

RESOURCES

Websites
• For more information about the rice hull house concept see: **thebiopod.com/pages/pages/articles**
• The ASTM testing results can be seen at: **esrla.com**; click on "download" under "Rice Hull House."

• For more information on the work in Vietnam, see: **dl.dropboxusercontent.com/u/22013094/Paper /Summaries/Alternative%20to%20Biodigestion.pdf**

Earthen Floors

47

SUKITA REAY CRIMMEL AND JAMES THOMSON

Earthen floors are a great option for those who want to bring earth into their homes. The technique is relatively easy to learn, and the floors can be installed in a variety of situations and conditions, including both new and existing buildings. They could sell themselves on aesthetic appeal alone, let alone their unique feel, low toxicity, thermal benefits and minimal environmental impact.

SUKITA REAY CRIMMEL *has installed over 20,000 square feet of earthen flooring, and is one of the preeminent experts in the emerging field of earthen floors. She has created a ready-mix flooring product and a line of finishing oils, manufactured under the name Claylin.*

JAMES THOMSON *has spent a decade introducing students to the joys of building with earth with House Alive, one of the leading natural building training organizations in North America. He is an accomplished public speaker and event planner, having facilitated several professional conferences for natural builders.*

The concept of an earthen floor is not new. Homes have been built directly on the earth for millennia. In many parts of the world, people still live on floors made of earth. Most traditional earthen floors are just the raw earth, tamped down with human feet and moistened frequently with water to keep the dust down. Sometimes sealers are used to stabilize the earth more permanently.

Over the last few decades, earth builders in North America have been improving earthen floor installation techniques to the point where now even people living in conventional houses are willing, even enthusiastic, to live on a floor made out of earth. Today's earthen floor practitioners

FIGURE 47.1. The appealing texture and slight softness of an earthen floor invite one to remove one's shoes. [Credit: Mike O'Brien]

carefully select, process and mix their raw materials and install them with the assistance of laser levels, steel trowels and insulation to make floors that are flat, smooth and warm. Oil and wax sealants provide durability, water-resistance and shine. Some earthen floors are installed in conjunction with radiant heat systems, a wonderful heating option for modern homes.

Earthen floors are remarkably versatile, but may not be suitable for every application. It's useful to understand a few of their key characteristics to determine where they should and should not be installed.

FIGURE 47.2. Mark Mazziotti installing an earthen floor at Red Earth Farms. The floor mix is flattened with a steel pool float. [Credit: Mark Mazziotti]

Weight: Earthen floors are heavy; they require a stable and strong subfloor. Most typically they are built "on grade" (i.e., directly on the ground), over a strong base pad made of concrete or compacted gravel (road base). They can also be built on raised wooden subfloors, even on second or third levels if the structure is strong enough to support the additional weight; consult with an engineer if in doubt. An advantage of heavy floors is that they are a good source of thermal mass, which helps moderate indoor temperature fluctuations.

Hardness: The surface of an earthen floor can look and even feel like concrete, but it does not have the same compressive strength. Earthen floors can be dented by point loads or scratched by heavy objects. Their hardness can be compared to that of a wood floor. Experience has shown that because they are softer, earthen floors are more comfortable to stand and walk on than concrete floors.

Water resistance: Sealing with the right kind of oil gives earthen floors a durable, waterproof finish. You can spill water on them and even mop them without any problem. But below the sealed surface, the floor is still unstabilized earth. Prolonged exposure to lots of water could have negative consequences, as the water seeps through cracks and pores into the layers beneath. Earthen floors have been successfully installed in bathrooms, but shouldn't be used in showers or in basements that flood.

Thickness: Earthen floors are usually ¾–2 in. (2–5 cm) thick. It's important to consider this added thickness when planning for transitions to adjacent rooms or entryways, or in rooms with already-low headroom.

Installation time: Earthen floors are not a quick flooring solution. Drying and curing are the most time-consuming stages. Sometimes installers employ fans, heaters and dehumidifiers to speed up the drying process. Under the proper conditions, a floor could be completed and ready for use in two weeks, but three to four weeks is not uncommon.

Toxicity and flammability: More people are becoming concerned about toxic materials in building products, such as glues, polymers, preservatives and flame retardants. Earthen floors are a natural, non-toxic flooring option; the main ingredients come from the earth beneath our feet. The oils used for sealing, while extracted from natural ingredients, do contain some volatile organic compounds (VOCs). Once the VOCs have evaporated (this takes one to three days), they no longer pose any risk to the inhabitants, but any adjacent occupied rooms should be sealed off during the oiling and drying process. Earthen floors are naturally non-flammable, and are good options for areas around stoves and fireplaces.

Testing an Earthen Floor Mix

Many earthen floors are made from locally sourced and processed ingredients. The basic ingredients are sand, clay soil and a short natural plant fiber (chopped straw is a common choice). Sand is the main building block, giving the floor its strength. The fiber provides tensile strength to minimize cracking, and an aesthetic touch. The clay is the binder that sticks it all together. There is a lot of flexibility in the recipe for

a floor mix, but good testing is critical to ensure a successful installation.

Start the testing process by making several batches of sand and clay soil mixed together in different ratios. Earthen floors are mostly sand. The final recipe will depend a lot on the amount of clay in the soil; if it is very clay-rich, you will need to add a lot of sand to compensate. Try starting with three test batches with different clay-to-sand ratios, say 2:1 (sand to clay), 3:1 and 4:1. For each test, carefully measure

FIGURE 47.3. Like the sculptural cob fireplace surround, the floor in Sudip Biddle and Rosalind Wu's straw bale home in Pagosa Springs, Colorado (built by Kelly Ray Mathews) also serves as a thermal mass for storing heat and moderating temperature fluctuations. Note the use of a stone under the stove, where people might be tempted to split firewood; an earthen floor could be damaged by high-impact activity. [Credit: Catherine Wanek]

the ingredients into a bucket, mix them dry and then add water slowly until the mix reaches a thick but spreadable consistency like cake batter. Use a wooden float to spread the mixture on a stable surface. Each test patch should be about ¾ in. (2 cm) thick and at least 18 in. (45 cm) in diameter. Smooth it with a steel trowel and allow it to dry. Repeat this process for each of the other tests, carefully labeling the ratios of each.

When the test patches are dry, check them for cracks, dusting and durability. Cracks are caused by the shrinkage that naturally occurs when clay dries. If a test patch has a lot of cracking, the clay content is too high. If sand grains easily come loose when the surface is rubbed, this is an indicator of too little clay. Finally, the test patch should be resistant to scratching with a fingernail. You will be able to mark it, but it should not crumble away as it is scratched. A surface that is too fragile indicates low clay content.

Once you have determined a good sand-to-clay ratio, make new test mixes with fiber added. Try several tests with fiber content ranging from 10–20 percent of the volume of the clay/sand mix. The "right" fiber concentration is mostly personal preference. Fiber in the floor will affect workability and aesthetics. More fiber makes the mix harder to spread and smooth out; too little could mean a weaker floor. Chopped straw is light in color and contrasts against the darker background of an earthen floor. The more fiber, the more this effect will be visible. Once a suitable recipe is determined, do a final round of testing that includes burnishing, oiling and waxing, to see what the finished floor will look like.

Mixing and Pouring the Floor

An earthen floor needs a stable, strong and level subfloor. Subfloors that settle or flex will eventually cause cracks in the finished floor. If it is a wood-framed subfloor, cover the wood with a vapor retarder to prevent damage from moisture during the installation process. Insulating under the subfloor is highly recommended to improve energy efficiency and occupant comfort. The insulation material must be strong enough to support the weight of the floor above without shifting or compacting over time. Typically, a high-compressive-strength rigid foam insulation is used. Unfortunately, there are few good natural options. Pumice rock has been used with some success. Straw or straw-clay combinations are not recommended.

Before beginning the pour, protect any surfaces in the room that could become damaged or dirty during installation. Set up

FIGURE 47.4. Mixing an earthen floor mix in a wheelbarrow with two hoes. The ideal consistency is similar to cake batter. [Credit: Mira Stebvika]

fans and dehumidifiers for drying in advance. Determine how thick the floor will be and mark the walls with a line to indicate the finished height. There are various methods for ensuring a flat and level floor. A laser level is great tool if it is available and the installers are familiar with its use. Other options include screed rails and boards (a technique commonly used for concrete pads), or using a depth gauge (a simple stick with a mark on it) to measure the floor thickness as it is installed.

Mixing the floor material is a messy process that is best performed outside. Organize all the materials in a central location and make sure they are processed and ready for use. Determine an appropriate measuring container (usually a five-gallon bucket) and translate the predetermined recipe for that measuring volume. Mixing can be done by hand in a wheelbarrow or with a machine like a mortar mixer. For small floors, hand mixing works fine. Have two people with hoes stand at opposite ends of the wheelbarrow. Mix the sand and clay first, dry, then slowly add water to achieve a cake batter consistency. Then add the chopped straw, and more water if necessary. If using a mortar mixer, put water

FIGURE 47.5. The final layer of an earthen floor should be one of the last steps in constructing a natural home. All of the finish plaster, carpentry and rough plumbing have been completed in this cob house prior to installing the finish floor. [Credit: Michael G. Smith]

FIGURE 47.6. Burnishing an earthen floor at the leather-hard stage polishes the floor and removes trowel marks. [Credit: James Thomson]

and clay in first, and then power up the mixer. Add the sand next, followed by the straw and more water if needed, then dump into a wheelbarrow for transport. For either method, add water slowly until you are confident about how much is needed to make an acceptable mix. It's easy to make a dry mix wetter; drying out a too-wet mix requires adding more dry ingredients in the correct proportions, which can be complicated.

Dump some wet mix onto the work area. Keep the piles of material to a manageable size, about enough to cover a 2×2 ft. (60×60 cm) area. Flatten the mix with a wooden float. Check frequently for uniform thickness and level. Use a back-and-forth sawing motion to remove small amounts of mix from high areas without making holes in the floor, or add more mix to low spots and blend it in with the flat part of the float. Once a section is flat and level, swipe a steel trowel lightly over the surface to make it smooth and glossy. It should only take a couple of passes. Do not overwork the material! Any irregularities up to $\frac{1}{16}$-inch (1.5 mm) deep can be taken out in the burnishing step.

Burnishing, Oiling and Finishing

Burnishing is the process of polishing the still-damp floor with a steel trowel to further smooth and compress it. This step is not necessary, but it will improve

A Tamped Road-Base Floor

by Frank Meyer

I made my first earthen floor over 20 years ago. I started the process by collecting samples of all the soil types available in our area. After weeks of playing in the dirt, mixing in stabilizers and trying to strengthen and harden the earth to make it suitable for a floor, I came to an interesting conclusion. One particular road base made the hardest, prettiest and quickest floor without any stabilizers at all. Its rich red color and excellent blend of silt, clay, sand and gravel made test bricks that were more impressive than anything else I came up with.

Not all road bases are created equal. The one I chose is what is known here as "city base," and is approved for building roads and streets in Austin, Texas. It originates in a quarry where the material is taken from the earth and the silt, clay, sand and gravel are separated, then re-blended to specified proportions. By using this material and applying basic road building techniques, we have a big advantage over traditional poured-earth floors. The process uses relatively little water, thereby requiring a much shorter drying time. It can typically be walked on a day or two after installing.

To begin the process of building a tamped road-base floor, make sure the ground is fairly level, smooth and compacted to at least 6 in. (15 cm) below the planned finished floor height. If a vapor barrier is used, spread a layer of sand 1–2 in. (2.5–5 cm) thick both below and above the barrier to prevent gravel from puncturing it. Apply the first layer of road base to a thickness of about two inches and wet it with a hose or watering can, just enough so that the silt and clay stick to the aggregate.

Compact the first layer. A plate compactor, available at tool rental outlets, works well. (Be sure to vent the building with fans if using a gas-powered compactor.) Hand tamping is slower but much quieter and doesn't produce fumes. Hand tampers are easily made from wood or concrete or by welding a steel plate to a piece of pipe. Hand tamp-

the final appearance of the floor. Burnish within 24 to 48 hours after pouring. The floor should still be damp but not too soft; if it's possible to make a trowel mark deeper than about an ⅛ in. (3 mm), the floor is still too wet and needs more time to dry. Once it reaches the necessary stiffness, carefully walk out to the far end of the floor, using foam pads or steel floor pans to spread your weight. Mist down a section with a spray bottle and smooth it out by applying pressure with a steel trowel. The surface should be shiny and smooth when done. If you find areas that are particularly low, you can add a little more wet mix to fill them out. This is your opportunity to make the floor perfect!

After the floor is completely dry, it can be sealed with a drying oil like linseed oil. Linseed oil is made from flax seeds, and there are many types and grades available. The recommended oils do not contain heavy-metal drying agents and come premixed with solvent to allow increased absorption. See under "Resources" for suppliers. If a premixed oil is not available, mix four parts linseed oil with one part solvent (mineral spirits, citrus oil or turpentine) to make your own oil blend.

Proper sealing with an appropriate oil is what gives an earthen floor its hardness and resistance to moisture. The oil is absorbed by the dry earth mix and polymer-ing the edges works best, even if a powered compactor is used.

Repeat layers as necessary until they reach about 1 in. (2.5 cm) from the finish height. At this point, you need to level the floor. Sift the road base through a piece of ⅜ in. (1 cm) hardware cloth to produce a mixture of silt, clay, sand and small gravel. Layer it on and level it out, using screed boards (much like concrete workers use).

After leveling, moisten and tamp the mix again, making sure that it bonds with the layer below. For the top coat, we screen the material again, this time using ⅛ in. (3 mm) hardware cloth. The top coat is not compacted but hand troweled and burnished, using just enough water to make it bond and be workable. The most important thing is to make sure it bonds with the layer below. Trial and error will give you a feel for it. Although many of the floors I have done have no straw in them, adding chopped straw lessens the likelihood of cracking. Getting a smooth, slick finish is more difficult with straw in the top coat, so I recommend chopping the straw very finely if a glassy finished is desired.

Traditionally earthen floors were sealed with fresh blood from a cow or ox, but most builders today use boiled linseed oil or tung oil to seal the floor so it will not dust up, and it can even be cleaned with a damp mop. The floor must be thoroughly dry before sealing or the finish may turn cloudy, or even moldy in a moist location. I like to put no less than six coats of oil on, making sure each coat is totally dry before adding another coat. There are now many commercial products available for sealing that may even dry harder than linseed oil, but they are more expensive. Consider using them only for the final coat. With time, patience, lots of hard work and an affinity for getting dirty, anyone can do this. Enjoy!

FRANK MEYER of Thangmaker Construction has over 45 years of construction experience. His focus is sustainable and green building. He specializes in straw bale construction and earthen floors and is available for consultation and workshop facilitation: **thangmaker.com**

izes as it dries, binding the earth together and making a hard and water-resistant layer on top. Keep in mind that the unoiled floor is fragile—walk and work on it carefully! The oil can be applied with a brush, a paint roller or rags. Apply four to six coats of oil in the same day, one right after the other. Do not leave any puddled oil on the floor; clean it up with a clean rag. Make sure the room is well ventilated while applying the oil, and also while it cures, which can take a week or more.

Once the oil has cured, the floor is ready for use. At this point, there are some additional optional finishing steps that can make the floor even smoother and shinier. Many choose to apply a floor wax for added durability and shine. The recommended waxes are fairly liquid and can be applied with a brush or rag. After drying, the floor should be buffed with an electric buffer to remove excess wax. Another optional step is to lightly sand the floor after the oil has cured and before waxing. This leaves a smoother finish.

The earthen floors of today are a synthesis of ancient and traditional practices melded with modern materials and building science. Until recently, the only way to have an earthen floor was to make it yourself. Now, in some parts of the country, there are contractors who offer the technique, and a ready-mix floor product is available to take out some of the guess work for the novice builder. More people are finding that earthen finishes are not merely appropriate for our modern lifestyles, but are in fact a highly desirable choice. They offer all of us the opportunity to experience the joy of living with earth in our homes.

RESOURCES

Books
• Crimmel, Sukita Reay and James Thomson. *Earthen Floors: A Modern Approach to an Ancient Practice*, New Society Publishers, 2014. The first complete handbook for owner-builders and professionals wishing to install successful earthen floors.

Organizations
• The Canelo Project: **caneloproject.com**. Classes and consultation on straw bale and earthen finishes, including earthen floors. Canelo, Arizona.
• From These Hands: **sukita.com**. Sukita Reay Crimmel offers consulting, trainings, design and contracting services for earthen floors and other natural building installations. Portland, Oregon.
• House Alive: **housealive.org**. Workshops in earthen building techniques including cob and earthen floors. Jacksonville, Oregon.

• Thangmaker: **thangmaker.com**. Frank Meyer offers workshops, consulting services and installations using many natural building techniques including earthen floors. Austin, Texas.

Suppliers
• Claylin: **claylin.com**. Founded by Sukita Reay Crimmel, this company provides formulated earthen floor mixes and sealers. Portland, Oregon.
• Heritage Natural Finishes: **heritagenaturalfinishes .com**. High quality oils and waxes for sealing wood and earthen surfaces. Grand Junction, Colorado.
• Tried & True Wood Finishes: **triedandtruewood finish.com**. Non-toxic wood finishes, also suitable for earthen floors. Trumansburg, NY.

Earthen Plasters and Alis

CAROLE CREWS

48

In touching clay, the finest particles derived from the stones of the Earth, we are connecting to her in a loving way, caressing our Mother as we caress our children. We witness something soft, slippery and malleable become hard by releasing water from its molecular structure. We watch the diverse elements of a clay plaster submerge into one another and transform themselves and

behold—this wondrous concoction has become a magical skin in beautiful shapes and delightful colors, sparkling with reflected light.

Just as in baking a cake where you need fat, sugar and flour, we need clay, sand and fiber to make nearly all plasters. The final goal of plastering is a smooth, durable, attractive surface for whatever kind of wall you are finishing. Small details matter. For example, you may not mind at first the way a rough-textured surface looks, but you will probably start to mind how much dust it collects over time.

After growing up with the adobe tradition still intact in her neighborhood, **CAROLE CREWS** *studied art, then came to natural building through making her first home in 1981, and later a 16 ft. diameter adobe dome. This brought her in contact with the budding natural building movement where she spread her alis techniques through numerous colloquia. After making a career of earthen interior finishes, she wrote* Clay Culture: Plasters, Paints and Preservation *to help others avoid mistakes and extra work. She rents out her adobe dome home for short-term retreats so others can experience off-grid living in a magical setting.*

FIGURE 48.1. Earth plaster being troweled smooth after having been pneumatically sprayed onto the straw bale walls of Ridge Winery, Healdsburg, California. [Credit: Joseph F. Kennedy]

Clay

Clay is composed of fine platelet-shaped particles derived from the erosion of stone by water. Clay's capacity to bind aggregates (sand, gravel and other coarse particulate materials) and fibers together makes it indispensable for plasters and alis. Alis is a thin paste made of clay slip mixed with very fine aggregate, traditionally brushed onto an adobe wall with a sheepskin. I use a paintbrush to apply it, then burnish the alis with a sponge as it dries.

I like to use native clays when I can find them for both earthen

FIGURE 48.2. Breaking up straw for fine plaster using a weed whacker.
[Credit: Janine Björnson]

plasters and alis. My favorite way to separate pure clay from sand or silt is through levigation (suspending fine particles through grinding in a liquid). To separate clay in this way, put equal amounts of dirt and water in a barrel, stir or whip with a drill mixer to the consistency of a thin milkshake and leave it overnight to settle. This is like a giant shake test (which is a way to see how much clay is in your native dirt), so do a small test first in a jar to determine whether or not your material has enough clay.

Nature will usually separate the clay for you; once the water in the barrel is clear again, all you have to do is skim off the smooth layer that is the last to settle (that is the clay slip). In wet climates with very hard wet clay, it can take a lot of work to make slip; it is difficult to add more water to leather-hard clays. You may have to wet-sieve it through a screen to get the lumps out, or find a more saturated clay by a pond. In the desert southwest US, you can sift many clays dry and use them that way. Most sieves will not deliver as fine a material as will the levigation technique. That's not important with most plasters, but is for finish coats: you don't want any coarse particles in a final coat of alis.

Make sure to test mixes made with native clays to avoid unhappy surprises later. Shrinkage rates vary greatly, so there are no guaranteed recipes. Vary the amount of sand and fiber, and test by making test blocks. Often, a native dirt will have silt, gypsum, mica, fine sand or other desirable minerals already mixed into it. Finely sifted, and with a binder such as buttermilk added, it may make a fine alis as is. If it cracks, add any combination of whiting, mica, silt or fine sand. If it dusts, add more clay or binder. Keep testing until you like the results.

Binders

Binders make clay plasters and finishes stickier when wet and harder, less dusty and more waterproof when dry. The most common natural binders are made from various starches, or casein derived from milk.

Flour paste is a binder made from wheat or rice flour, or even cornstarch. Start with a pot of water on the burner, no more than two-thirds full. Whisk together approximately one cup flour and one cup cold water in a separate bowl for each quart of water in your pot. When the water comes to a rolling boil, pour in the cold mixture and keep whisking, as if making gravy.

Remove it from the stove as soon as it thickens and turns opaque, which should happen quickly. You don't want to scorch it. Flour paste sours quickly and smells terrible, so make only as much as you can use in one day, or refrigerate the leftovers.

Milk binders are stronger than starch binders, so use less of them in proportion. You can make your own casein from skim or powdered milk. The milk must first be curdled by adding lemon juice or vinegar and, ideally, left to sit. If you're in a hurry, add vinegar to the milk as it warms on the stove until it separates into curds and whey.

Pour through a cheesecloth in a colander, rinse the curds and blend them in a blender with one tablespoon dissolved borax for each quart of milk you used to begin with. It's convenient to store cold in its concentrated form, but thin it out with four to six times as much water before adding it to an alis or using in a wash. Buttermilk can substitute for casein in most recipes, but make sure you do tests.

Straw-Clay Mud for Shaping and Sculpting

If a wall is very rough, uneven or soft, it will need more than one coat of plaster. In this case, a base layer of straw-clay mud may be used to shape it. [Note: This mud has more straw than traditional earth plasters, but more clay than light straw-clay (*leichtlehm*). Some natural builders call this material "strob," a contraction of straw and cob.—Editors] Straw bale walls go up quickly, but they require more plaster than any other wall type. I figured out early on that if a pure clay slip is worked into the straw bale, or if the bale is dipped in clay slip before being placed in the wall, the thicker straw-clay mud sticks very nicely to this "primed" surface. This sculpting layer is best applied with your hands. However, I recommend wearing rubber gloves, especially if you have or want a lover.

The easiest way to make a load of straw-clay mud is to fill a wheelbarrow one-third full with water, then add sifted clay, or place a half-inch screen over the wheelbarrow and sift dirt directly into it until there is just a small dry pile of dirt sticking up above the water. By adding clay to water, rather than water to clay, you avoid dry pockets at the bottom of the mixing tub. Let it soak while you do something else, and in five minutes, capillary action will have created a perfect soupy mud. Now start adding long straw.

I like to reach down to the bottom of the wheelbarrow with both arms, then lift them through the mixture, turning the mix over and over. Keep adding straw until

FIGURE 48.3. A silage mixer is here repurposed as a plaster mixing machine. [Credit: Joseph F. Kennedy]

you can pick up a huge handful and it holds its shape with only a slight slump. You won't believe how much straw this takes, but make sure the straw is well coated and the mix is sticky. If there is too much water, it won't hold together. If your clay is very pure and shrinks a great deal, you may also add some sand before mixing in straw, but don't overdo it.

Straw-clay mud also works well to create sculptural elements, though you may wish to add some manure and/or wheat flour paste to make it stronger, smoother and even stickier. Wheat paste darkens the plaster when it dries and can ferment and stink if it stays wet too long in the thick mud. For exterior plaster, adding wheat paste makes a tougher, more weatherproof coating. In fact, this long-straw-clay-with-additives mud is perfect as a one-coat exterior finish over many wall systems. For a tougher, smoother surface, one can leave it to partially dry, then compress it with a trowel when leather-hard. For less maintenance over the years, be sure to design your natural house with roof overhangs sufficient to protect your exterior plasters.

When applying straw-clay mud, dampen the surface to be plastered, then toss big handfuls of it into the low spots. Spread it out and smear it with the base of your palm, near the wrist, feathering it into a thin layer around the edges. The next handful covers that thin edge. Pay attention to the overall shape of the wall as you go; curves are great, but lumps and bumps, not so much.

Straw-clay mud is great for smoothing over lumps, since it does just as well at four inches thick as it does at one inch. Smooth it out with the palm of your hand, spread flat, with your fingers extended. It's also easy to take a wet 2×4 or a long darby (a straightedge often used in concrete finishing) or wooden float and go over this mud soon after applying it to make the wall even flatter. On interior walls, smooth, flat walls catch less dust. The goal is to get this layer so nicely shaped that you need only one very thin even coat of finish plaster to complete the surface.

Finish Plasters

Some people prefer a troweled finish plaster to an alis finish on their walls. (I have always preferred the action of brushing with a large brush and the wide arcing strokes of sponging to using a trowel, which I find overly exacting.) To make such a finish plaster, just add extra sand to an alis mixture and *voila!* The mix should be the consistency of cake batter and slide onto the wall in a creamy way. The final proportions will usually be twice the volume of aggregates to clay, but always

FIGURE 48.4. Applying an earth plaster to a straw bale wall in Mexico. [Credit: Joseph F. Kennedy]

do a test before applying the mix to your wall. Add more sand if your test sample cracks as it dries, or adjust your application technique (see "Drying and Cracking," p. 345).

The finer your aggregates, the thinner your plaster can be. You can experiment with fibers, too, but they can cause problems, like straw bits getting caught on the trowel. I stick to aggregates and plenty of whiting (with clay of course) for very thin plasters. Often, two coats are recommended to make a very smooth wall. The second coat benefits from being burnished with a trowel when leather-hard, spraying with water as you go. Japanese trowels are lovely for this sort of work. A plastic disk cut from the top of a yoghurt container also makes a fine trowel, especially for curves.

One-Coat Plasters

Owner-builders are smart to look for ways to reduce the amount of plastering needed; it's normal to get very tired of building by that time, and to want to move into your home. This is where a one-coat troweled plaster really shines. It works well on any wall that has been evenly shaped as it was built and just needs ½–¾ in. (13–19 mm) of plaster to make it perfect. Well-formed and laid

adobes or carefully trimmed cob are good candidates. If some irregularities remain, cob or adobe can be further shaped with a piece of metal lath attached around a short piece of 2×4, as a kind of rasp. Straw-clay, pumicecrete and various other systems take one medium coat of plaster very easily.

To make a one-coat plaster, start with a color of clay you like, adding kaolin if it is too dark, then add sharp plaster sand, which already has a variety of grain sizes, followed by soaked manure and chopped straw. Soaked and beaten paper pulp may be substituted for the manure, but it holds an incredible amount of water, so it slows drying time.

I find that when several sizes of aggregates and fibers are added to the clay, the mix is stronger and less likely to crack than when fewer are added. Start with equal proportions of clay, sand and fiber and do some tests. You may need more sand to prevent cracking. Or perhaps your soil is not very sticky, already having a large proportion of sand and silt, and you need to add less sand.

Make sure your wall is completely dry, but dampen the surface before applying plaster. I find the easiest method is to apply the plaster quickly to a vertical strip of wall about four feet wide, running from the bottom of the wall to the top. Once a section of plaster is troweled on, I sponge it to

FIGURE 48.5. This pattern was produced by incising the earth plaster after application. [Credit: Joseph F. Kennedy]

smooth out the trowel marks and bumps, and move on to the next section. You sometimes need to wait a little while for the plaster to set up before sponging, as the sponge will tear up a surface that is too soft.

After you apply plaster to the next wall section, the first section you sponged is usually ready to be hard troweled; if it's still soft, wait a bit longer. If it feels too hard, you might need to dampen the surface a bit so the trowel will slide across more easily. I use a 7 in. (18 cm) steel pool trowel for this. An oval-shaped pool trowel

FIGURE 48.6. This adobe meditation room in Taos, New Mexico, features a micaceous clay plaster by Carole Crews. [Credit: Catherine Wanek]

has no corners to leave marks. Remember to sponge the joint where two sections meet before hard troweling.

If the finished color is uneven for some reason, one can always come back with an alis or a casein wash after the plaster dries thoroughly. Sponging the dry finished plaster with a damp sponge often makes it look much better. Otherwise, a quick coating of casein mixed with whiting gives an antique look to a plastered surface and lightens the color easily. The additional casein binder also makes the surface harder.

Alis

The word "alis" comes from the Spanish word *alisar*, meaning "to polish." Traditionally, in the old adobe village in New Mexico where I grew up, the women painted their walls with a fine clay called *tierra blanca*, found in the nearby hills. Lori Lawyer and I developed a new form of alis in 1989 while repairing an historic adobe home which had a traditional *tierra ballita* coating. Unfortunately, we found that this traditional silty finish dusted badly, and we wanted our work to be lustrous, smooth and tough.

After some experimentation, the basic alis recipe we developed was half kaolin porcelain clay

from the pottery store and half mica powder, which we gathered from a mine site in the mountains. We found that if we added 25 percent cooked wheat flour paste to the water before mixing in the clay and mica, and rubbed the wall with a damp tile sponge about half an hour after brushing the alis on (at the leather-hard phase), there emerged a lustrous finish with slivers of straw, mica and sometimes granite granules reflecting the light, shattering the dull, flat quality of the wall.

There was no dust, and the surface was smooth as a baby's bottom. A damp sponge, dipped and squeezed often in warm water to keep it clean, will smooth and reveal bits of mica or straw, or unique elements of native clays, which can make the surface have an appealing random visual quality reminiscent of tweed fabric or Japanese paper.

We added fine sand to make the alis thick enough to complete or repair rougher or damaged wall surfaces. The sand works its way into the deeper areas with no need to laboriously trowel each divot. This sandy first coat also covers a floated gypsum base plaster surface beautifully. A sandy base coat also helps alis to stick to smooth or slick materials such as sheetrock. If you add acrylic glue to a sandy base alis, it will even stick to a painted wall.

Often two layers of alis are required to achieve the maximum aesthetic benefits. The first coat need not be buffed with the sponge unless it is very rough. The second coat usually needs little, if any, fine sand. I've come to appreciate adding whiting or marble dust to my alis recipes. This very fine calcium carbonate material adds a smooth, spreadable quality to the plaster.

When mixing alis, I start with a bucket or barrel not more than one-third full of water. I whisk in three scoops of clay a little at a time, then one scoop of whiting, one of ground mica, one of fine silica sand and repeat until it is the consistency of thin cream. Then I whisk in the binder—one quart (0.95 liters) of starch paste per gallon (3.8 liters) of alis— which thickens it more, so more water might have to be added to achieve the desired consistency (like medium to thick cream). If adding pigment, put the powder with a small amount of water in a jar and shake well. Measure out an exact amount of dissolved pigment in proportion to the other ingredients, so every batch will be the same.

Apply alis with a small flat natural-bristle brush to corners and edges first. Then switch to a larger brush and start at the top of the wall to avoid drips on the completed area. Old sheets on the floor reduce cleanup time, as does tape over rough wood, though alis can easily be wiped off smooth surfaces before it dries. Wait until the wall dries leather-hard, then buff with a damp tile sponge. When almost dry, buff again with a dry flannel cloth for the ultimate finish.

Drying and Cracking

People are often mystified when one person's work cracks while another person applying the same mix to the same wall gets no cracking. It takes a while to become familiar with why things happen with these materials. When earth plasters or paints crack, it's often a matter of timing. It is important to give the moisture an opportunity to evaporate before the plaster is compressed. When the surface is compacted prematurely, the water can't evaporate evenly, causing cracking.

Working with a trowel also pulls the clay to the surface; if you work it too much and make it really slick and pretty right away, it will definitely crack. If the plaster is allowed time to dry and shrink before it is compressed, the same mixture will crack far less. Everything works much better when you find the right moment to take the next step.

Don't rush plastering. If the weather is cold, make sure you have heaters or a fireplace going; otherwise the wall will not dry and you will be uncomfortably cold while working. Make sure each layer of plaster or alis is completely dry before adding the next or you will get cracks in subsequent layers. While we have to spray a little water on the surface of a dry wall before the

FIGURE 48.7. A bas-relief plaster sculpture by Carole Crews. [Credit: Joseph F. Kennedy]

FIGURE 48.8. This plastered cob wall is protected from the elements by a shake roof. [Credit: Joseph F. Kennedy]

next layer of plaster will stick, the dry inner layer of plaster will help the subsequent layer to dry more quickly.

Don't rush it; if the inner layer is still wet, it will stain the next layer of plaster or, in the worst-case scenario, grow mold. The alis layer, especially, needs to be put on a dry surface because it can discolor easily (due to the wheat paste) if it does not dry evenly.

My advice is to enjoy your life while you're working on such projects. Make your life the priority, not the building project. I have worked very slowly on my own natural building project for the last 22 years, on and off, between working on many other people's houses in order to make a living. Now my 16 ft. diameter (5 m) adobe dome is teaching me to sing, and I have finally made window quilts and roofed the bathing area. It is a huge healing blessing in my life to use and share this sacred retreat space I have managed to materialize with my own hands and with the help of many dear friends. I recommend the process, and the finished product, but only as long as you can keep the joy in it.

RESOURCES

Books

• Bourgeois, Jean-Louis with photos by Carollee Pelos. *Spectacular Vernacular: The Adobe Tradition*, Aperture, 1989. This book will inspire in ways well beyond most people's imaginations, and although it is not a how-to book, one can often figure out the techniques by observing the outstanding photographs from the author's and photographer's far-flung adventures.

• Crews, Carole. *Clay Culture: Plasters, Paints and Preservation*, Gourmet Adobe Press, 2010. Starting with an historical overview, this book informs the reader about various wall systems and the basics of plastering them with the least effort possible. Become inspired by the artistic possibilities of earthen materials and the use of color, and learn to make and apply simple, durable, elegant surfaces to walls or art projects.

• Guelberth, Cedar Rose and Dan Chiras. *The Natural Plaster Book: Earth, Lime and Gypsum Plasters for Natural Homes*, New Society Publishers, 2002. This well-illustrated book provides an excellent overview of the range of plastering techniques, with a particular emphasis on their interaction with other natural building systems.

• Henderson, James. *Earth Render: The Art of Clay Plaster, Render and Paints*, Python Press, 2013. This 72-page Australian guide to tools and materials offers good basic instruction on how to mix the mud and get it on the walls.

• Reynolds, Emily. *Japan's Clay Walls: A Glimpse into Their Plaster Craft*, CreateSpace Independent Publishing Platform, 2009. The Japanese are known for their craftsmanship, and this book reveals many of their ancient secrets and techniques for working with bamboo and avoiding the shrinkage cracks between earth and wood, their exceptional tools and many other helpful pieces of information.

• Weisman, Adam and Katy Bryce. *Using Natural Finishes: Lime and Earth Based Plasters, Renders and Paints*, Green Books, 2008. This thoroughly researched document with excellent layout and photos gives recipes and techniques that will guide the reader in the right direction.

Working with Lime

49

BARBARA JONES

Lime is a binder and finishing material derived from the burning of limestone or sea shells. Lime has helped create some of the most beautiful, memorable and enduring buildings in the world. Think of the great rotunda of the Pantheon in Rome, 142 ft. (43.3 m) across. It was built from lime two thousand years ago, and we still cannot replicate the workmanship today. Or imagine a sleepy village on the Greek coast, houses painted with a variety of naturally colored limewashes. Indeed, lime has been used all over the world as a binding material (mortar), a surface protector (plaster, render and stucco) and flooring (limecrete, mosaic) for thousands of years—long before the advent of Portland cement.

In order to use lime successfully, you must understand the processes involved in its manufacture and how, once applied, lime plasters will slowly turn back into limestone through the slow process of carbonation. The practice of lime work is relatively simple, but understanding the role of variables in the materials and of the weather during application and drying is crucial to its success and durability.

The Qualities of Lime

Lime's physical flexibility is essential for durability, as it allows a building to move over time without causing structural failure. It is breathable, allowing the passage of water vapor. Limewashes come in many natural colors with rich and varied hues, in contrast to the monotone look of synthetic paints. Lime is a natural material that will return to the earth safely after use.

We use lime as a plaster in large part because it provides exceptional weather protection. It regulates humidity by absorbing excess moisture from the environment, then releasing it as humidity drops. This makes lime ideal for interior surfaces, especially in areas of high humidity such as kitchens and bathrooms. When it is raining, an exterior lime render will absorb moisture till saturated. This saturation actually prevents any further absorption of moisture, and the lime surface will repel water until the humidity level drops again, protecting the wall behind it.

There are two types of natural lime, those we call lime putty, fat lime or pure lime, and those we call hydraulic limes. Their properties vary along a continuum. At one end, we have the pure limes, which are very flexible and vapor permeable, then further along

BARBARA JONES *is a carpenter, roofer and straw bale builder with over 30 years experience in construction and 20 years working with straw, lime and clay in the UK and Europe. With her team at Straw Works, she designs straw bale buildings, runs training courses on real building sites and builds houses made only from natural materials. She aims to encourage ordinary people to be involved in the building process, as we all would have been in the past:* **strawworks.co.uk**.

the continuum are the natural hydraulic limes (NHL). An NHL 5 lime has increased strength but less flexibility and permeability compared to an NHL 2 lime. At the far end of the scale, we have Portland cement, which is not a lime at all but a manufactured product; it is rigid and not vapor permeable.

The modern construction industry has nearly forgotten the wonderful and versatile material that is lime. It instead tries to find chemical additives that will make cement behave more like lime, or hydraulic lime more like cement. We now know that cement is not the miracle material it seemed to be in the 1940s, and that it has physical qualities that can cause moisture problems or structural cracking. Far from being a water-proof material, cement is porous. If you sit a concrete (cement) block partly in water, the whole block will become wet, and when it rains on a cement plaster, water is similarly transferred through it. To counteract this, waterproofing chemicals can be added.

Cement is also not permeable to vapor, which means that vapor-laden air from the normal use of a house cannot pass through it to the outside, and usually condenses instead on the inside surface of the wall. This is

in contrast to lime, which actually protects a building from further ingress of water when it gets wet. To protect our buildings from cement, damp-proof courses are required *above* cement rather than below it.

Knowledge about lime was traditionally passed down from one generation to the next, and a wealth of experience was built up over time. However, we almost lost the knowledge of how to use lime in the 20th century as it was almost entirely replaced by cement in new building construction. Fortunately, a bunch of enthusiasts rediscovered it and over the past several decades have been working tirelessly to raise awareness of its superior

properties, researching recipes and mixes used in the past and experimenting with limes made today. Mainly through the work of the Building Limes Forum in the UK, and now with researchers and practitioners working with lime throughout Europe and across to the US and Canada, we have a much better capacity to use lime in the 21st century.

Limestone and Lime Burning

The basic ingredient of lime is natural limestone. Lime can also be made from coral or sea shells as these are all calcium carbonate ($CaCO_3$). The process of making lime putty from the raw material is quite straightforward. Traditionally, limestone is broken up

FIGURE 49.1. These chunks of limestone were mined, then will be heated, or "burned," to produce quicklime. Highly reactive and dangerous to touch, quicklime is mixed with water to form putty. Lime putty is combined with sand to create lime plaster. [Credit: Catherine Wanek]

into small chunks, placed in a specially built kiln (sometimes a pit or a heap), layered with fuel such as brushwood and burnt for about 12 hours. At the end of the burning process, whitish lumps of calcium oxide are left, along with bits of burned and unburned fuel. Over-burned limestone appears as black glassy pieces, and these are removed and discarded.

The kiln needs to reach a temperature of 2,200° F (1,200°C). At 1,650°F (900°C), carbon dioxide (CO_2) is driven off, and 2,200°F

FIGURE 49.2. Mixing quicklime with water is called slaking. Lime plasters are a global tradition, from China to England to South Africa. [Credit: Joseph F. Kennedy]

is required for the heat to penetrate through to the center of the stone. As it heats up, steam (H_2O) is driven off, and a chemical change occurs. Heat acting upon calcium carbonate ($CaCO_3$) produces calcium oxide (CaO) plus carbon dioxide (CO_2). The chemical reaction is usually more complicated than this, due to other carbonates and silicates being present in the limestone, but it's important to understand the basic changes that are taking place at this stage.

Calcium oxide is very reactive and can be dangerous. It is called "lump-lime" or "quicklime" and may be left as lumps or ground down into powder. It must be kept dry, as it reacts very quickly with water (even the water in the air or the moisture in your skin) to form calcium hydroxide, which is the first step to reversing the process back to calcium carbonate. Just as making quicklime needed heat, the reverse process produces heat: calcium oxide (CaO) plus water (H_2O) produces calcium hydroxide ($Ca(OH)_2$) and heat. Quicklime added to water gives us lime putty.

How to Make Lime Putty

The process of making putty from quicklime is called "slaking" (slaking the thirst of lime).

Always add quicklime to water. Never do it the other way around or it can explode! Great care must be taken in the making of lime putty, and protective clothing should be worn, including mask, goggles and gloves. The tremendous amount of heat that is generated by slaking lime produces highly alkaline steam that can spit hot lime in all directions.

First, pour the water into a metal bathtub. Take care to position the bathtub on a fireproof surface, as the heat generated can burn any grass or wood underneath it. Gradually add the quicklime to the water in the ratio of one part quicklime to two parts water, by volume. As the mixture bubbles and boils, constantly rake and mix it; a garden hoe is the best tool for the job. Keep raking until there are no lumps left, and the boiling has subsided. The purer the quicklime, the faster this process happens. The resulting putty, which should have a consistency like double cream is then sieved through a 1/16 in. (2 mm) grid to take out any pieces of unburned or over-burned limestone, which will not react. Unburned pieces can go back in the kiln for burning next time.

Slaked lime putty must be stored for at least three months before use, but the longer it is left, the better it becomes. Calcium oxide takes a very long time to hydrate, and three months is considered the absolute minimum time to make a usable putty. The Romans never used putty younger than 3 years old, and their finest plaster work was made from limes over 12 years old. The longer the lime remains as putty, the better its stickiness, ease of application and readiness to carbonate. Once lime is exposed to the air, it takes in carbon dioxide and changes from hydrate to carbonate. So if the lime has already begun to carbonate before you use it, it will no longer be reactive and won't bind with the sand when mixed.

Traditionally, lime putty was stored in a pit in the ground, covered with sacking and straw, where it would remain for months or years before use. In fact, lime putty in pits would often be passed on from one generation to the next. Nowadays it is usually stored under a thin layer of carbonated water in a bucket and sealed to keep the air out.

Making Lime Render (Stucco) and Plaster

When making a lime render or plaster from lime putty, the usual recipe is one part lime putty to 2.5 or 3 parts sand, by volume. Ideally, the sand should contain particle sizes ranging from very small (dust) to quite large ($\frac{1}{6}$ in. or 4 mm), and these should be angular, not rounded. The aim is to use only as much lime putty as necessary to fill the void spaces between the grains. The mix is usually one to three because the void spaces take up about one-third of the volume of most sands, but more lime can be added for greater stickiness and flexibility.

The only real difference between a plaster (for inside work) and a render or stucco (for outside work) is the fineness or coarseness of the sand used, and the choice of finished texture. Render may contain aggregate up to $\frac{1}{6}$ in. (4 mm) in size in areas that experience lots of wind-driven rain; usually people prefer a smoother finish on their inside walls, and so they would choose a sand with smaller grain sizes.

The longer a lime putty has matured, the more solid it becomes, and the better a render it makes. It can be hard to work at first, but by pounding and beating it with wooden mallets or posts in a large bathtub or on a sheet of plywood, the putty becomes more plastic and can be worked into the sand. The beating process can be very labor-intensive, but should not be left out.

In the past, it was a completely separate trade to be a lime render beater. Nowadays, it is increasingly common to use a paddle mixer. This crushes the mix, scoops it up and turns it to be crushed again as the mixing pan turns. A cement mixer won't do a good job, as the mix stays in a lump and can knock the machine over. The tendency is to add water to soften it, and the resulting mix will crack due to too much shrinkage.

The most common method of making lime render in the UK historically has been to mix one part quicklime powder with three parts sand, by volume. The quicklime is added to damp sand and mixed with a shovel. It is raked and mixed continuously, and may not need any extra water depending on the dampness of the sand. The mix heats up as the quicklime reacts, and it is usually used while hot, especially when used as a mortar. (Putty is left to mature, but a hot lime mix with sand is used straight away.)

When the time comes to use a premade lime mortar or render, it should be beaten and worked to a malleable consistency, so sticky that it can be held upside down on a trowel. It will always become more plastic with lots of beating. There is no need to add water to it, which would increase the risk of shrinkage cracks. Too much water in the mix itself will leave voids in the lime render.

The second (body) coat render usually contains fiber to increase tensile strength. This was traditionally cow hair, but is often chopped hemp fiber today. It is increasingly common in the UK to buy ready-mixed lime renders, delivered to site, to reduce the risk of inconsistencies in the mix.

How to Use Lime Render and Plaster

For straw bale walls, we apply the first (key) coat of lime by hand (with gloves!) because it can be worked more effectively into the straw this way. It's also more fun, and the straw tends to flick the stuff back at you if you use a trowel. The lime needs to be well rubbed in to get a good bond between it and the straw. I would never use a stucco wire in the render. Not only is it unnecessary, but as we are aiming to build durable buildings with a lifetime of at least 100 years, metal in stucco will fail before this time—the evidence is all around us.

Apply the first coat of lime render thinly, leaving stubbly bits of straw sticking out. It is usually ready for the second coat after 24–48 hours, unless there are

pockets of thicker mix in places. Before putting on the second coat, wait until the first is hard enough that you cannot push your thumb into it. Wet the walls down with a mister (not a hose) before putting the second coat on. Apply the second coat with hands or a wooden float. The render is kept damp by misting it.

If the render cracks, rework it (several times if necessary) with a wooden or plastic float before the surface hardens, to squeeze and compress the sand particles together. The aim is to compress all the render so that there are no air spaces left. Using a steel trowel on a lime render tends to draw the lime putty to the surface, and then this can be lost from the render coat, making the surface crumbly when dry.

For the first few days, protect the render from direct sunlight, rain, forceful wind and frost. It's important to encourage the render to cure all the way through,

FIGURE 49.3. Lime plasters are applied with a hawk and trowel and smoothed out with a wooden float. Here, Kaki Hunter and Doni Kiffmeyer plaster the BWB Straw Bale Ecohouse at the US Botanic Garden in Washington, DC. [Credit: Catherine Wanek]

not to let the outside skin carbonate too fast and prevent carbonation behind the surface. Therefore, keep the applied render or plaster surrounded by humid air by hanging wet sacking from the eaves, especially in a dry climate. Hang sacking from eaves or scaffolding and keep them moist, creating a humid atmosphere close to the lime.

Mist the surface, not to add water to the render, but to make sure that carbon dioxide can be carried into the render. Ideal weather conditions are cool and damp, with very little wind, and no frost forecast for at least three months. In the UK, we would only lime render between the months of April and September, whereas in the hotter states in the US, it should only be done during winter.

It is essential to understand the chemical change that takes place in lime once the render is exposed to air, so as to know how best to care for it. Once render is on a wall, it begins to carbonate, a chemical process whereby carbon dioxide is absorbed from the air, which begins to change the calcium hydroxide back into the original limestone (calcium carbonate). Calcium hydroxide $(Ca(OH)_2)$ plus carbon dioxide (CO_2) produces calcium carbonate $(CaCO_3)$ and water.

This chemical change happens very slowly. Lime absorbs carbon dioxide from the air only in the presence of moisture, but too much water inhibits the process. It should take a pure lime putty/sand mix several days to harden, which does not mean that all the lime is carbonated at the end of this time. Some of our renders are hundreds of years old, and still not all of the calcium hydroxide in them is carbonated.

Plastering onto Earthen Walls

On the whole, it is straightforward to render with lime directly onto an earth/clay/adobe wall. This is what the English traditionally did with cob houses. However, there have been some failures when lime is used on top of a clay plaster. This usually takes the form of cracks developing at the corners of buildings, with occasionally whole sheets of lime plaster falling off.

There are two problems occurring here. The first has to do with different rates of expansion and contraction in the clay and the lime, the second with poor adhesion. Clay plasters will absorb more moisture than lime, so in conditions that would cause

FIGURE 49.4. Lime plasters, like all "hard plasters," do not stick well to other plaster coats. There must be a mechanical bonding, or "keying in" of each layer of plaster with the coat below it. Also, all plasters should be cured before freezing weather sets in. Otherwise, the consequences can be complete failure. [Credit: Catherine Wanek]

expansion and contraction—such as significant changes in temperature or humidity—the clay backing coat may move more than the lime finish coat, and cause the latter to crack. This problem is accentuated at corners because that is where the render coat is in tension.

The solutions are to: (1) make corners curved rather than right-angled to reduce tension; (2) add lots of fiber (chopped straw) to the clay and hair/hemp to the lime, to increase their tensile strength; and (3) make sure the clay coat is moistened to make it sticky by spraying lightly with water before applying the lime.

The problem of the lime coat dropping off in pieces from the clay is caused by a poor bond between the two materials. This can be solved by: (1) making sure the clay coat is moistened and sticky before applying the lime; (2) leaving the clay coat rough to provide a good key for the lime; (3) applying a coat of limewash to the clay before rendering; and (4) rubbing the lime well in to the clay backing.

Hydraulic Limes

Since the raising of awareness of limes around the world, and the development of an industry aiming to make a profit, there are now many types of lime available in Europe and the US, as imports or as manufactured blends. It's important to understand the nature of these products as some of them may not actually be pure lime. There is often confusion between the terms "hydrated lime" and "hydraulic lime." Hydrated lime is quicklime that has been slaked just enough to make

FIGURE 49.5. In this traditional Welsh cottage and the stone wall in front of it, stones were laid up in lime mortar and rendered with a thin coat of lime plaster. This plaster has recently been renewed with a coat of lime wash. Note the traditional slate roof. [Credit: Catherine Wanek]

it into powder, but not enough for it to become putty. It can be made from a pure limestone, or one with hydraulic properties. A hydraulic lime is a lime that can set under water, and reacts with carbon dioxide. It is made from a burnt limestone that contains clay.

Natural hydraulic limes (NHL) have similar properties to pure, putty limes, but also have the ability to chemically "set" so that they feel hard to the touch sooner. This is caused by a small percentage of burnt clay (less than 20 percent) naturally occurring in the limestone. NHLs can reach higher strengths than putty limes, but also have less permeability and flexibility. Their full strength is usually not reached for a year or more, but they are quite strong at about three months. These limes do not need water to set, unlike cement, and they can be used under water, for example, for lighthouses and bridges.

It is possible to make artificial hydraulic limes by adding what are known as pozzolans to a pure lime. Pozzolans have the same effect as burnt clay and make it possible for lime to set under water. It is very important to get the proportions of pozzolan correct, because adding too much burnt clay to lime causes it to have the properties of cement instead of lime.

Bagged Limes: Type S and Type N

The bags of lime bought at a builder's supply store are hydrated lime. In the UK, our hydrated limes are made from quite pure limestone, otherwise known as high-calcium lime. In America, due to differing geology, much of the limestone contains proportions of magnesium, which still produces a good material, but is a hydraulic lime. Hydrated lime is far less reactive and dangerous than quicklime but does not have the same quality as lime putty or hot lime mixes. This is because calcium oxide (quicklime) takes a long time to change to calcium hydroxide in the presence of water (slaking).

The partial slaking of quicklime to make hydrated lime means that this process has not been completed, which can cause two problems. First, once water is added in order to use it, more slaking can occur, which can result in "popping" of the surface. Second, unless the bags are totally airtight, the partially slaked hydrated lime will begin to carbonate in the bag, thus when it comes time to use it, an unknown

How to Make Lime Renders from Dry Hydrate

1. Always use fresh hydrated lime, less than one month old.
2. As far as possible, check the ingredients and buy from a reputable company—although this still doesn't guarantee the quality of the product.
3. Make up the hydrate into a lime putty by putting it into a bucket and adding water. Stir well, and only add enough water to make a very stiff mix. Leave it for 24 hours or longer, and then make up the render as described previously.
4. Use 1 part lime putty to 2½ parts sand, by volume, to compensate if you think your dry hydrate is not quite pure calcium hydroxide due to carbonation. If you have reliable information that your hydrate is pure, then stick to the usual 3-to-1 mix.
5. Once mixed up with sand, use in the same way as any other lime render.

quantity will no longer be active lime, but inert, thus making it impossible to get the recipe correct.

Limes containing magnesium were often less favored when slaked outside of factory conditions, due to the fact that the magnesium component took longer to slake. However, this is no longer the case with Type S hydrates. Type S hydrates are autoclaved, ensuring that all the magnesium oxide has been slaked, as well as the calcium oxide. Although Type S dry hydrate can be used right out of the bag, it improves when made into putty and gets even better the longer it is left in the putty stage. In Type N hydrate, only the calcium oxide portion of the lime is hydrated, not the magnesium oxide part, so it must be made into a putty and aged to make sure that all the magnesium oxide has slaked.

When you buy powdered hydrated lime it is difficult to know

RESOURCES

Books

• Holmes, Stafford and Michael Wingate. *Building with Lime: A Practical Introduction*, revised ed., Intermediate Technology Publications, 2002. This technical yet very readable book contains everything you ever wanted to know about lime, including classification, preparation, tools, use of lime mortars, washes and especially plasters and lots more.

• Weismann, Adam and Katy Bryce. *Using Natural Finishes: Lime and Earth Based Plasters, Renders and Paints*, Green Books, 2008. Step-by-step instructions with illustrations to show working with lime- and clay-based plasters, renders and paints from design, preparation, materials and execution.

• Schofield, Jane. *Lime in Building: A Practical Guide*, Black Dog Press, 1998. A simple and straightforward guide to using lime plasters, mortars, etc,. to repair traditional buildings, based on over 25 years practical experience.

• McAfee, Pat. *Lime Works: Using Lime in Traditional and New Buildings*, Associated Editions, 1998. A guide to the many uses of lime in building, aimed at building owners, practitioners and specifiers. Highly illustrated and cross-referenced, previous technical knowledge is not necessary.

• Taylor, Charmaine. *All About Lime: A Basic Guide for Natural Building*, Elk River Press, 1999. This excellent booklet contains lots of useful information combed from other books and the Internet, with references. For the beginner, this may be all you need. It is available in both booklet and download from **papercrete.com**.

Periodical

• *The Last Straw: The International Journal of Straw Bale and Natural Building*: **strawhomes.com**. Issue #29, Spring 2000 was dedicated entirely to lime plaster. Packs a lot of excellent information into 40 pages.

Organizations

• National Lime Association: **lime.org**. This industry association offers technical booklets and information on products and applications. Arlington, Virginia.

• OK OK OK Productions. Kaki Hunter and Doni Kiffmeyer offer lime application workshops and consulting and supply high-calcium lime putty. Moab, Utah; 435-259-8378.

• The Building Limes Forum: **buildinglimesforum.org .uk**. Facilitates the exchange of experience, information and opinion amongst its members. Members form a community of lime enthusiasts and practitioners, many of whom are producers, suppliers, specifiers or users of lime. Glasite Meeting House, 33 Barony St., Edinburgh, EH3 6NX, UK; admin@buildinglimesforum.org.uk.

• The Canelo Project: **caneloproject.com**. Workshops on lime plastering as well as straw bale and other natural building techniques. They also provide special harling trowels and limewash brushes by mail order. Elgin, Arizona, USA; 520-455-5548.

Website

• Lime-Online: **limeonline.it**. An Italian site (in English) with many articles on using lime.

anything about the lime unless it conforms to one of the categories above (where the ingredients must be disclosed). However, with any lime, if the dry hydrate has been in the bag too long, it may have already begun to absorb moisture from the air and thus to carbonate, thereby declining in quality. Some manufacturers date their bags. If not, you can always ask when a shipment arrived. Beware of anything which says it is "lime-based," as this will almost certainly contain other ingredients such as cement or fly ash and not be a pure lime product.

Care of Lime Renders and Plasters

It is sensible to give external lime renders a few coats of limewash, painted on very thinly, as part of the rendering process. The first coat can be applied before the final render coat has completely hardened. Otherwise, wait for a couple of weeks or more before applying. If the rain erodes the limewash over a season, then re-paint it; otherwise, a new coat of wash can be added as necessary to freshen up the appearance.

Limewash is basically a more dilute form of lime putty, made from well-aged putty. Use approximately two parts water to one part lime putty, mix well, and continue to mix at intervals during use as the lime will settle out to the bottom. Small amounts of other substances such as lin-seed oil or casein, may be added for greater durability in the final coat but be careful not to add more than about one percent by volume or the breathability of the wash will be affected. Lime renders have the capacity to "self-heal," as the slow buildup of limewash carbonates and fills in cracks.

Lime renders should be lime-washed at least every five years—every two or three is better—and perhaps once a year on the most exposed surfaces. In England, there used to be a tradition of limewashing houses on May Day each year. Limewash is much quicker to use than ordinary paint, because it's very watery.

As long as a lime render is limewashed as needed, there should be no need for other main-tenance, unless something else is causing problems, for example, a broken gutter, an overgrown gar-den or an accident of some kind. If you do need to patch a section of render for any reason, first make sure to remove any loose or crumbly render.

Cut the sides of the hole or crack to be patched so they are angled, then add fresh render in layers no more than $\frac{2}{5}$ in. (10 mm) thick, allowing each layer to harden before adding the next. The patch will adhere well to the rest of the render, and can be limewashed afterwards. Old render can be pounded up and used in addition to or instead of sand as aggregate in the new mix.

Natural Paints and Finishes

50

JANINE BJÖRNSON

Natural homes and ways of living are the key to a healthy world for us and future generations. We have many choices at hand to create healthy buildings from the inside out. One of the easiest places to reduce toxins and create beauty within our homes is in the finishes we put on our walls and furnishings.

Human beings spend up to 80 percent of their time indoors, and we deserve dwellings and places of business that support our health, not compromise it due to poor indoor air quality. You don't need to live in an entirely natural house to receive this benefit. In fact, you can choose to finish the interior of your home with natural finishes even if the structure is built using conventional materials. The surfaces of walls and ceilings take up most of the square footage in our buildings, so why not grab a paintbrush and begin there?

History

Human beings have been mesmerized by color since the dawn of time. The magnificence of an azure blue sky on a clear day or the colors of a sunset that defy the imagination send our spirits soaring. For thousands of years, we have used colored earth, pigments and binders to create paints to express ourselves in art and to seal and protect our objects and living areas.

Paints have allowed humans to record history through murals, paintings and the written word. The use of natural pigments in the Paleolithic murals of Chauvet in southern France date back 33,000 years, and cave dwellings

FIGURE 50.1. Traditional house in Beer, England, showing this traditional use of lime and pitch as finishing materials. [Credit: Joseph F. Kennedy]

JANINE BJÖRNSON is a natural builder, educator and consultant. She specializes in natural paints and plasters, and loves the concept of naturalizing any kind of home. She is the natural materials cyber panelist at greenhomebuilding.com. You can contact Janine and see her work at claybonesandstones.com.

from the American Southwest have remnants of clay paints dating back to the 12th century. Our long journey with paint has created a world of magic through color, a way to communicate across time and cultures.

Paints are made from pigments suspended in a liquid vehicle (binder) that helps to adhere the pigments to different surfaces. Historically, binders included saps, gums, animal glues, resins, oils, fats, waxes and proteins such as milk or blood. Over time, recipes have resulted in paints with varying uses, durability and longevity.

Modern paints became available in the late 19th century, when the sealable metal can was invented. Oil paints surged to the forefront at this time because milk paints would spoil. During the last century, the process of developing new paint recipes has emphasized long storage life, bright colors, ease of use and durability on the wall. Durability and color performance may give the gift of lasting beauty, but often come with the trade-off of toxic ingredients such as lead and mercury.

Modern paints are typically made from petroleum and contain volatile organic compounds (VOCs). VOCs are offgassing compounds of paint (and other materials) that are released during installation and for many months afterward. These compounds contribute to ozone depletion and smog formation. They are also linked to respiratory illnesses and memory impairment; long-term exposure can even cause cancer. While the current paint market offers a plethora of VOC-free paint choices, most VOC-free paints still contain formaldehyde, ethylene glycol and other solvents and substances that are known carcinogens, mutagens and reproductive toxins.

Homemade paints from natural materials do not contain VOCs, and therefore do not pose health risks during installation or during the life of the building, and they are often biodegradable. They are typically made from local, renewable ingredients, which use less energy to produce. But they often have a short shelf life, so be sure to use them as soon as possible.

I have been "naturalizing" conventional modern homes using natural paint (and plaster) finishes for over a decade. It is a beautiful way to bring the healthy, healing qualities of nature into your home. Natural paints offer a variety of textures, colors and finishes, which can be applied to sheetrock, or even on top

FIGURE 50.2. Applying a clay paint to a straw bale house. [Credit: Courtesy Janine Björnson]

of previously painted surfaces, with the right wall preparation. Natural finishes allow the walls to "breathe," ensuring that moisture moves out of the walls swiftly, which is imperative for most of the wall systems showcased in this book.

Paint Ingredients: Binders, Pigments, Fillers, Solvents and Preservatives

A binder is the fluid vehicle that pigments are suspended within. It assists the pigments in adhering to the object it is painted upon, preventing the pigment from dusting when dry. There are two types of binders: natural and synthetic. Modern synthetic binders like acrylic are by-products of the petroleum oil refining process. These synthetic binders are derived from a non-renewalable resource. Natural binders such as plant oils, resins, latex, cellulose, casein and animal glues have been used for thousands of years and can be produced in a renewable fashion.

Pigments can be found in a variety of colors and sources. Plant- or animal-derived pigments can yield lovely colors, but they typically fade over time. Therefore, there are two categories of pigments I like to use for making paints:

1. Natural inorganic pigments are minerals harvested from the earth, then washed and ground into powders such as ochres, siennas and oxides.
2. Synthetic inorganic pigments are made by chemical interaction or by heating (e.g., cobalt blue or violet). Natural earth colors like Mars red and yellow oxides can also be synthetically produced.

You can purchase powdered pigments from pigment suppliers (see "Resources") or landscape supply companies. Please note that the word *natural* does not mean non-toxic. In the past, naturally occurring pigments such as lead oxide were used, and in today's synthetic paints some pigments are derived from natural heavy metals.

Solvents or thinners are added to paints to create a workable consistency or to assist drying. The most common natural solvent is water. Other natural solvents are turpentine, citrus

FIGURE 50.3. A clay-based logo for a "green" automotive company created by Janine Björnson. [Credit: Janine Björnson]

thinners and plant alcohol. Examples of synthetic solvents include denatured alcohol and turpentine substitute.

Fillers are added to dilute more expensive ingredients and create bulk and texture in paint. Examples of fillers are chalk, talcum, whiting, mica, silica, marble dust and clay.

Preservatives in modern paints are toxic and should be avoided. Natural paint preservatives are refrigeration, borax, salt and essential oils (e.g., clove, lavender).

Types of Paint
Milk Paints

Milk paints, also known as casein paints, have been used for thousands of years; they were discovered on artifacts and furniture in King Tutankhamen's tomb. The ingredients for milk paints have been readily available throughout the ages, as most households had milk-producing livestock and lime on hand for building. You only needed to add pigment to create a colorful paint.

Using non-fat milk, you extract the protein to produce a binder known as quark. When mixed with an alkaline substance like borax or lime (hydrolyzers), the result is a strong binding agent. If you are using lime as a hydrolyzing medium, make sure to use lime-compatible pigments that will not bleach. You can also purchase powdered dry casein from artist supply stores or buy premixed colors from The Old-Fashioned Milk Paint Company (see under "Resources"). Follow instructions carefully to ensure success and use swiftly to prevent spoiling. Casein adheres well to most surfaces and can even be used as a sealer over or an additive to other kinds of paints, but it is not recommended in moist areas.

Carole Crews, author of *Clay*

FIGURE 50.4. Translucent tinted casein washes applied over a light-colored alis over a dark earth plaster at Emerald Earth, Anderson Valley, California. [Credit: Joseph F. Kennedy]

Culture: Plasters, Paints and Preservation, adds, "Colored casein washes give the most intense color possible for the least amount of pigment, and their transparency can be lovely. Casein wash is very drippy, and with pigment added, drips will show, so start at the top of the wall with a large natural bristle brush and go back and forth sideways, working your way down and brushing

FIGURE 50.5. The color here is actually mixed directly into the plaster and applied by Janine Björnson as part of a "naturalizing" process for an existing wall. Sonoma County, California. [Credit: Janine Björnson]

out all the drips. Keep brushing until the texture changes and becomes satiny and a little sticky. The milky smell will disappear after it dries. When planning your wall colors, be careful to choose similar values in color washes to the plaster underneath, such as medium grey plaster beneath a blue casein wash, not white or dark brown, otherwise minor scratches will show through easily."

Egg Tempera Paint

Tempera paint predates oil painting as a professional painting medium. Using egg as a binder, this ancient recipe makes a water-soluble paint that dries swiftly and has a luminous look. This paint is great for stenciling or work on absorbent surfaces such as wood and paper.

Water-Based Paints

Water-based paints (clay, milk, lime, etc.) tend to be the most commonly used in natural building because they are easy to work with and they are free of noxious solvents. They are not as durable as oil paints; therefore they are not suitable for all areas of the house. That said, all of the wall treatments in my home are water-based except for the bathroom.

Oil Paints

Oil paints take a long time to dry; some may never completely harden. This makes them more flexible and less prone to cracking. Oil paints are durable and excellent for wood, exteriors and wet areas.

Clay Paints

Clay paints (some are also known as alis) have taken the natural building world by storm. They are easy to make and easy to use, delivering beautiful results. Clay paints can be made from naturally

FIGURE 50.6. The Moroccan tadelakt natural finishing technique. Tadelakt is a polished and compressed lime-based finish that incorporates soap to create a glossy, water-repellant surface that can be used for bathrooms and other wet areas. [Credit: Joseph F. Kennedy]

Paint Recipes

Egg Tempera

- 1 egg yolk
- pigment

Separate the egg. Gently place the yolk on a paper towel for about five minutes to allow it to dry. Pinch the yolk between your fingers and pierce the sac to allow the yolk to flow out into a bowl. Discard the sac. Gradually mix in pigment to the desired color. Add water to thin the paint if needed. A drop of clove oil will slow spoilage.

Oil Paint

- 1 cup linseed oil
- 3 tablespoons pigment (guideline)
- ½ cup solvent (I recommend citrus thinner)

Put the pigment in a bowl and add enough oil to blend into a paste. Gradually add the rest of the oil and the solvent. Allow time to dry between each coat and wipe away excess. Use on untreated wood.

Limewash

Slowly add five parts water to one part lime putty, mixing thoroughly. Add pigment mixture and let stand overnight before use. Maximum pigment added is seven to ten percent by weight of lime. Pigments should be premixed in limewater before adding to limewash mixture. Additives you can use to increase durability are raw linseed oil, casein or salt. Limewash must be applied in circular motions with a limewash brush to work it into the surface. It should be applied as thin as possible to facilitate the carbonation process and to prevent crazing and cracking.

FIGURE 50.7. A chocolate brown alis. [Credit: Janine Björnson]

occurring clays harvested in the wild or from bagged dry clay purchased at pottery shops. Clay soils are naturally pigmented so you may not need to add anything other than a binder to create your paint. Clay also acts as a binder, but many clays do not have enough binding power to prevent dusting. A common binder used in clay paint and plasters is made from flour. Wheat paste is high in gluten, which makes it very sticky, and an excellent binder for pigments and fillers.

You can make your own clay paint (see "Earthen Plasters and Alis," p. 339, for wheat paste and alis recipes), or you can purchase beautiful premixed clay paint from Bioshield Healthy Living Paints (see under "Resources"). Clay paints are most suited to interior applications. Have fun and explore!

Limewash

In the vernacular architecture of Greece and other European countries, the annual use of limewash has been used to renew and protect buildings for centuries.

Limewash has many benefits: it is vapor permeable, anti-bacterial, anti-fungal and an insecticide due to its high alkalinity.

Limewash is made from slaked lime putty derived from limestone or chalk (see "Working with Lime," p. 347), water and pigment. It produces a soft matte finish that is pleasing to the eye. Limewash must be used with lime-compatible pigments (mainly natural earths) to prevent bleaching.

You can buy slaked lime putty or make your own using Type S

RESOURCES

Suppliers
• Bioshield. Natural paints, sealers, waxes, thinners and resins: **bioshieldpaint.com**.
• Kremer Pigments. Pigments, casein, gums and more: **kremerpigments.com**.
• Sinopia Pigments. Pigments, casein, mediums and more: **sinopia.com**.
• Building for Health Materials Center. Paints, plasters, sealers, etc.: **buildingforhealth.com**.
• Earth Pigments. Pigments, fillers, additives, clove oil and more: **earthpigments.com**
• Old-Fashioned Milk Paint Company. Environmentally safe and non-toxic milk paint: **milkpaint.com**.
• AFM Safecoat. Sealers for offgassing, finishes, paints: **afmsafecoat.com**.

Books
• Crews, Carole. *Clay Culture: Plasters, Paints, and Preservation*, Gourmet Adobe Press, 2010. A thorough look at clay as a building medium through the ages. This book includes recipes and directions for working with clay paints and plasters, including recipes developed by Janine Björnson.

• Delamare, Francois and Bernard Guineau. *Colour: Making and Using Dyes and Pigments*, Thames and Hudson, 2000. A close look at the history of dyes and pigments over time: where they come from, who used them and how to use them.
• Edwards, Lynn and Julia Lawless. *The Natural Paint Book*, Rodale Books, 2003. An excellent resource for a variety of paint recipes you can make from scratch.
• Massey, Robert. *Formulas for Painters*, Watson-Guptill, 1967. Two hundred formulas for painters. Great reference for testing and developing paint recipes.
• Mayer, Ralph. *The Artist's Handbook of Materials and Techniques: Fifth Edition, Revised and Updated*, Viking Adult, 1991. Known as "The Painter's Bible" this reference book is rich with information on the chemical and physical properties of materials used in all types of paints.
• Weismann, Adam and Katy Bryce. *Using Natural Finishes: Lime and Earth Based Plasters, Renders & Paints, A Step by Step Guide*, Green Books, 2008. This book has instructions for applying earth- and lime-based plasters and paints. Lots of wonderful photos and tips from experts in the trade.

builders lime. Make sure to wear gloves, goggles and protective clothing to prevent contact with this caustic material. Lime-wash is suitable for absorptive surfaces such as plaster, brick, earth, stucco, wood and stone. It is not suited to non-porous, smooth surfaces such as drywall, hard-troweled plaster or painted interior surfaces.

Sealers and Protectants

Sealers are used to protect walls, floors and objects from wear and tear and moisture. The most suitable natural sealers for wall finishes are casein, glazes and waxes. Each of these treatments will yield different results, so be sure to do your testing beforehand. You can make your own or purchase manufactured products from eco-building supply stores.

Sealing wood furniture and floors is best done with oils (tung, linseed and blends), waxes (beeswax or carnauba) or shellac. Shellac is a natural resin excreted by the tiny lac insect that creates a clear durable finish. This resin is collected and sold as shellac flakes. Shellac flakes are then soaked in solvent to prepare for painting.

There are myriad recipes for sealing and protecting. Determine what kind of protection you are trying to achieve and consider what material you are putting your sealer on to find the most suitable sealer for your project. Please use gloves, masks and appropriate safety equipment when making your own paints and sealers. And please have fun!

FIGURE 50.8. Applying natural pigment by hand in an age-old tradition, a Mauritanian woman decorates the walls of her mud house

PART FOUR

Building the Global Village

*The creation of humane environments
and livable cities is within our grasp.
No revolutionary new technology is required;
we know the methods and have seen them work.
The will to implement what we know and the determination
to succeed in doing so is what is needed....
This is the challenge before us.*

« Ismail Serageldin, *The Architecture of Empowerment,* 1997 »

Shelter and Sustainable Development

Susan Klinker

51

> *If all countries successfully followed the industrial example,*
> *five or six planets would be needed to serve as mines and waste dumps.*
> *It is obvious that "advanced" societies are no model at all; rather they are most likely*
> *to be seen in the end as an aberration in the course of history,*
> *in other words, a blunder of planetary proportions.*
>
> « Wolfgang Sachs, *The Development Dictionary: A Guide to Knowledge as Power* »

Human populations continue to multiply at exponential rates while increasingly inequitable distribution of resources leaves greater percentages of the world's people in poverty. The 1948 Universal Declaration of Human Rights (Article 25) recognizes the right to shelter as an important component of the right to an adequate standard of living. Despite this, a United Nations report in 2005 estimated that 100 million people are homeless worldwide and 1.6 billion people are living without adequate housing.

The barriers that limit us from finding real solutions are rooted in basic questions such as: How do we define "adequate" shelter? Can the human right to shelter be sustainably realized within the ecological limits of "Spaceship Earth?" Who is responsible for providing shelter? How can current processes of shelter development become more socially equitable for all?

According to the 1988 United Nations Center for Human Settlements (UNCHS) Global Strategy for Shelter, adequate shelter means "adequate privacy, sufficient space and security, adequate lighting and ventilation, adequate infrastructure in a location with adequate access to employment, and basic services at a price which is affordable to the user." UNCHS recommends that criteria for selection of a technology should include the affordability of its initial cost, the ability of local labor to utilize and maintain it and the viability of adapting it to local needs. Affordability, as defined by UNCHS standards, usually falls between 15 and 25 percent of household income.

As long as humankind has been building, people have

SUSAN KLINKER *holds a Master's Degree in International Development, focused on grassroots development. She currently serves as the Cultural Program Director at the Utah Cultural Celebration Center.*

creatively used materials available in their immediate surroundings and constructed shelter with their own hands. With the Industrial Revolution, a variety of non-native resources such as kiln-fired bricks, roofing tiles, cement and metal products became available in many countries at favorable prices. Specialized tradesmen became necessary to manage the rising complexity of materials and tools available. Little by little, ordinary people worldwide lost their knowledge of local building practices and the ethic of self-reliance in providing shelter.

When considering global population growth and the finite limits of "Spaceship Earth," it is clear that contemporary building technologies, lifestyles and patterns of consumption are neither sustainable nor appropriate. Contemporary building technologies inefficiently use natural and synthetic materials manufactured from resources from across the globe. Rich countries continue to build and "develop" their nations, importing goods from remote hinterlands, aggressively consuming disproportionate amounts of the world's natural resources, and projecting images of their standards and ideals for contemporary lifestyles to the far corners of the Earth.

Barriers to Sustainable Development

Advances in natural building provide solutions that meet and often exceed consumer expectations in the level of comfort, esthetics and quality demanded of modern buildings. A growing number of owner-builders in the US have explored the use of low-tech natural building and have created cost-effective, comfortable housing built with their own hands. Luxury natural homes have also become increasingly trendy for high-end custom-built homes in the US. Such natural building technologies

can be applicable in nearly all geographic regions and climates around the planet.

However, in new housing programs worldwide, appropriate low-tech natural building alternatives may not be fully considered because they do not seem to fit with contemporary societal ideals and standards. Barriers can be both social and institutional. At a social level, families want their housing investment to reflect a positive image of modernization and increased social status. They often reject traditional methods and styles that they have been conditioned to perceive as being

FIGURE 51.1. The empowerment of volunteers and the community is one of the greatest attributes of natural building. Here, a crowd of friends and strangers come together as one team to achieve a common goal. [Credit: Michael Rosenberg]

backward. At the institutional level, many government and financial institutions may also associate traditional building methods with lack of progress. Capital investment may be considered high risk or even a waste of financial resources until market values for natural built homes are proven over time.

The image of "primitive" building styles can only be changed through the sharing of information and the promotion of successful projects that demonstrate affordability, longevity, beauty and overall excellence in design. Lessons learned from individual projects can help solve common problems regardless of cultural or socio-economic context. Reconsideration of traditional vernacular architecture throughout the world, integrated with modern materials and methods, can provide a vital link to hybrid building solutions that honor local heritage and offer innovative new paths for others to follow.

By working together with traditional builders, concentrating on the cross-pollination of ideas through reciprocal learning, then sharing knowledge across cultural, economic and political boundaries, the collective wisdom of the past can be integrated with new scientific understand-

ings of what works and why. A critical mass of individual and larger-scale housing projects demonstrating excellence in natural building is needed to create a global paradigm shift toward more widespread acceptance and use of ecological building practices and systems to better serve people and our planet.

Intervention, Empowerment and Participatory Development

The World Commission on Environment and Development defined *sustainability* as "those paths of social, economic, and political progress that meet the needs of the present without compromising the ability of future generations to meet their own needs." The word "development" implies improvement, from worse to better, and from inferior to superior. Yet all too often, well-intentioned development projects have had disastrous effects on local people, including disrupting social and political environments, invalidating traditional values and means of production and creating of new desires and dependencies. Therefore, any project intended

FIGURE 51.2. This demonstration building in Oaxaca, Mexico, was constructed in two weeks as a collaboration between local architect Valentina Marquez Mendez, instructor Michael G. Smith, paid builders and volunteers. Such projects have been instrumental in introducing natural building techniques to communities all over the world. [Credit: Valentina Marquez Mendez]

to effect change through the intervention of outsiders must be carefully considered.

Beyond basic material gain and the physical outcomes anticipated by a project, it is important to consider how the proposed project will change community consciousness and empower local people. Who will be empowered and with what? Will participants gain knowledge, skills, status or confidence? Will everyone benefit equally, or only those who meet specific criteria? What kinds

of short-term and long-term relationships will the project develop? Will information exchange be reciprocal? Will the proposed process increase independence or improve local community relations?

It is critical that intervention workers maintain a sense of humility and respect for the process, recognizing what things will be changed through the project and why. Sensitivity to the subtle responses of the community to the project and a sincere, conscious

effort to monitor impacts and nurture people's empowerment at every level will help to keep initiatives on target.

When community members are involved in establishing priorities and making key decisions, they are invited to become true stakeholders in a project. Their grassroots involvement helps to expand their access to resources in the future and allows them to experience the immediate results of their decisions as the project proceeds. A well-orchestrated

FIGURE 51.3. This vaulted HIV/AIDS hospice in South Africa was constructed of earth blocks by local builders and features innovative sustainability features for passive cooling and lighting, solar hot water production and local food production. [Credit: Joseph F. Kennedy]

community design and planning process can improve physical conditions, build pride and raise a community's sense of responsibility for creating and maintaining a healthy environment. While working together, residents from varying social and ethnic backgrounds often find new understanding of each other and create new common ground for moving forward as supportive neighbors.

It's true that the more people involved in the decision-making process, the longer it can take to get things done. But strengthened relationships and partnerships within the community reinforce local capacities and help ensure the long-term sustainability and health of the community once planners or supporting NGOs withdraw upon project completion.

Nabeel Hamdi's book *Housing Without Houses* provides diverse perspectives and tools for navigating community-based participation toward outcomes that are socially, economically, architecturally and environmentally viable. In the process, he notes, it is important that development agencies carefully consider their goals and their use of resources and make conscious decisions about potential opportunities for public education, network-

ing and capacity building in the bigger picture. Even though such decisions may seem to be diversions, or may create scheduling challenges, this process may ultimately lead to greater long-term positive impacts regarding the sustainability of a project and its public presence.

Housing that Serves People

Planners and development professionals often misunderstand the hierarchy of basic needs and priorities of the poor. For many families, the need to provide food is a much higher priority than shelter, particularly in temperate climates where it is relatively comfortable to be outside. Opportunities for employment, healthcare and education may also take precedence over improved shelter.

John Turner's writings in the late 1960s helped draw attention to the rationality of the poor living in spontaneous settlements on the fringes of cities worldwide. He described how a "supportive shack" could provide a family with adequate shelter from the elements and still allow them to spend what income they had on other urgent needs. When families are forced to allocate too high a proportion of their income to housing, they can become

destabilized in many other areas of their lives.

Turner also introduced the concept of housing as a verb, recognizing "what housing does" rather than "what housing is." Turner's view stresses the "use value" of a house (as determined by how well it serves the needs of its occupants) rather than its "market value" (which is defined in dollars and cents). A "use value" perspective encourages alternative forms of housing, variety in the ways people attain shelter, and the use of the housing process itself as a means by which people can fulfill their hopes and dreams for their future.

Intervention programs aimed at sustainable development need to consider the broader issues of economic opportunity, social justice and ecological responsibility. These issues go hand in hand in enabling people to improve their livelihoods and their futures by creating physical and social environments that truly serve their needs.

Many self-help housing projects are specifically designed to advocate incremental building. Rather than requiring a large initial loan, incremental construction allows a household to upgrade or add more space as financial resources become

FIGURE 51.4. Local South African students work with a volunteer architect at this sustainable building workshop in Dennilton, South Africa. [Credit: Joseph F. Kennedy]

UN Recommendations for Human Settlements

More than 100 world leaders participated in the 1992 Rio Earth Summit. The publication of their proceedings, Agenda 21, includes, among others, the following recommendations for the management of human settlements:

- The use of local and indigenous building sources
- Incentives to promote the continuation of traditional techniques and self-help strategies
- Improved construction materials, techniques and training in recognition of the inequitable toll that natural disasters take on developing countries
- The regulation of energy-efficient design principles
- The use of labor-intensive rather than energy-intensive construction techniques
- Appropriate restructuring of credit institutions
- International information exchange
- Recycling and reuse of building materials
- Decentralization of the construction industry, through encouraging smaller firms
- The use of "clean technologies."

available. The quality of the house may be much lower during early phases of a project, but the overall security of the family is enhanced. For example, a typical "sites and services" project will provide water, sewer and electrical service to a specific plot of land. Many also include a simple foundation and a concrete slab floor. Beyond these basic sites and services, families are free to build as they wish, within their own time frame.

Physical planning decisions can have a significant effect on community economic opportunities, such as making allowances for income-generating activities within the home and providing easy public access to home-based commercial enterprises. The intentional development of local cottage industries to support the building trades can have a significant impact on a community's overall ability to afford sustainable housing improvements. Any number of local and renewable materials can be harvested and prepared for use as building products. Encouraging micro-enterprise opportunities along with architectural development projects can foster self-reliance and increase the rate of expansion and improvement of local affordable housing stock.

Although women in developing countries are often active in community-based planning and construction projects, there may be many additional factors that come into play when considering the role of women in a project. Women's ability to equally participate may be limited by cultural values and mores, physical limitations and severe time constraints related to their complex responsibilities as mothers, homemakers and economic supporters of their families. Personal security and modesty may also be factors in women's participation. With increasing percentages of the world's urban households headed by women, there is clearly a need for a gender-sensitive approach to project planning and to devise ways in which women may participate fully and access equal benefit.

Policy, Affordability and Building Codes

Definitions of adequate shelter vary widely in different nations, cultures and social circumstances. What is perceived to be very adequate by members of a traditional society living in a rural agricultural area may be considered highly inadequate to those accustomed to Western-style urban dwellings.

Balancing economic extremes and establishing appropriate standards for health and safety without infringing on people's right to access shelter poses challenges for policymakers. Many building codes are modeled after those used in industrialized countries and often favor high-tech, import-based materials that can be scarce and expensive in developing countries. Codes sometimes even prohibit the use of traditional building methods. Although these types of requirements may be inappropriate,

RESOURCES

• Day, Christopher. *Places of the Soul: Architecture and Environmental Design as a Healing Art*, Aquarian Press, 1990. Discusses how built environments impact us physically, emotionally and spiritually, challenging us to design organically to nurture the richness and depth of human experience.

• Hamdi, Nabeel. *Housing Without Houses: Participation, Flexibility, Enablement*, Van Nostrand Reinhold, 1995. Practical guide to community participatory design in a development context. Case studies from around the world provide specific tools to enhance communication, measurement and evaluation.

• Rudofsky, Bernard, *Architecture Without Architects: A Short Introduction to Non-Pedigreed Architecture*, University of New Mexico Press, 1987. Challenges architects to expand project processes in order to expand opportunities for enabling the poor. Case studies from across the world demonstrate how people can be empowered in the development of sustainable environments.

• Norberg-Hodge, Helena, *Ancient Futures: Learning from Ladakh*, Sierra Club Books, 1991. Provides a rich and engaging account of the impacts of rapid modernization in Ladakh, reflecting on how changes in global society are endangering traditional societies and questioning the spiritual cost of popular notions of "progress." This is a great read for practitioners of "development" projects worldwide.

• Steele, James. *An Architecture for People: The Complete Works of Hassan Fathy*, Thames and Hudson, 1997. Critical review of the philosophies and works of Hassan Fathy whose work served to revitalize ancient mud brick building technologies and open new paths for modern thinking.

• Turner, John F.C. and Colin Ward. *Housing by People: Towards Autonomy in Building Environments*, Ideas in Progress, 2000. Provides a reflective view of self-help solutions to empower people as rational consumers and managers of their own lives and destinies in the provision of shelter.

many governments are unwilling to change their defined standards because they fear criticism that they are sanctioning the development of low-quality housing and, therefore, the further growth of slums.

The adoption of distinctive codes and construction standards for traditional or alternative building techniques could significantly affect the availability of safe and affordable housing worldwide. In many cases, ecologically benign or recycled materials are perfectly adequate for simple construction needs, and have tremendous potential for improving the quality of existing housing when used in the right way.

What is still lacking in most building codes are adequate guidelines for artisans and professionals regarding the safe use of indigenous materials and low-tech appropriate technologies, and allowance for the adoption of feasible innovative technologies as they emerge. Ongoing public demand, activism and lobbying efforts by those who have demonstrated an ability to produce sustainable shelter effectively are critical to continuing the reform process.

Sustainable Building as Appropriate Technology

52

David A. Bainbridge

*A thing is right when it tends to preserve
the integrity, stability and beauty of the biotic community.
It is wrong when it does otherwise.*

« Aldo Leopold »

"Appropriateness" reflects the ability of a society to produce, use, repair and dispose of technology and materials without disrupting the society and its natural environment, limiting future options or harming future generations. The concept of appropriate or sustainable technology is foreign to most industrialists, designers, developers and engineers raised with the notion that all that is new is good. But this unfailing faith in technology is increasingly eroding, as materials previously thought safe are found to be harmful to human health, the environment or both.

As researchers more deeply analyze the benefits and impacts of modern industrial technology, the effort to create more sustainable alternatives has gained momentum. These appropriate technologies seek to solve problems such as housing, food production, economic activity, etc., while doing no harm to the society and improving the environment. These alternatives are rooted in tradition, yet make use of selected modern inputs as well. The result is a hybrid approach to solving the unprecedented challenges of our age.

Economist E. F. Schumacher helped encourage a reevaluation of technology, international assistance and development with the creation of the Intermediate Technology Development Group (now Practical Action) in 1966. In his seminal text, *Small Is Beautiful* (1973), he encouraged others around the world to develop

David Bainbridge *was educated at UC San Diego (earth sciences) and UC Davis (ecosystem science and environmental planning). His interest in planning, microclimate and renewable energy led to work with Living Systems, the California Energy Commission and the creation of the Passive Solar Institute. David helped develop the City of Davis's climatically adapted building codes (teaching workshops for building code officials) and its planning for energy conservation. He also led the fight there for narrow streets and above-ground drainage, water conservation, daylighting and passive solar heating and cooling. He was awarded the American Solar Energy Society's Passive Solar Pioneer Award in 2004.*

technological solutions that better fit local conditions.

Before these groups arrived on the international development scene, advice to local communities had been (and, sadly, often still is) woefully ill-suited to local cultures, developed by so-called experts who often had a very poor idea of the challenges facing the people they intended to help, and little or no knowledge of their local resources and cultural and environmental limitations. In contrast, Practical Action and other like-minded groups stress the importance of finding locally adapted sustainable solutions to complex problems, based on a clear analysis of the situation, working in partnership with local people.

Practical Action's research showed that it is important to understand the root causes of problems, not just the symptoms. Ask: What is the problem? Is it economics? Land tenure? Resources? Culture? This information helps avoid the basic errors that have caused well-intentioned aid projects to be disastrous to local people. Two guiding principles are to first do no harm and, second, to empower people to find their own solutions. This is the challenge for builders today!

FIGURE 52.2. Local production and transport of building materials in the Sahel helps keep money in a community economy. [Credit: Development Workshop]

FIGURE 52.1. Creative and appropriate use of available materials is demonstrated by this straw bale project in Mexico. [Credit:Catherine Wanek]

Sustainable Building Materials and Building Systems

For most of our existence on Earth, we humans have lived without architects, engineers, designers or manufactured building materials. In many societies almost everyone knew how to make most of their own tools, clothes and homes. Many of the design solutions these cultures developed were remarkable for their beauty, longevity and efficient use of materials. They learned from observation, testing and practice.

The grass dome houses of the Great Plains Indians are a good example. Found from Kansas to Texas, their light wood frame with grass thatch shelter was energy efficient, comfortable and easy to build. The construction process served as a community-building exercise as well.

When a house was needed, the leader would leave a twig at each house that was to provide a prepared roof rib. In the morning the "project coordinator" would establish the site, and then all the designated families would plant their rib in a circular set of holes.

One man climbed on an oak stump placed in the middle of the floor and used a rope to lash all the ribs together. Then horizontal ribs were attached and ten inches of thatch were tied on. The house was finished by midday and celebrated with a feast cooked inside.

We can find hundreds of other innovative and sustainable solutions to the challenge of shelter around the world. The vernacular architectures of China, Korea and Japan make excellent use of earth, straw, bamboo and paper. The mud houses of Africa are often stunningly beautiful and tolerably comfortable. In Europe, straw-clay walls are still in use after hundreds of years. The reed houses and churches of the marsh Arabs in southeastern Iraq are remarkable for their elegance and material efficiency. Traditional Mayan houses with thatched roofs and thick limestone walls were comfortable, and the walls could resist even the strongest hurricanes. Worldwide use of straw-reinforced mud is worth careful review, as is the rich history of rammed earth construction.

Traditional building techniques are not a panacea for the worldwide housing crisis. Many traditional designs are imperfect as a result of limited understanding of engineering principles and materials properties. For example, some earthen housing designs are uncomfortable in extreme climates and may fail during earthquakes. Because of these limitations, traditional

FIGURE 52.3. These student-built earthbag shelters at CalEarth demonstrate a quick and inexpensive solution to housing needs due to natural disaster or human conflict. [Credit: Joseph F. Kennedy]

materials were often abandoned once modern materials became available.

Sadly, despite advances in engineering and the use of modern materials, many new buildings are more uncomfortable than traditional designs, and can be equally dangerous in earthquakes. Fortunately, traditional structures of stone or earth that are weak in resisting tension and shear forces from earthquakes can be reinforced with locally available materials. By adding wire mesh or fabric and plaster skins, or internal and external tension and shear-resisting elements to these buildings, vernacular traditions can be improved, rather than abandoned.

Successful appropriate building solutions will often use composite materials, combining materials with different properties to get better performance. Reinforced concrete is a conventional example of a composite—it combines steel rods, which are very strong in tension, with cement, which is very strong in compression. Ecocomposites combine natural materials for improved performance—as, for example, when straw (with good tensile strength) is combined with mud (with good compressive strength). Examples of ecocomposites range from cob (a heavy mix of straw in mud once used in England and Europe) to straw-clay or *Leichtlehm* (a lightweight clay slip-coated straw mix developed in Germany).

Integrated system design can offer the same benefits. The Plains Indian tipi and the Mongolian *ger* (also known as a yurt)

FIGURE 52.4. This youth development project in Gbarnga, Liberia, utilizes locally produced compressed earth blocks. [Credit: CRAterre, A. Douline]

both combine a strong skin cover with a light wood frame. Putting the skin under tension strengthens the structure and improves the performance of the assembly dramatically.

Making Sure Things Work

It takes hard work, persistence and careful consideration of the social and environmental setting to create successful appropriate technology transfer projects. More projects founder on social concerns than on technical problems. Demonstration projects and continuing education efforts are critical. Researchers in California found that it took nine interactions with extension agents and their demonstrations for farmers to add one new best management practice.

Humility and a willingness to listen are crucial tools for sustainable building advocates. Local people often have the best understanding of the causes of a problem and the potential solutions, yet because they are not technically trained or accustomed to presenting information to experts or to other audiences, they are often ignored or scorned. Acknowledging their skill is rewarding to all concerned. Women must be included, as they are often key resource managers.

"Builder to builder" programs can be very effective, as information is always lost in the communication chain from builder to

FIGURE 52.5. An American Indian youth carries a straw bale to construct an energy-efficient home on a reservation in North Dakota. Creating comfortable homes using local materials was initiated in 1999 as part of a collaboration between the Red Feather Development Group, the University of Pennsylvania and the University of Washington. [Credit. Michael Rosenberg]

Sustainable Building Criteria

Truly sustainable building must:

- Improve quality of life
- Be comfortable and aesthetically pleasing
- Improve access to homeownership for the dispossessed and poorest members of society
- Be healthful, soft, fun
- Use materials that are safe to work with (for all ages and skill levels)
- Have minimal impact on the environment
- Be easily recycled, reused or returned to nature
- Support biodiversity and avoid eco-toxicity
- Be resilient to changing environmental and social conditions
- Be locally built, maintained, repaired and capable of being disposed of safely
- Promote community-building processes
- Be energy- and material-efficient
- Build asset value over time
- Be socially equitable and empowering

researcher to advisor to builder. The straw bale building movement offers many lessons about how to do this: Hear and see one (attend a lecture or a tour); do one (attend a workshop and build a house); then teach one.

Why Sustainable Building Projects Fail

The most common reasons for failure in building and technological assistance include:

- Asking the wrong questions: isolate and define the problem carefully and identify causes rather than symptoms
- Not considering risk
- Misconstruing land tenure and economic relations
- Talking to the wrong people (men only, for example)
- Not researching historical solutions
- Failing to provide maintenance support (training and supplies)
- Promoting untested solutions: prototype and test carefully; demonstrate successful examples
- Failing to match solutions to environment and/or culture: in some cases modern solutions are adopted because they are modern, even if they are worse than traditional practices

FIGURE 52.6. A Darfuri woman cooks with a solar oven constructed of recycled cardboard and aluminum foil in a refugee camp in Chad. Using such ovens has helped to reduce the need to scavenge for firewood in this desert region, improving both environmental and community well-being. [Credit: Patricia McArdle]

A Seven-Step Approach for Improving Housing, Resources, Health, Sustainable Food Production and Environmental Restoration

1. Define the problem(s).
2. Assemble a research team representing a wide range of stakeholders.
3. Research the cultural, environmental and technical environment.
4. Work with stakeholders to develop ideas and draft solutions.
5. Prototype, test, demonstrate and educate.
6. Monitor, revise, refine.
7. Report and let other know what works and why.

RESOURCES

Books

• Bjorn Berge, Chris Butters and Filip Henley. *The Ecology of Building Materials*, Architectural Press, 2009. One of the only books that looks at the sustainability of building materials. Translated from the Norwegian. More Eurocentric but still a great resource (first published 1992). Free online: **sciencedirect.com/science/book/9781856175371.**

• Schumacher, E.F. *Small Is Beautiful*, Blond and Briggs, 1973. The founder of what is now Practical Action wrote this seminal book that sparked the appropriate technology movement. It is still relevant more than 40 years later.

• Snell, Clarke and Tim Callahan. *Building Green: A Complete How-To Guide to Alternative Building Methods*, Lark Books, 2009. Recommended for beginners interested in more sustainable materials and buildings. Excellent illustrations and photos.

• Wilson, Alex and Mark Peipkorn. *Green Building Products*, New Society Publishers, 2009. The most comprehensive directory of green building products currently available. Products are grouped by function, and each chapter begins with a discussion of key environmental considerations and what to look for in a green product.

Articles

• David W.-L. Wu, Alessandra DiGiacomo and Alan Kingstone. "A sustainable building promotes pro-environmental behavior: an observational study on food disposal," PLoS ONE 8(1): e53856, 2013. One of the challenges of sustainable building is how to change current practices. Reading on the diffusion of knowledge can help; this paper shows that green buildings encourage broader adoption of green behavior. Free online: **plosone.org/article/info%3Adoi%2F10.1371%2Fjournal.pone.0053856**

• Fisk III, Pliny. "Availability and spatial coincidence of indigenous building materials," 2nd Regional Conference on Earthen Building Materials, 1982. Austin, Texas-based Fisk has been a pioneer in sustainable materials and innovative design for sustainability including rainwater harvesting, straw bale, earth materials and mapping. **cmpbs.org/sites/default/files/ad4.4-spatial_coinc.pdf.**

Organizations

• The Canelo Project: **caneloproject.com.** Bill and Athena Steen have been leaders in the sustainable building movement. Their workshops are the best!

• Center for Maximum Potential Building Systems: **cmpbs.org.** Access to much of Pliny Fisk III's work and ongoing projects. Highly recommended!

• Development Center for Appropriate Technology: **dcat.net.** David Eisenberg has done more to make building codes sustainable than anyone else in the world. His essays on building codes for a small planet are priceless.

• Ecological Building Network: **ecobuildnetwork.org.** Engineer Bruce King is one of the few engineers working on ecological building materials. His books and papers have covered straw bale, earth building and much more. Look for interesting conferences and future papers. He is also available as a consulting engineer for appropriate tech and straw bale projects: **bruce-king.com.**

• Practical Action: **practicalaction.org.** The first appropriate technology group is still active and working around the world. Excellent material for hands-on projects, rainwater harvesting, water storage, improved low-cost stoves. Start with their document library.

• The Wuppertal Institute: **wupperinst.org.** Based in Germany, it has done excellent work on the environmental cost of materials. A comparable effort is needed for the US.

Website

• Whole Building Design Guide: **wbdg.org.** A very detailed resource for architects and engineers but useful for the beginner as well. Detailed reports and material for specific topics, see for example "Natural Ventilation."

- Neglecting education and training
- Ignoring infrastructure and marketing limitations
- Hurrying: technology transfer takes time and patience
- Making big leaps rather than little steps: sometimes small steps are best
- Neglecting details: the devil truly is in the details
- Neglecting maintenance costs and technical and material demands for repairs
- Using non-renewable, unsustainable energy or material resources
- Ignoring equity or fairness

Although progress may be slow, it can be speeded up if the causes of inertia are recognized and addressed. Inertia can result from the fact that:

- Information is only a small part of the decision-making process
- Information is a political resource
- Human information processing is based on simplification and biased toward experiential learning
- Many communities reward stability rather than change

- People and communities are understandably risk averse
- Institutions are very effective at self-preservation
- Even if they are very poor, people are usually busy, without free time for new cheap, elegantly simple but labor-intensive practices
- Solutions for "the poor" may be avoided by those who do not see themselves as poor

David Eisenberg from the Development Center for Appropriate Technology (DCAT) emphasizes the importance of finding a shared commitment at the beginning. Perhaps the community is not willing to make a big step but can support a small first goal or project. An incremental approach works well with an ongoing adaptive review and evaluation process.

Taking many small steps allows everyone to learn more about environmental and social systems as well as sustainable building systems. Encouraging participation in this step-by-step process of muddling through can also minimize the problems caused by political mismanagement of informa-

tion. Persistence and patience are essential. Marketing viable solutions can be helpful, but good innovations will spread by themselves.

To sustain life on Earth, we must make building more sustainable. In developed countries, building represents about a third of the energy and material flows; in less developed countries this is often higher. Sustainable building is appropriate technology. It is something we, as a species, have done for most of our time on Earth.

We need to rediscover and refine the locally adapted designs and materials that make housing efficient, comfortable and sustainable. Sharing the best ideas from around the world and improving them with the current understanding and insight of science and engineering can create new solutions that are even better then the best traditional designs. Never be intimidated by the magnitude of the task—a single person with a good idea and the courage to implement it can change the world.

Woodless Construction in the Sahel

53

JOHN NORTON

The Sahel region of Africa lies immediately to the south of the Sahara and includes Mauritania, Mali, Burkina Faso, Niger and Chad. Local geography ranges from desert in the north to savannah in the south. Climatically, the Sahel is a region of extremes—very hot for most of the year, with daytime temperatures at 104°F (40°C) or more. Nights in December and January can be cruelly cold. Rainfall is low, from 4 in. (100 mm) in the north to 30 or 40 in. (80 or 100 cm) further south, but there are many signs that climate change is taking place. Flooding and unseasonal rains are both becoming more regular events that have to be taken into account when building. When rain does come, it can fall violently for an hour or more.

Multiple ethnic groups call the Sahel their home. Some 40 percent live below the poverty line, and about 80 percent of the active population lives from agriculture and herding, which can be very precarious. The search for alternative revenues is constant, and seasonal migration to larger towns and to the coastal countries further south for work drains young people (males in particular) from the region, making work in the villages harder for those who remain. More recently, thousands have turned to work in gold mines, often a terrible existence.

During years of drought in the 1970s, many communities shifted from a nomadic lifestyle with a light footprint on the environment to a more sedentary lifestyle. Traditionally, most nomads and pastoral families lived in relatively light structures; in the new sedentary settlements, earth walls and flat timber roofs covered with earth predominate.

This change plus a growing population have increased the pressure on scarce timber resources (for wood for beams, battens, etc.), outstripping the capacity of the land to support demand.

People's footprint on the environment is no longer light. Where once they could walk a few yards to collect wood, now they have to travel many miles by vehicle. Where wood was once free, it now costs money, and, moreover, a permit is required to cut wood, without which there are fines and confrontations with the forestry agents.

Many of the preferred species of tree, such as the "doum" palm (*Hyphaene thebaica*), have disappeared from parts of the region, and continued demand for wood prevents tree regeneration. In the past, good wood could last 50 or 60 years, but now finding that quality of wood has become ever

ARCHITECT JOHN NORTON *co-founded Development Workshop in 1973. In 1985, he established a DW office in France and now works principally in Southeast Asia and West Africa.*

more difficult. Some families find themselves replacing rotten roof beams after only two or three years because their poor quality makes them susceptible to termite attack, and so the spiral of timber replacement in roofs increases. And much as they might wish to, very few families can afford to use non-local resources such as cement, tin sheeting or steel.

The NGO Development Workshop (DW) has been working in the Sahel since 1980 to develop and promote the use of woodless construction—a construction method in which all structural elements, including vault and dome roofs, are made of hand-molded, unstabilized mud blocks. Woodless construction uses no wood and requires no presses nor cement. Instead, it uses four readily available resources: earth for building; seasonal water supplies; local transport, such as donkeys and carts; and a large and young labor force looking for work.

The introduction of woodless construction responds to four main objectives: (1) to develop skills and income-generating opportunities in the community; (2) to reduce pressure on threatened natural resources in the Sahel; (3) to make decent, affordable and durable building easier for the population to achieve using local resources; and (4) to encourage the integration of the use of local human and material resources into development policy. Since 1990, DW has contributed to the introduction of woodless construction in Niger, Mali and Mauritania; since 1995 the group has had a major focus on Burkina Faso.

Origins

Woodless construction techniques had their origin in Egypt and Iran. Thousands of years ago, both these countries experienced the problem that the Sahel faces today—a shortage of wood. In the 1970s, DW worked in Egypt with architect Hassan Fathy and Nubian builders skilled in the ancient techniques of building vaults and domes from mud bricks. DW went on to work for more than five years in Iran, where even more refined vault and dome techniques were still being used to roof whole towns. In 1979, a "South-South" technology transfer to West Africa seemed feasible, and the first demonstration buildings using vaults and domes were built in Niger in 1980.

FIGURE 53.1. A roofscape of earthen domes and vaults in the Sahel. [Credit: John Norton]

Although the basic idea of using vault and dome building was sound, the Sahel has its own particular conditions, climate, cultures and needs which require understanding and respect. For example, although arid, the Sahel experiences torrential rainstorms that are often accompanied by violent winds. Thus, unlike in upper Egypt where there are almost no gutters, in the Sahel special provision has to be made to quickly evacuate rainwater off the roof and protect the walls from erosion.

So, the early years of our work in the Sahel involved both demonstrating that woodless construction techniques were viable and durable, and adapting these techniques to local conditions. Time was needed to listen to what local people had to say about their building needs, to observe existing practices and buildings, to assess problems and benefits, and to make changes that would help further woodless construction techniques in the area. Working with and training local builders, for example, pro-

vided information about the difficulties that individuals encounter in learning particular techniques and highlighted areas where a change to the actual structure can make both the buildings safer and the building process easier.

Compared to the original techniques used in Iran and Egypt, major changes have been made over the years to make the construction process easier for the novice builder. Examples include determining a simple way to draw vaults based on dividing the desired span into thirds,

FIGURE 53.2. Starting vaults on a training structure. [Credit: John Norton]

introducing a mobile rotating guide that specifies every brick's position in the building of a dome, and changing the way the lower parts of vaults are built to make them safer and quicker. This process of change and improvement is ongoing, and despite the fact that woodless construction was first introduced to the Sahel over 35 years ago, there is still room for improvement with the techniques, the designs, and the training methods.

Moreover, in both Egypt and Iran, these ancient construction techniques were passed down through apprenticeships lasting many years, with learning taking place on building sites in an environment where there were many examples to learn from. But in the Sahel, with mounting pressure to find a viable and accessible construction solution, time was of the essence. Skills had to be developed both much faster and more methodically to ensure that all trainees got a comprehensive training.

The Training of Builders

In the early years of the project, training was conducted on building sites, with a lack of clear pedagogic structure. Learning how to do woodless construction "on the job," had clear defects. One could not tell who had learned which part of the process, which could be very dangerous when building masonry roofs. On-the-job training created pressure to get the building done and thus poor incentive to ask a builder to take down bad workmanship—and worse, public shame for the builders concerned.

In 1990, DW started to structure a formalized training program. By 1996, the model was fully developed, using an illustrated handbook that guided trainers through every stage of the program on a day-to-day basis. The trainer's handbook provides the structure for training the trainers, all of whom are selected from among previously trained Woodless Construction builders. Since the mid-1990's, all training has been done by local assistant

FIGURE 53.3. The test of successful technology transfer is when buildings are constructed without the input of the original importer of the innovation, as demonstrated by this "spontaneous" mosque. [Credit: John Norton]

trainers under the supervision of a head trainer on each course.

Trainings serve either 16 or 32 trainees at a time, with one assistant trainer allocated to either four or six students; higher ratios are difficult to manage. This large team of trainers constitutes an enormously important resource. Based locally, they provide the first level of technical assistance to new builders, and when not training they work on site supervision at their own construction sites.

Since 1996, our woodless construction trainings have been broken into two stages. The first part is a three-week instruction period covering both theory and practice. Trainees learn all aspects of the woodless construction process from testing bricks, site selection and layout, right through to learning how to start and build arches, vaults and domes, and to finish the building. The training takes place on specially designed small structures, all of which teach good masonry techniques, but in each case, teach a specific skill: building different types of arches, starting vaults and then building whole vaults; and starting domes and building a complete dome.

The masons are tested at the end of this period. Because the

How to Introduce a Technology Over Many Years

- Choose suitable techniques
- Adapt the techniques to local conditions
- Develop a training capacity and trained builders
- Take time to listen to local opinion and to observe local ideas
- Convince through demonstration
- Encourage individual initiative so builders will think for themselves

training structures are small, there is absolutely no stigma if a trainee is asked to take something down and start again; on the contrary, this is the expected process, and many training structures are destroyed at the end of training.

The second stage of training is completely different. Unlike the process in the 1990s, when DW looked for clients who wanted a woodless construction building on which trainees could get experience (a process that created dependence amongst the trainees rather than independent initiative), since 2003 every trainee builder engages to build his (or more rarely her) own small woodless house, which is on average between 90–120 sq. ft. (9 and 12 m²) with either a domed or vaulted roof.

Builders work in small teams of two to four with the part time guidance of an assistant trainer. Each trainee pays for the materials and additional labor. DW helps

them with some food, and by giving them one door and window and two ceramic gutters made by local potters—also part of DW's program. The finished house, the same size as most neighboring homes, serves as a local demonstration—or visiting card—of the skills that they have acquired. These small houses, many decorated in interesting ways, generate great pride and confidence amongst the trained builders.

The future village or small town builder is the central participant in the woodless construction process—both as builder actor and as agent of dissemination of the techniques. DW does not require that a trainee has previous building skills—indeed, sometimes these are a handicap, as bad habits have to be overcome—but does require that the community will vouch for his seriousness and commitment. Since people most often build using skills available within their extended family, by extending training to as many people as possible in a community, DW increases the chance that woodless construction will be used.

Many of these builders are illiterate, and some have only limited numeric skills. To address these difficulties in groups where people speak different languages, the training process is very hands on. Although trainees receive an illustrated *aide mémoire*, a document that visually recaps all the key points covered in the training, these documents never substitute for hands-on experience and are only provided as a reminder. All the handbooks use a mix of illustrations, photos and minimal text so that literacy (while helpful) is not essential.

Nearly all builders receive the offer of a refresher course a year or two after their initial training, which covers building maintenance, site management, marketing, drawing plans and the training of woodless construction trainers. All these programs are supported by teaching tools (the trainer's handbook being an example), and there are guides for doing cost estimates and drawing plans, with many of these available in local language versions.

One aspect of training that began in 2003 has been support to women potters. The production of ceramics in the region traditionally used extremely inefficient firing methods with no kilns and huge losses. DW designed a very fuel-efficient kiln that reduces energy use by 90 percent and breakages to less than 2 percent. To date, there are 80 of these kilns managed by women's groups, serving nearly 5,000 women who make terracotta floor tiles (a new, highly prized product) ceramic gutters, fuel-efficient stoves and other products in the Sahel. For the first time the women are able to earn a living from a non-agricultural activity.

Working in the Community

Training is mobile. DW takes the training to the community, village or town and runs the program in a manner that responds to local realities, uses local materials and labor and involves the community. Woodless construction builds on local skills and experience, rather than replacing them. So, for example, builders adapt woodless construction to local brick sizes and use local wall-plastering techniques whenever

FIGURE 53.4. Woodless construction has been popularized in the US largely due to the efforts of Simone Swan in Presidio, Texas, who was an early promoter of the work of the Egyptian architect Hassan Fathy. Here an earthen dome is replastered by an intern during a workshop. [Credit: Catherine Wanek]

possible. Different builders adapt the appearance of their structures to incorporate local and even individual styles and taste, and one can often identify the mark of an individual builder by sight. DW monitors the content and quality of the work.

Based on the experience of woodless construction in Niger and Mali, when DW started activities in Burkina Faso, it revised the way its program operated in order to stimulate much greater local engagement. DW now receives requests from communities to participate in its program. This request is followed by a community meeting to discuss local environmental, economic and infrastructure problems, and to consider what DW can offer. The community identifies which men and women might benefit from training and vouches for them. They also agree on what they can contribute, and DW draws up a Cooperation Protocol between each municipality and DW, spelling out each partner's roles and contributions.

The measure of the project's success is the degree to which spontaneous woodless construction takes place with no support from DW or local project staff. Trained builders are free agents who are actively encouraged to go out and find their own clients. Some builders remain to work in their villages, which is ideal, but many split their time between work at home and work elsewhere that generates an income for them. Such a mix of clientele contributes to the local economy and broadens the experience of the builders.

As builders move out into their societies, more and more people become involved in spreading woodless construction as a viable building solution. Local families needing homes and communities wanting facilities such as grain stores, literacy centers or kilns for making pottery (these can be built with woodless construction) learn how to incorporate woodless construction in their buildings. Public sector workers (NGOs and government workers) have built clinics, hospitals and schools. Parallel projects working on rural development, food security or

RESOURCES

Books
• Aquilino, Marie J. (editor), Beyond Shelter: Architecture and Human Dignity, Metropolis Books, 2011. A compendium of experience about disaster prevention and recovery. DWF's work in West Africa is framed in the context of a largely manmade slow onset environmental disaster and decades of climate change.
• Fathy, Hassan. *Architecture for the Poor*, University of Chicago Press, 2000. Describes Fathy's experiments with reviving ancient Egyptian building techniques, including the woodless construction techniques further developed by Development Workshop.
• ——. *Natural Energy and Vernacular Architecture*, University of Chicago Press, 1986. While unfortunately out of print, if you should find a copy, pick this book up for a technical discussion of the benefits of woodless

construction and other ancient innovations from the desert.
• Khalili, Nader. *Ceramic Houses and Earth Architecture*, Cal Earth Press, 1996. Khalili's inspiring text describes how masons in Iran build domes and vaults without formwork. It also describes his experiments in firing such structures to create "ceramic" houses.
• Koch–Neilsen. Holger, *Stay Cool: A Design Guide for the Built Environment in Hot Climates*, James & James, 2002. A concise climate design handbook very much channeled to the building needs of West Africa.
• Norton, John, *Woodless Construction: Unstabilised Earth Brick Vault and Dome Roofing without Formwork*, Lund University, 1997. Provides a more detailed account of the woodless construction program in West Africa.

environmental management have added woodless construction to their programs, identifying it as a major contributor to good resource management.

Today there are thousands of trained builders and as many woodless construction buildings spread throughout the Sahel. In many places, woodless construction has become part of the local building vocabulary. One builder has replaced nearly all the roofs on the houses in his village. Just as importantly, pride has been restored to the Sahel for the many people who have taken a hand in producing quality buildings using their own skills and local resources.

Woodless construction is undoubtedly a success story in the Sahel. It is sustainable—15 years after DW stopped training in Niger, the builders are still active, the practices have been found to be environmentally sound and they are now in the hands of the local population. There is just one problem—while DW has been aided over many years by the European Union and other smaller partners, DW and its partners need additional support. In a region covering half the width of Africa, there are simply not enough trained builders. To have an impact in every village, we need to train many more builders.

Straw Bales in China: Housing for the People

54

CATHERINE WANEK

All the flowers of all the tomorrows are the seeds of today and yesterday.

« Chinese proverb »

A modestly successful housing initiative in the People's Republic of China may be the most promising solution to sustainable housing for rural populations almost anywhere on the planet. Beginning with one school in 1998, the program expanded to build more than 600 fuel-saving straw bale homes, schools and clinics in a span of seven years. In 2005, this achievement was honored with the prestigious World Habitat Award.

Six hundred homes may not seem like many, when in China many millions live in substandard housing or have been displaced by earthquakes, floods and desertification. But this innovative and affordable housing model, a hybrid of Chinese traditional brick construction with an American innovation—straw bale walls for insulation—has reduced the use of coal for heating by a whopping 68 percent!

The implications of this energy reduction are huge, because in China, home to well over a billion people, coal does not just fuel electricity—most households heat and cook with it, too. The acrid smell of carbon combustion fills the air with eye-watering particulate matter and contributes to respiratory illnesses, especially during northern China's long cold winters. Even if global warming wasn't looming on the horizon, if energy-efficient housing is accepted in China, it would be an enormous benefit to the health of the Chinese people.

In China, commercial buildings are largely constructed with concrete, and brick houses are aspired to by anyone who can afford them. Both are heavy mass materials, without inherent insulating qualities, so they require lots of heating energy to keep their occupants warm. Coal is also relatively expensive for the rural populace; at the same time, rice and wheat are staple crops, so straw is readily available. Even so, straw bale homes started out as a hard sell in China. New ideas, even good ones, take time to gain cultural acceptance.

The successful housing program was the brainchild of Scott

Cathine Wanek is a former editor of The Last Straw Journal: The International Journal of Straw Bale and Natural Building, *and a founding member of Builders Without Borders.*

Christiansen, the Asia director of the Adventist Development Relief Agency (ADRA). He chose US architect Kelly Lerner as designer and technical consultant, and together they created a most remarkable building program in China. By offering partial funding, creating partnerships with local governments, training builders and overseeing projects, these two Americans spearheaded the creation of straw bale housing communities in five provinces in the coldest regions of the country.

Through a process of dialogue with Chinese builders and potential homeowners, Kelly suggested a solar design that incorporates a brick structural framework filled in with straw bales. While not ideal from an energy standpoint, due to the thermal bridging of the bricks, it satisfies the Chinese safety perceptions. And it still manages to reduce by two-thirds the amount of coal needed to keep a home habitable during the long cold winters.

This translates to a savings of about one-third of the annual income of rural farmers while significantly reducing carbon emissions. In terms of greenhouse gases, during the course of 30 years, a 600-square-foot straw bale home in China will save more than 150 tons of carbon from entering the atmosphere. Not to mention greater comfort, increased seismic safety and improved health and air quality for the residents.

Most impressive is a community of 42 small homes with detached greenhouses near Tangyuan, Heilongjiang, China's northeastern-most province. The greenhouse community is particularly efficient, as the living/working arrangement eliminates commuting. Although the lots are small (about 75 ft. wide × 150 ft. deep), residents grow an amazing amount of food on the tiny plots, which also might house chickens, ducks, pigs and cows. One mother funded her child's college education with the revenue from raising vegetables and hogs.

Many residents found they could completely eliminate coal as fuel, cooking and staying warm by burning corn stalks and other agricultural "waste." This is made possible with the *kang*, a traditional bed platform fashioned from bricks. Similar in principle

FIGURE 54.1. In northeastern China, this community of 42 modest homes was built with brick structure, with straw bales filling in the walls. Normally Chinese homes are heated with coal, which is expensive and contributes to smoke-related illness. Incorporating straw bales as insulation reduces the need for coal by two-thirds. [Credit: Catherine Wanek]

to the masonry stove, the Kang contains a system of circuitous channels that function as the chimney flue for their cooking stoves. When food is cooked, the smoke and excess heat pass through the massive bed platform, which absorbs the heat before the smoke exits through a chimney. This ingenious use of excess cooking heat dates back thousands of years.

Since 2004, ADRA has eliminated financial subsidies for building with bales, hoping that its money-saving energy efficiency will allow straw bale building to survive on its own in the marketplace. One encouraging sign is that the government of Heilongjiang has been distributing blueprints for a school and five small straw bale homes for replication throughout the province. And in 2009, Kelly Lerner again traveled to China to initiate a new straw bale housing pilot project in Szechwan province—a warmer climate, but an area where earthquakes regularly devastate traditional homes.

As in the United States or Europe, adopting new methods of housing, even clearly superior building methods, happens slowly. Knowledge must be exchanged, habits changed and prejudices overcome. If the buildings serve their residents' needs, keeping them safe and saving them money, then likely they will be replicated over time. So far the Tangyuan greenhouse community provides a significant endorsement for straw bale technology in China, and for the hard work of the committed visionaries who planted the seeds.

FIGURE 54.2. This typical Chinese living room features a *kang,* or raised sleeping platform, which is heated by the circuitous flue from the kitchen coal-burning cooking stove on the other side of the fired-brick wall. [Credit: Catherine Wanek]

Sustainable Straw Bale Housing in the People's Republic of China *by Kelly Lerner*

There is a severe need for adequate housing in northeastern China, exacerbated by an environmental refugee population fleeing desertification. Existing housing is frequently damaged by snow, flooding or earthquakes, and a significant proportion of the 160 million people in this region live in substandard and dangerous housing. Often built of mud and rocks, the houses offer little protection from the severe cold of the region, with temperatures as low as −40°F (−40°C). These mud, stone and rubble houses collapse easily even during a minor earthquake.

Super-Insulated, Seismically Resistant Construction

Especially well-suited to the local conditions and climate in northeastern China, building with straw bales was first tested in China in 1998. The pilot project was a straw bale school to replace a brick school destroyed by a minor earthquake. The new school has been very successful, with much reduced heating costs, and it has withstood a subsequent earthquake of 5.6 on the Richter scale, while other buildings around it collapsed. This is due to the relatively lightweight straw bale walls, which resist earthquake loads and absorb seismic energy through deformation.

Most new construction in China is carried out using locally made bricks, which adds to the removal of scarce topsoil and increases the already high levels of air pollution, while providing poor seismic performance. The new home designs retain some bricks (about a third the number used in an all-brick house), mainly to convince homeowners of the strength of the construction.

Involvement of the local communities is critical. The project only works in communities that have serious housing needs and have expressed interest in the project. Interested communities are invited to visit an existing project village to talk to straw bale homeowners and members of the local project management office. In order to participate in the project, there must be a local political commitment to provide matching funds, to establish and support a project management office and to manage the project with complete transparency.

Homeowners work with the designer and are encouraged to modify the basic designs by moving doors, windows and interior partition walls to meet their individual

FIGURE 54.3. This ADRA straw bale workshop is implementing a design by architect Kelly Lerner, which was informed by Chinese vernacular homes. In 2005, this ADRA initiative won the United Nations World Habitat Award. [Credit: Catherine Wanek]

needs. It is important that the houses are culturally and aesthetically pleasing in order for the new technology to be accepted. A post-occupancy survey of 159 families has shown 90 percent satisfaction with layout and design. Owners of straw bale homes also report that their houses are warmer, with more stable temperatures and that they have fewer respiratory ailments. Owning good-quality homes for the first time in their lives has increased the wealth and sense of well-being of the people living there.

Technology Transfer

To date, the project has trained 464 people and built 603 houses in 59 villages in 5 provinces of northeastern China where there are large straw surpluses. The direct beneficiaries of these developments have been farming families. These include low-income as well as middle-income groups. Those of middle income are included to avoid the perception of straw bale housing as appropriate for low-income groups only.

Some local building codes have

been modified to include provision for straw bale construction. Other NGOs in China have adopted straw bale technology, and it is also being used in the Ecologically Sustainable Model Village in Benxi Liaoning. A range of other NGOs, including World Vision, United Nations Development Programme (UNDP), and Pakistan Straw Bale and Appropriate Building (PAKSBAB), have similar projects in Mongolia, Mexico, Argentina, Belarus, Iraq and Pakistan.

Lessons Learned

- For real environmental impact and long-term sustainable development, there needs to be large-scale transfer of the technology.
- Local community interest, enthusiasm and commitment are essential to the success of the project. It is a waste of time and resources to train a community which will not support the project.
- The involvement of all stakeholders helps to maintain motivation to successfully complete the project, and it keeps costs down.
- It is important to build to the best possible quality that local

FIGURE 54.4. The ADRA straw bale initiative has been a life-changing improvement in terms of both economics and health for farming families in seismic and cold climate regions of China. [Credit: Catherine Wanek]

materials, local skills and budget allow to ensure the highest possible standards.

- Building construction systems should be allowed to develop organically over time in relation to the local climate, building skills and materials.
- Straw bale technology should be developed by studying and adapting existing local technologies.

- Adequate time must be given to the early phases of research, training, cooperative design and planning.
- Good technical training should be integrated with local design and local building skills.

KELLY LERNER *is co-author of* Natural Remodeling for the Not-So-Green House, *principal architect of One World Design Architecture in Spokane, Washington, and a project manager for the state of Washington.* Natural Home *magazine named her one of the top ten eco-architects in the United States, and in 2005 she received the UN World Habitat Award for spearheading straw bale construction in China. Her ecological design work and writing have been published in* Metropolis, Dwell, Natural Home *magazine,* Design of Strawbale Buildings, The New Straw Bale House *and* Green by Design.

RESOURCES

Websites
- One World Design: one-world-design.com
- The World Habitat Awards: WorldHabitatAwards.org
- ADRA China: adrachina.org

Improving Vernacular Housing in Western China

55

LIU YANG, JIAPING LIU AND DAVID A. BAINBRIDGE

Green building techniques are getting new attention in western China. This is critically needed, as annual energy consumption by people in rural areas in China has been rising with living standards, and this population now uses nearly 200 million tons of coal a year. Unregulated emissions from all this burning adds to the global greenhouse gas problem. The smog-filled air from coal burning is often appalling, and doubtless impacts the health of all of the area's residents.

Despite heavy use of this polluting energy source, millions of people still live in traditional buildings that, while mostly inherently sustainable, can be dark, poorly ventilated, damp and at times uncomfortable. But these traditional houses, imperfect as they are, are often more comfortable and energy efficient than modern concrete buildings. The challenge in western China (as indeed throughout the world) is to merge the best of traditional designs, often very energy efficient and made with sustainable materials, with modern understanding and improved details to make them more comfortable and healthy for their residents and safer in earthquakes.

Compared with the east, western China covers a vast territory with a sparse population, complex geography and a wide range of climates, most with strong solar radiation. Economic development lags behind coastal eastern China. In the rapid urbanization of China, the western area faces the double challenge of improving people's living standard while reducing energy consumption.

Xi'an University of Architecture and Technology (XAUAT) is the major architectural school for western China. A research group from XAUAT has played a leading role in the rediscovery of green building and passive solar design in western China, emphasizing rural areas. Passive solar design is nothing new in China. As John Perlin discovered in his research on the history of solar energy, the Chinese were using solar design long before Greek and Roman architects.

LIU YANG *is vice-director of the Green Building Center at Xi'an University of Architecture and Technology, and the leader of the low-energy architecture research group in Shaanxi province in China. In the past 20 years, she has undertaken four China Natural Science Fund Projects and won a National Science Award and a scholarship for International Cooperation and Exchange.* JIAPING LIU *has worked on a wide range of green building projects in western China.* DAVID A. BAINBRIDGE *has worked with alternative building materials, seismic safety and passive solar design for more than 40 years. University programs interested in cooperation or student exchanges should contact Dr. Liu Yang, School of Architecture, Xi'an University of Architecture and Technology, No. 13 Yanta Road, Xi'an 710055, PR China.*

Building and planning strategies derived from traditional models include passive heating (window placement, building orientation, thermal mass), cooling (through shading, radiant sky cooling and evaporation), ventilation (cross and stack), daylighting and microclimate modification to improve human comfort and safety. These passive systems will function without mechanical parts or additional power supply but may be enhanced with small fans, operable shades and window control systems.

The Green Building Center at XAUAT has searched for a design approach that incorporates traditional construction methods, protects nature and meets people's needs while using local ma-terials to build climate-adapted buildings. XAUAT has helped analyze and define climate zones, developed a climate-adapted building code, studied building performance in the field, explored appropriate designs for different climate zones through computer simulations and pioneered new designs based on traditional practices and materials. XAUAT also participated in the 2013 Solar Decathlon in China. The entry from XAUAT included straw bale insulation, passive solar heating and a hydronic radiant cooling and heating system.

Climate Analysis

Due to China's vast territory and rich climate resources, passive design approaches must be tailored to different regions and climates in order to be both economic and effective. Developing a better understanding of the climate challenges was the first step. We at Xi'an University used bioclimatic building design charts to define China's passive solar map.

Eighteen cities, representing five major climatic types (severe cold, cold, hot summer and cold winter, mild and hot summer and warm winter), were used for climatic analysis. Monthly weather data was plotted on psychrometric charts for each city and used to develop bioclimatic charts. These charts made it possible to explore the potential use of passive design strategies such as solar heating, natural ventilation, thermal mass with or without night ventilation and evaporative cooling. Nine passive design zones were identified, and appropriate design strategies were developed for each, for both summer cooling and winter heating. The analysis found that the combined use of passive solar heating and thermal mass with ventilation is very well-suited for western China, where it can reduce building energy consumption by at least 40 percent.

This information was used to shape a climate-adapted building code for residential building in

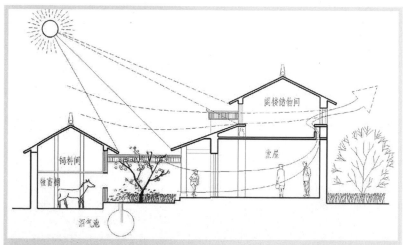

FIGURE 55.1. Sectional drawing for a new adobe house, showing passive solar heating and cooling strategies, daylighting, ventilation and micro-climate modification. [Credit: Wei Zhou]

Tibet. The Tibet plateau is the only area where most houses lack central heating systems in the coldest climate condition in China. The winter here is long and cold. Though short of conventional energy, it has rich solar radiation resources. If the architectural design in this region does not take solar radiation into account wisely, south-facing rooms are generally comfortably warm, but north-facing rooms are cold as ice cellars.

The code encourages new buildings to make the most use of solar radiation by using passive strategies such as sunspaces and Trombe walls, supplemented by active solar heating. The mean heat transfer coefficient in this area allowed us to determine the south-facing window-to-wall ratio should be greater than 50 percent. We found that when we comprehensively applied the strategies described in the code to houses in Tibet, indoor mean temperature increased from 50°F–61°F (10°C–16°C) while the conventional energy needed to heat the house decreased from 40 watts/m² to 16 watts/m².

Our research team demonstrated comprehensive utilization of solar energy in Tibet during the period of 2006–10. We worked to popularize low-energy climate-adapted designs by making basic meteorological information and solar architecture strategies available to builders. We also contributed to the uptake of these improved building systems by creating and testing model buildings.

Reworking Traditional Designs with Modern Understanding

The goals of the Green Building Center are to improve living conditions for rural people; to build public awareness of sustainability in western China, including energy conservation, farmland conservation and protection of the natural environment; and to enhance villagers' and local institutions' ability to design, plan and improve their homes to meet much higher living standards. At the same time, these more energy-efficient homes must be affordable. The designs must also respect appropriate vernacular housing traditions.

We have researched the performance of traditional designs, mostly looking at building orientation, shape and window placement to optimize performance. But without good windows and with little or no insulation, performance continued to be compromised after applying best practices elsewhere.

The use of traditional renewable materials in these designs was also studied. Many buildings in western China are built with adobe, mud and straw, or rammed earth with very little wood. They can and do return to the earth when maintenance is stopped— the ideal green building. But if maintenance is timely they can

FIGURE 55.2. XAUAT's entry house for the 2013 solar decathlon included straw bale insulation, passive solar heating and a hydronic radiant cooling and heating system. [Credit: Liu Yang]

stay in use for hundreds of years. Two examples illustrate the challenges and the design solutions we came up with.

The traditional cave dwellings common in the Yao Dong cave area of the Loess Plateau are warm in winter and cool in summer, but they are often both dim and damp inside. They can't satisfy the demand for the modern lifestyle aspired to in China. The modern brick masonry and concrete structures that have replaced them fail to recognize the rich regional architectural culture. These modern buildings are less thermally comfortable and therefore lead to greater energy consumption.

Reinterpreting the traditional cave dwelling with new technical measures, such as penthouse spaces, thermal storage, passive solar heating and natural lighting and ventilation, has led to the creation of a more energy-efficient cave dwelling that has proved popular with residents. These new dwellings not only save energy, materials and land, but maintain the traditional cave dwelling culture with a modern flavor. More than one thousand green cave dwellings have been built in Yan'an (over 1.1 million sq. ft. [100,000 m²] of total floor area), with an energy savings of 81 percent compared to traditional cave dwellings. Each dwelling unit is approximately 860–1,080 sq. ft. (80–100 m²), and construction costs are US$2.50 per sq ft. (US$27 per m²). Total cost per dwelling is thus US$2,160–$2,700. Owners

FIGURE 55.3. Traditional Yao Dong cave dwellings, viewed from the south.
[Credit: Jiaping Liu]

FIGURE 55.4. A new Yao Dong cave dwelling. These new dwellings not only save energy, materials and land, but maintain the traditional cave dwelling culture with a modern flavor that has proved popular with residents.
[Credit: Jiaping Liu]

building alone or with community support not only reduced construction cost but also enhanced neighborhood harmony. This design was a finalist in the World Habitat Awards in 2006.

The adobe buildings in the upper reaches of the Yangtze River have also been improved. There are billions of square meters of adobe buildings in this area. The traditional construction method results in uncertain seismic safety, cold and damp indoor environments, rudimentary spatial function and poor living environment quality. The research team studied the thermal and mechanical performance of raw soil materials, completed seismic performance tests of improved adobe building envelopes and used computer modeling to improve energy saving and seismic design.

Technologies such as raw soil thermal storage, passive solar heating, natural ventilation cooling, biomass energy utilization and domestic wastewater treatment have been comprehensively applied. More than 4.9 million sq. ft. (455,000 m²) of low-energy buildings that are energy-saving, low-carbon emitting, material-saving, water- and earthquake-resistant, cost-effective and simple to build have been constructed in Yunnan province.

The Future

For much of western China, the primary need is winter heating, which has proved an easy fit with traditional Chinese building design, green building materials and passive solar principles. Going beyond improving thermal performance, new designs will also often include space for commercial activity with the goal of rural economic development. Another professor is working on improved primary school design, with the hope of replacing many less satisfactory buildings now in use, and adding new uses as community centers to help restore the sense of community in these often remote rural areas.

Future work will involve cooperation across the Pacific to make more information from these Chinese experiences available in English and the reverse. It will also include more work on design solutions and further exchanges of students, professors and teachers, builders and architects.

FIGURE 55.5. New district of adobe houses in Yunnan province. [Credit: Wei Zhou]

RESOURCES

Books
• Perlin, John. *Let It Shine: The 6,000-Year Story of Solar Energy*, New World Library, 2013. A fully revised and expanded edition of *A Golden Thread*, the author's classic history of solar technology,
• Yang, Liu. *Bioclimatic Architecture*, Building and Architecture Press, 2010 (in Chinese).

PAKSBAB: Seismically Safe Straw Bale Buildings in Pakistan

56

CATHERINE WANEK

Many countries experience loss of life and housing due to the destruction of inadequately built houses in earthquakes. After Pakistan's 7.6 magnitude earthquake in 2005, which demolished 600,000 unreinforced homes built with stone, brick and solid concrete block, US civil engineer Darcey Donovan responded by starting an organization dedicated to affordable rebuilding with more appropriate materials. "The statistics of the earthquake disaster hit me hard," says Donovan. "There were approximately 86,000 dead, 69,000 injured and four million made homeless."

The organization, Pakistan Straw Bale and Appropriate Building (PAKSBAB), has adapted super-insulating straw bale designs to utilize indigenous

Cathine Wanek is a former editor of The Last Straw Journal: The International Journal of Straw Bale and Natural Building, *and a founding member of* Builders Without Borders.

renewable materials, local labor and traditional building techniques. They pay close attention to seismic resistance as they build, as well as to the cost of materials. Their pilot project was a women's community center, in Khyber Pakhtunkhwa Province

of Pakistan, in the foothills of the Himalayas, near Kashmir. As of 2014, PAKSBAB has completed 40 homes in the region.

The buildings are simple yet high-performance structures, with foundations of stone or woven plastic vegetable bags

FIGURE 56.1. Finished with clay and lime plaster, the PAKSBAB straw bale homes are sturdy and comfortable, and are built for about half the cost of a conventional Pakistani home. [Credit: PAKSBAB]

filled with gravel and load-bearing straw bale walls reinforced with fishing net, encased in earthen and lime plasters.

To prove the seismic capacity of this building system, PAKSBAB built a full-scale prototype house and conducted shake table tests at the University of Nevada, Reno, NEES facilities in March 2009. The 14×14×11 ft. (4.3×4.3×3.35 m)

structure was subjected to a series of eight increasingly forceful tests simulating the acceleration/shaking of real earthquakes. In the final, most powerful test—twice the acceleration of the Canoga Park record of the 6.7 magnitude 1994 Northridge, California, quake—the house shook and swayed violently, cracked at the seams and sent out a small cloud

of dust and straw, but remained standing.

"We now have the necessary and convincing engineering evidence that our straw bale building system is structurally safe and sound," says Darcey Donovan. "Heavy roofs which collapsed were one of the main causes of death in the 2005 Kashmir earthquake. Our lightweight roofs

FIGURE 56.2. After the 2005 Kashmir earthquake that impacted hundreds of thousands of Pakistani people, this straw bale system was developed to help the rebuilding process. [Credit: Catherine Wanek]

are made from site-built wooden trusses, covered with corrugated metal and insulated with light straw-clay. This inexpensive and local insulation keeps the homes warmer in the winter, cooler in the summer and provides sound-proofing."

"The key element tying the structure together," Donovan explains, "is nylon fishing net that is placed under the foundation, stretched up both sides of the walls and attached to the top plates. The 1×1×2 ft. (30×30×60 cm) straw bales are smaller than those used in typical straw bale buildings, and are compacted one at a time with a human-powered bale press. Exterior opposing bamboo pins help to keep the wall plumb during construction and provide resistance to transverse loads, such as wind, acting on the face of the walls. The walls are then covered with earthen or lime plaster which structurally transfers the lateral (earthquake and wind) and vertical (roof weight and snow) loads down to the foundation, as well as providing protection against fire and pests."

PAKSBAB's earthquake-resistant designs are comparable in cost to indigenous construction, and are half the cost of concrete and brick construction in Pakistan. This building system could also be an affordable solution in many other places around the world, due to its use of local labor and materials to create safe and comfortable homes.

FIGURE 56.3. In the creative quest to find local materials to meet seismically resistant building goals, fish netting emerged as a solution to tie the building together structurally. Plastered with clay, on a soil-cement foundation, this system survived a comprehensive shake-table test at the University of Nevada. [Credit: PAKSBAB]

RESOURCES

Organization
• Pakistan Straw Bale and Appropriate Building: **paksbab.org**.

Website
• Straw bale seismic test: **nees.unr.edu/projects/straw-house**

Earthen Building Comes to Thailand

JANELL KAPOOR

57

The story of modern earthen building in Thailand started on a little fishing boat. I was visiting Thailand for the first time with my boyfriend, who was there on a seed-saving mission. As we sat on the boat, we overheard the man behind us discussing the relationships between minority tribal practices and mainstream Thai religions. I turned around and introduced myself. Within ten minutes, I discovered that this man, Pracha Hutanuwatr, was the director of Wongsanit Ashram, one of Southeast Asia's largest activist training centers of Engaged Buddhism. In the same ten minutes, Pracha had learned about my background in natural building, and he invited me to teach at Wongsanit. This was the beginning of an amazing three-year journey.

As founder of Kleiwerks International, an organization that uses dirt to build community, I work with cornerstone principles that helped guide me through the journey to come. These include: (1) recognizing that natural building is a gateway into living in balance with the natural world around us; (2) working from invitation rather than assuming that I know what people need in a country that is not my own; (3) collaborating with people within those communities so their gifts and skills are at the forefront; (4) developing strategies for scaling up natural building from the micro- to macro-level, so that it becomes available to as many people as possible; and (5) trusting that there is always a way forward, and finding ways to align with what works. Starting from this baseline, the unexpectedly large consequences for earthen building in Thailand unfolded before our eyes, and hands and feet.

In preparation for that first training at Wongsanit, I clarified my intentions. Ideally, I wanted to design myself out of the system. This was about Thai people gaining the tools and techniques to lead their own projects, as part of a larger aim of independently designing and creating their own lives. Another goal was to tap into existing networks of grassroots groups and media so that as many people as possible could learn about natural building.

JANELL KAPOOR *is the founder of Kleiwerks International, a non-profit organization and global network of ecological design-build specialists. She has taught people from 45 countries and led trainings that launched natural building movements in Southeast Asia, the southern cone of South America, the Southeastern United States and Turkey. Janell also founded and lives at the Ashevillage Institute and Sanctuary, an eco-urban demonstration center that offers educational programs in Asheville, North Carolina.*

The organizers of that initial training could not have known just how quickly and extensively these intentions would be met. At the time, we figured that if ten people attended, it would be worth our efforts. Well, 10 turned into 125 in no time, and I soon came to understand that those who joined us represented tens of thousands of people as part of established organizations and coalitions that spanned Southeast Asia. Almost every person who joined us either had a follow-up project in their own community or intended to help spread the mud gospel by sharing it with others. This was one of the golden lessons of working in Thailand.

Scaling from micro to macro could happen quickly because of pre-existing relationships, networks and shared values.

Jon Jandai

As a matter of course, I asked Pracha if there were any earthen builders already practicing in Thailand, and if so, could they be invited to participate in the training. To my inquiry, there was only one reply: Jon Jandai. Jon, a rice farmer from the poorest region in Thailand, had visited the United States years before, and on a bicycle trip to New Mexico, he got to experience just how cool it was inside the earthen-walled pueblos, even on a scorching summer day. Jon realized: *I could build one of these back in my village for my mother.* And so he did.

"Crazy." That's what Jon's fellow villagers thought when he returned from the US and they saw him building with mud. They'd never heard of such a thing. Earthen building was not a tradition in Thailand (yet!). That didn't stop him. After building his mother's house, Jon invited the village kids to build a community library and, later, an organic food cooperative. Jon was dedicated to supporting fellow villagers to return to a more natural way of life. He believed in staying out of debt and maintaining a happy way of life.

He often recollected about how it was when he grew up: "Money and debt did not exist for us. If we needed something, we made it. We grew our food without chemicals. We didn't work too hard, and we had everything we needed. We especially had time to laugh, play music and be with our families and community. We were happy. Then the promise of development came, and too many people forgot their happiness. They went for 'progress,' but for us, the common villager, it was a path to suicide, depression, factory labor, prostitution in big cities and separation from our

FIGURE 57.1. Our second training took place at Jon Jandai's farm. Here Jon (right) works with Jo, a young architect who later quit his job and traversed the country to share with village groups how to build their homes. [Credit: Janell Kapoor]

families. It's a noose around our necks. But now we have the earth house, and we don't need to sell three generations of our family's hard work to have our homes."

Spreading the Word

Wongsanit tapped into its networks and helped generate a lot of media coverage during that first ten-day training. Word spread quickly, and invitations came from all directions. Jon and I, with the help of Wongsanit, decided to host Training #2, with the aim of supporting key pioneers of this budding movement. They would join in, get dirty and pass it on to many others.

The early pioneers who caught the mud bug were a dedicated bunch. Amongst them was Phairin Phongsura, a single

FIGURE 57.2. The first *bahn din* or "mud house" in Thailand was this meditation hut built at Wongsanit Ashram near Bangkok in 2001.
[Credit: Janell Kapoor]

mother who attended the first training. A couple years later, I got an email from Phairin, saying "Look teacher, what I do." Attached was a photo of one of the most beautiful earthen buildings I had ever seen. Apparently, Phairin had gone on to form a natural building collective with some of the villagers we had worked with. Their project won a national award for its architectural beauty.

Just Do It

During my three years of working in Thailand, one of the things that really impressed me was this: Someone with zero experience in earthen building, no workshops, no books, would just go do it. They didn't need to be told what to do. I had never seen anything like their willingness and capability in the West. They were not afraid of doing something wrong, and they did not need anyone to show them the details. For them, it was obvious what to do, and if they didn't know, they would figure it out. Making it happen, experimenting, having fun and being comfortable enough to just give it a try was the norm.

One day, Jon and I visited a monk who had dropped by our second training site for a few hours. By the time we showed up at his place, a couple of weeks

later, he had already built a whole hut! It had cute sculptures of flowers and mud lizards on it. All he had needed were a couple hours visiting our project, and voilà, he had made it happen.

By the time we arrived at a few other sites, people said they had seen us in a magazine or visited one of our projects and then gone home to build. There they were, smiling in front of their homes, ready to give us a tour. A common saying, coined by Jon, was "Just do it!" And that's exactly what was happening.

Assembly of the Poor and Mun Yeun

Attendees at our second training were part of a coalition called

FIGURE 57.3. Two years after the first earthen building training in Thailand, I received an e-mail with this photo from Phairin Phongsura. "Look teacher, what I do!"
[Credit: Phairin Phongsura]

"The Assembly of the Poor." This was a national alliance of hundreds of thousands of villagers who were saying *no* to modernization, and *yes* to their more traditional way of life. This coalition held a powerful presence in the country, including a seat in the government.

One of the groups of villagers that made up the Assembly had been flooded off their original homelands by a dam project. For four years, they fought to keep their land but ended up losing. In the process, they had become known for their struggle and garnered support from people all over the country. After a long, hard fight of demonstrations and petitions, they were given new land, and were ready to build their homes again. This group was called "Mun Yeun."

This amazing group of villagers asked if we could help them build the first earthen village in Thailand. "Of course!" was the only reply we knew. The villagers of Mun Yeun led the way, having their usual blast of fun throughout. I remember the first day of the month-long encampment in 2002. Many of the people there were brand new to both building and the mud, and in some cases, even new to Thailand.

None of this mattered as we joined together to move over one thousand adobes by hand. About a hundred of us formed a human chain from the adobe-making yard to the building site about a five-minute walk away. We could have stacked the bricks in batches on the one truck we had access to, but the classic brick toss got everyone involved and built community…just like that! It also created solidarity between us out-of-country volunteers and the villagers who were hosting us. Typically, they'd be a bit shy, but after the brick toss that first day, social barriers broke down more easily.

What does cross-cultural collaboration, rather than top-down "aid," look like? Through the international natural building network, I had spread the word, and over the course of our month at Mun Yeun, about 500 volunteers from 13 countries came to help. On a dirt-poor budget, we built a large council hall, completed four houses, and started five more. All the materials came directly from the land: an incredible variety of clays, sands and even several kinds of straw, as well as bamboo.

In the final week, a truck showed up, and a neighboring village dropped off enough palm fronds to thatch the 2,100 sq. ft. (195 m²) council hall. I still remember being mesmerized by the grace and deftness with which a couple of village guys fastened each sheath of thatch with tiny

FIGURE 57.4. A human chain of 100 international participants carries adobe bricks from the brickyard to the building site on the first day of the Mun Yeun encampment. Working together towards a common goal helped us to quickly break down cultural and language barriers. [Credit: Janell Kapoor]

bamboo twists that they had soaked and split with a machete just moments before. *Everything* came from the land. This was truly building from place—by community, for community.

Santi Asoke: Peace, No Sadness

Another opportunity to see how a little work could have far-reaching effects was with the group called Santi Asoke. This started with one of their lead monks who visited Jon and me at a training site. He was gracious, humble and ready to help spread earthen building. We forged a collaboration to build a project at one of the 18 Santi Asoke centers across Thailand. Every month, each center trains hundreds of villagers in self-reliance skills to support community-oriented ways of living while staying out of debt. Over the years, Santi Asoke created incredible community hubs, where everything was made in-house. Everything, that is, except the houses themselves.

So, we helped Santi Asoke with their first earthen building endeavor. It was mostly the youth of their community who came to help, like a school project. To this day, they are some of the best builders I've worked with. They worked hard for eight days until the walls and roof members of our 2,100 sq. ft. building (195 m²) were complete. After this, Santi Asoke's network officially adopted earthen building into its core curriculum; they would be sharing these new/old technologies with over 100,000 people per year. This was an amazing example of leverage—how one small project could scale up to that degree was deeply invigorating.

FIGURE 57.5. Local volunteers roofed the village council hall with palm fronds. The fronds were attached to the frame with bamboo "twist ties" split with a machete. [Credit: Janell Kapoor]

A Great Teacher

In Bangkok, there was a well-known center for nuns. It had beautiful and extensive grounds. Hundreds of people visited each day to walk the grounds and meditate in their hall. Jon and I were invited to support a building project there. The experience was profound. They made one of the most beautiful earthen buildings I have ever seen. They did it so swiftly, efficiently and with such grace, they barely got a drop of mud on themselves the whole time.

During the three years that I mudded it up in Thailand, I was deeply touched, profoundly inspired and incredibly motivated. I came to understand how potent natural building can be. Not as a building technique alone, but as a gateway for a regional movement to catalyze the future that so many want to create for themselves and their families.

Through stomping and lay-

FIGURE 57.6. People of many ages and nationalities cooperated to build Mun Yuen village. Here a Thai youth prepares *alis* or clay paint from local ingredients. [Credit: Janell Kapoor]

ing mixtures of mud, straw, rice husks and bamboo, people strengthened their connections to themselves and to each other and forged a new understanding of "home." They regained tactical tools and knowledge to live lives of peace, coherence and dignity. For me, this was a time that strengthened my ability to vision, to restore hope, to see new possibilities for humanity and to be in a rooted relationship with this most beautiful planet we are blessed to inhabit. I knew I would never be the same, and to this day, my time in Thailand is one of my greatest teachers.

RESOURCES

Organizations

• Ashevillage Institute and Sanctuary: **ashevillage.org**. Accelerates the design and implementation of local, nature-based, regenerative systems and thriving community-inspired culture.
• Kleiwerks International: **kleiwerks.org**. Hands-on natural building workshops with an emphasis on teacher training and movement building.

• Pun Pun Center for Self-reliance: **punpunthailand .org**. An organic farm, seed-saving center and sustainable living and learning center founded by Jon Jandai and Peggy Reents. They host workshops for both the Thai and international communities.

Natural Building Thrives in Argentina

58

MAX EDLESON

Argentina has experienced an incredible resurgence of interest in natural building since the turn of the millennium. Natural building is referred to as a "movement" there, and the term aptly describes that it is both a grouping of applied building techniques and a socio-cultural banner that brings people together and contains an expression of hope for a positive, non-violent future. I had the luck of being at the right place at the right time and with sufficient youthful naiveté to both witness and participate in this renaissance.

As I approached the end of a mostly intellectual college experience, I had identified that I wanted to learn to speak Spanish and to learn more about farming. This quest led me to the southern part of Argentina known as Patagonia where I apprenticed for a year at an organic farm and center for sustainability. Little did I know that I would spend the next seven years in El Bolsón, a small town tucked into remote Andean foothills with an interesting history and a thriving cultural environment.

This remote mountain valley had been home first to indigenous people, then for centuries was sparsely inhabited by only a few brave settlers. In the 1970s, it received an influx of people, many of them looking for refuge from the macabre hold that a military dictatorship had on the country at the time. When I arrived, I was immediately drawn to the families who had weathered cold winters and the hardships of homesteading, established functioning farms and craft businesses and emerged with their idealism intact. Round-pole carpentry was a standard method of construction given the abundance of wood, as was the use of river rock harvested from the two rivers that flow through the valley.

I traveled back to the US twice during my first years in Argentina. On my first trip back, my brother and I attended a gathering called "Build Here Now" held at the Lama Foundation in New Mexico. This gathering brought together many of the pioneers of the natural building resurgence in the US with those interested in learning. I met my wife-to-be Eva there as well as several other future friends and mentors, including Ianto Evans and Janell Kapoor.

On my next trip to the US, a year later, I engaged in a ten-week apprenticeship led by Janell who

MAX EDLESON *is a mason of devices for cooking and heating the home with wood. He also crafts metal, wood, words and web-sites, which are all guises for his main passion of growing food. Max lives with his family at the intersection of the Willamette Valley and the Oregon Coast Range. His work can be further explored at* firespeaking.com *and* handprintpress.com.

was actively involved in natural building education and empowerment through her organization Kleiwerks. She encouraged and coached us in the process of organizing workshops in our home communities as a means of propagating awareness about the techniques of natural building. At the time, I was working as a teacher at a Waldorf-inspired charter school in El Bolsón that needed a building to house the kindergarten. We organized a ten-day workshop in which Janell and Lydia Doleman, another North American natural builder, would join together with two knowledgeable local natural building enthusiasts, Jorge Belanko and Carlos Straub.

This ten-day workshop was a slingshot catalyst that helped launch natural building into the region with a momentum that is still growing a decade later. The *escuelita*, as the kindergarten building is called, was mostly built during the summer of 2003–04 and completed as the days grew shorter that fall. I remember fondly the days that the parents, many of them mothers, came each afternoon to apply the final burnished plaster so that their children could begin using the building. As a parent now, I understand more fully what these parents must have felt as they helped to complete a safe and inspiring place for their children to engage in their own first experience of community.

The building was designed by the parents under the guidance of Jorge and Carlos. One of the dads was an architect who was able to synthesize everyone's ideas into a floor plan. The specifics of wall and roof design were worked out through an organic process that involved discussion, model-making and full-scale mock-ups with sticks and strings. The children's needs drove the design and explain, for example, why the windows are at a comfortable height for kindergarteners to see outside rather than for adults. The desire to encourage the impulse for play led to both a recessed area and a loft that were designed with play and story time in mind.

The main part of the building was built with adobe bricks, many of which were made in work parties leading up to the workshop. One of Janell's many contributions to the project was to combine the sculptural possibilities of cob with the practicality of adobe bricks. A cob building of this size would have been a tremendous undertaking because of the volumes of wet

FIGURE 58.1. The *escuelita* kindergarten was built through a collaboration of parents, workshop students and both local and international instructors. The roofline and window placement were designed to let in a maximum of winter sunlight. [Credit: Max Edleson]

clay, sand and straw that would have had to be mixed and applied to the wall at a steady rate. With cob, the best bond results from a patient and continuous building process, much like building one huge clay coil pot. Adobe bricks, when viewed as predried units of cob, allow you to make, dry and stockpile ahead of time a large quantity of material that then can be laid in courses rapidly, because the dry bricks suck the moisture out of the mortar as you go.

Janell's style of hybrid adobe, complemented by a cobber's perspective that anything is possible, was a potent contribution to the region. Argentina has a very strong masonry tradition linked back through many generations to Italy, Spain and other European origins. Until quite recently, masonry construction was as commonplace there as stick-built houses are in North America. Adobe, with its low straw content, offered a lot of benefits, including economic savings and an investment in ecological conscience without some of the perceived limitations of straw-heavy mixes in a cool rainy climate. Passive solar considerations were paramount in the escuelita's design, and I think that the physical experience for many visitors of light flooding into the building during the cold but moderately sunny winters helped to solidify understanding of these important design criteria in the region.

The back part of the building, where a bathroom and small kitchen are located, was framed with round poles and then filled in with straw-clay. The straw-clay infill was done in the early autumn, and, as is too often the case, especially on the shady side of the building where good insulation is most valuable, we had challenges drying those walls out sufficiently before winter weather set in. The resulting mold growth was eventually brought in check by heating the space, which, of course, was only possible once the walls had been completed. This is a classic Catch-22 that many natural builders face, especially those interested in incorporating the exciting benefits of straw-clay. Jorge and other local builders have developed one solution to this dilemma in the form of predried straw-clay blocks.

This first workshop led to another one the following summer, which was equally successful. Two adjoining hexagons enclosed with straw-rich wattle-and-daub panels and a barrel oven were the start of a small bakery on school grounds in which parents could work to meet their quota of

FIGURE 58.2. Interior of the kindergarten at the escuelita, showing a recessed area designed for story time and a "tower" for playtime. The needs of the children drove the design process. [Credit: Max Edleson]

financial support for the school. These two workshops each attracted 20 participants, almost half of whom were from other countries. The support crew of teachers, collaborators and kitchen staff were almost as numerous, which contributed to the intense feeling of temporary community. Many of the participants from these two workshops have continued with natural building—some have even established centers and schools of their own where natural building is taught.

Before being swept up by the rising tide of natural building in the region, Jorge Belanko had already been fomenting the use of adobes, the building of barrel ovens and other appropriate technologies. His involvement in these workshops, and the results they had, inspired him to dedicate himself full-time to the craft, both through the construction of natural homes for others as well as through workshops; often times these two processes coincide. Jorge and a talented film producer named Gustavo Marangoni joined forces to create an educational DVD on natural building called *El Barro, Las Manos, La Casa* (in English: *Mud, Hands, a House*). Gustavo shadowed Jorge for a year and a half as he built several dwellings

and taught workshops. The result is an appealing and very useful primer on the why's and how's of natural building. In part thanks to this video, which was able to travel faster and more places than Jorge could physically, awareness of his work spread quickly and he has become a sort of alternative building national celebrity.

Carlos Straub, another of the original instructors, went on to help found Centro de Investigación, Desarollo y Enseñanza en Permacultura (CIDEP) (the Center for Permaculture Research, Development and Education), where ongoing workshops and many great examples of natural building have inspired hundreds of people. Carlos has a special talent for bringing people together; he counts human dynamics and the experience of the group as equally or more important than the construction of buildings, the design of supporting infrastructure and the agricultural methods in the adjoining fields. He has helped to coach the birth of a good number of sister organizations in other parts of Argentina and neighboring countries.

Paulina Avila was a participant in that first workshop. Her previous construction experience coupled with her immediate affinity for natural finishing tech-

niques set her on a path of prolific creation. She has spearheaded many projects, given the finishing touches to many more and been a tireless educator, organizing many workshops to share her skills. Among the workshops she has been instrumental in organizing is a natural building festival called BioConstruyendo, which has become an annual event and recently completed its fifth year. Imagine elements such as youthful energy, music, sacred geometry and community all mixed into a week-long natural building educational event.

Hundreds of natural buildings have been built in Patagonia during the last decade. Some of these are on private land in remote locations, but more and more are public buildings or very publicly visible. Jorge recently told me that never even in his wildest dreams could he have imagined the extent of interest in natural building techniques at this juncture in Argentina. Why was Argentina so ripe for this movement, and what can those of us in other lands learn from its example?

Many of the early natural buildings were built in part through workshop experiences, which has meant not only that the buildings stand as examples but also that the people involved in creating them have traveled and then returned to apply these techniques in their locales and thus helped to spread the ideas quickly. Another interesting phenomenon that has evolved is called the "Mingga." This is a word borrowed from the Mapuche, the indigenous people of Southern Argentina and Chile,

FIGURE 58.3. This photo was taken at the conclusion of a natural building workshop led by Jorge Belanko (center back, in white cap) and Max Edleson (to the left of him). The workshop took place in a Mapuche community that had reclaimed their ancestral land from the police, who had built a rural station there. [Credit: Firespeaking]

that essentially means "work party." In the natural building context, *Mingga* refers both to work parties as well as to a group of people who routinely rotate helping each other out on projects. Someone who is building a house may call a series of Minggas when they have reached the wall-building stage; a group of people will show up who the host has likely already helped in the past or will plan to help in the future. This is another way that exposure to natural building has spread quickly and is very different from most people's experiences with the building trades.

Argentina has gone through a lot of political changes in not so many decades, and it may be that the political upheaval has encouraged people to rely on themselves and their communities rather than waiting for the government to act. At the same time, I also observed what seemed to be an earnest investment on the part of the government in the cultural life of its people. One of the mechanisms by which cultural evolution occurs at the governmental level is through a novel and layered system of "declaration of public interest." In the last ten years, natural building has been declared of public interest at countless municipal levels, at several

of the provincial levels (akin to the state level) and then recently at a national level. This means that the equivalent of the House of Representatives has stated that natural building should be known about by citizens and legislators across the country. This declaration facilitates the provision of funds for projects within its umbrella. For example, Jorge's and Gustavo's DVD received some financial assistance through a national development grant. While natural building had a nonexistent role in architectural curriculums just a few years ago, there are now programs and specific classes at some of the largest and most prominent universities in Argentina.

What techniques are popular in Argentina? In some parts, particularly in Northern Argentina, adobe simply continues to be the way to build, as it has for centuries. For those in other areas just discovering adobe, there are brick and block masonry buildings everywhere to serve as references for basic technique.

In the region where El Bolsón is located, a version of wattle and daub, referred to as "pared francés" or the "French wall," was also very popular among early settlers. In this technique, a cane that grows abundantly in the area, like small bamboo but with a solid core, was attached horizontally to both the inside and outside faces of framing members, leaving a cavity into which soil was packed. The wall surfaces were then plastered. Jorge has found that adding sifted sand, which was probably a luxury then, and some fiber to these original plasters strengthens them in renovations.

In the more recent resurgence of interest, a simpler wattle-and-daub technique has been used widely. This involves nailing cane, willow or other coppiced wood horizontally onto the wall framing to create a single plane of lath. A first coat of earth mix,

usually containing some fiber, is integrated into this matrix. Subsequent layers, like very thick plasters, build the wall out to desired thicknesses. This technique finds wide application because of how easy it is to enclose and delineate spaces; it offers a very tangible way to make simple outbuildings and even dwellings.

A more modern approach to this technique substitutes new or recycled wire mesh or, often times, recycled fencing material, as a quick lattice. This method gives the additional advantage of being able to prehang elaborate designs of bottles and recycled glass to create low-tech stained

glass. The glass is carefully cut and tied to the metal mesh with wire. Once the first plaster coat has mostly set up and is structurally sound (ceramicists refer to this stage as "leather-hard"), any visible mesh or wire is snipped and the edges are detailed to further define the glass shapes. Many of these techniques are described in the DVD, *Mud, Hands, a House*.

One of the shortcomings of the initial experiences with natural building in this recent resurgence was a lack of emphasis on the importance of insulation. Many of the initial natural buildings followed the local custom of putting little or no insulation in roofs and walls. In response, my brother and I built a house mainly using straw bales—the first instance of bale walls that I knew of in the valley. It also had a living roof, whose insulative value is arguable, especially during the wet winter when the soil layer is saturated.

Exploration with different insulative techniques has picked up since then. Light straw-clay is employed to some degree. Of particular interest, however, is a variation of straw-clay called *bloques térmicos*; in English they can be referred to as light straw-clay blocks. These blocks are essentially predried units of

FIGURE 58.4. These earthen bas-reliefs and clay paints surround other artistic glass and carpentry work in a wire mesh wattle-and-daub wall. The clay finish work was applied during a workshop led by Eva Edleson at the community building of the Rio Azul community. [Credit: Eva Edleson]

straw-clay with two hollow cores, usually slightly larger than but shaped similar to the common cinder block. They are roughly 10×10×20 in. (25 × 25 × 50 cm) with two 5 in.-diameter (12.5 cm) cylindrical cores made by inserting a PVC pipe into the form. The hollow cores assist in drying, make them lighter for transport and also provide an opportunity for vertical reinforcement. Cutting a notch in the top surface of the blocks allows for horizontal reinforcement as well, making a grid of cane, bamboo or rebar to stabilize the wall.

Another interesting variation that they were developing at CIDEP was panels 3–4 in. thick (8–10 cm), made of a similar material with an embedded cane lattice. These panels were being experimented with for insulating ceilings and could potentially also be used in stud-framed walls. The panels were even made in such a way that the outer half-inch (one centimeter) of material included sand and smaller straw such that it would accept a coat of plaster better than the insulative mix.

The fact that these blocks and panels can be made, dried, stored and transported offers some great advantages. It allows, for example, for the construction of straw-clay walls at a later stage in the season when drying conditions have slowed or are nonexistent. Manufacturing blocks and panels also provides a good small business opportunity; several building collectives have been organized around their production.

Straw-clay blocks are now being used widely in Southern Argentina. A good example is the work of architect/engineer Claudio Rivero. Claudio is a "backwoods" engineer who, with his wife and design collaborator, Rosalín, left an engineering practice in a major city for the clear air and breathtaking views of Patagonia. They have developed a thriving design/build practice leveraged by their ability to apply engineering ingenuity to simple solutions and locally available materials. These credentials have allowed them to carry out very public projects, including a healing center in the middle of the town of El Bolsón, by providing sufficient engineering to satisfy building code officials while still being able to incorporate both the ecological and artistic aspects of natural building.

One design system Claudio has come up with and used on several high-profile buildings is to use discarded steel pipe from the petroleum industry in Patagonia to create a building superstructure that officials can understand and approve. The walls are then filled in with different natural wall systems and strategically situated glass to create a passive solar envelope. Claudio reminded me that if not repurposed in this way, the steel pipe would otherwise be discarded, and that it is the task of all of us in our locations to identify such useful

FIGURE 58.5. The author built this masonry heater with a heated bench to the left and water heating capacity. Everything for this heater was sourced within a mile from its location, except for the metal for the hardware, which was purchased but then fabricated within five miles. For more on Max and Eva's work with earthen building and masonry heaters, see firespeaking.com. [Credit: Eva Edleson]

materials in the waste stream and creatively incorporate them into our building strategies.

El Bolsón may have been the first municipality to incorporate a building code for the use of natural materials (other than wood), but many other cities in the country have followed suit. In fact, Jorge tells me that one of the challenges as more government-funded programs are training natural builders is that a parallel training will be necessary for code officials in the service of enforcing these new codes. The irony of the people whose work will be regulated having to conduct trainings for their future inspectors and enforcers demonstrates the organic process of cultural evolution which I think is typical in Argentina, where people seem to have an interesting mix of tradition, openness, perspective on changes in economy and government, resilience, fun and a great sense of humor about it all. Some of the early natural buildings may have looked primitive to tradespeople, but they reflected a democratic process of research out of which important innovation is still being developed.

At one point in Jorge's video, after talking about the negative ecological impact from the production of cement and describing how we have been made to believe that the products available at the hardware store are superior through calculated marketing backed by significant investment, he asks, "Who is doing the advertising for the soil beneath our feet?" If I learned one thing during the seven years I lived in Argentina, it is that cultural excitement, hands-on experience and the shared joy of working together are some of the few but potent elements that can compete with advertising by big businesses in helping us to make decisions that impact our own and other people's lives.

RESOURCES

Video
• *Mud, Hands, a House* (*El barro, las manos, la casa*). 2007, 116 minutes. An excellent how-to DVD which teaches many of the basic techniques of natural building and features Jorge Belanko. Spanish with English subtitles. Available at **handprintpress.com/mud-hands -a-house**.

Organizations and Businesses
• CIDEP (Center for Development and Education in Permaculture): **cidep.org**. A great team of people who offer courses in permaculture, natural building, organic gardening and nutrition. El Bolsón, Argentina.

• Firespeaking: **firespeaking.com**. Max and Eva Edleson's venture which specializes in the construction of masonry heaters, wood-fired ovens and natural finishes. An inspiring portfolio and example of a family-run craft-based business.
• Handprint Press: **handprintpress.com**. A cooperative publishing venture that offers relevant publications and updated articles, including a focus within natural building on wood-fired ovens and do-it-yourself home-heating.
• Kleiwerks: **kleiwerks.org**. Hands-on natural building workshops with an emphasis on teacher training and movement building.

Builders Without Borders

59

CATHERINE WANEK

Whatever you do will be insignificant,
but it is very important that you do it.

« Mahatma Gandhi »

A natural outgrowth of the revival of natural building is a desire to share these sustainable ideas with others. In 1999, during the war in Kosovo, I watched on TV how American bombs were destroying homes and infrastructure as winter was coming. After discussing this all-too-common situation with a few straw bale colleagues here in New Mexico, I hosted a gathering of a small group of natural building designers, builders and advocates to discuss how we might somehow offer help. Builders Without Borders (BWB) was created that chilly day in December.

Our ideas were informed and inspired by the activities of The Canelo Project in a poor but vibrant neighborhood in Ciudad Obregón, Sonora, Mexico. In this farming region, which produced two crops of wheat annually, Athena and Bill Steen were working with local builders and their families to create affordable straw bale homes from available materials. Together they had discovered simple solutions to working with poor-quality straw bales, including mixing mud and straw into lightweight adobe blocks, and a technique known as "exterior pinning," or the "corset system."

Conventionally, bale builders were pinning courses of bales together by pounding rebar, bamboo or wooden stakes down through them. The Steens discovered that it is both easier and stronger to place two pins vertically on each side of the bale wall, connecting the pins with twine or wire sewn horizontally between the bales. Cinching these pins tightly together firmed up an otherwise unstable wall. The Steens used a local reed called *carrizo*, but in other regions, bamboo or any plentiful sapling (or even plastic pipes or metal rods) can serve the same purpose.

The Steens' work evolved into an initiative they called *Casas Que Cantan* (Houses that Sing). They

CATHERINE WANEK *is a founding member and current codirector of Builders Without Borders. In 1999 she originated "Build Here Now" at the Lama Foundation in New Mexico, and in 1995 co-hosted (along with Pete Fust and the Cob Cottage Company) the first Natural Building Colloquium at her historic bed and breakfast, the Black Range Lodge, in Kingston, New Mexico.*

FIGURE 59.1. Working in Ciudad Obregón, Mexico, with extreme budgetary constraints, Athena and Bill Steen evolved a model of self-help housing by organizing week-long hands-on workshops in which participants and local families worked side by side building comfortable homes from locally available materials. [Credit: Catherine Wanek]

FIGURE 59.2. Builders Without Borders worked with the National Indian Youth Leadership Project (NIYLP) to build an earth-plastered straw bale hogan near Laguna Pueblo. [Credit: Catherine Wanek]

organized several families into a self-help cooperative in which each family helped the others build a decent home for around US$500 in materials. The Steens helped by raising the funds from US donors and brought workshop participants to build the walls and roof and get the first coat of earthen plaster on. These modest homes were often finished with limewash, and the floors made of salvaged concrete chunks from demolished construction, dubbed "urbanite."

Other inspirations for BWB were initiatives in Mongolia and China introduced by the Adventist Development Relief Agency (ADRA). In a multi-year project, they brought energy-efficient straw bale technology into areas with extremely long cold winters, saving up to 75 percent of the coal required to heat conventional buildings. Working mostly with local builders, ADRA brought only a few experienced architects and builders over the years to teach teachers, including Matts Myhrman, Steve MacDonald, Frank Meyer, Paul Lacinski and Kelly Lerner. In 2005, ADRA and architect Kelly Lerner received the coveted World Habitat Award for building over 600 energy- and carbon-saving homes in China (see "Straw Bales in China: Housing for the People," p. 391). And, in Belarus, a government initiative led by Evgeny Shirokov built nearly 100 straw bale homes for families displaced by the 1986 Chernobyl nuclear accident, at one-quarter the cost of a typical brick home.

Thus, BWB did not emerge in a vacuum, but as a logical extension of inspiring work that was already springing up in the straw bale network. Among those present at that first meeting were Alfred von Bachmayr, Steve MacDonald, Joe Kennedy, Derek Roff and several more. While we never made it to war-torn Kosovo, this coming together established a new network of natural builders with a desire to promote and educate about sustainable building solutions, especially in places of need, with a focus on utilizing locally available natural materials and human resources. BWB became a 501(c)3 non-profit entity, and funding was generally raised on a project-by-project basis.

We began with projects relatively close to home in New Mexico, working with the National Indian Youth Leadership Project (NIYLP) to build an earth-plastered straw bale hogan near Laguna Pueblo. Next we were asked to help across the border from El Paso, Texas, in Anapra, an unincorporated suburb of Juarez, Chihuahua, Mexico. Along this border, the typical home is built from shipping pallets, wired together to form walls, and finished with tar-paper siding. While concrete block homes represented a huge improvement, the price of a single bag of cement was equivalent to a week's wages for the average working man, so few families could afford this luxury.

By locating local sources of clay, free for the digging, and of straw, we sourced low-cost materials for BWB buildings. In the absence of affordable wood for roofing, architect Alfred von Bachmayr developed roof trusses that could be fashioned from shipping pallets. Over about a decade, working with local builders, Alfred helped create a cottage industry based on these "pallet trusses" and a local natural building vernacular using clay-plastered straw-clay infill in pallet walls, as a solution to the expense of cement, wood and other conventional materials (see "Mechanizing Straw-Clay," p. 250).

As individuals, we found it more practical to work within our geographical regions. Yet the rapid growth of the Internet allowed us to network globally. BWB began partnering with other organizations, supporting Joe Kennedy and the Next-Aid organization to teach and build with earthbags in South Africa, and designer Michal Vital and NGO Bustan to create

FIGURE 59.3. Builders Without Borders' first home building project in Anapra, Mexico, was for the family of José Luis Rocha, a respected builder in the neighborhood. [Credit: Catherine Wanek]

424 The Art of Natural Building

a straw bale clinic for nomadic Bedouins in Israel. In 2005, an international BWB design/build team (Colorado engineer Jeff Ruppert, builder Paul Koppana and plasterer Cindy Smith, and Hungarian Jakub Wihan) traveled to Russia to assist Alyson Ewald, of the Altai Project, in creating an education center in the majestic Altai region of southern Siberia. BWB also became a fiscal sponsor of the work of Darcey Donovan, who leads the Pakistan Straw Bale and Appropriate Building (PAKSBAB) organization (see "Seismically Safe Straw Bale

Buildings in Pakistan," p. 403). We also hosted educational workshops, organized a straw bale tour for the Mongolian code delegation (thanks to Susan Klinker), published a Straw Bale Construction Curriculum (in English and Spanish, thanks to Owen Geiger and Katia LeMone) and offered advice and educational materials where we couldn't give a physical presence or money.

In 2008, we were invited to build an exhibit at the US Botanical Garden (USBG) on the National Mall in Washington, DC as part of the "One Planet,

Ours!" exhibition. I organized and coordinated a talented team of builders and volunteers to create the BWB display that included a straw bale "Ecohouse," a bamboo shade structure and an adobe/cob arch which framed a view of the US Capitol.

During construction and the four-month exhibition, many thousands of passersby were exposed to the idea of straw bale and natural building. While initially somewhat skeptical (after all, we tracked mud into their hallways, and errant straw marred their impeccable planting beds),

FIGURE 59.4. The Builders Without Borders Ecohouse was an exciting opportunity to create a demonstration of traditional, sustainable building methods on the national mall in Washington, DC. The BWB building team was hosted by the U.S. Botanic Garden and supported by numerous sponsors. [Credit: Catherine Wanek]

the USBG ultimately extended our four-month tenure and kept the BWB Ecohouse onsite until the following spring. Early one magical morning in March 2009, a large crane lifted the Ecohouse onto a waiting trailer, and it was transported to Maryland and incorporated into a healing center. See a ten-minute video of this exciting project at the BWB website.

Do all of these efforts add up to anything more than a drop in the ocean? Often it seems that the need is endless and at the end of the day not much has changed. What we accomplished does sometimes seem insignificant, but it was important that we did it.

We found that staying small and working on one nearby building project at a time had the effect of focusing resources, time and energy within a local community. Also, by partnering with other organizations, we managed to contribute a small but important piece to a project far away on another part of the planet. Sometimes, even drops in the ocean produce ripples with meaningful and beneficial effects on the lives of others.

As an international network of ecological builders working together for a sustainable future, BWB is essentially all of you out there who are contributing to the art and joy of natural building. It inspires me to know that there are dozens, perhaps hundreds, maybe even thousands of grassroots organizations on this planet, made up of individuals giving of themselves to advance the health and comfort of fellow human beings by spreading the knowledge of natural building materials—because these materials are inherently available to all peoples, everywhere, if they can but (re)learn how to house themselves.

FIGURE 59.5. A Builders Without Borders straw bale training workshop in Kingston, New Mexico. [Credit: Pete Fust]

Sustainable (Re)Building in Haiti

by Martin Hammer

Within days of Haiti's devastating earthquake in January of 2010, I began thinking of how Haiti would rebuild, and how it could rebuild sustainably. Seven weeks later, I arrived in Haiti with a reconnaissance team from the Earthquake Engineering Research Institute, documenting building performance; then I went again a month later with a team from the World Monuments Fund, working to preserve historic buildings. But all the while, I was also exploring possibilities for sustainable rebuilding.

Most building materials in Haiti are imported (including cement, steel and most wood), and materials harvested in-country, such as sand and gravel, cause environmental damage when mined. Discussion began among my natural building colleagues about whether straw bale construction was viable in Haiti's tropical climate. Rice is grown in Haiti, and rice straw can be baled manually, as I learned when working with PAKSBAB in Pakistan. But would straw walls survive Haiti's high humidity, heavy rain and annual hurricanes? We decided the only way to know was to make a straw bale building and see how it held up.

Under the auspices of Builders Without Borders, I teamed with Andy Mueller of GreenSpace Collaborative to design and build Haiti's first straw bale building. The design team was rounded out with architect Dan Smith and engineer Henri Mannik, PE. We borrowed the construction system developed in Pakistan, but the building's architectural form was derived from the *ti kay* (small house), the traditional rural living unit in Haiti.

In 2011, the Ti Kay Pay, or "small

FIGURE 59.6. The Ti Kay Pay (small straw house) demonstration building, built with seismic and hurricane forces in mind, was Builders Without Borders' answer to rebuilding after Haiti's devastating earthquake in 2010. [Credit: Martin Hammer]

straw house," was constructed in Port-au-Prince, on the site of partner organization Haiti Communitere. It features a gravel bag foundation and straw bale walls stiffened with bamboo and finished with earthen plaster. Unlike the Pakistan buildings, we employed wire "X" braces instead of mesh to resist earthquakes and high winds. Wood from shipping pallets was used in the roof trusses, and bamboo rafters support the veranda roof. Roof-caught rainwater fills two rain barrels, and a small photovoltaic system powers the lights.

Haitian trainees Jean Louis Elie, Annio Baptiste, and Samuel Alcide became integral members of the construction team, along with Tina Therrien of Camel's Back Construction, and Mark Phillips, who contributed to both the funding and the building. During construction, in an interview with CBC Radio-Canada, Jean Louis Elie stated, "When people see the construction, then they really accept it. Because it's ours. The straw is ours. We make it, we live in it.... If we had this kind of house [before the earthquake], less people would have died."

In 2012, Andy Mueller initiated BWB's next project in Haiti. Named the Senp Kay, or "simple house," it was constructed with two wall systems: a tilt-up wood frame system with plastic bottle infill and wire mesh inside and out and a built-in-place wood frame with straw-clay infill. The plastic bottle walls, also called "bottle-and-daub," received cement plaster outside and earth plaster inside. The light straw-clay wall is reinforced with horizontal bamboo and received earth plaster inside and out. The plastic bottle system is seen as an urban solution (with more bottles generated in the city) and the light straw-clay system a rural solution, especially where straw is available from nearby rice farming.

How has the first house of straw bales performed in Haiti's climate? After three years and two hurricanes, the 29 moisture sensors installed in the bale walls have shown that straw can in fact last in Haiti's tropical climate when the building is well designed, constructed and maintained.

MARTIN HAMMER is an architect in Berkeley, California, and co-director of Builders Without Borders.

FIGURE 59.7. The Senp Kay (simple house) is a panelized system, using a simple wooden frame, filled with empty plastic soda bottles, covered with metal mesh, then plastered with clay, lime or cement plaster. [Credit: Andy Mueller]

RESOURCES

Organizations

• Builders Without Borders (BWB): **builderswithout borders.org**. An international network of ecological builders working together for a sustainable future.

• Bustan: **Bustan.org**. An Israeli NGO working in the Bedouin and Jewish communities in the Negev region of Israel since 1999, promoting sustainability and capacity building from within communities. Bustan and the village of Qasr A-Sir are working together to create a new development model for Bedouins in the Negev.

• The Canelo Project: **caneloproject.com**. Founded in 1989 by Bill and Athena Steen, this small non-profit offers high-quality workshops, internships, demonstrations and cross-cultural gatherings at their inspiring center in south-central Arizona.

• The Centre for Alternative Technology (CAT): **cat .org.uk**. An ecological demonstration center and a fun place to visit in Wales, UK, with interactive technology displays, permaculture gardens, a rammed earth bookstore, many other natural buildings, plus a series of sustainability workshops.

• Global Ecovillage Network (GEN): **gen.ecovillage .org**. This network of ecologically conscious communities includes early pioneers Findhorn in Scotland, Sieben Linden in Germany, The Farm in Tennessee, and Crystal Waters in Australia, plus a multitude of ecovillages springing up all over the world.

• Haiti Communitere: **haiti.communitere.org**.

• Help Hayti: **helphayti.org**.

• Kleiwerks International: **Kleiwerks.org**. An educational non-profit based in Asheville, North Carolina, that organizes events and trainings and promotes whole systems solutions to ecological regeneration and social transformation.

• Nordic Folkecenter for Renewable Energy: **folke center.net**. A research center with full-scale photovoltaic systems, biogas and wind technology—in a region that many days can produce 150 percent of its electricity needs from wind power. By offering training and technology transfer packages, their work reaches Asia and Africa. Their home base, the Village for Green Research, near Hurup, Denmark, is open to the public.

Periodical

• *The Last Straw Journal* (TLS): **thelaststraw.org**. *The International Journal of Straw Bale and Natural Building*, TLS provides online access to code information, organizational and human resources, while the quarterly journal keeps pace with the latest developments in the field.

Book

• Kennedy, Joseph F. (ed.). *Building Without Borders: Sustainable Construction for the Global Village*, New Society Publishers, 2004. An anthology of articles describing lessons learned from sustainable building and technology projects across the globe.

Websites

• BWB Ecohouse blog: **breathworkstudio.blogspot .com**. See how the Ecohouse built for the US Botanical Garden has transformed and evolved.

• Geiger Research Institute for Sustainable Building: **GRISB.org**. Good resource for code information and home plans, from Owen Geiger.

• Natural Building Network (NBN): **naturalbuilding network.org**. Membership-based non-profit education and outreach organization dedicated to making sustainable and regenerative healthy habitation more universally accessible, desirable and plausible. An online meeting place for the widespread community of natural builders, listing workshops, events, opportunities and human resources.

• The Natural Building Colloquium: **nbnetwork.org**. Natural builders coming together to share knowledge in the form of hands-on workshops, presentations and group conversations.

Ecovillages and Sustainable Communities

JOSEPH F. KENNEDY

The way we construct and inhabit human landscapes is destroying our capacity to live on this planet, and we have approached, if not exceeded, the ecological limit of human activities the Earth can sustain. If we are to have a tolerable planet to live on, we need to choose a new way to dwell. Ecovillages are one way we can manifest positive choices in how we live. They are communities that strive to combine the best of traditional approaches to building, farming and energy production (among others) with emerging innovations in those fields.

Why ecovillages? Why now? Ecovillages meet our fundamental need for community. In addition, ecovillages support the notion of right livelihood, where shared, local, satisfying work can minimize commuting and environmental impact. Ecovillages are diverse,

JOSEPH F. KENNEDY *has lived and worked in ecovillage projects in the US, Argentina, Ireland and South Africa.*

where people of different ages, races, incomes and spiritual paths are accepted within a common vision.

Although the term "ecovillage" is relatively new, perhaps dating from the mid-1980s, communities like these have been around for much longer. Communities inspired by Rudolf Steiner, like

Sólheimar in Iceland and Järna in Sweden, emerged in the late 1920s and early 1930s and continue to this day. The concept continued to evolve through the Danish cohousing movement. The first Ecovillages and Sustainable Communities conference was held in Scotland in 1994 and gave rise to the Global Ecovillage

FIGURE 60.1. In Bruges, Belgium, a farmers' market provides opportunity for commerce and social connection. Traditional urban environments have helped revive the idea of a "city of villages" now currently promoted in cities like San Diego, California. [Credit: Catherine Wanek]

Network, a non-governmental umbrella organization. Ecovillages have now been formed on five continents, and interest in the concept continues to grow exponentially.

Certain features characterize ecovillages. In order to maximize trust and cooperation, their populations are usually less than 500 people. The full range of human activity is supported through facilities for residence, work, leisure, social activity and commerce. In addition, ecovillages actively support the health of their residents on a physical, emotional and spiritual level. Ecovillages come in many sizes and shapes. A fundamental description is that they foster the intersection of community and sustainability on any scale.

Creating an Ecovillage

There are a number of challenges in the creation of a successful community. Ecovillage planners realize that a sustainable process is as important as a sustainable village and place a strong emphasis on all phases of the project, from initial research and development, through creation and implementation, to ongoing maintenance and renewal.

When people decide to build an ecovillage, they must first determine how decisions will be made and how things will get done. Ecovillages generally value democratic participation by all resident members, but there are often committees or "circles" charged with certain areas of responsibility. To live peacefully at the high densities typical of

ecovillages requires highly developed social skills and careful community design. This is perhaps the most challenging aspect of living in such a community. Ecovillages are at the forefront of the development and refinement of effective communication and decision-making processes for non-hierarchical groups.

Many ecovillages are in rural locations, which provide the natural resources and way of life sought by their residents. However, others in the ecovillage movement feel that taking land away from nature for human habitation is a serious breach of principle. As a result, some very exciting work is being done with urban restoration of brownfield sites into ecovillages. This is especially true in the cohousing form of ecovillage. Swan's Market in Oakland, California, is an inspiring example of reclaiming blighted urban space for regenerative purposes.

Whether rural or urban, numerous factors must be considered when deciding upon a site for an ecovillage. The more ideal the site, the better the chance for success. Some of the variables to consider when selecting a site include: the size and price of the land; climate; availability and quality of water and other natural

FIGURE 60.2. Gathering as a community at the Lama Foundation spiritual community near taos, New Mexico. [Credit: Catherine Wanek]

resources; existing buildings and other improvements; government regulations and restrictions; commercial development potential; access to roads, public transportation, electricity and other utilities; proximity to surrounding communities; and physical site factors such as slope, aspect and geology.

Once a site is chosen, the planning process is initiated. The process must be flexible and sensitive, engaging the future residents in a participatory process. Ecovillage designers draw on lessons from many disciplines, including architecture, planning, wilderness conservation, ecology and landscape design to create as rich and diverse a physical and social landscape as possible.

Before beginning any physical changes, the group undertakes a holistic land-planning process. This determines the carrying capacity of the site and the placement of elements, through a "zone and sector" analysis (see "The Permaculture House," p. 107). Access and energy flows, social zones and special places are all discussed and mapped through numerous iterations until a mutually agreed upon plan has been developed. Such a plan will consider the following.

Ecosystem

In creating an ecovillage, natural habitats for wildlife must be preserved. Soil, air, water and biodiversity are carefully preserved or improved. Waste products are

FIGURE 60.3. The FrogSong cohousing community in Cotati, California, features energy-efficient compact design, community spaces and permaculture gardens. [Credit: Joseph F. Kennedy]

recycled or managed onsite. Eco-villagers also endeavor to obtain food, wood and other biological resources from the region, or, ideally, from the site itself.

The Built Environment

Houses and other structures are designed to use ecologically friendly materials and renewable energy sources. Planning minimizes the need for automobiles in favor of walking and biking. Proper siting of buildings reduces the impact of construction on local plants and animals. For social harmony, a balance between public and private space is crucial. Cluster development encourages community interaction and minimizes the physical footprint of structures. The full range of human activity is designed for, from work to play and from quiet time to community gatherings. Some communities have strived to attain green certifications. An example is Sonoma Mountain Village, an ambitious reclaiming of a disused corporate campus in northern California, which is one of the initial One Planet Communities, and as such adheres to a very strict code of social and ecological sustainability.

Economics

Ecovillages attempt to reduce exploitation of other people, distant places and future generations through fair and sustainable practices and policies. Ecovillage residents must also discover sustainable economic activities for themselves. Some of the challenging questions include: Will ownership of land and buildings be handled privately or cooperatively? Are there alternatives to the money economy, including barter, local currency and the like? How can ecovillages be ecologically and economically efficient at the same time?

Governance

Ecovillage residents must create a structure for community decision-making. How will conflicts between people be resolved? How will group decisions be enforced? What will be expected of leaders, if any? How will the ecovillage deal with local and national governments? These social experiments are valuable laboratories for innovative strategies to better get along.

Group Vision

A strong shared vision is one of the most important factors that holds an ecovillage together. Is the community composed of

FIGURE 60.4. A volunteer and local child cooking together at Tlholego Village, South Africa. [Credit: Joseph F. Kennedy]

RESOURCES

Books

• Bang, Jan Martin. *Ecovillages: A Practical Guide to Sustainable Communities*, New Society Publishers, 2005.

• Christian Diana, Leafe. *Creating a Life Together: Practical Tools to Grow Ecovillages and Intentional Communities*, New Society Publishers, 2003. An amazing resource sure to save much time and heartache for those wanting to embark on the ecovillage adventure.

• ___. *Finding Community: How to Join an Ecovillage or Intentional Community*, New Society Publishers, 2007. Useful advice from an author who has studied intentional community more than perhaps any other.

• *Communities Directory: A Guide to Intentional Communities and Cooperative Living*, Fellowship for Intentional Community, 2000. This incredible book lists and describes over 700 intentional communities around the world, along with relevant books and organizations. More current information can be found at: **ic.org /directory**.

• Corbett, Judy and Michael Corbett. *Designing Sustainable Communities: Learning from Village Homes*, Island Press, 2000. A book with information and examples of how, through proper planning and development, it is possible to create successful communities.

• Dawson, Jonathan. *Ecovillages: New Frontiers for Sustainability*, Green Books/Chelsea Green, 2006. An important book from a European pioneer.

• *Directory of Ecovillages in Europe*, GEN-Europe, 1998. Available for DM30, Euro15 from GEN-Europe, Ginsterweg 5, 31595 Steyerberg, Germany. An excellent compendium of ecovillage projects in Europe, with useful descriptions of each one.

• Jackson, Hildur and Karen Svensson, eds. *Ecovillage Living: Restoring the Earth and Her People*, Gaia Trust, 2003. A profusely illustrated overview of ecovillages around the world.

• Joubert, Kosha and Robin Alfred, eds. *Beyond You and Me: Inspiration and Wisdom for Building Community*, Green Publishing, 2007. The first volume in the "Social Key" ecovillage anthology produced by GEN's Ecovillage Design Education (EDE) Program. Also available as a download (Google "Beyond You and Me.pdf").

• Park, Chad, Mike Purcell and John Purkis. *Integrated Community Sustainability Planning Guide*, The Natural Step, Canada. 2009. Is it possible to have a truly sustainable building in an unsustainable community? This is a thoughtful guide to making more communities more sustainable. Available free online at **norcalapa .org/wp-content/uploads/2012/04/ICSP-A_Guide.pdf**.

• Walker, Liz. *EcoVillage at Ithaca: Pioneering Sustainable Community*, New Society Publishers, 2005. The inspiring story of this pioneering ecovillage.

Organizations

• The Cohousing Association of the United States: **cohousing.org**. Central clearinghouse for cohousing information, with a directory of cohousing communities by state.

• Ecovillage Network of the Americas: **gen-na.eco village.org**. A whole-systems immersion experience of ecovillage living, together with classes of instruction; access to information, tools and resources; and on-site and off-site consulting and outreach experiences.

• The Fellowship for Intentional Community: **ic.org**. FIC promotes community living and cooperative lifestyles. Publisher of *Communities* magazine and the *Communities Directory*.

• Global Ecovillage Network: **gen.ecovillage.org**. Learn more about the concept of ecovillages as well as find where they are around the world.

• One Planet Communities: **oneplanetcommunities .org**. This is perhaps one of the most ambitious sustainability initiatives on the planet. By working with private and public property developers, One Planet aims to help create places where it is easy, attractive and affordable for people to lead healthy, happy lives within a fair share of the Earth's resources.

FIGURE 60.5. The performance space for the Youth With a Vision project, Dennilton, South Africa. [Credit: Joseph F. Kennedy]

individuals with divergent views, or are there common values regarding community life? What should be the balance between unity of purpose and diversity of views? Are the members close interpersonally, or do they lead separate private lives? How does the community relate to those outside the ecovillage? How will the ecovillage evolve over time?

There are no easy or right answers to these questions. Success depends on many factors, including the location and qualities of the site and the willingness of its residents to work through the many questions and conflicts that may arise. Good documentation of agreements is crucial for successful long-term community. Many believe that the process of creating ecovillages is crucial for human survival. Happily, increasing numbers of people are willing to take on the challenge. They see the manifestation of this new vision as not only necessary, but filled with immeasurable rewards—those of a life of hope.

Tlholego Village—A Sustainable Community in South Africa

PAUL COHEN

For diverse reasons—separation policies during apartheid, the proliferation of large farm systems and rapid industrialization and subsequent migration to urban areas—many South Africans have become alienated from formerly self-reliant rural areas in recent decades. Policies of mobile labor have disrupted family structures, forcing workers to leave their partners, dependent children and elders in depressed rural villages.

Despite newfound political freedom in recent years, many South Africans still face significant obstacles to achieving economic freedom. In addition to the challenges of entering a highly competitive global economy, the millions of South Africans living in poverty have an overwhelming need for land, jobs, housing and food. Efforts to resettle these

PAUL COHEN *was awarded an Ashoka Fellowship for his work at Tlholego. He loves the African land and the songs of its people.*

residents constitute one of the biggest challenges facing the new South Africa.

In response to South Africa's situation, low-cost housing products from around the world have flooded in as foreign and domestic companies vie for space in a potentially lucrative market. Yet the resulting years of building with these ill-suited imported "solutions" have resulted in shoddy developments that rarely meet residents' basic needs and leave little possibility for community growth. I came to the conclusion that creating sustainable rural villages was a necessary balance to increased urbanism, for the economic and ecological health of quickly shifting rural areas.

My work has been to develop something more appropriate in this changing rural environment. In 1991, after purchasing a 300-acre (146 ha) degraded farm near the city of Rustenburg in

the Northwest Province of South Africa, I formed with a number of other community leaders the non-profit organization Rucore (rucore.org.za) to initiate the Tlholego Ecovillage and Learning Centre. Here we have created a pattern of village development that introduces new forms of community organization for both

FIGURE 61.1. Some of the younger members of the Tlholego community; they are now all grown-up.

[Credit: Joseph F. Kennedy]

435

rural and urban areas of South Africa, using ecological principles for guidance.

Tlholego is a Tswana word meaning "creation from nature." Tlholego demonstrates and teaches sustainable approaches to land use, housing, food security and village development. It enables those who make their home here to live their dreams and values in tune with the natural environment. One of these values is living, learning and working in community, because economic, social and environmental needs can be more effectively met through both individual and collective engagement. At Tlholego we try to live by these values:

- We respect all people and paths, being open to learn, grow and support each other through our similarities and differences.
- We call on our humor when we feel challenged, because we know growth is often not easy.
- We stand tall in who we are, allowing our natural possibility to flow.
- We live in tune with nature, celebrating and finding inspiration in her intelligence.
- We co-create, earning livelihoods and security for our families as part of our common vision.

Working with leading professionals from South Africa and around the world, Tlholego has facilitated many of South Africa's primary training programs in ecovillage development, sustainable building technologies and permaculture design. This practical demonstration of village settlement and rural economic development integrates traditional African design, modern technology and lessons learned from around the world, giving hope and creating positive aspirations for communities living in rural or urban poverty.

Tlholego Ecovillage is comprised of three core components. Tlholego Enterprises, which owns and runs our commercial operations, develops training programs and provides a nurturing environment for economic development. The Tlholego Residential Village employs ecovillage design, permaculture and natural building to create a residential model for land ownership and sustainable housing. And the Tshedimosong ("Place of Enlightenment") Farm School, a primary/secondary school, provides basic education to 120 children from the surrounding farming community.

Our overall objective is to promote an integrated approach to sustainable development in South Africa guided by local needs; to create national, integrated and sustainable rural development strategies; and to

FIGURE 61.2. The nearby Iron Age settlement of Molokwane provides design inspiration for the work at Tlholego. [Credit: Joseph F. Kennedy]

influence government policies on climate change, sustainable agriculture and the UN Millennium Development Goals. By investing in rural communities' capacities to take a leading role in enterprise and community development, we are building the foundations for a healthier future. Tlholego's focus on livelihoods based on sustainable construction, organic farming and enterprise rooted in community development helps create solutions to the challenges of sustainability and development in South Africa.

Addressing South Africa's Housing Crisis

Despite some advances in housing, many of South Africa's marginalized urban majority still live in small corrugated metal shacks with no insulation from summer heat or winter cold. In some places, the situation is getting worse due to illegal immigration into South Africa from other countries. Further, during winter months, families are exposed to high levels of indoor air pollution from the combustion of fuels (wood, coal, kerosene and trash) burned for cooking and warmth.

The national government's housing subsidy provides basic sites and services in the majority of cases, often with a simple roof on four poles as the house. Most low-cost housing systems achieve cost efficiency by using standard house designs and standardized minimum cost materials. Governments and housing authorities generally accept these techniques as the best methods for producing low-cost housing en masse. Large building companies also like this approach because it results in maximum profit through repetition. The houses produced, however, are usually very low in quality—particularly regarding thermal, environmental and aesthetic characteristics. The thermal problems created by these designs can lead to high costs for heating and cooling. End users are usually not consulted in the design process or given alternatives, and they often experience low levels of satisfaction with the houses (particularly as a result of the houses being too small). Future additions at a later date are not planned for and can be difficult to bring about.

In owner-built sustainable building strategies, I found an approach that could provide better housing solutions, and for a similar or lower cost. In 1994, the founding residents of Tlholego began their practical training in sustainable building technologies. I invited natural builder and designer Joseph Kennedy to develop some prototype structures and help create a master plan for the site.

Over the following two years, owner-builders constructed a

FIGURE 61.3. The community gathering space (Lekgotla) under construction. This design was based on traditional Tswana architecture. [Credit: Joseph F. Kennedy]

series of experimental buildings. Some were built using traditional 2,000-year-old Tswana designs that make use of earth and thatch. Others were constructed from large earth-filled bags and had fired-brick dome roofs. Locally available and recycled materials were used for foundations, walls, floors and roofs.

In 1996, after accumulating experience with owner-builder methods, Tlholego began working in partnership with Brian Wood-ward (an Australian unfired-mud brick building expert) to develop the Tlholego Building System (TBS), a sustainable housing

FIGURE 61.4. Creating a traditional meal in the outdoor kitchen. [Credit: Joseph F. Kennedy]

system for South Africa. We first determined the minimum size and quality requirement necessary for a family home in South Africa. Then we looked for ways to construct this minimum house for the money available. Our goal was to create a flexible, affordable, high-quality owner-built housing system that addressed the serious shortcomings of typical low-cost housing construction in South Africa, while emphasizing environmental and resource issues not usually considered.

The resulting housing strategy combined the principles of sustainable building with natural waste treatment and the permaculture approach for designing food self-reliance. This strategy includes using modern techniques of unburned mud brick; passive solar design; appropriate technologies of rainwater collection, composting toilets, greywater irrigation (using water from sinks, shower, etc., excluding toilets); and solar water heating.

Our first prototype house in 1996 was a 4-room, 450 sq. ft. (42 m²) family home. It featured passive solar design with shower, laundry and kitchen area, along with damp-proofing, termite protection, insect screening, high-quality surface finishes, onsite waste treatment and electricity

in every room. The price limit we set was R8,000 (US$1,070). From the beginning we chose owner-building because of the cost savings it achieves. Tlholego's houses are designed to last far longer than those built of conventional materials. By establishing permanent food systems in the immediate vicinity of the home, we also create additional aesthetic and functional outdoor living environments that are far larger than the internal dimensions of the house—another asset that will appreciate in value.

Our approach to housing can be widely applied, with plenty of flexibility to allow designs to differ according to personal criteria. If the cost implications of alternatives are clearly spelled out, then the owner-builder can make an informed choice. The choice may be between different materials (based on cost or availability) or between quality and quantity (a larger, lower-quality house or a smaller, higher-quality house). The flexibility of this approach also facilitates staged construction and/or adding on at a later date.

Ecological Design and Construction

The building system most commonly adopted at Tlholego is a

wall made of locally manufactured mud bricks set on a concrete, block or stone foundation. The walls are well attached to a lightweight, insulated timber and metal roof. The walls are rubbed down with water to reduce cracks and provide a pleasing texture and are then coated with linseed oil and turpentine for weather resistance. We use passive solar techniques such as solar orientation, thermal mass and proper overhangs. Shade extensions are attached to the most vulnerable sides on the house, and vines or trees can be grown to provide protection from driving rains.

Natural Waste Management

The houses at Tlholego integrate onsite waste management for safely managing human wastes. The main system in use is a double-chamber composting toilet that is low-cost and easy to construct; it uses only the most basic available building materials, has no moving parts, is robust and has wide-scale application.

Water Harvesting

The harvesting of water is a key element of any sustainable housing and land use system. The more water a household is able to harvest, the greater the level of food and water security. This strategy can be applied equally well at the household level as at the village or watershed level. Ideally the first level of water catchment takes place on the rooftop through a gutter system that empties into a storage tank, which is then available as a high-quality water source for drinking or irrigation.

Excess water can be directed into below-ground storage and used for irrigation during the dry times of the year. If there is insufficient funding for water tanks and guttering in the initial stages of construction, water flowing off the roof during the rainy season can be directed along the ground into tree plantings, or to food gardens around the house. Wastewater is another source of water available at the household level. Our buildings incorporate greywater filtration, which cleans wastewater so that bathroom and kitchen wastewater can be used for irrigation purposes.

Permaculture Food Security

There is a natural integration between our buildings and the food security gardens that have been established in the immediate vicinity of the houses. Permaculture, now in wide use around the world, is a design system for human landscapes developed by Australians Bill Mollison and David Holmgren in the late 1970s. It integrates traditional knowledge with modern science and common sense to provide a complete system of self-reliance incorporating annual and perennial plants, small animals and useful trees. It relies on low external energy inputs. The beauty of this system is that, in addition to establishing a valuable source of healthy food, it increases the size of a family homestead's living environment and tangibly improves the quality of a rural or urban lifestyle.

Accomplishments

One of the most important accomplishments thus far has been the sustained transfer of building skills that Tlholego residents have experienced since 1994. This experience has grown through hundreds of hours of shared learning between professional architect/builders from around the world and Tlholego community members, most of whom come from a rural farm worker background with a minimal skills base. The techniques have stood up well to residents' expectations, and Tlholego is now proud of having established the first competent building team in southern Africa capable of training other communities and people from around the world in natural building systems.

TDP has become an internationally recognized reference point and demonstration center for sustainable living. In 2000, our village model was chosen by the National Department of Housing (DOH) as the most appropriate model to represent South Africa at the Africa Solutions Toward Sustainable Development conference.

As Tlholego approaches its twenty-fifth year, our work has expanded to include personal wellness and healing aspects. We regularly host eco-therapy groups for reintegrating liberation soldiers and others injured by the legacy of the struggle, as well as people from all walks of life seeking a deeper appreciation of the connections between our modern economy and nature. We continue to host international volunteers who come to experience this experiment in rural living. Our gardens have been revamped, and we continue to work to improve the conditions of the educational center, local community and public school. We always welcome your help.

Tlholego village has shown that even at our relatively small scale of activity, it is quite possible to harmonize the basic elements needed for sustainable development—land, people and know-how—into an integrated system that transforms current patterns of consumption and inequality. If, like a tree born out of a small seed, which is driven by still smaller genetic material, our projects ensure that core systems are designed sustainably, it is natural that what grows from this core will also be inherently sustainable. In this way, we will be able to create a world capable of nurturing our unfolding human potential.

FIGURE 61.5. Students from around the world making mud during a natural building workshop. [Credit: Joseph F. Kennedy]

RESOURCES

Books

• Architecture for Humanity, Kate Stohr and Cameron Sinclair, eds. *Design Like You Give a Damn: Architectural Responses to Humanitarian Crises*, 2nd ed., Abrams, 2012. This second edition of the best-selling book profiles innovative projects for the public good.
• Bell, Bryan and Katie Wakeford, eds. *Expanding Architecture: Design as Activism*, Metropolis Books, 2008. This book lays out the case for "public interest architecture" to solve our global shelter issues. Many of the ideas advocated here are applied at Tlholego.
• Clark University, et al. *Participatory Rural Appraisal Handbook*, Clark University, 1994. An excellent practical handbook on working with local communities. Available as download: **rosemike. net/religion/partner/part_large/ PRA.pdf.**
• Folkers, Anthony. *Modern Architecture in Africa*, Sun Architecture, 2010. An excellent overview of the current state of architecture in Africa.
• Frescura, Franco. *Rural Shelter in Southern Africa*, Ravan Press, 1981. While difficult to find, this beautifully illustrated book is a gold mine of ideas for natural builders.

Building with Earth in Auroville 62

Hilary Smith and Satprem Maïni

Auroville is an experimental international township in Southern India. As the founder of Auroville, The Mother, said at its founding in 1968, "Auroville is meant to be a universal town where men and women of all countries are able to live in peace and progressive harmony, above all creeds, all politics and all nationalities. The purpose of Auroville is to realize human unity." Auroville also lives up to its title as "the city that the earth needs" through the pioneering use of earth-based construction techniques for its public buildings and homes.

The Auroville Earth Institute (AVEI) has been at the forefront of this movement to develop and promote earth-based construction techniques since 1989.

Satprem Maïni *is an architect, director of AVEI and Representative for Asia of the UNESCO Chair Earth Architecture.* **Hilary Smith** *is AVEI's librarian and public relations director.* earth-auroville.com

French architect Satprem Maïni formed this institute to research how to optimize earth-building techniques; it holds training courses for students and professionals, and offers architectural design, construction, consultancy and technology transfer services.

AVEI has emphasized the use of compressed stabilized earth blocks (CSEBs) as a versatile, cost-effective and sustainable local building material (see "Compressed Earth Blocks," p. 195). CSEBs lend themselves well to vaulted structures, which can negate the need for conventional roofing materials such as wood and steel. Other earth-based techniques can be used in

FIGURE 62.1. Office of the Auroville Earth Institute. [Credit: Serge Maïni]

conjunction with CSEBs, such as stabilized rammed earth foundations and walls, stabilized earth plasters and "earth concrete" (also known as soil cement), a system that uses cement to stabilize a variety of earthen soils from degradation by water and for additional durability.

Manually produced CSEBs, made from locally sourced soil stabilized with five percent cement, correspond well to the building needs and economies of settings like Southern India, where labor-intensive building techniques can be both cost-effective and job-creating. The embodied energy of a CSEB is 10.7 times less than the average fired brick and 8 times less than reinforced cement concrete in India. To produce superior block strength and a diversity of forms, the AVEI developed the Auram 3000 manual block press in 1989. This press can produce 70 different types of CSEBs with 18 moulds, including hollow interlocking CSEBs suitable to earthquake-prone areas. As the cost of labor has increased dramatically over the last decades, an automatic mechanized block press (the Auram 6000) has been developed to increase production speed and reduce the physical strain of block production.

Projects designed and built by AVEI in Auroville showcase the versatility of CSEBs, including the Visitors' Centre, which in 1992 was granted the Hassan Fathy Award for Architecture for the Poor, and Vikas community, built from 1991 to 1998, which was a finalist for the 2000 World Habitat Award. Between 2007 and

FIGURE 62.2. Training center of the Auroville Earth Institute. [Credit: Serge Maïni]

2012, AVEI built the Realization community, which harmonizes environmentally responsive design and space economy, with 17 apartments on three floors. To create a participatory community environment and reduce construction costs, future residents were encouraged to participate in block production and construction.

For the Realization community, Aurovillians, newcomers and volunteers worked together as coordinated by the Auroville Earth Institute. Soil dug from the site of a rainwater harvesting tank was used to produce the CSEBs for the buildings. The team created foundations of stabilized rammed earth. The CSEB vaults and walls use earth mortar with a protective lime-stabilized earth plaster for exterior walls. To passively cool interior spaces, buildings were oriented toward established air currents and feature projecting eaves to protect against direct solar exposure. An earth cooling tunnel draws air from outside through pipes running under the rainwater harvesting tank, thereby cooling the air through a natural heat exchange before pumping it into the apartments.

The Sri Karneshwar Nataraja Temple, located on the Bay of Bengal 7.5 miles north of Auroville, is of a completely different shape and purpose. Designed as a square pointed dome according to the dimensions of the Great Pyramid of Giza, this temple is dedicated to Lord Shiva as the cosmic dancer Nataraja. Satrem led a team to build this innovative structure on the site of a former Nataraja temple that was

FIGURE 62.3. This Visitors' Center won the Hassan Fathy Award for Architecture for the Poor. [Credit: Serge Maïni]

destroyed by the tsunami in 2004. The design challenge was to create a structure that would resist a tsunami, while still remaining environmentally friendly.

The foundations of this building are of reinforced concrete placed over 3.5 ft. (1 m) below the ground level of the sand. Retaining walls extend out of the sand and are connected with a reinforced concrete slab. The team utilized CSEB and earth concrete for the basement, walkway and pyramid. The exterior surfaces were covered with a special type of CSEB, composed of a mixture of soil, cement, lime and alum, in order to minimize erosion from the sea air and monsoon rains.

In 1999, the Earth Institute designed and built a 247 sq. ft.

(23 m²) cost-effective and disaster-resistant house dubbed the Aum House. This prototype house was built in only 66 hours by an 18-man team in New Delhi, and was granted a Gold Medal by the India Trade Promotion Organisation (ITPO). The foundations were made with stabilized rammed earth and walls from hollow interlocking CSEBs, strengthened with reinforced concrete. The roof was made with interlocking ferrocement channels.

In 2001, following the 2001 Gujarat earthquake in India, AVEI built another Aum House as a demonstration in Khavda, Gujarat, with a 20-man team in under 63 hours. This house was the starting point of rehabilitation in Gujarat with the

techniques developed by AVEI, which were subsequently granted governmental approval. The Auroville Earth Institute assisted the Catholic Relief Services over a period of 6 months to build 2,698 earthquake-resistant houses and community centers, with 2,000 people participating in 39 villages.

The Earth Institute was also commissioned by Ar-Riyadh Development Authority in 2004 to build a mosque with CSEBs in the heart of Riyadh, Saudi Arabia, as part of a technology transfer program for earth construction techniques. The initial concept sketch for the mosque was done by the Riyadh Development Authority, which was interested in promoting indigenous-style architecture in Saudi Arabia, through using modern building techniques. They imagined building a mosque in the heart of Riyadh that could be a showcase for appropriate building technologies with earth blocks. The contracting company in Riyadh was unable to handle all the specialized design and work required. They contacted Satprem in July 2003 to design the mosque, start the earth blocks production and organize the building process. AVEI implemented a stone basement with walls, vaults and hemispherical domes made with CSEBs, creat-

FIGURE 62.4. This demonstration house was built in Delhi in 66 hours. [Credit: Serge Maïni]

ing an open interior interspersed with columns. The 4,520 sq. ft. (420 m²) building was topped with a minaret 59.2 ft. (18 m) tall.

The entire project required 160,000 blocks in 32 different shapes and sizes, which were produced by an Auram 3000 brought from India. The construction of the raw superstructure, from stone basement to the minaret, took 7 weeks, during which the Earth Institute team supervised 75 unskilled masons and 150 laborers. The semi-circular vaults

FIGURE 62.5. The Realization Community is built of compressed earth blocks, as are most buildings at Auroville. [Credit: Serge Maïni]

FIGURE 62.6. The Al Medy mosque, built in the heart of Riyadh, Saudi Arabia. [Credit: Serge Maïni]

were built using the free-spanning technique, developed by AVEI, and the hemispherical domes were constructed with a compass. The completed building was a finalist for the Aga Khan Award for Architecture in 2007 and was granted the Prince Sultan Bin Salman Award for Urban Heritage by the Al-Turath Foundation in 2010.

The potential for CSEBs and other earth-based techniques is still growing, as the Earth Institute and other research centers work toward improved production speeds, strength and alternative stabilizing agents. With proper planning and stability studies, CSEBs can be used for multi-story buildings and in disaster-prone areas. They present an appealing contemporary aesthetic, while responsibly managing natural resources and minimizing carbon emissions for future generations.

To date, the Earth Institute has taught over 9,700 individuals from 78 countries, who range from university students of architecture and engineering, to masons and contractors, to established architects. As the Asian Representative and Resource Centre of the UNESCO Chair for Earthen Architecture, AVEI actively participates in the global knowledge exchange in the field through collaborative consultancy and research projects, presentations at international conferences and hosting of foreign scholars. AVEI has worked in 36 countries to promote and disseminate knowledge in earth architecture, and has garnered 13 awards for its work (2 international awards and 11 national awards).

FIGURE 62.7. Interior view of the Al Medy mosque, winner of the Prince Sultan bin Salman Award for Urban Heritage. [Credit: Serge Maïni]

Friland: Affordable Housing in Community

63

LARS KELLER AND JOANNA MORANDIN

Friland (Freeland) is an intentional community located in the small village of Feldballe, 21 mi. (35 km) from Aarhus, which is the second largest city in Denmark. Friland was established in 2002, and has expanded twice, so that it now covers approximately 30 acres (12 ha). There are around 70 adults and 30 children, living in 43 homes of various stages of completion.

Although Feldballe is a commuter village, one-third of the working Frilanders work from home or in the village. Several of those who commute to Aarhus are aiming to have a different working life in the future. And

LARS KELLER *and* **JOANNA MORANDIN** *have been Friland residents since 2002, and they run a small business based at Friland. See* **smallplanet .dk** *for more information. Visitors are welcome to walk around Friland. To arrange a tour or for more information, see* **friland.org,** *or email ravnebooking @gmail.com.*

while nationally 6 percent of those working are self-employed, at Friland this number is 44 percent. This has led to more activity in the community. There are people home in the daytime, more opportunities for children to come home earlier from school and kindergarten and more social interaction between neighbours. It has also created employment and services in Feldballe.

One hundred people living together creates opportunities

for a better quality of life. At Friland, there are no obligations to work for the community or to socialize together; instead, there are various working groups and social groups that you can choose to be a part of. Examples include a food-buying cooperative that has organic food delivered once a week; a common garden, with a polytunnel and hens; a road-fixing group; a mediation group; car share constellations; clothes swapping evenings and shared

FIGURE 64.1. A bi-monthly membership meeting in the community of Friland, Denmark. [Credit: Lukas Wassberg]

dinners. The children at Friland have their own social network and are growing up like cousins.

Everyone living in Friland is a member, and most decisions are made at bi-monthly membership meetings. An annual budget (including membership fees) is approved at the annual General Meeting, while a steering committee deals with the everyday running of the community. Like all communities, we have disagreements and arguments, which can be interesting and challenging to solve, but are a good reflection of what happens in the "real world."

The intentions behind setting up Friland were to create a community where the inhab-itants are not tied up in debt, where people can work locally and where homes and businesses are built with sustainable materials without waste. While Friland is economically independent (not based on subsidies or other external support), links with Feldballe (population 500) remain important. Friland is not an isolated community trying to create a better way of life just for its own members. It is a part of Danish society, and is fairly well-integrated into the local village. Our children attend the same schools and kindergarten, we are in the same sports clubs and we socialize together.

One of the purposes of Friland is to promote natural building and mortgage freedom. We are open to the public, with guided tours and an open house day every summer when people can see inside the houses and visit stalls promoting natural building, organics and other relevant topics.

Mortgage-Free

It is very much the norm when buying or building a house, to take out a bank loan, which is then paid back over 20 or 30 years. One of the main goals of people living at Friland is to avoid this debt as much as possible. In Denmark the average household spends one-third of their income

FIGURE 64.2. The Friland home of Jonas and Birgitte has a greenhouse, a sauna and a swimming pond. [Credit: Lukas Wassberg]

after taxes on housing expenses (rent/mortgage, heating and electricity), one-third on basic needs (food, medicine, transportation and clothing), and one-third on extras (fashion, holidays, sports and hobbies). The size of the average household in Denmark is 2.2 persons, and new houses average 1,500 sq. ft. (137 m²), making them the largest in Europe.

While it is relatively easy to lower the cost of basic needs by buying different foods, growing food yourself, finding a local job or changing your mode of transport, and while the cost of extras vary according to the general economy and culture, once a mortgage has been incurred, it can be very difficult to escape. This is why Friland is focusing on housing-related expenses in its quest to free people. Our hope is that free people will have the mental resources and energy to make decisions that will benefit the common good. After 11 years of experience, our best answer to the question of how to be mortgage-free is to build a healthy house, at a low cost, with low running costs and for non-speculative purposes.

It is a part of the cultural mindset in Denmark (and in many other countries) to use land and houses to generate money. Selling a house or land without speculation passes the benefits of a low-expense life on to the next generation. Once the pattern has been established, this mind-shifting act of passing on a gift can continue for many generations. Deterring speculation is the most unusual and visionary experiment at Friland, and two things have been put in place to ensure that it remains an integral part of the community's constitution.

Maximum Sales Price

Putting a cap on sales prices is an old and well-established mechanism used in housing cooperatives in Denmark, aimed at making it easier for working class people to get access to

FIGURE 64.3. The Friland home of Niels and Inge seems in balance with their productive landscape. [Credit: Lukas Wassberg]

housing in the cities. While the average price for a house as of early 2014 is 14,000 Dkr/m² (US$242/sq. ft.), the maximum one can sell a house for at Friland is 5,000 Dkr (about US$1,000) for the first 50 m² (538 sq. ft.), 2,800 Dkr (about US$525) for the next 50 m², with the price per square meter decreasing gradually as the size increases. This means that an 860 sq. ft. (80 m²) house at Friland would have a maximum price of 334,000 Dkr (US$62,000), while a 3,000 sq. ft. (280 m²) house would cost 744,500 Dkr ($138,000), the average square meter prices being 4,175 ($72/sq. ft.) and 2,560 ($44/sq. ft.) respectively. This encourages people to build small houses.

No Security for a Mortgage

When the land for Friland was first purchased, the deed was altered to prevent land or buildings from being used to secure house loans. The direct consequence of this change is that Frilanders cannot get a low-interest mortgage loan from a bank or credit union, but must make do with higher-interest common bank loans. This may sound counterproductive, and although it does create problems, the positive spin-offs are stunning.

This detail ensures that Frilanders are not at risk of losing their home due to defaulting on debts, and it encourages Frilanders to consider the benefits of building small houses, using low-cost materials (such as unprocessed, natural and second-hand materials), doing the work themselves and, perhaps most importantly, building within their budget instead of within their debt limits.

Not everyone at Friland is debt-free. It is possible to borrow money from a credit union, or from family, but loans are well below the national average, and money is borrowed over a shorter

FIGURE 64.4. Help from community members, and the use of low-cost, high-performance materials, helps Frilanders reduce the out-of-pocket cost of their buildings, as well as minimizing their ecological footprint. [Credit: Catherine Wanek]

period of time. Frilanders are a healthy mix of young and old, students and professionals. Not everyone has arrived here after selling a house, or with a high-paying job. For some people, their house here is their first home.

Waste-Free Healthy Houses

Although Frilanders are free to use paid labor and expensive materials, and although our only stated regulation is an aim to build without producing waste, the reality is that houses at Friland are low-cost and rank high in regard to sustainability. As the very purpose for building a house is to provide shelter for yourself and your family, building with safe and healthy materials makes sense. Residents need to follow the normal building regulations, which are quite strict in Denmark. Houses need to be well-insulated in the walls, ceilings and foundations (at least 30 cm/12 in.), and windows and doors need to be of a high-energy standard. Friland has one important exception from the local building regulations, which is that the buildings do not need to conform aesthetically to other buildings in the village, so many of the houses have creative and unique designs. Friland does not impose its own building rules or approval procedures.

The low sales price—and a basic desire by Frilanders to live in healthy houses—has resulted in most houses being built from local, organic, recycled and waste materials such as straw, clay, lime, round timbers, mussel shells, paper or wood cellulose insulation, old bricks, granite and milled timbers. The short-term focus is to use materials without toxic

FIGURE 64.5. The wreath above the new house signals that this is a party to celebrate the completion of the roof structure. The community comes together for both the work and the celebrations. [Credit: Lukas Wassberg]

emissions (off-gassing), while the longer view is to use materials with as little embodied energy as possible—to build houses that last and can be repaired, and to use materials that are durable, but able to be reused or recycled instead of discarded.

Blue mussel shells (*Mytilus edulis*) are a waste product from the canning industry. At Friland, they are used by the truckload for house foundations and as a roof covering. Spread over a second-hand roof, they protect it from UV degradation, thus extending the life of the roof. In foundations, vibrated, compacted shells are used as an effective capillary moisture break, and also provide insulation under the floors. Exterior load-bearing straw bale walls and interior earthen subfloors are placed directly on top of the shells. In our own house, a 20 in. thick (0.5 m) layer of vibrated mussel shells extends 40 in. (1 m) outside the external walls, effectively draining water away from the house and substituting for a conventional concrete foundation.

Most houses at Friland have been built with straw in one way or another. There are load-bearing, non-loadbearing and hybrid straw bale buildings. Many ceilings are insulated with whole straw bales, plastered on both sides with clay as a fire retardant. We have also experimented with using chopped straw as blown-in insulation for ceilings, floors and walls. Other houses are insulated with paper or wood cellulose, hemp or flax batts and sea grass.

Good quality clay is available as an inexpensive waste product from local quarries. Many Frilanders have used this clay for internal and external wall plaster, earthen floors and plastering ceilings. With a good house design, clay plasters hold up well in the Danish climate, where the temperature on average crosses the 32°F (0°C) mark 100 times per year.

Low Running Costs

When building a new house in Denmark, the labor costs are typically equal to the costs of materials. Apart from a few obligatory authorizations from the electrician and the plumber, it is possible to reduce labor costs to a bare minimum by building the house yourself. The majority of Frilanders had no building experience before buying land at Friland, so they've had to learn a lot, but the results are impressive. Through using materials like mussel shells, straw bales, clay plasters, recycled roofs, etc., the material costs have been hugely reduced.

After a mortgage, the running costs of a house (heating, water, sewer, electricity, etc.) can be the next biggest budget expense. Most houses at Friland are built to keep these running costs low. Friland has its own wastewater treatment systems. Most houses have masonry stoves or rocket stoves for heating and hot water. Many people have installed low-consumption light bulbs or LEDs, and a few have installed photovoltaic panels and solar hot-water heaters.

As the families of Friland complete their houses and establish gardens, the village of Feldballe is also showing clear signs of vigor. This summer an arboretum will be planted between Friland and the local school, and next to it, other volunteers will be building an outdoor urban sports facility to serve the larger local community.

64

Evolving a Village Vernacular in Missouri

MARK MAZZIOTTI

It would be hard to overstate the impact natural building has had on my life. My watershed moment came at a Natural Building Colloquium in New Mexico in 2003. I picked up a piece of cob for the first time and started sculpting it onto a wall. The medium felt alive and in harmony with my body on a molecular level. The colloquium was the most exciting week of my life, and never have I felt more instantly at home with a group of strangers.

I transitioned out of a salaried job in San Francisco and into a natural building apprenticeship. I've been learning, practicing and teaching natural building ever since. I moved to Red Earth

Over the past ten years, MARK MAZZIOTTI has worked with some of the most respected folks in the natural building community, teaching and building in places ranging from Sedona to South Africa. He lives at Red Earth Farms Community Land Trust in northeast Missouri.

Farms in 2006 and started a homestead and a family. My quality of life has risen in inverse proportion to the decline in my income. I eat better food, get more consistent exercise and live with my partner and daughter, mortgage-free, in a house of our own creation. Only, I never would

have guessed it would all be happening *here*.

Northeast Missouri is a rolling sea of soybeans, corn, wheat and cattle. A landscape dominated by large-scale agriculture. Politically conservative. Amish and Mennonite communities can be found interspersed among its small

FIGURE 64.1. The author looking down through the oculus of a reciprocal roof that he helped install on a cob cottage at Dancing Rabbit Ecovillage. When building a reciprocal roof, the first rafter is supported by a "Charlie stick." Once the remaining rafters are in place, the geometry is self-supporting and the Charlie stick can be removed. [Credit: Mark Mazziotti]

towns. Not the kind of place one would expect to find a growing network of progressive-minded communities and a vibrant experiment in natural building and sustainable living.

But it is here nonetheless. It all started in 1974 near the small town of Rutledge with an egalitarian community called Sandhill Farm. Sandhill cleared the path for Dancing Rabbit Ecovillage in 1997. Red Earth Farms Community Land Trust formed in 2005, and Stillwaters Sanctuary, home of the Possibility Alliance, followed soon after in La Plata.

Each of these communities has a different approach to sustainable living. Sandhill grows most of its own food and produces sorghum and honey for income, which is shared among its members. Dancing Rabbit Ecovillage has covenants that require all lumber to be harvested within the bioregion or reclaimed and all electricity to come from sustainable sources. Personal vehicles are not allowed. Instead they have a car cooperative that serves about 80 people with 4 cars, one of which is electric, and the other 3 run on biodiesel whenever possible. Stillwaters Sanctuary members use no motor vehicles or electric power at all. They travel by bike or horse and buggy, and build with hand tools and draught animals. Red Earth Farms requires its members to create a land use plan and to audit their ecological footprint.

Natural builders spend a lot of time thinking about *what* and *how* to build, but an equally important question is *where*? Living alone in a remote location is often part of the natural builder's fantasy. But the reality is that the energy savings of a natural built house can be quickly lost by the need to drive many miles to work, play and do business with other people. By building sensible houses *and* sharing resources like

FIGURE 64.2. A modern wattle-and-daub application on the author's outhouse. The plaster is a mixture of clay and crushed sorghum stalks or "pummies," left over from sorghum syrup production. The long fibers are draped over the lath strips with a shingling effect. The sugars from the sorghum may have fermented this plaster; it has endured six years of driving rains in good repair. [Credit: Mark Mazziotti]

kitchens and cars, these communities in northeast Missouri have reduced their ecological footprint by as much as 90 percent compared to the average American.

Dancing Rabbit's vision is to become a village of 500 to 1,000 people. It is currently at about 70 members and growing. New houses are going up every year. By definition, an ecovillage is bound to reduce the life-cycle impact of its buildings. If you've already decided to build a smaller house with minimal use of concrete and other manufactured materials with high embodied energy, natural building becomes a logical choice. Being free from building codes, Dancing Rabbit has developed a strong DIY culture with a willingness to question the dominant paradigm. They have manifested 25 natural buildings with an average size of 532 sq. ft. (50 m²), about one-fourth the size of the average American single-family dwelling.

One reason this works so well for the villagers is their growing cooperative culture; sharing kitchens, for example, means fewer houses need to include them. And since part of their mission is outreach and education, the houses can be seen by the public through tours, internships and workshops. This works well

when folks are drawn to the look and feel of natural built houses, but it can be a downside when natural building looks foreign or strange to the mainstream or when the techniques are not applicable in their location due to codes or other urban issues.

Stillwaters Sanctuary, with its sister project the Peace and Permaculture Center, offers workshops in natural building and other sustainable living skills for free. They operate on the principle of "gift economy," where people are asked to give according to what makes them joyful and no one is turned away for lack of funds. They entertain hundreds of visitors each year, and all without the conveniences of computers and modern vehicles.

Counting all 4 communities, there are upwards of 40 houses using natural building technology in northeast Missouri and—knock on cob—none of them have fallen over yet. We've employed just about every typical technique and have built numerous hybrid structures that combine cob, straw bales, light straw-clay, earthbags, wattle and daub, earthen floors, urbanite foundations and living roofs in different configurations. We've even tried some new things.

I have been experimenting with fermented plasters based on

a recipe developed by the innovative French straw bale builder, Tom Rijven. It calls for mixing chopped hay (not straw) and a little sawdust with clay, adding water that's been spiked with fermenting fruit, and letting it sit for a week or two. The fruit water kicks off a fermentation process with the hay that somehow makes the plaster harder and more water resistant.

Another innovative idea I've put to use is the pallet-wood truss. This is a technique invented by

FIGURE 64.3. Pallet truss sections loaded up for transfer to Red Earth Farms. The owner of the pallet salvage operation let the author set up a jig and build the trusses at his mill. He was so impressed with the technology that he built himself an entire fishing cabin with repurposed pallet wood. [Credit: Mark Mazziotti]

the inspirational architect and natural builder Alfred Von Bachmayr, who passed away in August of 2013. He invented the pallet truss while working on low-income housing in Mexican border cities where trees are sparse and pallets are plentiful. It's basically a matter of reconfiguring pallet wood into triangles, which Buckminster Fuller called the strongest shape in the universe. The hardest part is getting the pallets apart. By some miracle I found a guy in the business of breaking down pallets for resale nearby, so I decided to give it a go. I adapted the concept to a gambrel roof shape as a concession to the local building vernacular.

FIGURE 64.4. Intern Monica Chaplin installing a pallet wood truss. The trusses were assembled on the second-floor deck and then erected in place to create the walls and roof for the second floor of the author's house. [Credit: Mark Mazziotti]

So, what have we learned?

We have cold winters, so it's no surprise that straw bale walls work best. Frost-protected foundations help a lot. Living roofs need additional insulation. There has been one honest attempt at a cob cottage, but the results were not promising. Cob walls are great in many situations but not, it turns out, where winter temperatures are consistently in the teens and below.

Rocket stoves are amazing. They burn less wood, combust it more cleanly and store heat in thermal mass so it pays dividends long after the fire goes out. There are six in our area, and they're great for folks who spend a lot of time at home in the winter and like to play with fire. If you do not meet these two criteria, you will probably not be happy with a rocket stove.

The bigger challenge around here is not heating a house in winter but keeping it cool in summer. We've found that ground contact works well on both fronts but brings with it the challenge of controlling humidity. We've had a lot of problems with mold. Some folks swear by vapor barriers, others think they cause as many problems as they solve. We didn't use one in our straw bale house, relying on a massive gravel trench as our only defense against ground moisture. So far we've had no problem with mold.

In our region, whether you're talking about functionality, durability or labor costs, it's all about the plaster. We've found that natural building presents some tricky challenges when it comes to airtightness. Earthen plasters tend to shrink away from edges, which can lead to air penetration if the details aren't handled well. Driving rain and freeze-thaw cycles take their toll on exterior plasters. We use both earth and lime, but they don't mix well here. Earth/lime plasters are standard in other places, but we've not had the same luck, probably because our clay is expansive and our temperature variations extreme.

It seems that natural builders rarely have the discipline to complete a house before they move in. We all know that a house is never finished, but I recommend having floors and plasters completed as a minimum goal. We moved into our house after two years of work. Three years later, we still have finish plaster work to do.

Details matter. But what's also important is that natural building is fun and accessible. People are drawn to it. It connects them to each other and to the land. Perhaps that's why so many folks are drawn to these communities each year to visit, intern and participate in workshops. Our population nearly doubles during the building season. That means there are plenty of helping hands, which make labor-intensive solutions like cob and natural plasters more attractive.

Work-exchange arrangements come in all shapes and sizes. The simplest is a straight trade—work for food and a place to camp. We've started to ask our interns to contribute to food expenses, reasoning that the learning opportunity alone is a fair trade for labor. Others have organized elaborate workshops with expert teachers, sometimes from outside the community. One of the nicest timber-framed straw bale houses at Dancing Rabbit was built mostly by workshop participants who paid a premium for the experience. This model requires organization and marketing savvy and a big investment in time up front, but the benefits are many. It's a winning formula when education and fun add up to a great house that doesn't cost a lot.

Having all this "free" labor around makes it hard to figure the true worth of the houses. Our 840 sq. ft. (78 m²) straw bale home cost about US$25,000 in materials, which included the solar/wind off-grid power system

FIGURE 64.5. The author's straw bale home, with earthen exterior plaster and gambrel pallet-truss roof. [Credit: Mark Mazziotti]

and a cistern for storing rainwater harvested from the roof. Then there's the labor. Most of us have more time than money so, for example, using reclaimed materials makes sense even if it takes longer. I don't even like to think about how many hours I have invested in our house, and I'd charge a king's ransom for it if I could. Houses around here have so far sold for prices that discount the value of labor, but that's beginning to change as skill levels improve and better houses get built.

If cob is the duct tape of natural building, then coopera-tion is the glue makes it work in communities like ours. Answers are only a neighbor away, and labor can be summoned on short notice. When there's a big job to do at Dancing Rabbit, they call a "swarm." Before long, folks are converging in numbers to do the heavy lifting together. Stillwaters Sanctuary follows the Ghandian ideal of bread labor, in which physical labor is seen as necessary and fulfilling in itself. When the physical work is shared by all, intellectual faculties can be used in the service of mankind instead of in competition for resources or amassing a fortune.

The original homesteaders in this area—like the Native Americans before them—were natural builders by necessity. They didn't have the luxury of ordering a load of sand to make cob. Neither did they have the technology to make a straw bale. There wasn't much wood or rock around, so they mostly cut squares out of the deep-rooted prairie sod and stacked them up to build their houses. Those deep roots are gone now, thanks to modern farming methods, but the spirit to build with what the land offers is alive and well.

RESOURCES

Organizations
- Dancing Rabbit Ecovillage. dancingrabbit.org
- Red Earth Farms. redearthfarms.org
- Sandhill Farm. sandhillfarm.org

Index

If you have enjoyed *The Art of Natural Building*, you might also enjoy other

Books to Build a New Society

Our books provide positive solutions for people who
want to make a difference. We specialize in:

Food & Gardening ◆ Resilience ◆ Sustainable Building
Climate Change ◆ Energy ◆ Health & Wellness
Sustainable Living ◆ Environment & Economy
Progressive Leadership ◆ Community
Educational & Parenting Resources

New Society Publishers
ENVIRONMENTAL BENEFITS STATEMENT

New Society Publishers has chosen to produce this book on recycled paper made
with 100% post consumer waste, processed chlorine free, and old growth free.

For every 5,000 books printed, New Society saves the following resources:[1]

74	Trees
6,739	Pounds of Solid Waste
7,415	Gallons of Water
9,672	Kilowatt Hours of Electricity
12,251	Pounds of Greenhouse Gases
53	Pounds of HAPs, VOCs, and AOX Combined
19	Cubic Yards of Landfill Space

[1]Environmental benefits are calculated based on research done by the Environmental Defense Fund and
other members of the Paper Task Force who study the environmental impacts of the paper industry.

For a full list of NSP's titles, please call 1-800-567-6772 or check out our web site at:

www.newsociety.com